THE MULTICULTURAL CHALLENGE IN ISRAEL

ISRAEL: SOCIETY, CULTURE, AND HISTORY

Series Editor: *Yaacov Yadgar*, Political Studies, Bar-Ilan University

Editorial Board:

Alan Dowty, Political Science and Middle Eastern Studies,
University of Notre Dame

Tamar Katriel, Communication Ethnography, University of Haifa

Avi Sagi, Hermeneutics, Cultural studies, and Philosophy, Bar-Ilan University

Allan Silver, Sociology, Columbia University

Anthony D. Smith, Nationalism and Ethnicity, London School of Economics

Yael Zerubavel, Jewish Studies and History, Rutgers University

ACADEMIC
STUDIES
PRESS

THE MULTICULTURAL CHALLENGE IN ISRAEL

Edited by
AVI SAGI and
OHAD NACHTOMY

Boston   2009

Library of Congress Cataloging-in-Publication Data

The multicultural challenge in Israel / Avi Sagi and Ohad Nachtomy, editors.
    p. cm. — (Israel: society, culture, and history)
  Includes index.
  ISBN 978-1-934843-49-9 (hbk)
1. Multiculturalism—Israel. I. Sagi, Abraham. II. Nachtomy, Ohad.
  HN660.Z9M846 2009
  306.44′6095694—dc22
                    2009031889

ISBN 978-1-934843-49-9 (hbk)

Book design by Ivan Grave

Published by Academic Studies Press in 2009
28 Montfern Avenue
Brighton, MA 02135, USA
press@academicstudiespress.com
www.academicstudiespress.com

Israel: Society, Culture, and History is a book series dedicated to the interdisciplinary study of complex interactions among culture, identity, history and power in Israeli society and politics. It encourages nuanced interpretation in a broad range of theoretical approaches, transcending ideological and disciplinary boundaries. Books published in this series contextualize the Israeli case study in a broadly comparative perspective sensitive to Israel's distinctiveness and its place in theoretical and socio-historical frameworks. In this spirit, the series promotes interpretive studies, based on empirical material, sensitive to social scientific as well as humanistic and ethical concerns.

*

THE MULTICULTURAL CHALLENGE IN ISRAEL explores various aspects of the multicultural face of Israel, which are ordinarily less familiar and appreciated for readers outside Israel. Bearing in mind that the constitution of Israeli society was shaped by the Zionist agenda of creating a Jewish state, the book reminds it readers that while most (though not all) Jewish groups support this agenda, non-Jewish groups do not and, at least in this sense, are marginalized by the constitutive ideology of the state. Furthermore, many of the groups making up Israeli society lead entirely disparate ways of life and occupy separate socio-cultural fields. For these reasons, Israeli society constitutes a fascinating 'testing ground' for studying a variety of particular case studies in multicultural life.

In this book, the various authors propose to study numerous aspects of the processes and struggles that currently shape the identities of Israelis and are thus determining the future of this state and society. This book offers ingenious insights into some of the essential debates and conflicts that currently shape Israeli society by experts and activists in their specific fields. Doing so it exposes important aspects of the character and structure of the current multicultural space of Israeli society.

The editors wish to acknowledge the financial support provided by the Continental Philosophy Fund at Bar-Ilan University for this project and to warmly thank Noa Shein and Liat Lavi for their wonderful work on bringing this manuscript to its final form.

CONTENTS

INTRODUCTION

AVI SAGI, OHAD NACHTOMY

At present, most societies in the democratic world are multicultural and comprise different identity groups. These identity groups shape their lives as culturally distinct communities. Israeli society presents a particularly interesting case of multicultural existence and experience. While it is well known that the very existence of Israel in the Middle East is endangered by external forces, it is less well known that Israeli society comprises many different communities and opposing identities, including Jews, Arabs, Muslims and Christian, Druze, and Bedouins. The majority Jewish group (roughly 75 percent of the current population) includes Orthodox, traditional, and secular, Ashkenazi and Sephardic, as well as new and old immigrants from many countries with different aspirations and purposes. These groups lead different ways of life and are often confined within separate geographical spaces. This book aims to reveal and explore aspects of Israel's multicultural face, which is less familiar to readers outside of Israel.

The constitution of Israeli society was shaped by the Zionist agenda of creating a Jewish state. Whereas most (though not all) Jewish groups support this agenda, non-Jewish groups do not and, at least in this sense, are marginalized by the constitutive ideology of the state. Furthermore, many of the groups making up Israeli society lead disparate ways of life and often cannot share a table, a marriage market, education, and sometimes even a language.

The homogenizing agenda of mainstream Zionism had sought to blend the variety of Diaspora Jewish communities into a single Israeli identity. This "melting pot" ideology, which had been dominant in Israel since its constitution, has been seriously challenged in the last two decades. During the last twenty years, Israeli society has been disintegrating into heterogeneous groups that challenge the ideal of a uniform Israeli identity. In effect, several different groups are consciously struggling to maintain an Israeli

1

identity of their own. In this sense, the very notion of what constitutes an Israeli identity has undergone a radical change: from a homogenizing "melting pot" — characterized by and implemented mainly through the institutions of common education, a common Hebrew language, a common ethos, and the obligatory military service — to a potpourri of heterogeneous groups that constitute a new map of identities in tacit or explicit struggle for recognition. A politics of recognition, together with internal struggles for recognition, have become a central part of life in Israel. Arguably, these internal forces and processes may well undermine any sense of unity and solidarity among Israeli citizens.

For these reasons, we believe that Israeli society constitutes a very interesting lab for a variety of particular case studies in multicultural life. We also believe that Israeli society provides a unique and fascinating context for observing the relations between multicultural theory and practical life. As theoreticians, our contention is that theoretical questions of this type require a concrete context. As residents of Israel, we feel that, in this small country, fundamental questions of multiculturalism reach a very high level of intensity. Much is at stake: could multicultural tendencies in Israel threaten the sovereignty of the state (here the question of unique versus uniform education is very pertinent)? Is Israel turning into a state of separate communities? Could and should Israel continue to exist as a national Jewish state? Is there a way of recognizing the plurality of diverse identities without losing a sense of common identity and solidarity?

This book examines various aspects of the processes and struggles that currently shape the identities of Israelis and are thus determining the future of this state and society. We do not pretend to be providing a complete picture here and we certainly do not attempt to represent all groups adequately. Such an attempt would require a far broader scope. Rather, what we offer here are glimpses and insights into some of the debates and conflicts that currently shape Israeli society. Our working assumption is that focusing on specific case studies will expose important aspects of the character and structure of the current multicultural space of Israeli society. Let us clearly state that the collection of articles presented here does not aim to cover all groups and/or problems in Israel. Nor does it aim to focus on most important or urgent issues. Rather, this selection of case studies calls for further research and can only be seen as a first step in a much broader project of observing and understanding the multicultural challenge facing Israeli society.

CONSTITUTIONAL INCREMENTALISM AND MATERIAL ENTRENCHMENT

HANNA LERNER

1. INTRODUCTION

Israel is one of the few democracies that have never adopted a formal constitution. This has not been for lack of trying. Since the first year of Israel's independence, the debates over the constitution had two dimensions: they concerned not only the content of the constitution but also the question of the appropriate method of crafting it. The debates reflected deep ideational schisms which polarized Israeli society over the foundational aspect of the constitution: over the underlying credo of "the people," which a constitution is expected to reflect. Constitutions do not merely establish the structure of government and regulate the balance of power. They also serve as a binding statement of people's aspirations for themselves as a nation.[1] For constitutions to be legitimate and popularly accepted in democratic societies, they are expected to outline the shared norms and common vision which underpin the state.

In the Israeli case, the deep internal disagreements over what should be those underlying norms and values were apparent from the very beginning of the constitutional debates, already in the pre-state era. In particular, these disagreements were between a religious and a secular vision of the Jewish state. The dispute over the meaning of Israel's definition as "Jewish and democratic" continued to be the center of a long and heated public, political and judicial dispute, which is still not resolved, nearly sixty years after independence.

This chapter will focus on the relationship between the controversy over the character of the Jewish state and the continuous avoidance of drafting a written constitution for Israel. It will trace the constitutional debates during the first Knesset, showing how the Israeli "founding fathers" preferred to adopt an incrementalist approach to constitution-making, deferring controversial decisions regarding the ultimate values and shared norms of the state to the future. In light of the deep internal divisions between the religious and secular perspectives, they chose to transfer controversies over issues of Israel's identity from the constitutional sphere of entrenched law to the more flexible realm of political deliberation.[2] Yet, nearly six decades later, the continued inability of the political system to decide on the appropriate relationship between religion and state is reflected in the recent Knesset constitutional discussions. Thus, the chapter will conclude, Israeli constitutional incrementalism may have unintentionally resulted in the entrenchment of a material constitution which lacks a formal mechanism of amendment.

Before continuing, however, a preliminary clarification is required with regard to the changing role of the Palestinian minority in Israeli constitutional developments. Although since independence, approximately twenty percent of the Israeli population has consistently been non-Jewish, constitutional deliberations during the formative years of the state remained exclusively internal to the Jewish majority. Some cite the wish to limit the civic rights of the Palestinian minority in Israel as one of the reasons that led the Knesset to avoid enacting a constitution including a comprehensive Bill of Rights.[3] In addition, since independence, the Palestinian minority was excluded from Israeli nationhood, which is understood in terms of "the Jewish people." This exclusion is reflected in the expressions of Jewish identity in the state's legislation, emblems, and ceremonies.[4] As such, the non-Jewish sectors in the population have been by and large excluded from the discussions over the constitution, which centered around the definition of the identity of the state.

Recent years, however, have been characterized by growing Palestinian demands for participation in decision-making on the character of Israeli collectivity. Thus, the constitutional debate over the definition of Israel as a "Jewish and democratic state" is no longer limited to Jewish religious and a secular interpretation of the formula. Rather, it now includes also the Palestinian perspective and demand for the transformation of Israel into a liberal-democratic state "for all its citizens," where Palestinians are guaranteed not merely individual rights but rather recognized as a national minority.

2. RELIGIOUS VS. SECULAR VISIONS OF THE JEWISH STATE

The intensity of the secular-religious conflict in Israel differs from social conflicts in other western democracies which tend to focus on allocation of resources and power between various groups. While European Christian parties chiefly aim to preserve the interests of their religious institutions and education systems, [5] the Israeli religious parties wish to leave an imprint of religious Judaism on the state institutions and on Israeli public sphere. The clash is between rival religious and secular conceptions of the optimal nature of the Jewish state. What is at stake is "a struggle over the ultimate values rather than distributive justice, over the whole rather than the parts."[6]

The controversy over Jewish identity has deep historical roots dating back to eighteenth-century Europe. In the context of the emergence of European Enlightenment, both Jewish Orthodoxy and the Zionist national movement represented opposing reactions to the confrontation between traditionalism and modernity. The emergence of Jewish nationalism and the mostly secular Zionist movement posed powerful, new challenges to Orthodox Jews. Zionism provided an option of a secular modern nationalist interpretation of Jewish identity. Moreover, the return to Zion was intended to create the conditions for defining Jewish identity in political-territorial terms rather than in religious-communal terms.[7] The negative reaction of most religious Jews to Zionism stemmed not only from its legitimating an atheist Jewish identity. The ultra-Orthodox also rejected the Zionist notion of self-emancipation which violated the doctrine that only God could ordain the timing of the redemption of the Jewish people and their return to Israel.[8]

In between secular Zionists and the ultra-Orthodox stood the Religious Zionists, who attributed religious meaning to the modern return to Zion. The foundation of the state was viewed by them as the 'beginning of redemption.' Thus, for the Religious Zionists, the political-territorial aspect of Jewish identity was seen as a supplemental component to the traditional national-religious definition of Jewish identity. [9]

After World War II, when the possibility of an independent Jewish state became increasingly more realistic, the religious-secular conflict concentrated on the construction of Israel's emerging legal system. The leaders of the Orthodox Agudat Israel demanded that it would be grounded in traditional Jewish religious law — the Halacha. As Y. M. Levin, the leader of Agudat-Israel declared in a meeting with the heads of the Jewish Agency: "After two thousand years of living in Diaspora, a Jewish state unregulated by the Halacha is a defamation of God, placing the Torah of the people of Israel in a remote corner, rebelling against the kingdom of heaven, and clearly nondurable."[10]

The Halacha is a comprehensive system of rules of conduct, grounded in what is considered to be divine commandment. As an autonomous system of law and procedures, it could comprise an alternative to the civil legal system of the state. From the perspective of the Orthodox Jew, the Halacha takes precedence over the law of the state whenever there is a contradiction between the two systems, and especially when civil law demands behavior that is contrary to Halachic rule.[11] The nature of the Halacha as a comprehensive legal system means that the problem of defining the relationship between religion and state is not a problem of deciding whether or not a certain religion shall have official status, as a state religion, as in many other states. Rather, the problem concerns the nature of the relationship between the laws of the state and the laws of the Halacha. This problem was clearly expressed, during the Knesset deliberations over the constitution, by Meir Levonstein, a representative of the Ultra-Orthodox party, Agudat-Israel, who declared: "There is no place in Israel for any constitution created by men. If it contradicts the Torah — it is inadmissible, and if it is concurrent with the Torah — it is redundant."[12]

3. Constitutional Incrementalism

Although the secular camp had a large majority within the Knesset and could easily pass a secular-liberal constitution,[13] in June 1950 the Knesset decided to refrain from writing a formal constitution in a single document. Following heated discussions, the Knesset passed a compromise resolution, named after its initiator, the chair of the Knesset Committee Haim Harari.[14] The resolution stated:

> The first Knesset charges the Constitutional, Law and Justice Committee with preparing a proposed constitution for the state. The constitution will be composed of individual chapters, in such a manner that each of them shall constitute a Basic Law in itself. The individual chapters shall be brought before the Knesset as the Committee completes them, and all the chapters together will form the state constitution.[15]

The compromise Harari resolution left much doubt with regard to Israel's future constitution. It was not clear from that bill what should be the content of the Basic Laws and their status relative to ordinary legislation. Other issues that were left undecided were the form of entrenchment and amendment of the Basic Laws, as well as the question of consolidation of all the "individual chapters" into one complete constitution. Even the constituent authority of the Knesset and its duty to adopt a constitution were subject to legal and political debate.[16]

The non-adoption of a constitution reflected a preference to circumvent potentially explosive conflicts within the Jewish population and to avoid definitive declarations on controversial questions concerning the identity of the state. This approach was commonly referred to as "the decision not to decide."[17] Instead of making clear-cut choices in the religious arena, the Knesset consciously adopted a suspensional strategy of constitution-making, transferring decisions regarding the nature of the state from the constitutional sphere of high and entrenched law to the political level of ordinary legislation. Thus the first Knesset left it to the political system to gradually construct accommodational arrangements.

By deferring controversial choices to future political institutions, the Harari compromise broke the link so common in modern politics between constitution and revolution.[18] It introduced a different understanding of the relationship between constitutions and time, by attempting to slow the process of radical change usually associated with a moment of constitution adoption. It was hoped that longer timeframe enable a consensus around the state's underlying norms and values to gradually evolve. Thus, instead of viewing the making of the constitution as a moment of radical transformation, the framers chose a long-term process of gradual adjustment. In this way, Israel's leaders opted for an "incrementalist" approach to drafting a constitution.

Adherence to the gradual rather than the revolutionary constitution-making approach did not emerge abruptly but rather materialized as drafting progressed. As the next section will show, when the discussions on the future constitutions began immediately after independence, the framers hoped that the drafting would mitigate the internal conflicts and would bridge between the competing visions of the state.[19] However, the inability to achieve consensus over the foundational and symbolic aspects of their constitutions led the drafters to recognize the limitations of the constitutional arena in resolving ideational disputes.

4. THE SHORT-LIVED CONSTITUENT ASSEMBLY

The operative section of Israel's Declaration of Independence stated, in keeping with UN resolution 181, that the constitution of the State of Israel would be adopted by an elected Constituent Assembly. The elections for the Assembly were planned for 1 October 1948, but were later postponed for three months, mainly because of the outbreak of the war between Israel and its neighboring states. In the meantime, a Provisional Council continued to function and appointed in July 1948 a constitutional committee, chaired by Zerach Vahrhaftig from the Religious Zionists. The Committee, which included representatives of all political parties in an attempt to service a consensual constitution, held twenty meetings until the February 1949 elections for the Constituent Assembly. It was during these deliberations that the question of the content of the constitution was replaced as the central question of the debate by the question of the very necessity of its writing.[20]

Several constitutional drafts were submitted to the committee, varying in their formulations with regard to the relationship between religion and state — from a completely secular and liberal constitution to a theocratic formulation, which suggested democratic representation based on separate electorates for men and women.[21] Yet the committee failed to achieve agreement over state-religion relationship in the emerging state. Zerach Vahrhaftig, the chair of the committee, described in his report the broad agreement among the committee members with regard to institutional and governmental issues. By contrast, the committee was bitterly split over the role of religion in the Jewish state. The tensions around this issue led Vahrhaftig to the conclusion that the opposing perspectives regarding the norms and values which should underpin the constitution were impossible to reconcile, and thus Israel should defer the drafting of the constitution.[22]

The challenge to the Declaration of Independence's directive to write a constitution received a legal dimension with the decision of the elected Constituent Assembly, on 16 February 1949, two days after its first meeting, to enact a *Transition Law*, which united the authorities of the assembly with those of the Provisional Council of the State. Through this Transition Law, the assembly transformed itself into the first Knesset, i.e., the first elected parliament.[23]

The first Knesset decided not to appoint a separate constitutional committee, but to charge the committee of Law and Justice with drafting a constitution. From the beginning, the discussions of the committee did not focus on the content of the future constitution, but rather on the question of whether a written constitution should be adopted at all.[24]

5. KNESSET DEBATES

On February 1950, one year after its establishment, the Knesset opened its formal deliberations over the issue of the constitution. Nine sessions were devoted to this topic. The polarization between the secular and the religious perceptions of the Jewish state was clear to all members. The position of religious representatives claiming to represent "loyal Judaism," was that a Jewish state should have Jewish laws. This was the position taken by Minister of Welfare Yitzhak Meir Levin when he stated that "the goal of religious Jewry is that only the law of the Torah will be established in all areas of life in the state."[25] The secular parties vehemently objected the religious representatives' aspiration to establish "a theocratic state."[26] Many of them shared the position of Mapai member Efraim Tavori who declared: "As a socialist and as an atheist I am unable under any circumstances to sign on a program which contains a religious formulation."[27]

Nevertheless, the Knesset debates over the enactment of the constitution did not focus on the polarization over the foundational content (whether religious or secular) of the constitution. Rather, in light of the intense ideological tensions, the acrimonious debate in the Knesset revolved around the question of whether, given the deep disagreements, a constitution should or should not be drafted. In other words, the issue at stake was what role should a constitution play given the presence of severe internal schisms over the most basic principles of the state, and what timing should be adopted for its enactment. The next section will trace three meta-constitutional issues that played a role in the Knesset constitutional deliberations: First, the question of whether the constitution can be an efficient instrument of conflict resolution; second, the method of decision-making most appropriate for deeply divided societies (majoritarian or consensual); and finally the dimension of time and the question of the pace of constitutional emergence (whether revolutionary or gradual).

Constitution-making as Resolving or Exacerbating Conflicts

The supporters of immediate enactment of a formal constitution, including the secular opposition parties on both the left (Mapam and the Israeli Communist Party) and right (particularly Herut), argued that precisely because of the deep ideological fragmentation, a written constitution, including a Bill of Rights, is needed. They believed that a formal constitution could serve as a vehicle for conciliation, helping to bridge between the competing visions of the state. For them, a shared constitution could have symbolic uniting qualities, which could "bring together and unify the various world views and diverse traditions" that existed within the constantly growing Israeli society.[28] The constitution, it was argued, was needed for educational purposes, as a common ethical guide for the culturally diverse immigrant newcomers.

> We live in the Land of Israel under unique circumstances of ingathering of exiles, of different ethnicities, emigrants from around the globe, with different customs, and also… different — and at times, clashing and contradictory — constitutions. And from this vast diversity, we strive to create one nation. To that end we must act in every direction: the direction of education, the direction of organization, throughout all the cells of our lives, in order that we may live cooperatively and not as we live currently: separately. And this goal must find an expression also in the law, through education for one law for all.[29]

According to this position transforming the multitude of immigrants into a united collective of active contributing citizens is the true nature of Israel's national revolution. A formal constitution could contribute to this goal.

By contrast, the opponents of immediate constitution-making (which included the religious representatives as well as most of the secular Mapai party) contended that given the extreme polarization over the normative basis of the constitution, the process of constitution-drafting would either, at best, still be incapable of diminishing the tensions, or, in the worst case, be likely to exacerbate the conflict.

Abstract constitutional declarations, contended several Mapai members, would have negligible impact on controversies over "form of life" issues. Hence, religious-secular disagreements should be resolved at the level of ordinary law, which could address particular problems more concretely:

> A constitution contains only abstract principles. A detailed set of laws is required to implement these principles in everyday life. This is the greatest challenge which the Knesset faces. It is not enough to declare independence. We need a legal system that would translate the abstract principles into practice.[30]

Opponents to the drafting of a constitution further claimed that doing so under conditions of severe internal rifts was not only unnecessary, but could be counter to the real interests of the state. They argued that the drawn-out philosophical deliberations which would be necessary for the drafting of the constitution would divert the national attention from the truly urgent necessities of the new state.

> We fear… that the philosophical and metaphysical part of the constitution does not facilitate the building of the state, the absorption of immigrants, and does not serve the needs of our time.[31]

The most fervent warnings against the potential polarizing effects of constitution-making in the context of unbridgeable ideational schism, came from the Orthodox representatives, who rejected its immediate drafting, fearing it would result in an entrenchment of secular principles. Such consequences could lead to a dangerous *Kulturkampf*, they contended:

> And when Mr. Nir stated cynically: "We will establish a constitution and there will be an uproar once and not every Monday and Thursday," I want to emphasize here: You are still unfamiliar with the nature of the Jewish people! The Jewish people are willing to resign themselves to many things, but the moment the issue touches upon the foundations of their faith, they are unable to compromise. If you wish to foist upon us this type of life or a constitution that will be contrary to the laws of the Torah, we will not accept it! We endured all the stages of suffering in the path of our exile and all the forces of the inquisition were no match for us! Do you think that what our haters were unable to accomplish, what blood and fire were unable to accomplish, you will be able to accomplish through the power of the state? No and no! You have yet to delve into the depth of the Jewish soul. It will awaken, and ignite a very large bonfire if, of all places, here in the Holy Land we strive to turn the bowl upside down, and make the lives of religious Jews unbearable.[32]
>
> I would like to warn: the experience of drafting a constitution would necessarily entail a severe, vigorous uncompromising war of opinions. A war of spirit, which is defined by the gruesome concept of Kulturkampf... Is this a convenient time for a thorough and penetrating examination of our essence and purpose? It is clear that there is no room for any compromises, any concessions or mutual agreements, since no man can compromise and concede on issues upon which his belief and soul depend.[33]

In the early years of the state, the destabilization of the polity was a real possibility, grounded in the fragile political order of the newly founded state. One of the most serious problems which the Israeli government faced after independence was the challenge of transforming the political culture of a voluntaristic community in the pre-sovereignty era into a society with the institutional structure of a sovereign state. During its first years, the government faced serious challenges to the state's authority. This dissent originated in the pre-state social and ideological fragmentation within the Zionist movement and outside of it.

The most notable example of an attempt to challenge the authority of the state's governmental institutions was the *Altalena* affair, the IZL paramilitary organization attempted to ship its own arms and soldiers into Israel in order to maintain its autonomy from the Israeli Defense Force. This threat to the fledgling state was considered serious enough to warrant the

IDF firing upon and sinking the ship.[34] Another underground group was "Brit Kanaim" (Alliance of the Fanatics), an organization of young zealous religious men, that condemned the state's desecration of religion. Its members were arrested in 1951 after planning to bomb the Knesset in protest against the draft of women into the army.[35] This was not the first time that extremist religious groups acted against the central Zionist institutions.[36]

Constitutional Decision-Making

Acknowledging the zealousness with which the clashing positions were held, several Knesset members challenged the principle of majoritarianism as the appropriate method of constitutional decision-making. While, as a central democratic principle, majority vote was an inherent element of the aspired-to national ideal, severe polarization over the foundational aspect of the constitution made apparent the difficulties of majoritarianism.[37] The pragmatic argument against majority-vote rested on the assumption that any imposition of a majoritarian decision on the minorities would result in exacerbation of the conflict and destabilization of the democratic order.

Those who advocated adopting a constitution only through consensus argued that a legitimate constitution should rest on wide popular support for the ideals and norms entrenched in the document. While it was clear to all that from a majoritarian point of view, secular Knesset members could easily pass a secular nationalist constitution, many contended that a constitution, expected to reflect the ultimate goals and common values of the citizenry, should be adopted on the basis of a wide consensus, since "sometimes, even the majority does not need to use the fact that it is a majority."[38]

Perhaps more importantly, the argument against immediate majority vote was made with reference to the unique condition of Israel at time of independence. The State of Israel was in fact a small community awaiting the ingathering of the Diaspora Jews. When founded, only 600,000 Jews inhabited Israel — less than ten percent of the world Jewish population. The government's goal was to double its Jewish population within four years. These conditions added a geographical dimension to the classic constitutional problem of precommitment.[39] The opponents of a written constitution argued that its drafting should await the anticipated arrival of the future Israeli citizenry, which would be subjected to the constitution. "We are not referring to future generations," claimed David Bar-Rav-Hay from Mapai, "we are concerned with the present generation... we are concerned with those who are expected to arrive in our country in the very near future."[40] David Levonstein from the Orthodox Agudat Israel party also used the democratic argument, when he declared:

> We all see Israel as a place which gathers in all parts of the Diaspora; we all look at world Jewry as our future citizens, if not actually, then at least potentially. What is the normative authority of the inhabitants of our country, which consists of seven percent of our people, and what is the authority of the members of Knesset, who were elected by five percept of the people, to adopt a constitution for the homeland and the entire people?

6. EVOLUTION OR REVOLUTION

Finally, the debate between the opponents and the proponents of a formal constitution included the question of the *pace* of constitution-making. The supporters of a written constitution argued that this "revolutionary" period of national transformation would be the optimal moment to construct constitutional principles likely to obtain general consent. The direction in which the state is going should be determined now, it was claimed, "Precisely because we are standing at the center of an immense process of ingathering of the Diaspora, which streams into the country as a 'mob' so diverse and multicolored in terms of its past, its habits, its development"[41]

The foundation of the state was viewed by the supporters of a constitution as a revolutionary moment, providing an extraordinary opportunity for the reconstruction of the nation: "It is only at this time of fermentation that the powers of the nation are reaching their peak … … I doubt we will be able to achieve later what we could probably achieve today."[42] Mapam member, Israel Bar-Yehuda declared:

> At this point we must force the issue … why can't we determine the direction of nation-building from the beginning of our work? … We forced the issue in many other areas and we must force the issue on this question as well. It is necessary, from the first moment of the state, to establish the healthy foundations, which would assist its emergence.[43]

By contrast, those who objected to immediate constitutional drafting argued that it was exactly because of the vast disagreements and the fragility of the newly established political order that the most controversial decisions regarding normative basis of the constitution should be adopted in an incremental, rather than radical, manner. The opponents of an immediate formal constitution rejected the revolutionary attitude, advocating a more "realistic approach": "I must believe in evolution" argued Avraham Hartzfeld from Mapai towards the members of Mapam, "and you prefer the way of revolution and force. My conviction is that the state could not be built in a revolutionary way, but only in an evolutionary way."[44]

The dispute over the timing of the constitution-drafting mirrored a longstanding schism within the Zionist movement over pace. Dan Horowitz and Moshe Lissak argue that the Zionist movement was historically divided over the question of whether the realization of the Zionist dream demanded a rapid pace or a slow one. In the pre-state era, the supporters of an incremental approach to the goal of Zionism aimed at building up a Jewish presence in Palestine step by step, whereas advocates of a radical approach aimed at rapid realization of this goal through dramatic political and/or military action.[45] Throughout the history of the Zionist endeavor, this "pacing" debate was waged between the radicals and the incrementalists/ pragmatists, involving such issues as whether to publicly proclaim the goal of the Zionist movement as creating a Jewish state in Palestine, whether European Jewry should be "evacuated" to Palestine en masse or gradually, in accordance with economic absorptive capacity; whether statehood should be achieved through gradual settlement and development of autonomous political institutions or by military force.[46]

During the Knesset constitutional debates it was argued by several Mapai members that the incrementalist approach, which was viewed as successful in terms of achieving independence, should be applied in the case of the constitution.[47] And, in the end, the compromise Harari Resolution, which postponed the drafting of the constitution while gradually adopting a set of basic laws, was passed. Yosef Burg, one of the central leaders of the Religious Zionists, claimed that this approach was particularly important due to the severe social and ideological fragmentation in nascent Israel. He defended the Harari Resolution by arguing:

> The contradictions which have been revealed here are, in my opinion, the strongest argument against unlimited empowerment of the Constitutional, Law and Justice committee. This is because we could not find the wide common foundation necessary for the framing of a constitution. I advocate the enactment of basic laws instead of a constitution not because I object to the notion of a constitution in principle. I prefer basic laws for reasons of method and chronology.... What we need at this time is to pause so as to clarify and deliberate

about our problems. We need to get used to each other and together construct our common political and public life.[48]

Unfortunately, Burg's prediction did not come true — "getting used to each other" only led to greater resentment and deepening of the conflict.

7. CONSTITUTION AND (NON) CONSENT

In the first decades since the Harari resolution, the conflict over the definition of the Jewish state was mitigated through accomodational means. The Harari Resolution enabled the first Knesset to bypass any explicit formulation of the relationship between religion and state and to circumvent controversial ideological decisions concerning the character of the polity. Lacking a written constitution, conflicting religious-secular claims were dealt with through a set of informal consociational arrangements, known as the *religious status quo*.[49] The status-quo is generally taken to mean the non-separation between religion and state in certain areas such as Sabbath observation, Kosher food in governmental institutions, exclusive jurisdiction of rabbinical courts over Jews on issues of personal law (particularly marriage and divorce), the autonomy of religious educational institutions, the exemption of religious students and religious women from military service.[50] This vague concept was first introduced in the coalition agreements of 1950. Since then, the term has been included in the coalition agreements of almost every Israeli government, as a manifestation of the delicate balance between religious and secular demands.[51] Nevertheless, the precise nature of the status quo that these coalition governments agreed to preserve has never been clearly or formally defined.

During the 1980s, the consociational character of Israeli politics in the religious sphere had weakened. Religious and secular Jews became progressively more strident in their opposing positions, and the accomodational relationship between the two sectors of Israeli society had deteriorated. Following the Likud victory over the Labor party in 1977, Israeli politics had transformed from a dominant-party system to a balanced two blocks, in which the religious parties enjoyed a special position of 'scale tipping,' affecting the formation of coalitional governments in Israel.[52] In face of the growing political powers of the religious camp, the liberal-secular population found support in the increasingly more activist Supreme Court. The Court became identified with one side in the political and cultural struggle over the character of the State of Israel. It turned to be the central arena for the promotion of the liberal-secular Jewish agenda.[53]

During the 1990s, the overlap between the societal conflict over the character of the Israeli polity and the institutional conflict between the Knesset and Supreme Court reached a climax following the legislation of two Basic Laws on Human Rights: Basic Law on Human Dignity and Liberty, and Basic Law on Freedom of Occupation. Chief Justice Aharon Barak lauded this legislation as a "constitutional revolution," claiming that the legislation implicitly granted the Court the power to strike down any Knesset legislation which conflicts with the Basic Laws.[54] While the Supreme Court has used its self-declared power of judicial review only in a number of minor cases, the Court's revolutionary rhetoric met with harsh reactions from the political system. The Knesset decided to override one of the Court rulings[55] and discussed the option of establishing a 'constitutional court' that would better represent the social fragmentation of Israeli society.[56] Eventually, the clash between the religious population and the Supreme Court became direct. In 1999, all subgroups in the religious camp from the religious Zionist (including the Chief Rabbis of the State) to the fanatic anti-Zionists — united in a massive demonstration against the Supreme Court in Jerusalem.[57]

The exacerbated religious-secular conflict, reflected in the growing inter-institutions tensions between the Knesset and the Supreme Court, had paralyzing effects on the process of constitution-making in Israel. The fear of activist interpretation of a liberal Supreme Court prevented any further Basic Laws from being legislated. In the words of religious Knesset member David Tal (Shas):

> "Even if the Ten Commandments would be proposed as Basic Laws we will oppose the legislation … because if I accept the Ten Commandments as Basic Laws ….the Supreme Court may interpret them and overturn them".[58]

On May 2003, in order to break this impasse, the Knesset Constitution, Law and Justice Committee initiated the "Constitution in Broad Consent Project," taking upon itself to consolidate a single constitutional document that would "enjoy a wide support among Israelis and Jews worldwide."[59] It was the most comprehensive endeavor since 1950 to develop a constitution for the State of Israel. In the next two years, the Committee held over 80 meetings, including hundreds of experts, legal advisors, public figures and politicians. Hundreds of documents were submitted to the Committee as background material. On February 2006, the Committee presented to the Knesset its final report, containing more than 10,000 pages of detailed protocols, and a constitutional draft.

The Committee, however, did not succeed in finding acceptable compromise formulations to the most controversial issues. Rather, the constitutional draft incorporated several alternative formulations for controversial topics on which committee members had not reached agreement. Amongst other issues, a number of alternative versions were presented on the issues of the relationship between religion and state and of the powers of the Supreme Court.

The Committee protocols, the Knesset debate around the Committee report, as well the public dispute in the weeks that followed, reveal that the divide between a religious and a secular-liberal perception of the Jewish state still appears to be the central obstacle for the adoption of a constitution.[60] Knesset members from both the Orthodox and the liberal-secular poles acknowledged the substantial distance between their positions and admitted that no agreement had yet been achieved on issues such as personal law, particularly marriage and divorce, conversion to Judaism and the question of "who is a Jew," Kosher food and public preservation of Sabbath.[61] As Deputy Minister of Welfare, member of the Orthodox *Yahadut Hatorah* party, Abraham Ravitz stressed during the Constitutional Committee discussions:

> "The main reason that for fifty years we could not make any progress towards a constitution is that... first, the Jewish people already has a constitution, and we should implement it in our daily life... and second, the fact that we cannot compromise on the most fundamental issues which, from our perspective, are essential to our existence as a people."[62]

However, in one important respect the contemporary constitutional, political and public dispute over the character of the state differed from that of Israel's formative years: it is no longer exclusive to the Jewish majority. In recent years, the Israeli Palestinian minority has expressed a growing demand to participate in the redefinition of the identity of the State of Israel. Leading Arab advocacy and lobbying NGOs, such as Adalah and Mosawa, have challenged the constitutional efforts made by the Constitution, Law and Judiciary Committee of the Knesset and published alternative constitutional proposals.[63] They called for the transformation of the state from its official definition as "Jewish and democratic" into a liberal-democratic state "for all its citizens," where the Palestinians will be recognized as a national minority.[64] The demands for special minority group rights and power sharing were echoed by Arab representatives in the Knesset.[65]

In spite of the attempt of the Constitution, Law and Justice Committee to find compromise formulations for the proposed constitution, regarding both the foundational and the institutional aspects of the constitution, many Knesset members expressed their pessimism that a constitution could be formulated which would enjoy a broad consensus. Hence, from a range of different factions — religious, secular and Arab — arguments were made for the preservation of the existing ambiguous and indecisive informal constitutional arrangements, rather than for the entrenchment of a constitution that would mirror the world-view of only part of the population. This position was expressed by religious representatives such as Yizchak Levi, who stated that "we are not ready yet for clear cut decisions", and Meir Porush of Orthodox *Agudat Israel*:

> "The constitutional draft may fit any state around the world, but does not represent the spirit of the Jewish people in its country…Israel cannot be like any other nation…we must be loyal to our identity, our heritage, our spiritual destiny, and stick to the holy Torah that was given on Mount Sinai. The draft constitution does not express that, hence we will vote against it…A constitution under circumstances of disagreement is a recipe for deepening divisions. Therefore, Israeli society should be allowed for few more years of internal discussions, until general consent is crystallized, and perhaps anchored in a constitution."[66]

Zehava Galon, representative of secular-left wing Meretz came to a similar conclusion:

> "I fear that the enactment of a constitution not only would not fortify the fragile protection of human rights in Israel, but rather fracture it and create big and dangerous breaches which will deepen the rotten compromise. Hence, it is better to leave us without a constitution, rather than use the term constitution in vain."[67]

Similarly, Abed el-Malech Dahamsha, of the Arab party Ra'am, claimed that the proposed constitution does not protect the rights of minorities in general, and those of the Arab minority in particular, for example by not declaring Arabic as an official language.

> "If the constitution does not guarantee entrenched minority groups, and since we lived for 57 years without a constitution, it is better to wait for better days in which a constitution will be enacted."[68]

8. MATERIAL ENTRENCHMENT

By refraining from making a controversial decision on the identity and underlying values of the state, the Israeli "founding fathers" may have believed that they were transferring these issues to the more flexible arena of ordinary politics. In the political sphere, it was argued during the 1950 constitutional debates, decisions could be arrived at gradually in accordance with an emerging societal consensus. However, in fact, postponing the drafting of a written constitution led to the emergence of a material constitution, which turned out to be, in ways, more rigid than a formal one might have been.

Hans Kelsen distinguishes between a constitution in the formal and in the material sense.[69] While the former denotes a written document created by a legislative act, the latter refers to the established structures of the political order, based on conventions, customs, and judicial interpretation, which may exist even in lieu of a formally entrenched written document. In Israel, the institutional structure of the government, while not entrenched in a constitution, was formalized in written Basic Laws. However, the definition of the relationship between the state and the Jewish religion, which is part of the foundational aspect of the constitution, was represented by the informal consociational arrangements of the status quo. In other words, they took the character of a material constitution.

A standard criticism of consociational arrangements points to their tendency to build "systemic constraints" to rapid societal change.[70] When constitutional arrangements are informal, the problem of rigidity may be even more acute, as unlike the case of a formal constitution, material constitutions do not include a clear mechanism of amendment. The lack of formal procedure for the alteration of material constitutions can result in an entrenched conservatism.

In the case of Israel, the incrementalist constitutional arrangements, which deferred the enactment of a written constitution, opened the door for a material entrenchment of the religious status-quo. The political inability to enact a Bill of Rights over half a century after the first constitutional debates, as well as the continuing inability to enact civil marriage in a mostly secular society, reveals the inherent rigidity of Israel's material constitution in the religious arena.

This is one of the shortcomings of the incrementalist approach to constitution-making. Although over the years the Israeli court has managed to establish the legal status of many individual rights through its precedents,[71] the material constitution in the religious sphere violates

19

liberal principles. For example, the Orthodox dominance in area of personal law infringes upon the basic liberties of hundreds of thousands of citizens who cannot marry or divorce according to the existent religious legal traditions[72] It is women, particularly, who are the main victims of the traditional patriarchal legal system. Jewish law enables men the power to deny their wives a divorce, hence prohibiting thousands of Israeli women from remarrying and allowing men to use the threat of withholding divorce in order to force divorce terms or avoid payment of alimony.

9. Concluding Remarks

Despite its effort, the 2006 Knesset could not avoid repeating the choices made by the first Knesset, re-affirming the incrementalist approach to constitution-making adopted by the 1950 framers. Recognizing the lack of consensus regarding the foundational aspects of the constitution, Knesset members from all over the political spectrum called for the preservation of existing ambiguous informal constitutional arrangements, rather than for the entrenchment of a constitution that mirrors the world-view of merely one sector of the population.

One of the fears expressed by members of the liberal-secular camp is that the fragmented political system will produce a "bad constitution," which would be worse than the absence of a formal constitution.[73] Perhaps it is not surprising, then, that the following statement, which was made during the Knesset constitutional debate in 1950, still sounds so very relevant today:

> The fundamental question is what are constitutions for? All constitutions are designed to unite the people. The people as a whole unite around particular known, supreme principles. Do we have the shared base, a uniting base which is required for enactment of this constitution, or are we still lacking this base, and hence it would be better to supress for now the issue of constitution-drafting? The truth is that we do not yet have the minimal common basis upon which we can build a constitution. Because this building depends on a difference in the approach to one cardinal question: what is the state of Israel? Is it a novel state, a new creature that never existed, or are we facing the renewal of the Kingdom of Israel?[74]

NOTES

1   Walter F. Murphy, "Constitutions, Constitutionalism and Democracy," in *Constitutionalism and Democracy: Transitions in the Contemporary World*, ed. Douglas Greenberg et al. (New York, Oxford: Oxford University Press, 1993), p. 10.

2   The Knesset decision not to enact a written constitution in 1950 is attributed by different studies to various ideological, coalitional, pragmatic and national factors. For further discussion see, among others: Giora Goldberg. "'When Trees Are Planted There Is No Need for Constitution': On State Building and Constitution Making," *State, Government and International Relations* 38 (1993); Philippa Strum, "The Road Not Taken: Constitutional Non-Decision Making in 1948-1950 and Its Impact on Civil Liberties in the Israeli Political Culture", in: S. Ilan Troen and Noah Lucas (eds.), *Israel: The First Decade of Independence* (Albany, N.Y: State University of New York Press, 1995), pp. 83–104.

3   Yonathan Shapira, *Politicians as an Hegemonic Class: the Case of Israel* (Tel Aviv: Sifriat Poalim, 1996), p. 33.

4   Baruch Kimerling, "Religion, Nationality and Democracy in Israel," *Zemanim* 50 (1994); Yoav Peled, Ethnic Democracy and the Legal Construction of Citizenship: Arab Citizens of the Jewish State, *American Political Science Review* 86, no. 2 (June 1992): 434-435.

5   Stathis N. Kalyvas, *The Rise of Christian Democracy in Europe* (Ithaca, NY: Cornell University Press, 1996).

6   Asher Cohen and Bernard Susser, *Israel and the Politics of Jewish Identity: The Secular-Religious Impasse* (Baltimore and London: The John Hopkins University Press, 2000), pp. 20–21.

7   Dan Horowitz and Moshe Lissak, *Trouble in Utopia: The Overburdened Polity of Israel.* (Albany: State University of New York Press, 1989), p. 139.

8   *Ibid.*

9   Cohen and Susser, *Israel and the Politics of Jewish Identity*, pp. 20–21.

10 Menachem Friedman, "The History of the Status-Quo: Religion and State in Israel," in *Brethren Dwelling Together. Orthodoxy and Non-Orthodoxy in Israel: Positions, Propositions and Accords*, ed. Uri Dromi (Jerusalem: Israel Democracy Institute, 2005), p. 72.

11 Horowitz and Lissak, *Trouble in Utopia*, pp. 59–60, 138.

12 *Knesset Records* 4 (14 February 1950), p. 744.

13 This was the party composition of the constituent assembly/first Knesset: out of 120 members of Knesset 46 were Mapai (Israel Labor Party); 19 Mapam (United Workers' Party); 2 minority lists connected with Labor parties; 16 United Religious Front (included the Religious Nationalists and the Haredi — Orthodox — Agudat Israel); 14 Herut (Freedom Party, led by Menachem Begin, the leader of the IZL pre-state underground); 7 General Zionists (Liberal Party); 5 Progressive Party (Independent Liberals); 4 Israeli Communist Party; 7 others. From: Dan Horowitz

and Moshe Lissak, *Trouble in Utopia*, Appendix 2. Mapai formed a narrow governmental coalition with the religious parties and the Progressive Party. Left out were Mapam, the central party from the left, and the General Zionists and Herut on the rights wing.

14 Out of 119 Knesset members (one passed away) 50 voted for the Harari bill, 38 voted against, 3 were absent and 16 abstained. *Knesset Records* 5 (1950), p. 1922.

15 *Knesset Records* 5 (1950), p. 1743.

16 Justice Mishael Cheshin argued that the Transition Law alters the authority of the Constituent Assembly and changes it to a regular legislator. According to Cheshin, the instruction to adopt a constitution was irrevocable, directed only to the Constituent Assembly, which had no authority to pass it to any other bodies, namely to the following Knesset. Cheshin expressed this view in a minority opinion in the case of *Ha'mizrachi Bank v. Migdal* (1995). See also infra note 23.

17 Yehoshua Segev, "Why Israel does not have and will not have (at least in the close future) a Constitution? On the Advantages of 'the Decision not to Decide'," *Moznei Mishpat* 5 (2006).

18 See for example: Ulrich K. Preuss, *Constitutional Revolution: The link between Constitutionalism and Progress* (Atlantic Highlands, N.J.: Humanities Press, 1995), p. 2; Bruce Ackerman, *We the People: Foundations* (Cambridge, Mass.: Cambridge University Press, 1991), p. 9; Hanna Arendt, *On Revolution* (New York: Viking Press 1965).

19 The preparation for the writing of the constitution began by Zerach Vaarhaftig already in 1947 within the Jewish Agency Executive. However, Mapai leaders objected this constitutional activity. Zerach Vahrhaftig, Zerach. *A Constitution for Israel: Religion and State* (Jerusalem: Mesilot, 1988), p. 60.

20 During that period Ben-Gurion began expressing his objection to the writing of a constitution. Preferring the British system of parliamentary sovereignty he rejected the delegation of arbiter powers to the court, which would weaken the legislature. For detailed discussion of Ben-Gurion's position towards the constitution see: Goldberg, "When Trees Are Planted There Is No Need for Constitution" (1993); Shlomo Aaronson, "Constitution for Israel: The British Model of David Ben-Gurion," *Politica: An Israeli Journal for Political Science and International Relations* 2 (1998); Shapiro, *Politicians as an Hegemonic Class*, pp. 31–33.

21 The drafts were written in either Hebrew, German or English. For details on the constitutional proposals submitted to the committee see: Zerach Vahrhaftig, *A Constitution for Israel: Religion and State* (Jerusalem: Mesilot, 1988), ch. 3 (Hebrew).

22 *Ibid.*, ch. 3–6.

23 The law did not explicitly acknowledge the first Knesset's duty to enact a constitution. The constituent authority of the Knesset was formally laid down by Supreme Court ruling in the case of *Ha'mizrachi Bank v. Migdal* (1995). Chief Justice Aaron Barak described the Knesset as wearing "two hats...first, a hat of constituent authority, and second, a hat of legislative authority." Aaron Barak, "The

Constitutional Revolution: Protected Human Rights," *Mishpat Umimshal: Law and Government in Israel* 1, no. 1 (1992): p. 16 (Hebrew). For the minority opinion see supra note 16.

In two respects Israel differs from other countries with dual-level legislative authority (e.g. Germany, Austria, India). In all other cases, the constitution was adopted previous to the establishment of the legislative body, granting it with the power to amend the constitution. Second, the Israeli constitutional law does not mandate a distinctive procedure, or a demand for special majority, for passing Basic Laws. See: Amnon Rubinstein and B. Medina, *Constitutional Law in the State of Israel*, 5th ed. (Jerusalem: Schocken, 1997), p. 368.

[24]   As the Chair of the Committee Nachum Nir reported to the Knesset in its first discussion on the constitution. see: *Knesset Records* 4 (14 February 1950), p. 714.

[25]   *Knesset Records* 4 (20 February 1950), p. 811.

[26]   *Knesset Records* 4 (20 February 1950), p. 814.

[27]   *Knesset Records* 4 (13 February 1950), p. 774.

[28]   Yaakov Gil, The General Zionists in: *Knesset Records* 4 (7 February 1950), p. 745.

[29]   Israel Bar-Yehuda, (Mapam, United Workers Party) in: *Knesset Records* 4 (7 February 1950), p. 734.

[30]   David Bar-Rav-Hai in: Mapai, *Knesset Records* 4 (7 February 1950), p. 726.

[31]   Efraim Tavori, Mapai, in: *Knesset Records* 4 (13 February 1950), p. 774.

[32]   Minister of Welfare, Rabi Yitzhak Meir Levi in: *Knesset Records* 4 (20 February 1950), p. 812.

[33]   Meir-David Levonstein (Agudat Israel) in: *Knesset Records* 4 (7 February 1950), p. 744.

[34]   The IZL (stands for Irgun Zvai Leumi, which means National Military Organization) was a right-wing nationalist paramilitary organization that conducted guerrilla warfare against British rule. Founded in 1931, it was associated with the Revisionist movement and did not recognize the authority of the central Jewish institutions of the Yishuv.

[35]   Dan Horowirz and Moshe Lissak, *Origins of the Israeli Polity: Palestine under the Mandate* (Chicago and London: University of Chicago Press, 1978), p. 429.

[36]   In the 1920s, an attempt of fanatic ultra-Orthodox groups to collaborate with the Arab leadership in Palestine against the Zionist enterprise ended with the political assassination of Israel De-Han by the Haganah. *Ibid.*, 417.

[37]   For a theoretical discussion on the difficulty of implementing majority rule in deeply divided societies see: Arend Lijphart, "Majority Rule Versus Democracy in Deeply Divided Societies" *Politikon* 4, no. 2 (1977).

[38]   Avraham Hirtzfeld, Mapai, in: *Knesset Records* 5 (2 May 1950), p. 1277.

[39]   The Jeffersonian argument against an entrenched constitution by which the founding generation limits the majoritarian decision-making of the future generations and thus infringes upon the most fundamental principle of democracy, was raised by

several members of the Knesset. See for example: *Knesset Records* 4 (7 February 1950), p. 727; *Knesset Records* 4 (13 February 1950), p. 777.

40 *Knesset Records* 4 (7 February 1950), p. 727.

41 Moshe Aram, from the United Workers Front, in: *Knesset Records* 5 (2 May 1950), p. 1267.

42 Ben-Zion Dinburg, Mapai, in: *Knesset Records* 4 (7 February 1950), p. 742.

43 Israel Bar Yehuda, Mapam, in: *Knesset Records* 4 (7 February 1950), p. 736.

44 *Knesset Records* 5 (2 May 1950), p. 1277.

45 Horowitz and Lissak, *Trouble in Utopia*, p. 101.

46 *Ibid*, pp. 101–2.

47 For example, David Bar-Rav-Hai, Mapai, *Knesset Records* 4 (7 February 1950), p. 728.

48 *Knesset Records* 5 (8 May 1950), p. 1310.

49 On consociationalism in the religious sphere in Israel see: Eliezer Don-Yehiya, *Religion and Political Accommodation in Israel* (Jerusalem: Floersheimer Institute for Policy Studies, 1999); Cohen and Susser, *Israel and the Politics of Jewish Identity*, Ch. 2.

50 On the origins of the status quo see: Menachem Friedman, "The History of the Status-Quo: Religion and State in Israel," in *Brethren Dwelling Together. Orthodoxy and Non-Orthodoxy in Israel: Positions, Propositions and Accords*, ed. Uri Dromi (Jerusalem: Israel Democracy Institute, 2005).

51 Eliezer Don-Yehiya, *Religion and Political Accommodation in Israel* (Jerusalem: Floersheimer Institute for Policy Studies, 1999), pp. 44–45

52 Cohen and Susser, *Israel and the Politics of Jewish Identity*; Giora Goldberg, Religious Zionism and the Framing of a Constitution for Israel, *Israel Studied* 3 no. 1 (1998).

53 Menachem Mautner, "The 1980s: The Years of Anxiety," *Iyunei Mishpat* 26, no. 2 (2002): 670.

54 Aaron Barak, "The Constitutional Revolution: Protected Human Rights," *Mishpat Umimshal: Law and Government in Israel* 1, no. 1 (1992).

55 Following the Supreme Court ruling in the case of *Mitrael v. Prime Minister 1993* the Knesset amended Basic Law: Freedom of Occupation. See: Hanna Lerner, "Democracy, Constitutionalism and Identity: the Anomaly of the Israeli Case," *Constellations* 11:2 (2004): 247.

56 Ibid.

57 It was one of Israel's largest demonstrations, with estimated 250,000 to 400,000 participants. Cohen and Susser, *Israel and the Politics of Jewish Identity*, p. 94.

58 *Knesset Records* 184 (14 July 1999), p. 537.

59 *Constitution in Broad Consent: Report of the Constitution, Law and Justice Committee regarding Proposals for the Constitution of the State of Israel*, 2006 (Hebrew). http://huka.gov.il/wiki/index.php

60 Avirama Golan, "Not a Good Way to Construct a Constitution", *Haaretz*, 13/02/2006. Suzie Navot, "Is it the Right Time for a Constitution?", *Yediot Acharonot*, 24/01/ 2006.

61 Knesset members Yischak Levi (National Religious Party), Ofir Pines (Labor), Zehava Galon (Meretz), Nissim Zeev (Shas) during the concluding discussion of the Constitutional, Law and Justice Committee, 2 February 2006, Protocol no. 658 in: *Constitution in Broad Consent: Report of the Constitution, Law and Justice Committee regarding Proposals for the Constitution of the State of Israel*, 2006 (Hebrew). http://huka.gov.il/wiki/index.php.

62 *Ibid*, p. 12.

63 See websites: www.adalah.org and www.mosawa.org. see also the Haifa Declaration at Mada-el-Carmel: www.mada-research.org.

64 Yoav Peled and Gershon Shafir, *Being Israeli: The Dynamics of Multiple Citizenship* (Tel Aviv: Tel Aviv University Press, 2005), p. 164.

65 Amal Jamal, "Strategies of Minority Struggle for Equality in Ethnic States: Arab Politics in Israel," *Citizenship Studies* 11, no. 3 (July 2007): 277; Amal Jamal, "Future Visions and Contemporary Dilemmas: On the Political Ethos of Israel's Palestinian Citizens," *Israeli Studies Forum* 32:2 (2008): 277.

66 *Knesset Records*, 13 February 2007, pp. 53–54.

67 *Knesset Records*, 13 February 2007, pp. 29–30.

68 *Knesset Records*, 13 February 2007, p. 76.

69 Hans Kelsen, *Pure Theory of Law* (Berkeley: University of California Press, 1967), p. 222.

70 Alfred Stepan, "Paths toward Redemocratization: Theoretical and Comparative Considerations," in: Guillermo O'Donnell, Philippe C. Schmitter and Laurence Whitehead, *Transitions from Authoritarian Rule: Comparative Perspectives* (Baltimore and London: The John Hopkins University Press, 1988), p. 80. For an extensive criticism of the consociational model see: Brian Barry, "Political Accomodation and Consociational Democracy," *British Journal of Political Science* 5, no. 4 (1975).

71 Dafna Barak–Erez, "From an Unwritten to a Written Constitution: the Israeli Challenge in American Perspective," Columbia Human Rights Law Review 26 (1994–1995): 315–317.

72 Pinhas Shiffman, "Civil or Sacred: Civil Marriage and Divorce Alternatives in Israel" (Jerusalem: The Association for Civil Rights in Israel, 2001). (Hebrew).

73 Mordechai Kremnitzer, in: *The Israel Democracy Institute's Proposal for a Constitution by Consensus* (Jerusalem: Israel Democracy Institute, 2005), p. 63.

74 *Knesset Records* 5 (1950), p. 1315.

WHO IS AFRAID OF LANGUAGE RIGHTS IN ISRAEL?

MEITAL PINTO

1. INTRODUCTION

The issue of language rights illustrates, and sometimes takes to the extreme, the complexity of the multicultural existence in Israel. Granting language rights to the Israeli Arab minority is perceived by many Israeli Jews as a controversial political matter that Israeli courts should refrain from discussing. Significant legal support for this common view has recently been given by Cheshin J. in his minority opinion in the *Adalah* Israeli Supreme Court case, which discusses the need for bilingual street signs in mixed Arab Jewish cities.[1]

Justice Cheshin raises three major problems with the rights the petitioners ask. I identify these claims with three allegedly distinctive features that language rights bear in comparison with other rights. The first dimension is their collective nature, which means that they legally protect groups rather than individuals. The second dimension is their positive nature, which not only requires a state not to interfere with a person's will to speak a minority language, but also requires that the state take active measures to support this language. The third dimension is their selective nature, which means that unlike general rights such as the right to freedom of expression, language rights protect the language of certain minority groups and not others.

By analysing *Adalah* and comparing it to previous linguistic legal cases in Israel, I observe that the common fear of language rights is mostly invoked in what I call 'multidimensional linguistic cases.' In such cases, demands for language rights involve at least two of the above dimensions and sometimes all of them. The more dimensions such cases involve, the more reluctant the court is to address them.

I then argue that many other well acknowledged rights in Israel involve at least one of the dimensions I have identified. I conclude therefore that the difference between language rights and other well-acknowledged rights in Israel is a difference in degree and not kind. If so, Justice Cheshin's reservation about dealing with language rights is unjustified. It seems to me that the general reluctance of courts to deal with language rights lies elsewhere. Many Israeli Jews fear that granting language rights to the Arab minority will damage the Jewish character of Israel. This fear is associated with the fourth distinctive feature language rights may bare — the public dimension.

This paper consists of four parts. In section II, I depict the facts of the *Adalah* case and analyse Barak C. J.'s majority opinion and Cheshin J.'s minority opinion. Setting out their arguments side by side will allow me to identify the challenge that language rights pose for courts. In section III, I provide a definition of language rights. I also analyse two different interests language rights may protect: instrumental and intrinsic interests. In section IV, I argue that language rights may manifest themselves in legal cases within three different dimensions. In section V, I show that other rights that are well-acknowledged by the Israeli legal system involve at least one of the dimensions I have identified. I conclude that the common fear of language rights is greatly unjustified as the difference between language rights and other well-acknowledged minority rights in Israel, is a difference in degree and not kind. The fear of language rights lies in their fourth distinctive feature — their public dimension, which brings Arab culture into the Israeli public sphere.

2. The *Adalah* Decision

The case of *Adalah* raises one of the most difficult questions in Israeli legal discourse with regard to language rights. Its special circumstances created new arguments, which had not been addressed by Israeli courts before. The petitioners in *Adalah* argued that in a municipality with an Arab-minority population, municipal signs should be bilingual, rather than in Hebrew only. The term 'municipal signs' refers to all kinds of signs that are published by the municipality: warning and guidance signs on roads and sidewalks and signs marking street names.

The petitioners' argument is based on constitutional principles as well as statutory interpretation. The constitutional part of their argument is based on discrimination and human dignity. The statutory part of their argument is based on Article 82 of the Palestine-Order-in Council, 1922,[2] which states as follows:

All ordinances, official notices and official forms of the government and all official notices of local authorities and municipalities in areas to be prescribed by order of the government shall be published in Arabic and Hebrew. The two languages may be used, subject to any regulations to be made from time to time, in the Government offices and the Law Courts.

The majority of the Supreme Court (Barak C.J. and Dorner J.) accept the petition, and require the respondent municipalities to ensure that municipal signs in their areas be in both Hebrew and Arabic. Justice Dorner bases her decision on art. 82. In her opinion, street signs are part of what is referred to in art. 82 as 'official notices' and therefore should be published in the two official languages, i.e., Hebrew and Arabic.[3]

Chief Justice Barak points out the ambiguity and weakness of art. 82 by noting that there is no way to know whether municipal signs are included in the legal term 'official notices' in art. 82.[4] Barak then concludes that the fact that Arabic is an official language does not oblige all the respondent municipalities to mark all municipal signs in Arabic as well.

Consequently, Barak C.J. provides other arguments on behalf of the municipalities' duty to add Arabic captions to street signs. According to Barak, the duty of the respondent municipalities is determined by balancing several considerations. First, municipal signs should include Arabic captions so the Arab residents of the municipalities will be able to find their way within the borders of their city, receive information and be warned from traffic hazards and the like. As, Barak puts it: "Municipal signs are designated to 'talk' to the residents of the city and therefore should be published in a language that they understand."[5]

Chief Justice Barak refers to other considerations, which he calls 'general purposes' of interpretation. The first consideration is the right of an individual to freedom of language. The second consideration is the right to equality. The right to equality is broadly interpreted by Barak C.J. as a guarantee not merely of equal formal access to state services, but also of equal use, or equal benefit from them. In Barak's own words:

...the municipality has to ensure equal use of its services. In a place where part of the municipal public cannot understand municipal signs its right to equal benefit from the municipal services is injured.[6]

Barak's equality argument is that Arab citizens are entitled to equal municipal services, and in order for them to enjoy these services they should be able to understand the language of signs. This argument is relatively weak in a case where an Israeli Arab is fluent in Hebrew. This is where the freedom of language argument comes into play. An Arab Israeli citizen has a right to fully live his life in Arabic even if he is capable of conducting some of it in Hebrew. That is to say, Arab citizens are entitled to live their lives in Arabic because this is the language to which their cultural identity is deeply attached.

The broad interpretation of the rights to freedom of language and equality allows Barak to deduce the positive duty of the municipalities to add Arabic captions to street signs. Thus, Barak C.J. overcomes the ambiguous language of art. 82 which allegedly imposes positive duties, but does not make clear what are the 'official notices' that should be bilingual.

After dealing with the positive dimension, Barak C. J. asks whether the positive dimension of the rights to freedom of language and equality should guarantee the right of every minority language in Israel to be added to street signs. In other words, Barak C.J. asks what distinguishes the Arabic language, and why is its status different from that of other languages — apart from Hebrew — that Israelis speak? Chief Justice Barak provides the following answer that justifies the selective application of the positive aspects of the rights to freedom of language and equality by pointing to the fact that:

> …Arabic is the language of the largest minority in Israel, which has lived in Israel since far far in time […] This is the language of citizens who, notwithstanding the Arab-Israeli conflict, wish to live in Israel as loyal citizens with equal rights, amid respect for their language and culture.[7]

Justice Cheshin, in a minority opinion, holds that the petition should be dismissed for several different but connected reasons.[8] According to Cheshin J., the requirement to add Arabic captions to street signs is not capable of being deduced from the right to freedom of language, which guarantees every individual's liberty to speak his or her language, but does not impose a duty on the governing authorities to act in this regard.[9] In Cheshin's view, this requirement also does not arise from the principles of international law, which also focus solely on the negative dimension of the right to freedom of language.[10]

In addition, Cheshin J. states that the petition lacks a minimal factual foundation because the petitioners do not show, even with minimal proof, that there are Arab residents who do not know Hebrew and are therefore injured as a result of the lack of street signs in Arabic.[11] Justice Cheshin also argues that there is no reason to provide bilingual municipal signs only in mixed cities because the life of Arab citizens in Israel are not confined to their home town. Many Arab citizens live in one city and work in another.[12]

Justice Cheshin also argues that the petitioners ask the court to recognize collective rights that aim to promote the collective culture of the Arab minority in Israel. However, according to Cheshin, Israeli courts have never acknowledged collective rights. Legal rights in Israel in general concern only individuals, not collectives.[13]

Justice Cheshin's central claim is that the court should not acknowledge language rights that protect the Arabic language because the question whether to recognize them or not is a political question. In Cheshin J.'s view, it is improper for the court to create a new right that independently strengthens Israeli Arabs' cultural and national identity. Such a decision should be left to the political arena. Therefore, the political authorities, and not the court, have the authority to formulate such rights. As long as the petitioners' ideological aspirations are not translated into a statute by the Knesset, the court is unable to assist them, and it is improper for the court to decide an issue that does not lie within its domain.[14]

Before delving into the definition of language rights, the different interests they protect and their distinctive features I would first like to counter Cheshin J.'s claim about the political character of the petition. It may be inferred from Cheshin J.'s view that when a controversial political matter is brought to the court, and there is no specific statute that regulates it, this matter is not justiciable. Let us assume that Cheshin's observation is true, and that the question whether to place bilingual signs in mixed cities does indeed have serious political implications. Has the Israeli Supreme Court refrained from deciding a case only because this case has serious political implications? The answer is negative.

From looking at the decision history of the Israeli Supreme Court, it becomes clear that it has very often made decisions on politically charged issues without hesitation.[15] Yaacov Ben-Shemesh reminds us that it was Cheshin J. himself who said that the fact that an issue is political does not prevent the court from dealing with it.[16]

Lorraine Weinrib locates Israeli courts within a specific value framework which is common among other liberal states such as Canada, Germany, and South Africa. Weinrib points out that courts' tendency to deal with political issues is rooted in a comprehensive normative framework which she calls "the post World War Two paradigm." As a court that operates in what Weinrib calls "a constitutional state," the Supreme Court of Israel has been committed to promoting constitutional liberal norms, such as liberty and equality.[17] These liberal norms govern and are superior to interests that are preferred by the majority.[18] In my view, the most important feature of the constitutional state is its commitment to the interests of all members in the political community: to the interests of those who are part of the majority, and most significantly, to the interests of those who belong to weak groups.[19]

While the general commitment of the Israeli Supreme Court to defend minority rights is rooted in the normative framework in which the court operates, it lacks the comprehensive doctrine of language rights that allows the court to deal with the challenge they face. In *Adalah*, Barak C.J. tries to cope with these challenges, while Dorner J. avoids dealing with them and Cheshin J. identifies them but wrongly argues that the court should refrain from dealing with them. In section III, I use Barak C. J.'s and Cheshin J.'s opinions to analyse three distinct dimensions in which language rights may manifest themselves in legal cases. Before delving into the four distinctive dimensions, I wish to provide a legal definition of the term 'language rights' and to discuss the two different interests they protect: the instrumental and the intrinsic interests.

3. What are Language Rights?

None of the Judges in *Adalah* uses the term 'language rights'. Nevertheless, the petitioners' claim is a claim for language rights. Language rights are defined in the legal and philosophical literature as rights that protect the use of particular languages, namely one's mother tongue or native language.[20] Language rights are regarded as minority rights because in a heterogeneous linguistic society, members of minority groups usually need their language to be legally protected. As opposed to members of majority communities, whose languages enjoy strong status without needing special legal protection, members of minority groups are usually under constant pressure to abandon their mother tongue[21] in favour of the majority language.[22]

According to Joseph Raz, the right to X exists if and only if some person's interest constitutes a sufficient reason for holding others to be under a duty to provide or secure X.[23] Following Raz's definition we ought to identify one or more interests in protecting particular languages that might be thought important enough to justify imposing duties on others. The following discussion of interests in language will focus on the interests in using a particular language, which may require protection, rather than on human interests in having language in the first place. In the same manner, I will not discuss the importance of language as a human enterprise for human culture in general.[24]

Viewed instrumentally, the use of a particular language is regarded as valuable because it is a tool, an instrument to achieve valuable human objectives. Viewed as a matter of intrinsic value, the use of a particular language is regarded as valuable on its own account and not because it promotes other valuable ends.

One may think of several instrumental interests in protecting a particular minority language. First, language is a person's main form of communication. It allows people to conduct their every day life, to exchange information with other people. People have an interest in communicating via their own mother tongue language because they are less comfortable using other languages in their communication activities.[25] Therefore, people's own language is the best means for them to accomplish the object of communication. However, since minorities can communicate in the majority language as well after they learn it, the mere interest in comfort does not seem to justify legal protection.

Second, one may appeal to some social good, such as peace and security, which society in general gains as a result of protecting minority languages.[26] However, language rights are only one of the means of mitigating conflicts between majority and minority groups. It is not the only means and, among available means, it is not a necessary means to achieve peace and security in a multilingual society.[27]

Third, one may embrace Will Kymlicka's argument of language as a context of choice. According to Kymlicka, people are deeply connected to their own culture in the sense that their culture enables them to make meaningful choices when they are confronted with questions about personal values and projects. People's capacity to form and revise their conception of the good is intimately tied to their membership in their own culture, since the process of deciding how to lead their lives is a matter of exploring the possibilities made available by their own culture.[28] Therefore, if individuals are entitled to protection of their ability to make meaningful choices, then their culture and the specific language that is attached to it[29] — the context that makes this choice possible — deserves protection. Kymlicka emphasises the difficulty of learning a foreign language. However, once one overcomes this difficulty by integrating into a new culture, one does not need one's original language in order to make meaningful choices. The newly acquired foreign language serves as an alternative means for achieving the goal of making meaningful choices.[30]

Since instrumental interests are relatively weak, I will turn to discuss the intrinsic interest in protecting a particular minority language. Denise Réaume provides an elaborate account of the intrinsic interest language rights may protect by stressing the link between language and identity. She argues that language has an intrinsic value as it can constitute a marker of personal identity. One's identity is derived from one's culture. Culture is a marker of identity and language as a central part of culture is itself a marker of identity. [31]

We can find support for Réaume's observation in current sociolinguistic and anthropological theories, which highlight three interconnected ways in which language constitutes a marker of identity. First, a specific language is an embodiment of cultural concepts. The language of a particular culture is best able to express the interests, values, and world-views of that culture. No language but the one that has been most historically and intimately associated with a given culture is as capable of expressing the particular artefacts and concerns of that culture.[32] An expression in a language refers to a concept in a culture and encapsulates a specific meaning that is grounded in a specific cultural context. Due to the intimate link between culture and identity, it is difficult for people of a certain culture to truly express their identity in another language.[33]

Second, components of a particular culture such as songs, prayers, laws, and proverbs are written and expressed by the language associated with that culture.[34] In other words, language is not only a repository of conceptual building blocks for the mind, it is also the medium used to produce cultural texts from building blocks. People therefore value their language which allows distinctive texts that express the uniqueness of their culture.[35]

The third aspect combines the first and the second aspects of language as a marker of cultural identity. When a specific language is embedded with distinctive cultural concepts and serves as a cultural text in itself, it is only natural that persons who speak this language view it as an object of cultural identification. Language has a strong symbolic meaning for people as an expression of their culture. It symbolically represents the particular culture of the people who speak it.[36]

Justice Cheshin refuses to discuss the intrinsic interest in Arabic because he perceives it as a political issue. In contrast, Cheshin J. perceives the instrumental interest as less problematic. Under the instrumental view, courts protect the minority culture and language not for their own sake but for the sake of other aims such as communication. I believe that the reason for it is that the instrumental aim of promoting communication between people is not a controversial aim as opposed to protecting and promoting the minority culture.

In contrast to Cheshin J., Barak C. J. does not concentrate solely on the instrumental value of Arabic as a means of communication, but also on its intrinsic value as a marker of cultural identity. Barak uses the *Re'em* decision[37] to stress the important role of language, which is not a mere tool of communication, but also an expression of cultural and group identity. As Barak puts it:

> [L]anguage is also a culture, history, mode of thinking; it is the soul of a person[38]...[V]ia language we express ourselves, our uniqueness and our societal identity. Take a person's own language and you take himself from him... Language has a special importance when it belongs to a minority...[39]

Up to *Re'em* and *Adalah,* the Israeli Supreme Court has ruled in favour of language rights only in cases in which the claimants proved lack of knowledge in Hebrew.[40] Chief Justice Barak's statement in *Adalah* reflects a new attitude towards the right to freedom of language (which is part of the right to freedom of expression). Traditionally, the right to freedom of language has been understood as protecting individuals' interest to freely express themselves. Chief Justice Barak gives new content to the right to freedom of language as protecting the intrinsic interest in culture. In sum, Barak C.J's opinion in *Adalah* is a pivotal point in Israeli ruling as it acknowledges the intrinsic interest in language rights. However, as we have seen, it is still countered by Cheshin J.'s dissenting opinion. As I will show in the next section, in addition to the fact that the intrinsic interest in language rights is viewed as a politically problematic matter, language rights may bare three distinctive dimensions which are also perceived as problematic.

4. Three Distinctive Dimensions

The Participatory Dimension of Language Rights

Justice Cheshin argues in *Adalah* that the petitioners ask the court to recognize collective rights that aim to promote the collective culture of the Arab minority in Israel. However, according to Cheshin, courts in Israel have never acknowledged collective rights. Rights in Israel concern only individuals, not collectives. I argue that Cheshin J.'s view is wrong. First, language rights protect the interest of individuals and not of collectives. Second, when the collective dimension of language rights is properly understood, it becomes clear that other rights with collective dimensions have already been acknowledged by the Israeli Supreme Court.

There is an abundance of literature about the definition of collective rights that are also called 'group rights'.[41] Two competing conceptions regarding the definition of group rights are articulated in the literature. Under the first conception, a right might be considered to be a group right because it is the group, acting through its leadership, which has the legal power to invoke or waive the right. For example, a group's right to its land may be considered a group right because only the group acting through its leadership has the power to make decisions about the disposition of that land.

Under the second conception, a right is a group right when the interests it protects are collective or shared by a group of individuals. These two conceptions are respectively called "rights of collective agents" and "rights to collective goods".[42] The former is distinguished by the agent who holds the rights, while the latter is distinguished by the good it protects.[43] In my view, the "rights to collective goods" conception best captures the collective nature of language rights. Moreover, the "rights to collective goods" conception is preferable for two reasons. First, in order to argue that a right is a group right under the "rights of collective agents" conception we have to show that the group holds the right as a collective. This right therefore must amount to something more than the sum of the rights of its individual members. We must assume that there exists a collective whole that is irreducible to its members in the sense that its welfare is independent from the welfare of each of its members. If we cannot point out the distinction between a group and its members, then the right is in fact an individual right as it relates to the separate well-being of every individual in the group. In most cases, such a holistic approach towards a group of people seems somewhat implausible.[44]

Second, groups are usually unable to play an active role in exercising, interpreting, and defending their rights. Groups often lack effective agency and clear identity. Unlike individuals, groups are often internally divided, unorganized, unclear in their boundaries, and are therefore unable to engage in actions as groups.[45]

The second conception of group rights, namely "rights to collective goods," requires that we observe the character of the object or the interest the right protects in order to decide whether the right is a group right. Denise Réaume argues that a right is a group right only if it protects a participatory good. There are two characteristics of a participatory good. First, a participatory good involves activities that require many in order to produce it. Second, a participatory good is valuable only because of the joint involvement of many in it.[46] It is the participatory character of the good that makes the right irreducible to the individual.

Language rights protect the interest of people in speaking their own language. Language is a participatory good. First, language requires many to produce it. The use of language has a social dimension in the sense that individuals learn to use their language from others, they use it to communicate with others, and by using it they express their affiliation with others. Second, as indicated above, a person's own language is a marker of his identity. As Réaume puts it: "the point of the interest in using one's mother tongue lies in sharing it, and the culture it embodies, with others. This interest cannot be satisfied for an individual in isolation from other speakers; it can only be enjoyed through participation with others".[47] These others must speak the same language as this person. Together they constitute a linguistic community.[48]

Language Rights' Positive Dimension

As Justice Cheshin and Barak C. J. stress, the petitioners in *Adalah* do not ask for the negative liberty of Israeli Arabs to speak Arabic. They ask the state to do a positive act — to communicate with them in Arabic. The *Adalah* case demonstrates the positive dimension that language rights may bare, which requires the state to actively associate itself with the protection of minority language (Arabic in this case). Justice Cheshin claims that there is no legal basis for their claim. Freedom of language, which is part of freedom of expression, does not impose any positive duty on the state. In order to challenge Cheshin's claim I will first discuss the distinction between negative and positive rights.

The roots of the familiar distinction between negative and positive rights are found in Isaiah Berlin's well-known distinction between negative and positive freedoms.[49] Crudely speaking, the term 'negative rights' refers to rights that create the duty of the state not to interfere with a citizen's freedom to do whatever he or she desires. The term 'positive rights' refers to rights that impose positive obligations on the state, i.e. actions that the state is obliged to do, if it is to take these rights seriously.[50] For instance, the right to religious freedom entails the negative freedom of every person to practice his or her religion without interference from the state. However, one may argue that a religion cannot thrive without any financial support from the government. The right to religious freedom therefore may also entail positive steps that the government should take, such as allocating resources for building and maintaining religious institutions.[51]

In some cases the court employs this distinction in order to deny positive rights, but many times it uses this distinction in order to grant positive rights. In section V I will give examples from cases in which courts interpret the rights to freedom of expression as a positive right. These examples will refute Cheshin J.'s claim according to which the right to freedom of language does not impose any positive obligation on the state.

The Selective Dimension of Language Rights

The petitioners in *Adalah* ask the court to instruct public authorities to speak their specific language (Arabic). In the absence of unlimited economic resources in most multilingual states, the positive dimension of language rights is inherently connected to another distinctive characteristic of language rights, which I will call 'the selective nature of language rights'. Most countries can only provide comprehensive legal protection for few minority languages. Because of pragmatic reasons, the state cannot provide comprehensive support for every language that happens to be spoken by one of its citizens. It needs to choose which languages it supports and which it does not. A multilingual state has to 'choose' one or two minority languages to which it offers strong legal protection such as access to state services, governmental and municipal publications, public education and the like.[52]

As Joseph Carens observes:

> There are certain issues on which the state cannot avoid making decisions that have a significant impact in culture, and, if the polity contains people from different cultures, that advantage some and disadvantage others. The most obvious and important example is that of language.[53]

In this sense, *Adalah* had to address the selective dimension of language rights, and the right to freedom of language, which generally applies to all individuals, could not suffice it.[54]

The task of selecting the minority languages most deserving of comprehensive protection by the state, which is inevitable because of pragmatic reasons, such as limited resources, requires a complex normative decision that privileges one linguistic minority over others. In *Adalah*, Barak C.J. chooses to protect the Arabic language over other minority languages in Israel such as Russian. In order to justify his decision Barak C.J. raises a distinctive argument in favour of the Arab minority, which I have already mentioned. Chief Justice Barak stresses that the Arab minority has lived in Israel since long ago and stayed in Israel as loyal citizens in spite of the Arab-Israeli conflict.[55]

As Ilan Saban argues, Chief Justice Barak's argument about the Arab national minority which has lived for a long time in Israel, as opposed to other immigrant linguistic minorities such as the Jewish Russian minority, echoes Will Kymlicka's famous distinction between national minorities and immigrant minorities.[56] In a nutshell, Kymlicka argues that in light of pragmatic limitations on multicultural states, comprehensive language rights should be granted to national minorities, whereas immigrant minorities are to be accorded weaker language rights.[57]

Elsewhere I have critically discussed Kymlickas's distinction extensively. I have argued that Kymlicka's empirical, normative and methodological assumptions are very problematic.[58] I have suggested an alternative criterion for distinguishing between linguistic minorities, according to which the interests of different linguistic minorities in protecting their languages should be comparatively evaluated. In the absence of unlimited resources, the minority that possesses the strongest interest in its language deserves the strongest protection. Language rights should therefore protect first minority members who have the strongest interest in their language as their exclusive marker of cultural identity. I have argued that in the Israeli case, the Arab linguistic minority has a stronger interest in the protection of Arabic than that of the Russian linguistic minority, because Arabic constitutes Israeli Arabs' exclusive marker of identity.[59]

For now, it is important to stress that the selective dimension of language rights in cases such as *Adalah* requires the state or the court to make a difficult normative decision about the 'chosen' linguistic minority. This normative distinction makes language rights in multidimensional cases more complex because the state not only identifies with one linguistic minority (in the case of *Adalah* with the Arab minority), but also prefers it over other linguistic minorities, such as the Jewish Russian linguistic minority, which may raise similar linguistic demands in its struggle for cultural recognition.[60] Such a decision always involves stereotypes, political interests in response to cultural and ethnic conflicts and the like. It is therefore the most problematic dimension of language rights, as it will always be subjected to criticism and challenges.

Cases that involve all of the above three characters of language rights, namely, their participatory nature, their positive dimension and their selective nature, constitute 'multidimensional linguistic cases'. As I will argue in the next section, multidimensional linguistic cases are more complex only because they deal with language rights that bear all these three distinctive dimensions. I will show that there are other rights which courts in Israel have already acknowledged, that bear one or two of these dimensions but do not bear all of them. The difference between language rights in multidimensional cases and other rights is therefore only a difference in degree, not a difference in kind.

5. A Difference in Degree but Not in Kind

Let us consider the right to freedom of religion. Gidon Sapir distinguishes between two interests that the right to freedom of religion protects. The first and the most common one is the interest in freedom of conscience.[61] The second interest that underpins the right to freedom of religion which Sapir identifies is the interest in protecting religion as a culture.[62] Religion is not just a belief system, it is more fundamentally a way of life, a normative system,[63] an encompassing culture.[64] As Sapir rightly argues, people in general, and minority members in specific, have a strong interest in the protection of their culture because it serves as their context of choice and as a marker of their identity.[65]

The main difference between the two goods that the right to freedom of religion protects is that the first one — the good of conscience — is an individual good, whereas the second good — the good of religious culture — is a collective good. Conscience is a good that belongs to individuals, but culture is a participatory good that can only be produced and exercised by a group of people. An alleged injury to an individual conscience therefore requires us to examine the individual soul and practice, whereas an alleged injury to culture requires us to examine the social reality, norms and beliefs that exist in a given religious community.[66]

The Supreme Court has acknowledged minority members' participatory interest in their religious culture. The decision in *Avitan*[67] deals with a Jewish petitioner who wanted to purchase a highly subsidized piece of land in an area in the south of Israel that was designed to be populated by Bedouins. The Supreme Court rejected the petition on the grounds that the selectivity of the program was justified as a compensatory measure, providing resettlement for Bedouin nomadic tribal groups, who had been moved off nomadic land areas and wished to sustain their unique lifestyle, religion and culture.[68]

In the case of *Kaadan*,[69] the same participatory interest in religious culture is acknowledged again. In this case, the application of an Israeli Arab family to reside as members in Katzir, a residential community, is refused. The Supreme Court holds that the residents of Katzir cannot refuse to accept membership applications merely because the applicants are not Jews,[70] but the court is careful not to close the door on all practices of private exclusion based on different criteria, such as unique cultural affinities.[71] The exception the court creates acknowledges the need for legal protection of the interest in the participatory good of a unique culture.

In the *Kabel* case[72] Cheshin J. said that "we agree that ultra-orthodox Jews are eligible and entitled, if they wish, that we will do the best we can to allocate distinctive accommodations for them, in order to allow them to keep their lifestyle."[73] In the *Am Hofshi* case[74] Beinisch J. explicitly says that:

> the acknowledgment of the possibility to allocate lands and allow separate accommodation to groups which have unique characteristics, according to their needs and aspirations, goes in accordance with the approach that allows minorities to preserve their uniqueness; This is an approach that represents a common attitude amongst lawyers, philosophers and people in the educational system, according to which the individual is also entitled — among his other rights — to realize his affiliation to his community and its unique culture as part of his right to autonomy.[75]

So far I have shown that the Supreme Court has acknowledged the participatory dimension of other rights. It is therefore not distinctive to language rights as such. Let us now consider the positive dimension of language rights. Do Israeli courts interpret other allegedly negative freedoms as positive rights? The answer is positive. Take, for instance, the right to freedom of expression. The Supreme Court in Israel has acknowledged that there are three rationales underpinning the right to freedom of expression: the truth rationale, the autonomy rationale, and the democratic rationale. The truth rationale refers to the good of seeking and attaining truth, which is better realized by protecting freedom of expression. According to the autonomy rationale, we become individuals capable of developing our thinking and identity when we participate in conversation with others.[76] The negative right to freedom of expression mostly refers to the freedom of individuals to express themselves without being interfered with by the state. This view emphasizes the autonomy rationale underpinning the right to freedom of expression, which concentrates on the individual as the spokesman, rather than on the audience.[77]

However, according to the third rationale that underpins the right to freedom of expression — the democratic rationale — public discourse should be open for the free flow of information about governmental acts, in a way that allows citizens to pass their will to their representatives.[78] Public discourse has to be based on three principles: information, participation and rationalism. The relevant principle to this paper is the principle of information.

Receiving information about governmental acts is a pivotal condition for the existence of true democracy.[79] The right of citizens to receive information is acknowledged in the Israeli legal system as part of the democratic argument.[80] The information requirement is not satisfied by the fact that the state does not interrupt individuals' access to information. It is satisfied only when the state holds its obligation to positively assure individuals' access to information.

The right to freedom of language is part of the right to freedom of expression. By appealing to the democratic argument, one may refute Cheshin J.'s argument with regard to the right to freedom of language in *Adalah*. Under the democratic argument, the state is not only obliged to allow every person to speak the language he or she chooses, as Cheshin J. understands, but also to provide recourses to support this language. For instance, the government should provide public information in the minority language if it is to ensure free access to this information for minority members. This line of reasoning may suggest that a democratic state is obliged to regulate the press by enacting legislation to prevent the press from becoming the captive of majority interests. In the context of language, the argument that may be drawn is that the state has a duty to regulate public television and radio broadcasting in a manner that includes the linguistic interests of minority groups. Justice Cheshin's claim that the right to freedom of language does not impose positive obligations on the state is therefore false.

What about the selective dimension of language rights? Has the court acknowledged the selectiveness of other rights in Israel? The answer again is affirmative. There are other Israeli legal decisions that acknowledge the selective dimensions of the participatory interest in protecting a culture. Think about the decisions of *Avitan*, *Am Hofshi* and *Kabel*, which I have discussed above. All of them acknowledge that participatory interest in a unique culture may require legal protection. However, when they discuss unique cultures they refer only to religious cultures. It seems to me that the chance for a secular group to be regarded as having a unique lifestyle that deserves legal protection is pretty low. The Supreme Court's recent decision in *Hasolelim*[81] indicates so. *Hasolelim* dealt with a secular Jewish settlement that refused to admit an Arab couple as residents. After The Land Authority of Israel overturned the settlement's decision, the settlement's members asked the Supreme Court to acknowledge their right as a small Jewish secular settlement not to admit Arabs and ultra orthodox Jews into their settlement because such an admission would change the lifestyle of their community. Justice D. Cheshin rejected the petition and refused to discuss the petitioners' claim about the danger to their communal lifestyle. Because the land that the Arab couple had asked to buy was the last land to sell, the court decided that the danger the petitioners were predicting was far from being realized.[82]

In summary, as I have shown, all the three dimensions of language rights in multidimensional cases are not peculiar to language rights. They are acknowledged with regard to other rights. Justice Cheshin's argument that the claim of the petitioners in *Adalah* was fundamentally different from other claims the court has accepted before is therefore false. The only difference between the language rights the petitioners asked the court to acknowledge and other rights that have been acknowledged before is a difference in degree and not in kind. The fact that *Adalah* was a multidimensional case of language rights that bore all three of the dimensions makes this case more complex than other cases.

But Cheshin J. is well-known for his breakthrough decisions in complex cases. Take for instance the case of Israeli Women's Network (IWN) in 1998.[83] In this case, a feminist NGO won a suit against the Minister of Labour and Social Affairs following the appointment of a male as a deputy director general of the National Insurance Institute, in violation of fair representation for women. In the absence of any statutory or contractual provision for the fair representation for women, Cheshin J. accepted the petition by ruling "a ground-breaking precedent,"[84] according to which the principle of affirmative action applies even when there is no official requirement for affirmative action in any specific statutory provision. The express requirement for fair representation of women in statutes concerning other public bodies was sufficient for Cheshin J. to establish a doctrine of fair representation going beyond specific statutory provisions.[85]

Just in the same manner Cheshin J. infers a general doctrine from affirmative action statutes, he could have concluded in *Adalah* that the great number of laws that require public authorities to publish information in Arabic[86] along with art. 82 create a general doctrine imposing the duty of public authorities to "speak" Arabic even when there are no official statutes that require it.

In my view, Cheshin J.'s real problem with the petition was its public character. The problem was not the peculiarity of the language rights the petitioners were asking for, but rather that they were asking for the Arabic language to be visible in the public sphere. While other minority rights such as the right to freedom of religion and the right to education are interpreted in Israel as imposing positive duties on the state such as to establish Muslim tribunals[87] and Arab schools, such tribunals and schools do not occupy a public space in the full sense as language rights do.

As Carens accurately puts it, language rights may go beyond the internal realm of the minority culture. Carens demonstrates his argument through the bilingual arrangements in Canada, which apply to all Canadians in their contact with public authorities and in their everyday life when they buy products with bilingual captions, apply for jobs, etc.[88]

It is true that Muslim tribunals and Arab schools are not invisible, but they do not occupy the same public space as language rights do. A Jewish Israeli who lives in Ra'anana or Herzliah (non-mixed cities in Israel that consist mostly of Jewish citizens) will not encounter Muslim tribunals or Arab schools if he or she does not wish to do so. In fact, if language rights are not taken seriously by the state, as has been the state of affairs in Israel until recently, most Jewish citizens in Israel will hardly ever encounter Arabic at all.

The language rights the petitioners in *Adalah* asked for therefore have a deep influence on the public character of Israel. Why is this deep influence so problematic? There is of course no problem with the visibility of the majority Jewish culture or religion. Such publicity does not seem to threaten most Israeli Jews. But the visibility of the Arab minority culture is perceived as a serious threat.

Many people in Israel, including scholars and judges, think that the visibility of Arabic may weaken the high status of Hebrew.[89] Some think that a state that gives equal status to two languages is not only a bilingual state but also a bi-national state.[90] Others think that the status of Hebrew is not threatened by the public visibility of Arabic.[91] Moreover, some of them also point out that a state can be bilingual but not bi-national.[92]

I tend to agree with the latter view. This is neither the time nor the place to elaborate on this point. I believe it is important to put this problem on the table. Justice Cheshin cannot hide behind legal terms such as 'collective rights' or 'positive rights' in order to justify his position. His vague argument about the political character of the petition is also not sufficiently developed.[93] As I have shown, the unique aspects of language rights that Cheshin J. discusses in *Adalah* as political are not unique to language rights, but common to other well recognized legal rights in Israel. The most political aspect of *Adalah* is actually not addressed in it at all.

6. Conclusion

This paper focuses on the common fear of language rights. This fear is manifested in Cheshin J.'s minority decision in *Adalah*. I have analysed the *Adalah* decision and observed that the common fear of language rights is mostly invoked in what I call 'multidimensional linguistic cases'. In such cases, demands for language rights involve at least two of the following dimensions: the participatory dimension, the positive dimension and the selective dimension. The more dimensions such cases involve, the more reluctant the court is to address them.

I have then argued that many other well acknowledged rights in Israel involve at least one of the dimensions I have identified. I therefore conclude that the difference between language rights and other well-acknowledged rights in Israel is a difference in degree and not kind.

Justice Cheshin's reservation about dealing with language rights is unjustified. It seems to me that the general reluctance of courts to deal with language rights lies elsewhere. Many Israeli Jews fear that granting language rights to the Arab minority will damage the Jewish character of Israel. This fear is associated with the fourth distinctive feature language rights may bare — the public dimension.

NOTES

This paper is based on my LLM thesis. I am most grateful to Lorraine Weinrib and Denise Réaume for supervising my thesis with great enthusiasm. Their comments have greatly contributed to my research and sharpened my arguments. I presented this paper at the Language Policy Research Forum in February 2009 at Tel-Aviv University. I am especially greatful for Elana Shoami, Miriam Shlesinger, Dafna Yitzhaki and Nira Trumper-Hecht for their insightful comments. I also wish to thank my husband, Boaz Miller for helping me work out my arguments, for his insightful comments, and for his endless patience.

1   H.C. J. 4112/99 *Adalah et al. v. The Municipality of Tel-Aviv-Jafa et al.*, 56(5) P.D. 393.

2   Drayton (1934) 3 Laws of Palestine 2569, 2588.

3   *Adalah, supra* note 1 at 478.

4   *Ibid*, p. 411.

5   *Ibid*, p. 412.

6   *Ibid*, p. 414 (my translation).

7   *Ibid*, pp. 417–418.

8 Amongst other things, Cheshin J. rightly argues that art. 82 of the Order-in-Council of 1922 does not establish the duty of the respondent municipalities to add Arabic text on all signs within their jurisdiction (*ibid*, at 425–431).

9 *Ibid*, pp. 431–436.

10 *Ibid*, pp. 431–438.

11 *Ibid*, pp. 441–446.

12 *Ibid*, pp. 447–448.

13 *Ibid*, p. 456.

14 *Ibid*, pp. 456–460.

15 See for example, the following legal decisions: H.C.J. 5100/94, 4045/95 *Public Committee against Torture in Israel v. State of Israel* 53(4) P.D. 817, which challenges the torture investigatory method of the General Security Service (the English version of this decision can be found on the Supreme Court's website — www. court.gov.il); H.C.J. 3267/97 *Rubinstein et al. v. The Minister of Defence*, 52(5) P.D. 481, that deals with a very controversial issue in Israeli society — the question of mandatory military service for ultra-Orthodox Jewish Yeshiva students (the English version of this decision can be found on the Supreme Court's website — www. court.gov.il); H.C.J. 6698/95 *Ka'adan v. Israel Land Authority*, 54(1) P.D. 258, which deals with the question of allocation of lands to Israeli Arab citizens in non-mixed cities. For a discussion about the judicial activism of the Israeli Supreme Court in these decisions see Suzie Navot, "More of the Same: Judicial Activism in Israel," *European Public Law* 7(3) (2001): 355.

16 H.C.J. 715/98. *Amnon Rubinstein and others v. Minister of Defence* (1998) 52(5) P.D. 481 at 533–534; Yaacov Ben-Shemesh, State Neutrality and the Right to Language," *Mishpat Umimshal* 8 (2005): 347. (Hebrew)

17 Lorraine E. Weinrib, "Canada's Constitutional Revolution: From Legislative to Constitutional State," *Isr. L. Rev.* 33 (1999): 24; Lorraine E. Weinrib, "The Postwar Paradigm and American Exceptionality" in Sujit Choudhry ed., *The Migration of Constitutional Ideas* (Cambridge: Cambridge University Press, 2006), p. 84.

18 L. Weinrib, "From Legislative to Constitutional State," *ibid*, p. 24.

19 *Ibid*.

20 See C. Michael MacMillan, *The Practice of Language Rights in Canada* (Toronto: University of Toronto Press, 1999), p. 11; Royal Commission on Bilingualism and Biculturalism, *Report*, vol. 1 (Ottawa: Queen's Printer, 1968), p. 41.

21 As Spolsky and Shohamy observe, the term 'mother tongue' and the concept behind it are both somewhat questionable. In any case, there is a common underlying assumption that whatever language a mother chooses to speak to her children will be stronger and form a better basis for later education (Bernard Spolsky & Elana Shohamy, *The Language of Israel: Policy, Ideology and Practice* (Clevedon, UK: Multilingual Matters, 1999), p. 76).

22 Denise G. Réaume, "The Constitutional Protection of Language: Survival or Security?" in David Schneiderman ed., *Language and the State: The Law and Politics of*

Identity (Cowansville, Québec: Editions Yvon Blais, 1991), pp. 46–47 [Réaume, "The Constitutional Protection of Language"].

23 Joseph Raz, *The Morality of Freedom* (Oxford: Clarendon Press, 1986), p. 166.

24 This account focuses on the aesthetic or beneficial value of a particular language for humankind as a whole. Under the aesthetic account, each particular language is compared to a rare piece of art or to an endangered biological species that makes the world more colourful, interesting, and dynamic. According to the aesthetic account, every language enriches the human experience by providing different ways of talking about the world and therefore should be preserved (Alan Patten & Will Kymlicka, "Language Rights and Political Theory: Context, Issues, and Approaches," in Will Kymlicka & Alan Patten, eds., *Language Rights and Political Theory* (Oxford: Oxford University Press, 2003), p. 44).

25 Leslie Green, "Are Language Rights Fundamental?," *Osgoode Hall L. J.* 25 (1987): 658–659 [Green, "Are Language Rights Fundamental?"]; Réaume, "The Constitutional Protection of Language," *supra* note 22 at 45.

26 According to Jacob Levy, providing minorities with language rights contributes to the formation of cross-culture frameworks that can mitigate the conflicts that result from interactions between ethnic or cultural minority groups and majority groups in multilingual societies (Jacob T. Levy, *The Multiculturalism of Fear* (Oxford: Oxford University Press, 2000), p. 40–41). Similarly, James Tully argues that recognizing minority cultures may strengthen minorities' allegiance to, sense of belonging to and identification with, their state (James Tully, *Strange Multiplicity: Constitutionalism in an Age of Diversity* (Cambridge: Cambridge University Press, 1995), pp. 197–198). Joseph Magnet raises a very similar argument, according to which the main justification for language rights is that they mitigate conflicts between Canada's linguistic communities (Joseph E. Magnet, *Official Languages of Canada: Perspectives from Law, Policy and the Future* (Cowansville, Quebec: Éditions Y. Blais, 1995), pp. 83, 250).

27 Other means can mitigate harsh conflicts between minority groups and majority groups, such as temporary economic support or affirmative action, which seek to put the minority and the majority at the same level.

28 Will Kymlicka, *Multicultural Citizenship* (Oxford: Clarendon Press, 1995), pp. 82–83, 105.

29 Kymlicka's argument refers to what he labels 'societal culture'. A societal culture is a culture that involves "a common language and societal institutions, rather than common religious beliefs, family customs, or personal lifestyles" (Kymlicka, *Multicultural Citizenship, ibid*, p. 76). Because under Kymlicka's account a culture is attached to a particular language, Kymlicka's argument regarding the importance of one's own culture can be rephrased with regard to one's own language as his or her context of choice.

30 Denise G. Réaume, "Official-Language Rights: Intrinsic Value and the Protection of Difference" in Will Kymlicka & Wayne Norman eds., *Citizenship in Diverse Societies* (Oxford: Oxford University Press, 2000), p. 247 [Réaume, "Intrinsic Value and the Protection of Difference"].

31 Réaume, "Intrinsic Value and the Protection of Difference," *ibid*, at 251; Green, "Are Language Rights Fundamental?," *supra* note 25 at 659; Réaume, "The Constitutional Protection of Language," *supra* note 22 at 45; Denise G. Réaume, "Beyond Personality: The Territorial and Personal Principles of Language Policy Reconsidered" in Will Kymlicka & Alan Patten eds., *Language Rights and Political Theory* (Oxford: Oxford University Press, 2003), p. 283 [Réaume, "Beyond Personality"].

32 See Joshua A. Fishman, *Reversing Language Shift* (Clevedon, UK: Multilingual Matters, 1991), p. 21.

33 This understanding of the connection between language and culture is supported by the work of the American anthropologist Benjamin Whorf, who argues that the perception of the world changes from one language to another. What is referred to as Whorf's 'weak hypothesis' emphasizes the role of a particular language as reflecting the concepts of the culture it is associated with, rather than determining these concepts. You may know Whorf's hypothesis from his famous example that Eskimo language has many words for snow, because the discrimination between different kinds of snow plays a significant role in Eskimo culture. For a detailed account of Whorf's argument see Benjamin Lee Whorf, *Language, Thought and Reality: Selected Writings of Benjamin Lee Whorf*, ed. John B. Carroll (Cambridge, MA: MIT Press, 1964).

34 Stephen May, "Uncommon Languages: The Challenges and Possibilities of Minority Language Rights," *Journal of Multilingual and Multicultural Development* 21(5) (2000): 374.

35 For example, prayers in the Jewish religion and other religious texts, such as the Haggadah (tales for Passover night) are written in Hebrew and publicly read in ceremonies and rituals. Secular Jews consider these texts as part of their culture as well. In fact, almost all cultural creativity in Israel is expressed in Hebrew: popular music, academic and popular literature, movies, and plays. The verbal components of a culture, which are expressed in a specific language, embody unique characteristics of a culture that will be lost if expressed by other languages (see Nancy C. Dorian, "Choices and Values in Language Shift and Its Study," *Int'l. J. Soc. Lang.* 110 (1994): 115).

36 Réaume, "Intrinsic Value and the Protection of Difference," *supra* note 30 at 251; May, *ibid*, p. 374.

37 *Adalah*, *supra* note 1 at 413; C.A. 105/92 *Re'em Engineers and Contractors Ltd. v. Municipality of Upper Nazareth*, P.D. 47(5) 189.

38 This phrase is taken from Justice Cheshin's decision in H.C. 2316/95 *Ganimat v. The State of Israel* 49(4) P.D. 589 at 640.

39 *Adalah*, *supra* note 1, p. 413.

40 See Meital Pinto, "Language Rights, Immigration and Minorities in Israel," *Mishpat Umimshal* 10 (2006): 242–244 [Hebrew].

41 See, for example, Michael McDonald, "Questions about Collective Rights" in David Schneiderman ed., *Language and the State: The Law and Politics of Identity* (Cowansville, Québec: Editions Yvon Blais, 1991), p. 3; James W. Nickel, "Group Agency and Group Rights" in Ian Shapiro & Will Kymlicka eds., *Ethnicity and Group Rights* (New

York: New York University Press, 1997), p. 235; Yael Tamir, *Liberal Nationalism* (Princeton: Princeton University Press, 1993), p. 42.

42   Leslie Green, "Two Views of Collective Rights," *Canadian Journal of Law and Jurisprudence* 4 (1991): 315.

43   *Ibid*, p. 320.

44   *Ibid*, p. 319.

45   This argument is also called the deficiency thesis, according to which many groups and particularly ethnic groups are deficient as right holders (Nickel, *supra* note 41, p. 235-237).

46   Denise G. Réaume, "Individuals, Groups and Rights to Public Goods," *U. of T. L. J.* 1 (1988): 10 [Réaume, "Public Goods"].

47   Réaume, "The Constitutional Protection of Language," *supra* note 22, p. 48.

48   *Ibid*, at 49.

49   Isaiah Berlin, *Four Essays on Liberty* (Oxford: Oxford University Press, 1969), pp. 121-172.

50   John William Salmond, *Jurisprudence*, 11th edition (London: Sweet and Maxwell, 1957), pp. 269-270.

51   The distinction between negative and positive rights has been rightly criticized as elusive. Some scholars argue that a sharp distinction between a negative and positive right cannot be drawn because the object of any right cannot be truly protected without minimal positive steps that are taken by the state in order to protect it (See Patrick Macklem, "Aboriginal Rights and State Obligations," *Alberta. L. Rev.* 36 (1997): 100-102; Ran Hirschl, "Negative" Rights vs. "Positive" Entitlements: A Comparative Study of Judicial Interpretations of Rights in an Emerging Neo-Liberal Economic Order," *Human Rights Quarterly* 22 (2000): 1072-1073). Although the distinction between negative and positive rights was rightly criticized by scholars as illusive, the Israeli Supreme Court still employs this distinction (Hirschl, p. 1073).

52   As Kymlicka mentions, "Not all interests can be satisfied in a world of conflicting interests and scarce resources. Protecting one person's cultural membership has costs for other people and other interests, and we need to determine when these trade-offs are justified" (Kymlicka, *Multicultural Citizenship*, *supra* note 28, p. 107).

53   Joseph H. Carens, "Liberalism and Culture," *Constellations* 4(1) (1997): 40.

54   Most scholars prefer the term 'universal rights' over 'general rights'. However, I am influenced by scholars who think that there are no universal rights. Joseph Raz, for instance, thinks that different people have different interests. It is therefore not accurate to talk about universal rights that protect the interests of all people. Raz thinks that the term 'universal rights' does not describe the nature of the right, but rather denotes the rejection of certain false distinctions between rights that are based on race, sex and the like (Joseph Raz, *Value, Respect and Attachment* (Cambridge: Cambridge University Press, 2001), pp. 54-58). Other scholars think that the term 'universal rights' implies that there are values that should be protected in every

legal system. Such approach may be paternalistic as it aims to enforce Western moral values on societies that hold different values (Martha Nussbaum, *Women and Human Development: The Capabilities Approach* (Cambridge: Cambridge University Press, 2000); William J. Talbott, *Which Rights Should Be Universal?* (Oxford: Oxford University Press, 2005). I therefore prefer the term 'general rights' over 'universal rights'. Justice Barak emphasized the general application of the rights to freedom of expression in *Re'em* by saying that a democratic society should allow individuals to express themselves in their chosen language, whether it is Arabic, Amhari or Russian (*Re'em, supra* note 37, p. 209).

55   Adalah, *supra* note 1 at 413.

56   Ilan Saban, "A Lone (Bilingual) Cry in the Dark?," *Tel-Aviv Law Review* 27 (2003): 121 [Hebrew]; Ilan Saban & Muhammad Amara, "The Status of Arabic in Israel: Reflections on the Power of Law to Produce Social Change," *Isr. L. Rev.* 36 (2002): 33.

57   Kymlicka justifies this distinction by claiming first, that it is usually the culture of national minorities that takes the form of a societal culture whereas members of immigrant minorities are part of subcultures, i.e. cultures that lack the range of activity and institutions that characterize societal cultures (Kymlicka, *Multicultural Citizenship, supra* note 28, pp. 77–94). Second, Kymlicka argues that immigrants freely and voluntarily choose to leave their society and join another existing society. Therefore, if they had the option to stay in their country of origin, but they decided not to do so, immigrant minorities should not expect to be given comprehensive language rights (Kymlicka, *Multicultural Citizenship*, pp. 95–96).

58   Meital Pinto, "On the Intrinsic Value of Arabic in Israel — Challenging Kymlicka on Language Rights," *The Canadian Journal of Law and Jurisprudence* 20 (2007): 143.

59   *Ibid.*

60   For Jewish Russians' claims for recognition see Meital Pinto, "Language Rights, Immigration and Minorities in Israel," *supra* note 40, p. 236, fn 42.

61   Gidon Sapir, "Religion and State — A Fresh Theoretical Start," *Notre Dame L. Rev.* 75: 644

62   Sapir, *ibid*, pp. 625–632.

63   Alvin J. Esau, "'Islands of Exclusivity': Religious Organizations and Employment Discrimination," *U.B.C Law Review* 33 (2000): 727.

64   Esau, *ibid.*; Clifford Geertz, "Religion as a Cultural System" in *The Interpretation of Cultures* (New York: Basic Books, 1973), pp. 87–125.

65   Sapir borrows Kymlicka's argument about culture as a context of choices, which I have discussed in section 3. Sapir does not use the term "marker of identity," but refers to Kymlicka's argument about the intrinsic value minorities attach to their own cultures, even when integration with the majority culture can be easily achieved (Sapir, *supra* note 61, p. 627). I borrow the term "marker of identity" from Denise Réaume, who suggests a more developed account of culture as a marker of identity (Réaume, "Intrinsic Value and the Protection of Difference," *supra* note 30, p. 247). I have discussed her account in section 3.

66 Sapir, *ibid*, pp. 625–632

67 H.C.J. 88/528 *Eliezer Avitan v. Israel Lands' Authority et al.* (1989) 43(4) P.D. 297.

68 *Avitan, ibid*, pp. 303–304.

69 *Kaadan, supra* note 15.

70 *Ibid.*

71 *Ibid*, pp. 279–280.

72 H.C.J. 1/98 *Eitan Kabel v. Israeli Prime Minister* (1999) 53(2) PD 241.

73 *Ibid*, pp. 258–259 (my translation).

74 H.C.J. 4906/98 *Am Hofshi Association v. Ministry of Construction and Housing* (1998) 52(2) P.D. 503.

75 *Ibid*, provision 3.

76 Richard Moon, *Constitutional Protection of Freedom of Expression* (Toronto: University of Toronto Press, 2000), p. 4.

77 For the autonomic rationale of the right to freedom of expression, see for example, H.C.J. 73/53 *Kol Ha'am v. Minister of the Interior* 7 P.D. 871 at 878.

78 For the democratic rationale of the right to freedom of expression, see for example, H.C.J. 399/85 *Kahane v. The Board of the Broadcasting Authority*, 41(3) P.D. 255 at 267.

79 As observed by Emerson in the very beginning of his book: "A system of freedom of expression, operating in modern democratic society, is a complex mechanism. At its core is a group of rights assured to individual members of society. This set of rights, which makes up our present-day concept of free expression, includes the right to form and hold beliefs and opinions on any subject, to communicate ideas, in any medium — in speech, writing, music, art or in other ways. To some extent it involves the right to remain silent. From the adverse side it includes the right to hear the views of others and to listen to their version of the facts. It encompasses the right to inquire and, to a degree, the right of access to information" (Thomas I. Emerson, *The System of Freedom of Expression* (New York: New York Random House, 1970), p. 3).

80 See H.C.J. 1601/90 *Shalit v. Peres* [1991] 45(3) P.D. 353 at 360–364.

81 H.C.J. 7574/06 *Hasolelim v. The Land Authority of Israel* (2007). The case was not published.

82 Section 7 to Cheshin D. J's decision. Their request for a further hearing was denied (see H.C.J.F.H. 1107/07 *Hasolelim v. The Land Authority of Israel* (2007).

83 H.C.J. 2761/98 *IWN v. Minister of Labor* (1998) 52(3) P.D. 630.

84 See Frances Raday, "Social Science in The Law: The Israeli Supreme Court: Social Science Insights: On Equality — Judicial Profiles," *Isr. L. Rev.* 35 (2001): 435. See also Meital Pinto & Hillel Sommer, "The Role of the Judiciary in Affirmative Action" in Anat Maor ed., *Affirmative Action in Israel — Policy, Application, Challenges* (Tel Aviv: Ramot Tel Aviv University Press, 2004), pp. 200–202 [Hebrew].

85   *IWN v. Minister of Labor* (1998) 52(3) P.D. 630 at 662.

86   Meital Pinto, "Language Rights, Immigration and Minorities in Israel," *supra* note 40, p. 227, fn 6.

87   The origin of the duty of the state to support religious tribunals is found in the Ottoman law. The Ottoman Empire recognized the religious laws of the Muslims, Jews and Christians according to the Millet System under which considerable autonomy was accorded to non-Islamic religious groups treated as 'nations'. This autonomy included the maintenance of the independent legal system with prescribed jurisdiction for each of the recognized religious communities (Izhak Englard, *Religious Law in the Israel Legal System* (Jerusalem: Alpha Press, 1975), p. 13); Asher Maoz, "Constitutional Law" in Itzhak Zamir & Sylviane Colombo eds., *The Law of Israel: General Surveys* (Jerusalem: The Harry Michael Sacher Institute for Legislative Research and Comparative Law, The Hebrew University of Jerusalem, 1995), p. 29).

88   Joseph. H. Carens, *Culture, Citizenship, and Community: A Contextual Exploration of Justice as Evenhandedness* (Oxford: Oxford University Press, 2000), pp. 67–68.

89   In *Re'em* and *Adalah* Barak C.J. balanced the value of freedom of language with the value of Hebrew as the major language in Israel (*Re'em, supra* note 37, p. 207; Gad Barzilai, *Communities and Law* (Ann Arbor: The University of Michigan Press, 2003), pp. 112–113; *Adalah, supra* note 1, p. 412).

90   Ilan Saban calls this argument "the slippery slope argument," according to which acknowledging the Arab culture in the Israeli public sphere will gradually turn Israel into a bi-national state (Saban, "A Lone (Bilingual) Cry in the Dark?," *supra* note 56, pp. 123–125).

91   See Alon Harel, "Book Review: The Judge in Democratic Society, by Aharon Barak," *Isr. L. Rev.* 39 (2006): 282; (Saban, *ibid*, p. 130).

92   Ilan Saban rightly argues that bi-national state is a state in which there is equal partnership between two national communities. Israel is far from that (Saban, *ibid*, p. 124)

93   For more developed arguments about the political character of *Adalah* see Gershon Gontovnik, "The Right to Culture in a Liberal Society and in the State of Israel," *Tel-Aviv University Law Review* 27: 67–70. (Hebrew); Eyal Benvenisti, "National Courts and the Protection of National Minorities," *Alei Mishpat* 3: 493–494. (Hebrew)

THE VOICE OF THE PEOPLE: LANGUAGE AND STATE IN ISRAEL

TAMAR HOSTOVSKY BRANDES

1. INTRODUCTION

This article examines the issue of language in Israel and the question of language rights of the Arabic-speaking minority and the Russian-speaking minority. It challenges the traditional distinction between immigrants and national minorities in the context of Israel. It rejects the traditional justifications often brought for this distinction and argues that alternative justifications that were offered to justify this distinction in the case of Israel are equally problematic. It then presents and examines, using the concepts of self-determination and self-defense, an alternative justification, which is based not on the nature or characteristics of the members of each of the two groups but on the cultural nature of the state. The conditions for admission of Russian immigrants into Israeli society, I argue, contain an implied expectation that these immigrants abandon their culture and language of origin and identify with the Hebrew language and culture. This expectation, however, is not always realized, and, standing alone, is a poor basis for upholding the distinction between immigrants and national minorities and rejecting on a sweeping basis the possibility of recognizing the language rights of Russian-speaking immigrants in Israel.

2. LANGUAGE, CULTURE AND THE STATE

The relationship between language and culture is twofold: language is a component of culture, but it is also a tool through which other components are constituted and a vehicle for passing a culture to future generations. This unique nature of language led many to argue that language is an important component of culture and that language survival is the key to cultural survival.[1]

In no case is this relationship clearer than in the case of the Hebrew language and the Zionist movement. The Hebrew language played an important role first in the Zionist enterprise and, after the establishment of the State, in the development of Israeli nationhood. The phrase 'Ivri, daber Ivrit' (Hebrewman, speak Hebrew), which was coined by the Zionist movement in Israel in the early 20th century to promote the use of Hebrew, reflected the attitude that only through speaking the same language, the language of the bible and of their ancestors, could Jews once again become a nation. The creation of a nation, in turn, was viewed as necessary for the success first of the Zionist enterprise and then of the new state. The view that a state is a cultural institution and that cultural and linguistic reproduction takes place through the state's various institutions is therefore inherent to the perception of a state in Israel.

The centrality of the Hebrew language to the enterprise of the State of Israel raises difficult issues since Hebrew is not the primary language of all of the citizens of the State of Israel. Hebrew is not the primary language of the Arab minority in Israel. It is also not the primary language of many new immigrants. The two largest linguistic minorities in Israel today are the Arabic-speaking minority and the Russian-speaking minority, both of which will be discussed in this paper.[2]

While many have acknowledged and discussed the relationship between language and culture and the relationship between language and the nation, few have emphasized the interrelation between language, culture and the state, and the important role the state as an institution, through its various institutions and mechanisms, plays in enabling the preservation and maintenance of language.

Scholarly debates on the rights of linguistic groups within a state usually take place as part of a larger discussion of minority rights. These discussions tend to revolve around the degree of autonomy that should be awarded to cultural minorities. Under the autonomy model, a linguistic minority receives a certain degree of linguistic autonomy in one or more areas of public life, in a defined territory. This model usually offers a solution that is based on separation and does not offer cultural minorities an opportunity to access and shape the linguistic character of the state at-large.

3. INSTRUMENTAL AND NON-INSTRUMENTAL LANGUAGE RIGHTS

Ruth Rubio-Marin proposes a classification of language rights that is based on the justification for particular rights: rights that aim at ensuring the language is not an obstacle to the enjoyment of other rights, that happen to have a linguistic dimension, can be classified as instrumental language rights. The right to have a translator in criminal proceedings, for example, is an instrumental right necessary to ensure that language barriers are not an obstacle to the enjoyment of the right of due process. Instrumental language rights are usually tied to the communicative aspect of language. Because language is seen as a means to achieving the realization of another right, the justification for instrumental language rights depends on whether they are effective at achieving this goal, as well as on the availability of alternative measures.

Non-instrumental language rights, on the other hand, are justified by the intrinsic value of language. They are concerned not with the opportunities provided by a language, but with the importance of language in itself. Because the value of language derives from its nature as a collective enterprise, protection of this value can often be achieved only through group, rather than individual rights.[3] Rubio-Marin describes non-instrumental language rights as rights that are concerned with a group's right to enjoy, maintain and reproduce its language. The distinction between the different interests that lie at the heart of each type of right does not mean, of course, that each language-related right can promote only one of these interests. Instrumental language rights can facilitate non-instrumental language interests and vice versa, but when discussing the justification for recognizing rights it is important to be aware of the interest that is at the core of such rights.

Both discussions on instrumental language rights and discussions on non-instrumental language rights focus on examining the characteristic of a specific minority group and trying to determine whether these characteristics justify recognizing any language rights. The particular cultural nature of a state itself, however, and the legitimate requirements and expectations a state may present to its members is a key issue that is often ignored. This article examines the manifestation of the relationship between language, culture, and state in Israel by looking at the measures a state may legitimately take to defend a particular cultural and linguistic nature.

4. LANGUAGE, SELF-DEFENSE AND SELF-DETERMINATION

Two concepts borrowed from the area of international law may be useful in illuminating the special role the state plays in the preservation of culture and language. The first is the idea of self-determination. The right to self-determination is recognized in article I (1) of both the International Covenant on Civil and Political Rights and the International Covenant on Economic, Social and Cultural Rights, which state that:

"All peoples have the right of self-determination. By virtue of that right they freely determine their political status and freely pursue their economic, social and cultural development."[4]

The interpretation of this Article is a matter of much controversy and the conditions under which self-determination would be justified, as well as the criteria identifying those who have a right to it, are a matter of much debate. The recognition of the principle of self-determination suggests, however, that the exercise of group rights may take a political form, and the right of a group to economic, social and cultural development finds expression through the institution of the state. While many identify self-determination with statehood, I bring the analysis of the principle of self-determination not to advocate a right of every cultural minority to statehood, but rather to illuminate the importance of the state as an institution through which groups fulfill their right to culture. The state's various institutions and systems, including the legislative system, the public services system and the public education system, create spaces and spheres in which the process of cultural and linguistic reproduction takes place. They are spaces in which members of a community interact, deliberate and debate and in which the culture is shaped and changed. Since these spaces comprise the state apparatus, the activity that takes place within these spaces creates, defines and shapes the cultural and linguistic character of the state itself.

The second concept of international law that may be helpful in analyzing the issue of language is the concept of self-defense. In general, the principle of self-defense in international law constitutes an exception to the general ban on the use of force. It allows a state to use force to defend its territory against an armed attack and to protect itself from eradication. A right to self-defense emerges when a state is facing an immanent threat, and the measures taken under the right to self-defense must be proportionate to the pending threat.

Borrowing this concept of self-defense, George Fletcher presents the concept of linguistic self-defense. While the right to self-defense is understood as protecting national territory, argues Fletcher, the importance of the national territory, and the reason why use of force is allowed to protect it, lies in the meanings people invest in it.[5] The territory of the state provides a physical space in which the enterprise of the state operates, and the enterprise of the state provides a powerful tool for the preservation of culture and language. The state's right to self-defense thus protects the right of the cultural group to continue to exist, as the state provides a space necessary for such existence.

Even if we are willing to accept the existence of a right to linguistic self-defense, we still need to be cautious about the extent of such rights and the conditions under which it may be exercised. The argument I present is that when a language group tries to recruit the state's institutions to the cause of defending its language, the distinction between insiders and outsiders becomes imperative. A right of self-defense may be valid against outsiders, but it cannot be employed internally against those who are already members, and to which these institutions and resources also belong.

Claims made on such resources usually take one of two forms. Under the first form, linguistic minorities demand to have "their piece of the pie," which usually involves some form of autonomy and self-government in the area of culture and language. An example of such possible claims is demands for separate schools in a minority language. Under the second form, claims made by linguistic minorities may challenge the exiting cultural nature of the state at-large. An example of such demands is a demand to recognize a minority language as an official or public language, to be used in all of the state's institutions.

Examining the relationship between various language groups and the state through the concept of self-defense may offer new insights on the considerations involved in rejecting or accepting claims to the resources of the state. This discussion cannot replace an examination of the right of different groups to cultural self-determination or other forms of language rights. This article will not examine how language-related claims should be realized when such claims are valid, since the answer to this question is case-specific and depends on a large number of particular factors. Rather, it will only examine whether and when the state may have legitimate grounds for rejecting such claims altogether.

The first stage of the analysis requires us to identify a state and understand which language or languages are the state's languages in the sense that they are preserved through the state's apparatus. I use the term "state language" rather than official language because an official status is not required for a language to become de-facto the language of a state. An official status, in turn, does not in itself guarantee that a language will actually be used by a state. State languages do not necessarily need to be explicitly chosen by a state, but when they are, they are usually chosen in "constituting moments" in a state's life, when the foundations of a society are established or reexamined. Such moments can be the foundation of a new state, as was the case in Israel, a change in regime, as was the case in South Africa or an adoption of a new constitution, as was the case in Canada.

It is important to remember, however, that while it is legitimate for a state to choose to use a certain language or languages, not every choice of language is legitimate. The choice of a state language or languages, whether official or not, can easily be used as a tool of oppression. A common example is Afrikaans, which played an important role in the rule of the white minority in apartheid South Africa. Even if the choice of a particular language was initially legitimate, this may change over time due to social and demographic changes within the state.

The second stage of the analysis requires us to ask whether there are any additional linguistic groups who may have valid claims upon the state, so that the state's institutions will, at least to a certain extent, operate to preserve their language. Even if we determine that such claims are indeed valid, there can be various ways in which they can be realized. As I have indicated earlier, a discussion of these different ways will require a separate article.

5. STATE AND LANGUAGE IN ISRAEL

Although the population in Israel speaks an estimated 33 languages,[6] three main languages can be identified in the linguistic landscape in Israel today. Hebrew is spoken by the majority of the citizens of Israel, and although it is not the single official language, it is effectively the main language of the state. Arabic, the second official language, is spoken by the large Arab minority. Russian is the third most common language and it is spoken by many of the new immigrants who arrived to Israel during 1990's from the former USSR.[7]

Of the above-mentioned languages, only Hebrew and Arabic currently have an official status in Israel. Prior to the establishment of the State of Israel in 1948, the legal status of languages in Mandatory Palestine was determined by Article 82 of the Palestine Order-in-Council.[8] Subtitled 'official languages,' Article 82 stated that:

> "All ordinances, official notices and official forms of the Government and all official notices of local authorities and municipalities in areas to be prescribed by order of the High Commissioner, shall be published in English, Arabic and Hebrew. The three languages may be used in debates and discussions in the Legislative Council, and, subject to any regulations to be made from time to time, in the Government offices and the Law Courts."

With the establishment of the state of Israel the provisional government, which was established in anticipation of the British withdrawal, enacted the Law and Administration Ordinance to ensure that there would be no legal gap during the transition period.[9] Section 11 of the Ordinance stated that the law that existed in Palestine on the eve of the establishment of the State of Israel would continue to be in force subject to any enactments of the new legislature and also subject "to such modifications as may result from the establishment of the State and its authorities."[10] One such modification was the cancellation of any law that requires the use of English, the language of the former rulers of the land.

English was therefore omitted from Article 82, leaving Hebrew and Arabic as the two official languages. Article 82 continues to be in force to date and English has no official status in the State of Israel. The legal status of both Hebrew and Arabic in Israel is, therefore, a result of an arrangement that was intended to be temporary but turned to be permanent,[11] and is the product of an administrative order issued by a prior colonizer rather than an explicit expression of the intentions and will of the people of the newly established state.[12]

The fact that the main legislation regarding the status of languages is a mandatory administrative order has several implications. The first regards the normative weight of the arrangement determining the status of the two languages. When the draft of a proposal law, stating that Hebrew will be the single language of the land, was brought before the second Knesset, it was rejected. However, David Ben-Gurion, Israel's prime minister at the time, indicated that it was not the proper timing to enact such law and that, when the time comes, the government itself would present to the Knesset a bill regarding the language of the state, which would be Hebrew. Ben-Gurion therefore represented the view that the Article 82 would not be the final act regarding the status of languages in Israel. Moreover, Ben-Gurion's main concern was with the many new "Olim," the Jewish immigrants to Israel, whose needs would need to be taken into consideration when determining the language of the state.[13]

Throughout the years, a large number of bills have proposed to alter the existing status-quo regarding the official status of Hebrew and Arabic in Israel and express the superiority of the Hebrew language by either a regular or basic law. In May 2008, for example, Knesset member and former Minister of Education Limor Livnat, together with additional Knesset members, submitted a bill proposing to define Hebrew as the primary official language in Israel and to define Arabic, Russian and English as secondary official languages.[14] In 2006, Knesset Member Zvi Hendel of the

Mafdal, suggested to determine by law that Hebrew is the official language of the state of Israel and change the subtitle of Article 82 from "Official Languages" to "Use of Languages," removing any doubt regarding the superiority of Hebrew in Israel.[15]

Because of the minimalist language and specific historical circumstances by which Article 82 became part of Israeli law, it is difficult to draw from it meaningful conclusions regarding the status of both Hebrew and Arabic in Israel. Even the specific instructions included in Article 82 are not followed in reality: laws are enacted in Hebrew and only later translated both to Arabic and English.[16] Court decisions are written in Hebrew. While Article 82 prescribes that Arabic may be used in the Knesset and in correspondence with government officials and in the courts, due to administrative lack of translators this can significantly slow the procedures. Indeed, at least until recently, Article 82 has served as a weak basis, if any, for recognizing language rights.

The status of Article 82 was recently invoked in the case of *Adalah v. the Municipalities of Tel Aviv-Jaffa*.[17] In this case, Adalah, a local NGO, filed a petition with the High Court of Justice, based in part on the official status of Arabic as expressed by the subtitle of Article 82. The petition requested that municipal authorities of mixed cities add the Arabic language to all public signs within their jurisdiction. The case, however, was resolved without a conclusive decision regarding the status of Hebrew and Arabic in Israel or regarding the legal implications of Article 82. In fact, three of the municipal authorities involved in the case, together with the legal counsel to the government, requested a second hearing of the case. They requested that the High Court of Justice reexamine the case and argued that the court's decision did not set a definitive standard regarding article 82 and the status of the Hebrew and Arabic languages in Israel. The request for second hearing was denied.[18]

6. THE STATUS OF HEBREW IN THE STATE OF ISRAEL

The centrality of Hebrew to Israeli nationalism and the story of the revitalization of Hebrew have been discussed and written about extensively. The renaissance of the Hebrew language, which resulted in its transformation to the principal language of the Jewish population in Palestine by the 1920's, is often identified (although some argue, erroneously) with the efforts of Eliezer Ben-Yehuda, who is known as the "reviver of the Hebrew language."[19] This renaissance was a result of conscious and directed attempts to establish a "new Hebrew man," the climate of which was the 1913 battle over the language to be used in the Technion, the technological higher education institute.[20]

The creation of a people was viewed as necessary for the success first of the Zionist project and then of the new State of Israel. The young state was a state of immigrants stemming from different places and speaking different tongues. Ensuring that all new immigrants learn to speak the Hebrew language served both practical causes, as Hebrew was to be the one language in which these people could communicate, and symbolic ones, as it was the language of the historic and religious narratives that were meant to tie them together. Shlomo Kodesh, one of Israel's first Hebrew language educators, expressed the common feeling that the new immigrants, "Holocaust survivors, persecuted Jews and Jews expelled from Muslim counties" were "miserable people full of fears, without nationality or an emotional tie to their place of residence," and that "only an act that would expedite the assimilation of the different communities and of each immigrant into work and society could have prevented a disaster… 'One language, one people, one country' was no longer a slogan… but a necessity of life and existence."[21]

In a way, the transformation the Hebrew language went through mirrored the transformation the Jewish people were experiencing, from a religious minority to a nation. The prosperity of the Hebrew language was considered to be so important that an Academy of the Hebrew Language, which role was to "direct the development of the Hebrew language," was created by law in 1953 and operates till this day.[22] The standards prescribed by the Academy and published by the minister of education are supposed to be binding on the government, educational institutions and local authorities.

The "Ulpan" is another institution that exemplifies the commitment of the state of Israel to the Hebrew language. An Ulpan, meaning studio or school, is a school for the intensive study of Hebrew to adults, primary new immigrants. The purpose of the Ulpan exceeds the mere study of the language and is to "expedite the transformation of the new immigrant to Israel into a citizen with consciousness and an emotional sense of belonging to his people and his country."[23] While schools for the study of Hebrew existed in Israel before the establishment of the state, the first Ulpan in its current form was created in Jerusalem in 1949. Ulpanim (the plural for Ulpan) are sponsored by the government or the local authorities, or by institutions or organizations that receive public funds. The state is therefore actively involved in assimilation of new immigrants. According to the Jewish Agency for Israel, 1,220,000 individuals have studied in Ulpanim since 1949.

7. THE ARABIC LANGUAGE AND THE ARAB MINORITY

While Arabic is an official language of the state, it is clear that Hebrew is the dominant language and that Arabic plays little, if any, role in the public sphere. Arabic is spoken almost exclusively by and within the Arab minority, and its status as an official language is mainly declarative.[24] While most of the Arabs in Israel know Hebrew, the majority of the Jewish population does not know Arabic. Studies conducted among Jewish students indicated that the desire to study Arabic was low as Arabic was considered by the participants to be a non-prestigious language (Arabic only became a mandatory part of the curriculum in 1996).[25]

The Arab minority in Israel falls into the category often referred to in political science literature as a "national minority". A national minority can be described as a group that is a historical community living within a state, which shares a language and culture that are different from that of the majority in such state.[26] A group can become a national minority either voluntarily, through the formation of a federation, or involuntarily.

When a multination state is created through a voluntary process, the specific rights of the minority and the relationship between the majority, the minority and the state are usually negotiated in the process of formation. The results of this negotiation are often embodied both in the governmental structure and in the constitution of the state. When a group, however, becomes a national minority through an involuntary process, establishing this relationship in a fair and just manner becomes a more difficult task.

The general democratic process is inherently flawed since without taking special measures, it favors the majority. Such special measures, however, are exactly the issue at stake. Courts, in turn, are willing to address the protection of individual members of a minority group, but are usually reluctant to discuss issues involving the group rights of national minorities. These matters are considered by courts in many states, including Israel, as matters that belong in the political rather than the legal arena. In the area of language rights, courts are more willing to protect individual, instrumental language rights than they are to recognize a group's right to non-instrumental language rights.

The Arab minority in Israel clearly falls into the category of national minorities that found themselves within the boundaries of a state as a result of an involuntary process. Because of the strong ties between Zionism and Hebrew and the historical circumstances under which the Arab minority became part of the state of Israel, there is little argument that it cannot be expected to assimilate or acquire Hebrew as its main language. This does not mean that Arabs in Israel don't speak Hebrew. To the contrary, most Arabs speak and understand Hebrew quite well because it is the language of economic opportunities and social mobility. Arabic, however, is the first language spoken by them. Research conducted among Arab students indicated that most students felt that it was the Arabic language that defined their identity.[27]

Despite the centrality of Arabic to cultural identity of the Arabs in Israel, there is no comprehensive legal arrangement regarding the language rights of the Arab minority. A number of laws require the use of Arabic in particular circumstances. Tender offers published by the government, for example, must be published in an Arabic language newspaper in addition to a Hebrew language newspaper,[28] and one of the purposes of the Second Authority for Television and Radio is to broadcast programs in Arabic.[29] These laws, however, are specific arrangement that are limited to particular situations and are often executed poorly, if at all. There is no developed comprehensive body of law that specifies and explains the language rights of the Arab minority in Israel.

Many view the existence of a public education system in Arabic as the most critical tool for maintaining the Arab culture and language in Israel and as the main non-instrumental, "group right" accorded to the Arab minority. This is because an education system in the language of the minority is one of the most common demands raised by linguistic minorities around the globe. I use the term "group right" in inverted commas, however, because the existence of the Arabic language education system is not (or at least not directly) the result of recognizing any group rights of the Arab minority. With the establishment of the state of Israel, the education committee of the Knesset decided to continue the British policy of allowing Arab schools to use Arabic as the language of instruction, a policy that was enabled due to the geographical separation of the Arab and Jewish populations.[30] While the contribution of this policy to the maintenance of Arabic among the Arab minority cannot be undermined, there are many controversies regarding its scope and application. Indeed, some of the most heated debates concern the degree of autonomy the Arab minority should enjoy in determining the content of the teaching material and managing the Arab schools. Because a group right was never recognized, however, there is no available legal context in which these debates can take place.

As Chief Justice Barak acknowledged in the *Adalah* case, there can be little dispute that Arabic poses no real threat to the Hebrew language in Israel today.[31] In examining the petition in the *Adalah* case, Chief Justice Barak indicated that whenever an official authority uses its power, it should consider and balance between the various different and legitimate considerations and purposes of both the authority and the law. In this particular case, Barak listed as the relevant considerations the specific purpose of the authority discussed (the authority to put up public signs), which goal was to provide residents guidance around the city, as well as several other "general" purposes: the right of an individual to protect his language, the right to equality (and to enjoy equal services in particular), the status of the Hebrew language, which, according to Barak, is one of the expressions of Israel being a Jewish state and the importance of language to national unity and the definition of a sovereign state. The proper balance in this case, according to Barak, required that the Arab residents equally enjoy the services, in this case signs, provided by the municipally, especially since the status of the Hebrew language faces no real threat. The subtext of this argument, however, suggests that if Arabic did pose a serious threat to the status of the Hebrew language in Israel, such threat would be a legitimate consideration (although not necessarily determinative) in deciding the case.

In light of the clearly superior status of Hebrew, how are we to understand the constant attempts to challenge the current arrangement regarding the official status of languages in Israel and express the superiority of the Hebrew language by either a regular or basic law? Arab leaders have called these attempts racists and demanded that the official status of Arabic expressed in Article 82 be given real substance.

The Israel Democracy Institute, a prestigious Israeli think tank, published in 2005 a draft of a proposed constitution for the State of Israel, entitled Constitution by Consensus.[32] According to this draft, the future constitution would determine that Hebrew is the language of the state and that Arabic has an official status in the state. The implication of such "official status," however, are not specified in the proposed constitution and are to be determined be law. The drafters explain that the suggested draft not only reflects the existing reality, in which Hebrew is clearly the language of the state, but sets an appropriate and desired hierarchy between the two languages. Since Israel is not a bi-national state, they explain, the constitution should determine explicitly that Hebrew is the exclusive language of the state.

The proposal of the Israel Democracy Institute sheds some light on some of the motives behind the various suggested legislation concerning the status of the Hebrew language. The fact that Arabic does not pose a real threat to the Hebrew language in Israel does not mean that it is not perceived, at least by some, as a threat. This can be attributed to two main reasons. First,

Arabic is the language of the Arab states which Israel has been in a state of war with since the establishment of the state. Arabic is therefore perceived as the language of the enemy.[33] More importantly, however, is the fact that many of the Jewish citizens of Israel express fear from a demographic change that will shift the majority/minority numbers in Israel. They are concerned that this will influence the nature of Israel as a Jewish state. Becoming a bi-lingual state is viewed by many as the first step in Israel becoming a bi-national state. Legislation aiming to give Hebrew a preferred status over Arabic aims, to a large extent, to prevent this from happening.

Measures that aim to prevent the impact of demographic changes, although formally possible, are problematic from a democratic perspective. Establishing the relationship between different groups at the time when a society is established is one thing. Once the basic relationship is established, however, any changes made by the majority to disadvantage the minority are a potential abuse of power that should be examined with scrutiny. In addition to these difficulties, changing the existing status unilaterally by the Jewish majority, even if it has few practical implications, sends a message of exclusion to the Arab minority. When viewed through this angle, it is understandable why Arab leaders and organizations view such proposals as offensive.

From a self-defense perspective, it is clear that the Arabic language poses no immanent threat to the Hebrew language in Israel. Even if a real threat existed, however, the concept of self-defense applies to a situation in which a state is threatened by an external aggressor. It is unlikely that it can be applied by a state to its own members, even if the goal is to preserve the self-determination right of the majority.

8. RUSSIAN IMMIGRATION AND THE STATUS OF RUSSIAN

Israel has experienced two large immigration waves from the former USSR. The first wave was during the 1970's; the second was during the 1990's. Research indicates that immigrants arriving to Israel as part of the last wave of immigration retain, for the most part, the use of the Russian language. Indeed, these immigrants also learn Hebrew, but Russian continues, in many cases, to be the main language they use for both personal and cultural purposes and, for many, the language they identify with culturally.

A number of factors have been suggested to explain the maintenance of the Russian culture and language among the recent immigrants. One factor is the large number of immigrants, which enabled them to settle in

"Russian" communities within Israel, in which Russian continues to be the dominant language. Another factor is the socio-economic profile of many of the new immigrants, many of which hold higher education degrees. Interviews conducted with these immigrants revealed that they view Russian culture as superior to Israeli culture. An alternative explanation points to the motives that lead these immigrants to immigrate to Israel. As opposed to past immigrations, it is argued, the current Russian immigrants arrived to Israel not out of Zionism but out of economic considerations. While they are eager to pursue the economic opportunities that knowledge of Hebrew provides, they are not interested in integrating into the Israeli society.

As a result, Russian has become highly visible in the Israeli linguistic landscape. There is an unprecedented prosperity of Russian language newspapers and publications, as well as in other cultural institutions. Advertisers, banks and commercial companies address the Russian sector as a separate sector, in Russian. The perception of Russian immigrants of themselves as a separate sector with particular needs lead to the establishment of several "Russian" political parties.

What is the approach that is taken by the state of Israel with respect to the Russian language? Although many governmental services are in fact provided in Russian (even the Knesset has a Russian language website), Russian is not an official language in Israel. When the law does require the use of Russian, it is usually in the context of regulating services that a person would not be able to enjoy otherwise. While some might argue that Russian speaking citizens are de-facto awarded language rights through such regulations, any rights awarded under these regulations fall under the limited category of instrumental language rights. Language itself and the right to maintain and preserve it are not at the core of such rights.

What about non-instrumental language rights? Does the Russian-speaking minority in Israel have a right to cultural self-determination? Does the Hebrew speaking majority have a right of self-defense against a potential threat the Russian language may pose to the status of Hebrew in Israel?

A negative answer to the first question is often explained by drawing a distinction between immigrants and national minorities based on the idea of consent. Immigrants, goes the argument, choose to leave their old culture and therefore cannot claim to have a right to preserve it.[34] By uprooting themselves and moving to a new state, immigrants have either waived their right to culture or have chosen to change their culture.

The validity of this argument has been widely criticized for a variety of reasons. Critics have questioned whether a right to culture can be waived, in particular due to the implications on future generations. In addition, it has

65

been argued that even if immigrants agree to waive such right, in order for such consent to be morally valid it needs to be free and informed. The harsh economic realities that often drive immigrants to immigrate can raise doubts regarding the moral validity of such consent. Moreover, many immigrants may choose to immigrate based on a belief that they will actually be able to maintain their culture and language, especially if they choose to immigrate to a country in which a large number of members of their original culture already live, as is the case with the Russian community in Israel.[35]

Others reject the general distinction between immigrants and national minorities but offer alternative explanations justifying a distinction between rights awarded to the Arab minority and those the Russian-speaking minority may be entitled to. One such suggestion concentrates on the specific characteristics of each of these two specific groups and the connection between language, culture and identity.[36] The interest the Arabic speaking minority has in Arabic, goes the argument, is stronger than the interest the Russian-speaking minority has in Russian. This is because the Russian immigrants belong to the Jewish nation and therefore can identify with the Hebrew language as well as with the Russian language.

This argument is interesting because history actually tells us otherwise. For thousands of years, the majority of Jews did not feel that knowledge of Hebrew was an essential part of their identity. In addition, the continuous importance of Russian language and culture in the life of immigrants indicates that Russian continues to be a constituting element of their identity, even after they learn Hebrew, and that although most immigrants are able to function in Hebrew, many feel that Russian language and culture continues to define them.

The key issue, however, is not whether or not the Russian-speaking minority does or can potentially identify with the Hebrew language. The real issue at stake regards the implications of membership in the state and the expectations the state has of its various members. In Israel, the expectations the state has from its Arab members are different from the expectations it has from Russian speaking immigrants. In this sense, the distinction between national minorities and immigrants is indeed relevant.

Understanding this argument requires a brief review of the concept of membership in a state. Michael Walzer argues that membership in a human community is the primary good we distribute to one another. He also explains that those who are already members of a community get to choose, based on their understanding of what sort of community they want to have, who will be admitted as a member of the community. Indeed, it is generally accepted that a state can determine its own admission policy.[37]

Under international law, there are two common ways for acquiring nationality. An individual can become a member of a state by virtue of blood, through being a descendent of a national (the jura sanguinis principle) or by soil, by being born on the territory of a specific state (the jura soli principle). Both principles require that a certain link exists between individuals and the state, and the choice between these principles is tied to the nature of the state as viewed by its members.

States also enable individuals to become members through naturalization. The criteria for naturalization are determined by each state and, therefore, vary from state to state. Many states, however, require familiarity with the state's history and political system as well a certain degree of fluency in the state's language or languages as preconditions for naturalization. Thus, naturalization laws often reflect the perception that the admission criteria is there to ensure the protection of a certain cultural nature of the state.

Although international law does not prescribe any principles regarding admission standards set by states, not all admission policies can be morally defendable. Nevertheless, when determining their admission policies, states are generally entitled to apply principles that would be considered unjust if applied to their own citizens (for example, a distinction based on the place of birth). This is because the duties a state owes to its own members, including the duty to treat them equally, are different than the duties a state owes to outsiders.

In Israel, an individual has two main ways, in addition to being born to an Israeli citizen, to become a citizen.[38] The first way to become a citizen is by taking residency in Israel under the Law of Return.[39] A person may also become an Israeli citizen if he complies with the requirements of the Nationality Law and is awarded citizenship by the Minister of Internal Affairs.[40] Under the law of return, any Jew, child and grandchild of a Jew, the spouse of a Jew, the spouse of a child of a Jew and the spouse of a grandchild of a Jew may immigrate to Israel and is granted the status of "Oleh," under which he becomes a citizen immediately and is entitled to a variety of benefits and privileges. No knowledge of the Hebrew language is required in order to become a citizen under the Law of Return.

In order to acquire Israeli citizenship under the Nationality Law, however, an individual must fulfill a number of preconditions. The Nationality Law requires an individual to be in Israel for three years out of five years proceeding the day of the submission of his application, to be entitled to reside in Israel permanently, to settle, or intend to settle in Israel, and to have some knowledge of the Hebrew language.

Two additional requirements distinguish between those acquiring Israeli citizenship under the Nationality Law from those becoming citizens under the Law of Return. Individuals acquiring citizenship under the Nationality Law are required to renounce all prior nationalities, while individuals acquiring citizenship under the Law of Return are allowed to maintain additional citizenships. Individuals acquiring citizenship under the Nationality Law are also required to make a declaration stating they will be loyal nationals of the State of Israel.[41]

A requirement of knowledge of the Hebrew language as well as the requirements to renounce all other citizenships and to declare loyalty to the state of Israel appears in the Nationality Law but not in the Law of Return. This is because Jews becoming citizens under the law of return are not considered to be complete outsiders. Their loyalty is not questioned but is assumed, and they therefore are not required to prove it.

In this context it is interesting to note the frustration some members of Israeli society express with respect to the cultural, ideological and religious characteristics of the new immigrants. Many in the Israeli society question their "real" motives for immigrations and accuse the new immigrants of not being Jewish, not being Zionists and therefore "abusing" the Law of Return. The Law of Return itself, however, does not require an individual to be Jewish and certainly does not require him or her to identify with a certain ideology.

The issue at stake, therefore, is not explicit requirements but implied expectations. Those immigrating to Israel under the law of return are seen as "lost brothers," and are therefore expected to behave like a family member. This includes a duty of loyalty to the state, but also includes adopting its culture and its language.

But what happens if this expectation is not realized? This brings us back to the issue of members and outsiders. Once immigrants become citizens they become full and equal members of society and the state cannot defend itself against them. They are equally entitled to make claims upon the resources of the state and are therefore also entitled to try and affect the cultural nature of the state. Whether they achieve these goals in practice is of course also an issue of political power. If we believe, however, that culture and language are important, and that the state is crucial to their maintenance, we cannot dismiss, at least on a sweeping basis, claims for non-instrumental language rights brought by new immigrants who have already become members of the state.

NOTES

1   See, for example, Davis Crystal, *Language Death* (Cambridge University Press, 2000), p. 38.

2   According to Israel's Central Bureau of Statistics, at the beginning of 2008, the Arab minority in Israel constituted 20% of the population. *The Demongraphic Situtation in Israel*, published by Central Bureau of Statistics, available at: http://www1. cbs.gov.il/reader/newhodaot/hodaa_template.html?hodaa=200711262. In 2004, approximately 800,000 people were immigrants from the former USSR. See: http://www1.cbs.gov.il/www/publications/migration_ussr01/migration_ussr_h.htm.

3   Ruth Rubio-Marín, Language Rights: Exploring the Competing Rationales, in *Language Rights and Political Theory*, ed. Will Kymlicka and Alan Patten (New York: Oxford University Press, 2003), p. 56.

4   International Covenant on Civil and Political Rights, December 16, 1966, 999 U.N.T.S. 171, International Covenant for Economic, Social and Cultural Rights, December 16, 1966, 993 U.N.T.S. 3.

5   See George Fletcher, The Case for Linguistic Self-defense, in *The Morality of Nationalism*, ed. Robert McKim and Jeff McMahan (New York: Oxford University Press, 1997).

6   See Raymond G. Gordon, Jr., *Ethnologue: Languages of the World* (Dallas: SIL International, 2005).

7   It should be noted that the immigrants from the former USSR do not form a homogenous linguistic group and that many of these immigrants speak languages other than Russian. Knowledge of Russian among immigrants from the territories of the former USSR in which Russian was not the local language is usually tied to the nature of the place of origin (urban versus rural) and the level of education.

8   Palestine Order-in-Council, 1922, Article 82.

9   The Law and Administration Ordinance, 5708–1948.

10   *Ibid*, Section 11.

11   Amnon Rubinstein, *The Constitutional Law of Israel* (Tel-Aviv: Schoken, 1997), p. 88–89.

12   Although Ilan Saban and Mohammad Amara argue that the cancellation of English but not of Arabic as an official language indicates that Arabic was left as an official language intentionaly. See Ilan Saban and Muhammad Amara, The Status of Arabic in Israel: Reflections on the Power of Law to Produce Social Change, *Isr. L. Rev.* 36(2) (2002):5.

13   The Knesset and the Hebrew language, published by the Knesset Information and Research Center on January 5 2005 in honor of the Hebrew Language Day in the Knesset. http://www.knesset.gov.il/mmm/doc.asp?doc=m00993&type=pdf.

14   See Shahar Ilan, *Proposed Legislation: Arabic Will Not Be an Official Language*, Haaretz, 19/05/2005, at http://www.haaretz.co.il/hasite/pages/ShArt.jhtml?itemNo= 984862&contrassID=1&subContrassID=0&sbSubContrassID=0.

15 The bill, entitled "The Hebrew Language Law (Legislation Amendments)" was presented by Knesset member Hendel on June 19, 2006. See the Knesset website at http://www.knesset.gov.il/privatelaw/data/17/533.rtf.

16 According the Interpretation Law of 1981, the binding version of any law is in the version in the language in which it was promulgated. This gives the Hebrew version of the laws a superior status. In addition, the failure to translate a law to Arabic does not affect the law's validity, although an injustice caused due to a failure to translate a law to Arabic may entitle the injured to a relief. See more in David Kretzmer, *The Legal Status of the Arabs in Israel* (Westview Press, 1990).

17 H.C. 4112/99, *Adalah, et. al. v. The Municipalities of Tel Aviv-Jaffa, et al.*

18 The decision was delivered on 25 July 2002. The request for a second hearing was denied on 14 August 2003.

19 Bernard Spolsky and Elana Shohamy for example, argue that the role attributed to Ben Yehuda's personal efforts is often too significant. See Bernard Spolsky and Elana Shohamy Language in Israeli Society and Education, *Int'l J. Soc. of Language* (1999).

20 Ben Yehuda himself was influenced by the revival of the Bulgarian nation and the revival of the Greek and Italian nations in the 19th century. See Jack Fellman, Eliezer Ben-Yehuda: A Language Reborn, *Ariel*, Vol. 104, 1997.

21 Shlomo Kodesh, Teaching the Hebrew Language in Israel, in *The Adult Education Philosophy of Shlomo Kodesh*, ed. Shlomo Haramati (Jerusalem, Ministry of Education, Culture and Sport, 1997), p. 182.

22 The Supreme National institution for the Hebrew language Act, 1953-5713.

23 Kodesh, *Supra* note 15.

24 See Saban and Amara, *Supra* note 9.

25 See Muhammad Hasan Amara and Abd Al-Rahman Mar'i, *Language Education Policy: The Arab Minority in Israel* (Dordrecht: Kluwer Academic Publishers, 2002).

26 See Will Kymlica, *Multicultural Citizenship: A Liberal Theory of Minority Rights* (Oxford: Clarendon Press, 1995), p. 11.

27 See Amara and Mar'i, *Supra* note 19.

28 The Mandatory Tenders Regulations, 5753–1993, Section 15.

29 Law of the Second Authority for Television and Radio — 1990.

30 See Amara and Mar'i, *Supra* note 19.

31 See also Amara and Mar'i, *Supra* note 19, p. 6.

32 *Constitution by Consensus*, proposal of the Israel Democracy Institute leaded by Justice Meir Shamgar (Israel: Israel Democracy Institute, 2005).

33 Amara and Mar'i, *Supra* note 19.

34 See, for example, Kymlicka *Supra* note 20, p. 95.

35   Ruth Rubio-Marin, Exploring the Boundaries of Language Rights: Insiders, New-comers, and Natives, in *Secession and Self-Determination, Nomos XLV*, ed. Stephen Macedo and Allen Buchanan (New York: New York University Press, 2003).

356   See Meital Pinto, Immigration and Language Rights in Israel, Exclusive Identity Marker as a Criterion Distinguishing between Arabic and Russian [Hebrew], *Mishpat Umimshal*, Vol. 10 No. 1: Citizenship, Immigration and Naturalization in Israel (November 2006).

37   Walzer notes that admission policies of countries are criticized, it is usually in terms of charity rather than justice. See Michael Walzer, *Spheres of Justice, a Defense of Pluralism and Equality* (USA: Basic Books, 2003).

38   A special provision is made in the Nationality Law for former citizens of British Mandatory Palestine, stating that those who remained in Israel from the establish-ment of the State in 1948 until the enactment of the Nationality Law of 1952 became Israeli citizens *by residence* or *by return*.

39   Law of Return, 5710–1950.

40   The Nationality Law, 5712–1952.

41   *Ibid.*

THE HAND IN HAND
BILINGUAL EDUCATION MODEL:
VISION AND CHALLENGES

MUHAMMAD AMARA

1. INTRODUCTION

According to the general Israeli language education policy, the mother tongue is learned first for several years, after that the second language is studied (English for Jews and Hebrew for Arabs), and this is followed by a third language, English for Arabs and Arabic or French for Jews. This type of limited bilingualism in Israeli schools may be called '**functional bilingualism.**' This model of language education seems to suit the Israeli reality in the context of the Israeli-Arab conflict, the definition and perception of Israel as a Jewish-Zionist state, and the complex Jewish-Arab relations within the state of Israel.

In 1997, the Hand in Hand: The Center for Jewish-Arab Education in Israel (henceforth Hand in Hand) initiated a new model of bilingual education in the Israeli landscape. The new model is based on balanced bilingualism, where both Arabic and Hebrew are equally used as the languages of instruction in the three integrated schools of Jews and Arabs learning together. The main purpose of the new model is to offer dignity and equality to the two national groups. The basic idea behind the initiative is to create egalitarian bilingual educational environments.

Several studies of the new model have been conducted, providing rich information, mainly about the educational, cultural and national issues (Amara, 2005; Amara, Azaiza, Mor-Sommerfeld & Hertz-Lazarowitz, 2007; Bekerman, 2003a 2003b, 2004, 2005; Bekerman & Horenczyk, 2004; Bekerman & Maoz, 2005; Bekerman & Shhadi, 2003; Mor-Sommerfeld 2005; Mor-Sommerfeld, Azaiza, & Hertz-Lazarowitz, 2007). So far, however, no systematic studies have focused on actual language practices in the classroom and the entire school environment. This paper will attempt to answer the following questions:

- What are the characteristics of the new bilingual education model? What differentiates it from other bilingual education models in Israel?
- What are the actual linguistic practices of both Hebrew and Arabic in the classroom and the entire school environment?
- What are the language achievements of both groups, Arab and Jewish students, in the mother tongue and the second language?
- What are the major obstacles and challenges facing the implementation of the new bilingual education model?

For data collection, we employed observations, interviews and questionnaires in order to answer the research questions. Our analysis is based on more than 200 hours of recorded and tape-recorded observations both in the classrooms and in the school environment gathered over more than two years, from January 2004 till the end of 2005. The observations were meant to provide answers to the question of who uses which language/s with whom, when, where, and for what purposes? (Fishman, Cooper & Ma, 1971). We also conducted 57 structured interviews with teachers and headmasters, and the directors of Hand in Hand. Through the interviews, we hoped to learn about the interviewees' experiences, feelings, expectations, perceptions of Arab-Jewish relations, and commitment to the new enterprise. One hundred and nine parents of students attending the three schools filled out a questionnaire designed to assess their satisfaction with educational, pedagogical, social, and linguistic aspects of the schools.

The importance of language here is not confined to linguistic competence per se: Language has as special importance because Hand in Hand puts special attention on bilingualism as a means for creating a population of students who recognize and respect the other culture, while preserving their own culture. In other words, language in the new model is employed as one of the main means for reconstructing power, dominance and political relationships in the wider society.

2. THE ARAB-JEWISH CONFLICT-RIDDEN RELATIONS IN ISRAEL AND BILINGUAL EDUCATION

Bilingual education cannot be properly understood unless it is dealt with in relation to the socio-political contexts. The Israeli-Arab/Palestinian conflict and the concept of the State of Israel and its definition as a Jewish-Zionist State constitute two important components that determine the character of the relations between the Arab minority and the Jewish majority in the State of Israel. These relations are wrapped in tension and persistent friction. (See Amara and Mar'i, 2002.)

The Israeli reality points to a number of deep divisions among the population, such as between Sephardim and Ashkenazim, Orthodox and secular, men and women, and Arabs and Jews. The Arab-Jewish division is probably the deepest of all, and there is still no solution. Over the course of time, Arabs in Israel have consolidated an identity for themselves outside the hegemony of the Jewish state (Amara, 2003). Exacerbating this situation, there are heated political disputes between right and left wing ideologies. Such a structure inhibits the prospect of successful social integration (Schildkraut, 2005).

The Arab minority is an indigenous minority which was a majority in Mandatory Palestine,[1] and became a numerical minority with the changing socio-political situation and the establishment of Israel (see Smooha, 2005). It is also a distinctive minority, different from the Jewish majority in many important ways, including those related to ethnicity, religion, nationality, language and culture. The Arab minority is considered a national minority. Consequently, the Arabs seek to achieve not only individual rights in Israel but also national rights, such as cultural autonomy, Palestinian national identity, and recognized national leadership. Add to that it is a non-assimilated minority. The non-assimilation of the minority is increased by the non-assimilated nature of the Jewish majority. It is also a minority of low socio-economic status; the standard of living among the Arabs stands substantially below the average level of the Jewish population.

Furthermore, it is a minority which has an internal conflict with the state over two major issues: the Arabs reject the state's Jewish-Zionistic character, and they also reject the Jewish and Zionist narrative regarding the Palestinian/Arab-Israeli conflict and have an alternative, Palestinian narrative.

Fen Olser et al. (2002) define the Jewish-Arab conflict within the state of Israel as intractable and frozen. It is also integrated within other cycles of conflict: the Israeli-Arab conflict in the Middle East and the conflict that has developed in the last few years between the West and both the Muslim and the Arab world. Furthermore, the Arab citizens of Israel, though officially offered full rights as citizens, have chronically suffered as a putatively hostile minority with limited political representation and a debilitated social, economic and educational infrastructure (Beckerman & Maoz, 2005).

The Jewish-Arab conflict within the state of Israel is not only a *material conflict*, but also an *identity conflict.* The focus on identity gives birth to and nourishes a "victim-victimizer" narrative. Each side feels that the other has usurped its legitimate rights. The conflict may be termed an "identity conflict" if at least one of the sides denies the adversary's narrative regarding its national identity and its right to national sovereignty in the territory claimed by the two protagonists as their exclusive property. The total negation of the legitimacy of the other as a national entity, and the ensuing active efforts to nullify its demands, are perceived by the deprived side as injustice and gives birth to a feeling of victimization (Auerbach, 2005a, 2005b).

Montville (1993) believes that conflict resolution in this type of situation entails *a process of forgiveness and reconciliation*. This process can be achieved, according to him, through *a direct dialogue* between the two sides. Direct dialogue may bring about the delegitimization of existing prejudices and stereotypes. It is only this meeting of identities that can generate a new interpretation of 'other' and "otherness." According to this approach, only direct contact can create empathy for the human suffering of the other side, pave the way to rapprochement and engender cognitive dissonance that will challenge negative stereotypes and create social change.

Kacen and Lev-Wiesel (2002) summarize the research dealing with conflicting groups, Arabs and Jews, in Israel as follows: it is not sufficient to provide an opportunity for an encounter between conflicting sides, especially when the conflict is historical, ideological and national. Real dialogue can be created only provided emotional and cognitive barriers have been overcome first. Otherwise, any attempt to create a mutual openness will probably fail from the start.

Bilingual education is an approach to conflict resolution and the improvement of inter-group relations. Research has demonstrated that bilingual education results in socio-cultural outcomes that are not just linguistic (Crawford, 1997; Paulson, 1994; Ricento & Hornberger, 1996; Valdes, 1997). Mor-Sommerfeld et al. (2007) believe that bilingual education is a bridge for cooperation, sharing and equality. Skutnabb-Kangas and Garcia (1995) summarize the major benefits of effective bilingual education as achieving a high level of multilingualism, improving equal opportunity for academic achievement, and engendering a strong, positive, multilingual and multicultural identity including positive attitudes towards self and others.

However, though bilingual education has the potential to overcome a wide variety of societal and cultural tensions, it remains controversial. Bilingual education, it is claimed, can be a patronizing exercise, because schools can do little to reconstruct power (Cummins, 1986). In order to reconstruct power, changes must be made in areas of dominance and political relationships in the broader society and attempts must be made to eradicate prejudice, fear, and victimization (Baker, 1993).

In light of the above considerations, the study of bilingual education offers us in-depth insights into power structures and political systems in society. Bilingual education does not just reflect curriculum decisions. The rest of this section describes bilingual education in Israel.

Though Hebrew and Arabic are both recognised as official languages in Israel, the status of the two languages is not at all equal. The status accorded to Arabic in Israeli law is quite limited, so that for all intents and purposes Hebrew is the language of public civic life. Hebrew is the regular language of bureaucracy, the medium of instruction in higher education, the dominant language of the domestic electronic media, and most importantly, it is the language of those sectors of the labour market that are open to the Arabic-speaking minority. Although Arabic is recognised as an official language, its significance is not in regard to the society as a whole, but in the degree of protection it affords to the internal life of the minority, especially in regard to the right to education in the minority tongue (Saban & Amara, 2002). Due to the dominance of Hebrew in the national language landscape of Israel, it is extremely difficult for Arabs in Israel to function outside their home villages and towns without sufficient competence in Hebrew.

Generally speaking, Jewish and Arab students in Israel study in separate schools, and they do not have many opportunities to meet. Hebrew is the language of instruction in Jewish schools (except in some ultra-orthodox schools, where Yiddish or other languages are used). Arabic is the language of instruction in Arab schools. Hebrew is learned as a second language by all minorities from the third grade on. Arabic is studied by tens of thousands of Jews as a foreign language. English is learned as a foreign language by both Jews and Arabs (Amara, 2002; Amara & Mar'i, 2002). In short, under the general Israeli language education policy, the mother tongue is learned first for several years, after that the second language is studied (English for Jews and Hebrew for Arabs), and this is followed by a third language, English for Arabs and Arabic or French for Jews (Abu Rabi'a, 1998). This type of limited bilingualism in Israeli schools has been termed "**functional bilingualism**"[2] (Amara, 2005). The model of functional bilingualism in the separate schools seems to suit the Israeli reality in the context of the Israeli-Arab conflict, the definition and perception of Israel as a Jewish-Zionist state, and the complex Jewish-Arab relations within the state of Israel.

In 1997, Hand in Hand was established in order to challenge and attempt to change the conflict-ridden Israeli reality, characterized by segregation and hostility, and based on functional bilingualism. Hand in Hand initiated a new model of Hebrew-Arabic bilingual education in the Israeli landscape, assuming that direct contact and dialogue between Arab and Jewish students would bring about far-reaching changes in the conflict-ridden Israeli reality.[3] So far three schools have adopted the model.

3. THE HAND IN HAND MODEL

The Schools

The biggest of the three schools is located in Jerusalem, and was established in 1998. In the 2006–7 school year, 370 students were enrolled in the school, from pre-kindergarten to grade eight. There are about 50 teachers, including kindergarten teachers. The school is regional, and the students come from many neighborhoods in Jerusalem and from other localities near the city of Jerusalem.

Established in the same year, the Galilee school is an elementary and junior high school, located between the Jewish community of Misgav and the Arab city of Sakhnin, in the lower Galilee. The Jewish students come from the various communities that make up the Misgav regional council. The Arab students come mainly from Sakhnin and Sha'ab. There are 230 students and 25 teachers.

The third school is called Bridge over the Wadi. The school was established in 2004, and currently operates classes up to fifth grade. Unlike the Jerusalem and Galilee schools, it is located in the heart of an Arab village, Kafar Qara, in the Little Triangle. There are about 200 students and 25 teachers and kindergarten teachers (See the map on p. 78).

Characteristics

Whereas regular Israeli schools for Arabs and Jews have distinct curricula, Hand in Hand schools use the same school curricula in all subjects. Hand in Hand's objectives, as stated on their website (http://www.handinhand12.org/), are as follows: "Hand in Hand schools are fully egalitarian, with classes team-taught by one Jewish and one Palestinian teacher. The curriculum is innovative, bilingual and bicultural, allowing students to strengthen their own identities while attaining a better understanding of their classmates."

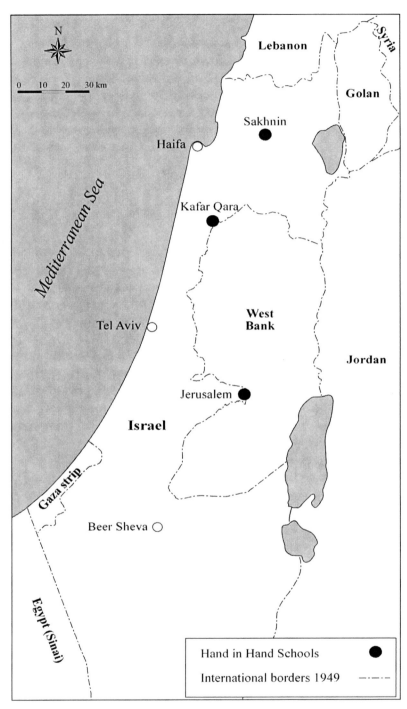

The location of the schools

The central goal of Hand in Hand is to develop a new educational scheme for Jewish-Arab schools that integrates children, parents, and the rest of the community jointly with governmental institutions (Ministry of Education and local authorities), in the hope of changing the existing, conflict-ridden reality.

The main purpose of the new model is to offer dignity and equality to the two national groups in Israel — Arabs and Jews. The basic idea behind the initiative is to create egalitarian, bilingual educational environments. The desired outcome is people who can respect and appreciate the culture of one another while remaining loyal to their own cultural heritage.

According to this model, language is a tool that can be used to change reality by breaking down the cultural and linguistic barriers between the two nations and strengthening civil society in Israel. Hand in Hand aspires "to create a new model of relations between Palestinians and Jews, enabling children, parents, and educators at school and in the community to develop continuous relations of equal cooperation, co-existence and education for peace" (Hand in Hand *Weekly Planner*, 2006–7).

The Hand in Hand bilingual education model is different from other bilingual educational models in Israel in that it aims to place Hebrew and Arabic on an equal footing.[4] It is not the first enterprise chronologically, but today it is undoubtedly considered the leading educational enterprise in this type of bilingual education. Neve Shalom[5] was the first to adopt bilingual education of this type, but it encountered many difficulties and has not succeeded in generating significant Arabic-Hebrew bilingualism among its Jewish students (for more details see Amara, 2005; Mor-Sommer-feld, 2005; Mor-Sommerfeld et al., 2007).

Hand in Hand schools are recognized as non-religious and are supported by the Israeli Ministry of Education. In part, they use the standard curriculum of the state non-religious school system. Enrollment in the schools is open to everyone at any time. No linguistic pre-requisites are set even for students enrolling after students of their grade level have become bilingual. Parents are interviewed before children are enrolled in the school and required to make two commitments: one is to the school's pluralistic philosophy; the other is to volunteer their time at the school. The schools attempt to keep equal numbers of Arab and Jewish students in each class (50 %–50 %), but the balance is not always maintained, with some classes consisting of an Arab majority (situations in which there is a Jewish majority do not exist).

Students from both national groups are integrated in most lessons, except for the teaching of language 1 (L1) and language 2 (L2) in the Galilee and Bridge over the Wadi schools. In these schools, such instruction is conducted in separate classrooms. The situation in Jerusalem, however, is different. There, the classes are divided according to linguistic competence and the same level of linguistic competence is expected from all students, regardless of nationality, who study the same syllabus and materials together (Amara et al., 2007). The schools are open five days a week, from Sunday to Thursday, and observe the religious holidays of the three religions.

Team teaching by an Arab teacher together with a Jewish teacher in the same classroom is a central characteristic of the schools. Instruction, therefore, is given in both Arabic and Hebrew. Some lessons are taught by only one teacher (either an Arab or a Jewish teacher). "The presence of two teachers in the classroom requires adjustments" said Lily Mesch, a Jewish first-grade teacher at the Jerusalem school. "It is even more difficult when my partner comes from another culture, with another type of educational background, and a different outlook and set of values about education" (Sudilovsky, 2003). In principle, each teacher uses her/his first language for instruction.

The majority of the Jewish teachers in the Hand in Hand schools are not bilingual, have not experienced bilingual education, and are not sufficiently familiar with Arab culture. Consequently, they are not capable of functioning in Arabic either for educational matters or for personal-social purposes. In contrast, all the Arab teachers are bilingual in both Arabic and Hebrew, and are capable of using the two languages in different domains and for various functions. (Amara, 2005; Bekerman, 2005)

The teaching programs are one of the major means through which Hand in Hand schools can achieve their goals. As stated in the Hand in Hand *Weekly Planner*, 2006–7:

> The curriculum is based on principles, values and knowledge reflecting the two cultures and languages without giving a preference to one over the other, and also based on education for multi-cultural literacy. We seek to enhance the civil identity together with the personal identity of the students. Consequently, the purpose is to develop abilities and skills for qualitative learning of contents, tolerance and multi-faceted attitudes, thinking and social criticism, and education for effective citizenship and the ability to democratic functioning.

Linguistic Practices

Hand in Hand schools employ *a strong additive bilingual approach* in that they emphasize symmetry between the two languages in all aspects of instruction. More specifically, two teachers, an Arab and a Jew, jointly conduct most of the classes. Two principals, a Jew and an Arab, head each school. There is an attempt to keep a numerical balance of students in classes, even though in practice this is not always possible.

The classroom is possibly the most important arena in which language interaction takes place. First, students spend most of their time at school in the classroom. Second, this location is structured, because of the presence of the teachers and the influence of the curricula. In this section we will answer the following questions about the classroom: Who uses which language? In which subjects? In what contexts? How often?

The written languages in the classrooms are clearly biliterate. The biliteracy environment, as reflected in the signs, letters, and numbers hanging on the walls, in the books available in the classrooms, and on the trilingual computer keyboards (Arabic, Hebrew, and English), reveals an attempt at language equality.

However, this is not the case in other aspects of language practice in the classroom. The language used in a given class depends on several factors including the subject, the teacher, the language teaching concept, and the students' interaction in classroom.

Generally, both languages are used for instruction in all classes. The frequency and the dominance of one language over the other depend on the teacher. They also depend on whether one or two teachers teach in the same classroom. Whenever an Arab teacher is available in the classroom, both languages are always present. The only class where the presence of Hebrew is completely minimal (almost no Hebrew at all) is in the class of Arabic as a mother tongue where an Arab teacher teaches Arabic to the Arab students as L1 in the Galilee and Kafar Qara schools.

Math is jointly taught by an Arab and a Jewish teacher. Thus, each teacher uses her own language for instruction. The Arab teacher in the math classes uses much less Hebrew than the Arab teacher in science classes. According to the teachers interviewed, this is due to the presence of a Jewish co-teacher who can explain the material in Hebrew. The presence of a Jewish teacher thus lessens the use of Hebrew by the Arab teacher. In math classes, as in science classes, homework can be done in the pupil's L1.

There are also linguistic considerations when deciding which textbooks to use in which subjects at school. Some textbooks are available in separate Arabic and Hebrew versions, while others are in both Arabic and Hebrew, with alternating sections in either language (*Relationships and Context* for grades 1 and 2). An example of the latter is the arithmetic textbook in Kafar Qara. The science textbook at that school is available in separate

Arabic and Hebrew versions so that each pupil has a science book in his/ her mother tongue. In Jerusalem, although the textbooks used in history and geography are available in Arabic and Hebrew, all students have the Hebrew version. This is because the teacher is Jewish and understands only basic Arabic. The textbooks used for these classes (science, math, geography, history) are also used in regular state schools.

In some classes, such as science or geography, only one teacher is available in class.

Moreover, on some exceptional days such as when one of the co-teachers is sick, the other co-teacher has to teach the class. Language use and the dominance of one language over the other do not seem to differ in classes with only one teacher and in others with two co-teachers.

The language used by Jewish students during the lesson is Hebrew, regardless of what the lesson is. Even in Arabic classes Jewish students would reply to the Arab teacher with Hebrew, while the Arab teacher uses Arabic.

When a Jewish teacher teaches a class, Hebrew is used by the teacher as well as the students, Arabs and Jews. Hebrew is almost the ONLY language used in class except for some words here and there used by the Jewish teacher such as *mumtaz* (excellent). Thus, when the class is taught by a Jewish teacher, the atmosphere and the instruction in the class is almost monolingual.

Hebrew is present in all classes except for Arabic as a mother tongue or where there is only an Arab teacher and Arab students. Regardless of the teachers' linguistic background and the presence of only an Arab teacher or both teachers in class, Hebrew is always there. Only the frequency of its use varies.

More Arabic is used in classes with Arab and the Jewish co-teachers, but Hebrew is dominant even there.

To conclude, our observations reveal there is an attempt at language equality for the written materials in the two languages. However, in classroom conversations, Hebrew is the dominant and most frequently used language in most of the subjects taught at all three schools.

If Hebrew is more dominant when speaking in the classroom, it is much more so on the school grounds. Few interactions outside the class-room take place exclusively in Arabic, and Hebrew is obviously the most present and dominant language. Arabic is used as the only language in the few cases where there is an absence of Jewish interlocutors. It is sufficient to have one Jewish person involved in the activity for Hebrew to become the language of conversation (Amara, 2005).

The actual language practices are reflected in the students' linguistic competence. The bilingual instruction is more successful among the Arab students at all stages of education. In contrast, the overall success of bilingualism among the Jewish students is limited.

Specifically, after three or four years of education, many Arab students reached almost native skills in speaking and writing Hebrew, while most Jewish students were not able to communicate fluently and smoothly in Arabic, and had limited reading and writing skills (See Amara 2005; Bekerman, 2003).

4. Discussion: Challenges Facing the Model

The findings reveal that both Hebrew and Arabic are used on many occasions in the various environments, with Hebrew more dominant and salient. Arabic is used most often for educational purposes in obligatory contexts. However, when language is used for social and expressive functions, Hebrew is the more dominant language. The attempt to sustain full symmetry in the use of Arabic and Hebrew has not yet been achieved.

Considering the socio-political situation in Israel, creating Arab-Jewish co-education is a daring enterprise. Compared to other mainstream schools, the Hand in Hand schools have succeeded in overcoming difficult circumstances, such the Second Intifada[6] and the events of October 2000,[7] and offer encouraging signs of Arab-Jewish co-existence. The Hand in Hand schools are among the few locations in Israel where direct and genuine contact takes place between Arabs and Jews, where they can learn about each other's culture and heritage, study the same curricula and where instruction in all subjects is offered in the two languages.

Despite the serious and genuine efforts made by the Hand in Hand schools, there are many obstacles and challenges facing the model. One of the challenges is the issue of symmetry in the study and use of Arabic and Hebrew in the schools. This failure may be attributed to both external and internal factors. The external factors refer to the socio-political con-texts and the value and status accorded to both Arabic and Hebrew in the Israeli language market; by internal factors we refer mainly to the implementation of the Hand in Hand language policy in those spheres that the schools can influence (such as teachers, students, learning environment, parents, and the curricula).

The current Israeli socio-political situation does not encourage the teaching and learning of Arabic and accordingly, Arabic carries little symbolic power in the wider public arena. In Bourdieu's (1991) terms, Hebrew speakers have more cultural capital in the linguistic marketplace than Arabic speakers.

Researchers (e.g. Cohen, 1975; Collier, 1992; Hakuta, 1986; Pease-Al-varez & Hakuta, 1992; Snow, 1992) present several factors which encourage children to acquire two languages: a) the languages involved must have equal status in a community, b) both languages must be spoken by indi-viduals who are important to the child, c) the larger environment demands the use of two languages, and d) there are ample opportunities to speak and use the language in many social contexts (Escamilla, 1994, p. 22). In Israel, Hebrew is the status language, the preferred language, and the language spoken with the greatest frequency and fluency. Furthermore, Hebrew is the language used in the various domains of public life in Israel between groups from various ethnic groups (Saban &Amara, 2002).

However, there is a tremendous gap between the official or desired policy and the field, arising, among other things, from the status of the Arabic language, and from attitudes towards it and its speakers. In Israel, Arabic is usually taught to Jews as the language of the enemy. It is not taught because it is the language of the region, or the language of twenty percent of the population, or the original language of a large part of the Jewish population (Amara & Mar'i, 2002; Brosh, 1996; Mor-Sommerfeld, 2005).

The socio-political power distribution is reflected in the language learning of the two national groups: Arab citizens of Israel have a good command of the Hebrew language, whereas most Israeli Jews do not know Arabic. Such a situation may be described as 'asymmetrical bilingualism' (Landau 1987:128). Learning and using the language of an ethnic/national minority by members of the majority group has been characterized in the literature as **'language crossing'** (Rampton 1999). In situations in which the status of the minority group is low, language crossing is very rare, while in more 'relaxed' environments, it is a sign of interethnic sociability. Based on this observation, it is assumed that the existence of speakers from the majority who learn and use the minority language signals a more tolerant approach towards the minority.

The inability of the Hand in Hand schools to achieve symmetry in the use of Arabic and Hebrew is attributable not only to the outside world, but also to the policies of the schools and their implementation (for additional details, see Amara, 2005; Amara et al., 2007). The Hand in Hand schools can influence and significantly improve bilingual education, provided they seriously address weaknesses in five major areas: teachers, students, parents, the learning environment and the curricula.

Teachers — Teachers in strong bilingual education models (such as the Canadian immersion model) have native or native-like proficiency in both languages. Such teachers are able to use the two languages fluently in the classroom. "Teachers are thus important language models through their status and power role, identifying French with something of value" (Baker, 1993, p. 229).

Unlike in strong bilingual models, most of the Jewish teachers in the Hand in Hand schools are not bilingual (a key issue in the model), have not experienced bilingual education, and are not sufficiently familiar with Arab culture. Consequently, in interactions with students in the classroom, Arab teachers use both languages, Arabic and Hebrew, in contrast to Jewish teachers who use only Hebrew, with both Arab and Jewish students.

Students — Generally speaking, the Jewish children speak Arabic less than the Arab children speak Hebrew. In their national groups, the children talk to each other in their mother tongue. In a mixed group, Hebrew is generally the operative language. It is enough to have one Jewish pupil in the group for Hebrew to be the preferred language.

Our observations and tests reveal that bilingual instruction has been more successful among the Arab students at all stages of education (see also Amara, 2005; Bekerman, 2005). In contrast, the overall success in bilingualism among the Jewish students is extremely limited. More specifically, after three or four years of education many Arab students have acquired almost native-like abilities both in speaking and writing skills in Hebrew. The majority of Jewish students cannot communicate fluently and smoothly in Arabic, and their reading and writing skills are extremely limited (Bekerman, 2005).

As described earlier, Hebrew is the lingua franca between Arab and Jewish adults at the Hand in Hand schools. When students see adults enjoying informal conversations in Hebrew, while Arabic is mainly used in obligatory contexts, they get the impression that the adults at school enjoy Hebrew, while they merely tolerate Arabic. Students might infer that in order to be "enjoyed," "appreciated," and "rewarded" by the school, they must speak Hebrew.

Parents — The reasons for sending children to these schools can shed some light on the linguistic competence of both Arab and Jewish students. Arab parents do so to afford their children better opportunities for educational excellence, and to insure that their children become proficient users of Hebrew, a key skill if they are to succeed in Israel. Jewish parents do not send their children for educational reasons (they have many schools to which they can send their children). Their purpose is to provide their children with an opportunity to learn about Arab culture and society, in order to break the socio-political barriers between the two nations.

Clearly, parents from the two nationalities have different expectations as to linguistic outcomes. Arab parents want their children to be highly proficient in Hebrew, and they are worried about attrition in their children's mother tongue, Arabic. Jewish parents are not worried about Hebrew among their children, and do not have high expectations in terms of their children climbing to higher levels of functional bilingualism (Amara, 2005).

Learning Environment — Contexts outside the classroom are no less important linguistically than what happens in the classroom. The school personnel outside of the classroom (e.g. secretaries, administrative staff, playground monitors, etc.), also serve as language role models for the students. The attitudes toward the two languages the personnel exhibit may also influence the development of bilingualism in students.

In Hand in Hand schools, bilingual education has taken place mainly within the classrooms, and less effort has been made to influence the entire environment outside the classroom. Only in the last two years has some attention been paid to this issue, and structured activities have been created to enrich the learning environment outside the classroom. For example, the first 15 minutes of the teachers' meetings are conducted solely in Arabic. More and more Arab teachers in these meetings have started using Arabic with Jewish teachers. More Arab teachers have started using Arabic with Jewish students outside the classroom. The language landscape is dynamic and more presence and salience is given to Arabic. However, Hebrew is still the most frequently used and dominant language outside the classroom.

Curriculum — Some of the fundamental questions for those involved in bilingual education are: In what language should each subject be taught? When? What are the consequences of emphasizing one language over another?

Currently in Hand in Hand schools, Hebrew and Arabic are used as the languages of instruction in nearly all subjects. However, research on bilingual education reveals that it is preferable not to mix two languages during a single lesson, and that separating languages in instruction is more useful. When there is language mixing, students may wait for an explanation in their stronger language (Lindholm, 1990). Consequently, it is preferable that one language be used for one set of subjects; the other language for a separate set.

To date, almost all the subjects have been taught in both languages in the schools. This policy should be reconsidered, with the following options:

1. Maintain the existing policy in the first and second grades. 2. From grade 3 on, alternate the languages, for example, two days a week. Lessons can be conducted in both languages (like the current system), on one day.

5. CONCLUSION

The paper revealed a greater presence and dominance of the Hebrew language at Hand in Hand schools in various domains and functions. Arab students and teachers use the two languages extensively in the various domains, while the Jewish students and teachers use mainly Hebrew, and Arabic is used in limited domains and occasions.

Some researchers raise doubts about the capacity of bilingual education to reconstruct power and ethnic relations within society. They believe that multicultural education can be a patronizing exercise. They claim that for multicultural education to succeed, activities designed to reconstruct the power, dominance and political relationships in the wider society and to eradicate prejudice, fear, and victimization must first occur.

In the conflict-ridden Israeli reality, symmetry in the knowledge and use of both Arabic and Hebrew among the two national groups is not a real option under the current socio-political circumstances. However, highly functional bilingualism among Jewish students is possible if the right policies, language practices and teaching programs are devised.

REFERENCES

Abu-Rabi'a, S. (1998). *Bilingual/Trilingual Education*. Ra'nana: The Institute for Israeli Arab Studies (In Hebrew).

Amara, M.H. (1999) *Politics and Sociolinguistic Reflexes: Border Palestinian Villages.* Amsterdam-Philadelphia: *John Benjamins.*

Amara, M.H. (2002). The Place of Arabic in Israel. *International Journal of the Sociology of Language* 158, 53–68.

Amara, M.H (2003). The Collective Identity of the Arabs in Israel in an Era of Peace. *Israel Affairs* 9 (1& 2), 249–262.

Amara, M.H (2005). *Hand in Hand Model of Bilingualism.* Jerusalem: Hand in Hand — Center for Jewish-Arab Education in Israel (In Arabic).

Amara, M. Azaiza, F. Mor-Sommerfeld, A. & Hertz-Lazarowitz, R (2007). *Hand in hand Schools: Teaching Programs.* Haifa: The Jewish-Arab Center.

Amara, M.H, & Kabaha, M., Eds. (2005). *Identity and Belonging: The project of Basic Terms to Arab Students*. Tamra: Ibin Khaldoun and the Center for Struggle against Racism (In Arabic).

Amara, M.H., & Mar'i, 'A. (2002) *Language Education Policy: The Arab Minority in Israel*. Dordrecht: Kluwer Academic Publishing.

Auerbach, Y. (2005a) Conflict Resolution, Forgiveness and Reconciliation in Material and Identity Conflicts. *Humboldt Journal of Social Relations* 29 (2): 41–80.

Auerbach, Y. (2005b) Forgiveness and Reconciliation: The Religious Dimension. *Terrorism and Political Violence* 17 (3), 469–485,

Baker, C. (1993). *Foundations of Bilingual Education and Bilingualism*. Clevedon: Multi-lingual Matters (1st edition).

Bekerman, Z. (2003a). Reshaping Conflict through School Ceremonial Events in Israeli Palestinian Jewish Coeducation. *Anthropology and Education Quarterly* 34 (2), 205–224.

Bekerman, Z. (2003b). Never Free of Suspicion. *Cultural Studies and Critical Methodologies* 3 (2), 136–147.

Bekerman, Z. (2004). Potential and Limitations of Multicultural Education in Conflict-Ridden Areas: Bilingual Palestinian-Jewish Schools in Israel. *Teachers College Record* 106 (3), 574–610.

Bekerman, Z. (2005). Complex Contexts and Ideologies: Bilingual Education in Conflict-Ridden Areas. *Journal of Language, Identity and Education* 4 (1), 1–20.

Bekerman, Z. & Horenczyk, G. (2004). Arab-Jewish Bilingual Coeducation in Israel: A Long-Term Approach to Intergroup Conflict Resolution. *Journal of Social Issues* 60 (2), 389–404.

Bekerman, Z. & Maoz, I. (2005). Troubles With Identity: Obstacles to Coexistence Education in Conflict Ridden Societies. *Identity: An International Journal of Theory and Research* 5(4), 341–357.

Bekerman, Z. & Shhadi, N. (2003). Palestinian-Jewish Bilingual Education in Israel: Its Influence on Cultural Identities and its Impact on Intergroup Conflict. *Journal of Multilingual and Multicultural Development* 24 (60), 473–484.

Bourdieu, P. (1991). *Language and Symbolic Power*. Cambridge, MA: Harvard University Press.

Brosh, H. (1996). Arabic to Hebrew Speakers in Israel — "Second Language" or "Foreign Language". *Helkat Lashon* 23, 111–131 (in Hebrew).

Cohen, A. (1975). *Bilingual Education: A Sociolinguistic Approach*. Rowley, MA: Newbury House.

Collier, V. (1992). A Synthesis of Studies Examining Long-Term Language-Minority Student Data on Academic Achievement. *Bilingual Research Journal* 1 (1&2), 187–212.

Crawford, J. (1997). Best evidence: Research Foundation of the Bilingual Education Act. Unpublished manuscript, Washington, DC.

Cummins, J. (1986). Bilingual Education and Anti-Racist Education. *Interracial Books for Children Bulletin* 17(3&4), 9–12.

Escamilla, K. (1994). The Sociolinguistic Environment of Bilingual School: A Case Study Introduction. *Bilingual Research Journal* 18 (1&): 21–47.

Fen Olser H., Aall, P.R., & Crocker, C.A. (2002). Conflict Unending: Intractable Conflicts and the Challenge of Mediation. Paper presented at the ISA, 2002.

Firer, R. (1985). *The Agents of Zionist Education.* Tel-Aviv: Sifriyat Poa'lim (In Hebrew).

Fishman, J.A., Cooper, R.L., & Ma, R. (1971). *Bilingualism in the Barrio.* Bloomington: Research for the Language Services, Indiana University.

Hakuta, K. (1986). *Mirror of Language.* New York: Basic Books.

Hand in Hand Center for Jewish-Arab Education in Israel (2005). *Outline of a Core Program for Hand in Hand Bilingual Schools.* Jerusalem: Hand in Hand (Hebrew).

Hand in Hand Center for Jewish-Arab Education in Israel (2006). *Weekly Planner, 2006–2007.* Jerusalem: Hand in Hand.

Kacen, L., & Lev-Wiesel, R., Eds. (2002), *Group Work in a Multicultural Society.* Tel-Aviv: Tcherikover.

Landau, J. (1987). Hebrew and Arabic in the State of Israel: Political Aspects of the Language Issue. *International Journal of the Sociology of Language* 67, 117–133.

Lindholm, K.J. (1990). Bilingual Immersion Education: Criteria for Program Development. In A.M. Padilla, H.H. Farirchild & C.M. Valdes (Eds.), *Bilingual Education: Issues and Strategies.* London: Sage.

Montville, J. (1993). The Healing Function of Political Conflict Resolution. In Dennis J.D. Sandole & H. van der Merwe (Eds.), *Conflict Resolution in Theory and Practice.* Manchester: Manchester University Press.

Mor-Sommerfeld, A. (2005). Bilingual Education in Areas of Conflict — Bridging and Sharing. *Race Equality Teaching* 24 (1), 31–42.

Mor-Sommerfeld, A., Azaiza, F. & Hertz-Lazarowitz, R. (2007). Into the Future: Towards Bilingual Education in Israel. *Education, Citizenship and Social Justice* 2(1), 5–22.

Paulson. S. E. (1994). Relations of Parenting Style and Parental Involvement with Ninth-Grade Students' Achievement. *Journal of Early Adolescence* 14, 250–267.

Pease-Alvarez, L. & Hakuta, K. (1992). Enriching Our Views of Bilingualism and Bilingual Education. *Educational Researcher* 21(2), 4–6.

Rampton B. (1999) Deutsch in Inner London and the Animation of an Instructed Foreign Language. *Journal of Sociolinguistics* 3 (4), 480–504.

Ricento. T., & Hornberger, N. (1996). Unpeeling the Onion: Language Planning and Policy and the ELT Professional. *TESOL Quarterly* 30, 401–428.

Saban, I & Amara, M. (2002). The Status of Arabic in Israel: Reflections on the Power of Law to Produce Social Change. *Israel Law Review* 36 (2), 5–39.

Schildkraut, M. (2005). Linguistic Socialization and Social Identity: Arab Students in a Mixed College in Israel. In B. Preister, A. Fabricius, H. Haberland, S. Kjaerbeck & K. Risager (Eds.), *The Consequences of Mobility: Linguistic and Sociocultural Contact Zones* (pp. 197–211). Denmark: Roskilde University.

Skutnabb-Kangas, T., & Garcia, O. (Eds.). (1995). *Multilingualism for All? General Principles.* Lisse, The Netherlands: Swets and Zeitlinger.

Smooha, S. (2005). *Index of Arab-Jewish Relations in Israel–2004.* Haifa: Haifa University, The Arab-Jewish Center.

Snow, C.E. (1992). Perspectives on Second-Language Development: Implications for Bilingual Education. *Educational Researcher* 21 (2), 16–19.

Sudilovsky, J. (2003). Building Bridges in Israel Peace Path. *International Herald Tribune*, February 18, 2003.

Valdes, G. (1997). Dual-Language Immersion Programs: A Cautionary Tote Concerning the Education of Language Minority Students. *Harvard Educational Review* 67, 391–429.

http://www.handinhand12.org/

http://www.nwas.com/

NOTES

[1] Following the end of World War I, Palestine was placed for an interim period under the British Mandate, which formally began in 1922. The British Mandate was a turbulent period marked by continual violence between Palestinians and Jews, both of whom opposed the Mandate. The British Mandate over Palestine ended on May 15, 1948 and the establishment of Israel ensued (see Amara, 1999: 21).

[2] This type of limited bilingualism is called "mainstream with foreign language teaching" (See Baker, 1993).

[3] For more details about the goals of *Hand in Hand* bilingual education, see "Outline of a Core Program for Hand in Hand Bilingual Schools" (2005), and Amara (2005).

[4] For more details about the goals of *Hand in Hand* bilingual education, see "Outline of a Core Program for Hand in Hand Bilingual Schools" (2005), and Amara (2005)

[5] Neve Shalom/Wahat al-Salam (*Oasis of Peace)* is a village, jointly established by Jewish and Arab citizens of Israel, in 1972. The village is situated equidistant from Jerusalem and Tel Aviv-Jaffa. It is engaged in educational work for peace, equality and understanding between the two peoples. http://www.nwas.com.

[6] The **Second Palestinian Intifada** (Arabic word for "uprising"), also known as the **al-Aqsa Intifada** (Al-Aqsa refers to a prominent mosque in Jerusalem) broke out at the end of September 2000, following Ariel Sharon's provocative visit to the courtyard of the mosque. Palestinian protests against this visit resulted in the killing of several Palestinians on the holy grounds of the Al-Aqsa mosque. This event is

generally considered the spark for the Intifada. However, the real reasons lie in the failure of the Camp David negotiations of the same year between the Palestinians and Israelis, Israel's perceived lack of respect for signed agreements, and the continuing deterioration of the economic situation of the Palestinians. Palestinians consider the Intifada to be a war of national liberation against Israeli occupation. It was a bloody Intifada, in which Palestinians used weapons and suicide attacks against Israelis. The death toll, both military and civilian, for the entire conflict in 2000–2006 is estimated to be over 4,000 Palestinians and over 1,000 Israelis (Amara & Kabaha, 2005).

[7] In the first two weeks of the second Intifada the Arabs in Israel protested against what happened in the Aqsa mosque. There were bloody confrontations between the Israeli forces and Arabs citizens of Israel, 13 Arabs were killed, and scores were wounded. This situation led to the deepening of the divide between the Arabs and Jews, as reflected in informal economic sanctions against the Arab sector, mainly by the Jewish population (Amara & Kabaha, 2005).

CULTURAL AND NORMATIVE DUALITY IN ISRAELI SOCIETY

YEDIDIA Z. STERN

1. INTRODUCTION

The centrality of state law and of legal bodies in Israeli society is axiomatic. The long arm of the law reaches everywhere, and recently, it has been meeting with popular resistance. The law's prominence and its increasing involvement in our lives have been of constant concern to Israeli politicians, academics, and journalists.

A similar development, though less obvious to the wider public, is presently taking place concerning the place of *Halakhah* (Jewish religious law) in Israel's Jewish religious communities. For many religious individuals, Halakhah is the central, almost exclusive expression of contemporary Jewish culture. Halakhah is the source from which they derive most of their life practices, as well as the substance of their Jewish identity. Although the religious space is not devoid of values, philosophy, creativity, and historic memory, primacy is unquestionably reserved for normative statements, such as ritual injunctions, responsa, commandments, and transgressions.

Is there any room for comparison between these two developments? Can a single cause-and-effect narrative, one unified frame of meaning, explain the tendency of Israel's Jewish society toward the "lawlization" and "halakhization" of reality? Leaders within both normative systems may not be unduly pleased with these parallels, and may even view the very comparison as an affront to the ethos of their own system. Scholars of the two systems may also argue that each system needs to be considered separately, resting their case on a series of substantive distinctions that can and must be examined. Thus it may seem, for example, that these systems differ in the source of their authority (a social contract v. a divine command), in their purpose (social-material attainments v. religious-spiritual perfection), in their target audiences (the citizenry v. the members of the Jewish religion), and so forth. Yet, given that both function within one socio-cultural reality, the question of whether they have a common denominator is worth asking. This paper will present a unifying theory that can clarify the preference of Israelis, both religious and secular, for legal solutions. In so doing, I will indicate the price we pay because of the heavy shadow that state law and Halakha cast upon Jewish society in Israel. The analysis will also suggest parameters for the necessary reform.

Let me open with a personal remark. I belong to those segments of the Jewish Israeli public who are simultaneously subject to the rule of the political sovereign and to the rule of God. We observe *mitzvot* [the commandments] on the strength of our religious responsibility, and abide by the law on the strength of our civic responsibility. For me and others like me, normative duality in its more common Israeli manifestation creates a genuine existential difficulty, unique in its character and entailing considerable practical implications. We are fully and unreservedly committed to the rule of law (except for obvious reservations anchored in widely accepted democratic principles). At the same time, we are fully and unreservedly committed to the Halakhah (as interpreted within the religious circles to which we belong). Subjectively, we approach both legal systems as part of our primary and unconditioned responsibility. State law cannot coerce freedom of religion; as part of its adherence to values of tolerance, it is also wary of harming religious sensibilities. Hence it is difficult — though not impossible — to find actual conflictual situations that require choosing between these different loyalties.[1] The main point, however, is that the very consciousness of this normative duality — both elements of which are dominant — is not easy for people who are aware of and sensitive to their twofold commitment.

When faced with the inner discourse of either of the two legal systems, such persons become conscious of their alternative commitment, which, as noted, represents a cultural perspective (sometimes) antagonistic toward the discourse in which they are participating at a given moment. This realization is even more pronounced for the religious judge, lawyer, or law professor. In court and in the law schools they are challenged by Halakhah; at the *beth midrash* (where Talmud is studied) or in their Torah studies they are challenged by the law. Although they are at home in both worlds, they are doomed to observe each of them also as outsiders. Their cultural and professional world is nurtured by both sources, and therein lies their advantage; but their yearning to attain full intimacy with both is marred by the emotional and intellectual difficulties stemming from their dual commitment. Sometimes their friends in each of these worlds, who are usually aware of this dual pledge but do not share it and have difficulty internalizing its complexity, may ascribe to them a touch of strangeness or a distancing from their own "truth," when they discover the "other side" of the religious jurist's commitment.

This "confession" may clarify why, notwithstanding my legal training, I am tempted to suggest in some parts of this paper a strain of social criticism. My writing here is sometimes of a personal nature, and I have deliberately refrained from weeding out evaluative or judgmental statements. I write here as a man of a time and a place who has a unique perspective because, for better or worse, I am rooted in two worlds. The "situation" I describe is personal but definitely not private, since it is relevant to my surroundings. The cautious reader should certainly take into account my personal background, as well as the limitations of the legal prism through which I observe the world outside the law.

I will open with a description of normative duality within the context of a wider duality between Western and Jewish culture (Chapter Two). The main communities in the Jewish public arena in Israel — ultra-Orthodox, religious, and secular — find contending with cultural duality an arduous endeavor. In the past, each of these three communities had developed unique strategies for coping with cultural duality (Chapter Three). Recently, however, these strategies have been collapsing, given that Israel has shifted from being a consensual democracy to a democracy in crisis (Chapter Four). At present, I submit that the Israeli marketplace of ideas offers no significant ideological paradigms that might enable coherent functioning and the consolidation of a solid identity combining the two hegemonic cultural approaches. Given this lack, the ethical-ideological contest intensifies and, in part, spills over onto the normative battleground. The analysis suggested here argues that "lawlization" and "halakhization" were meant to create a clean field for deciding the *kulturkampf* (Chapter Five). Each of these competing normative systems developed different attitudes toward its own values, with the law externalizing these values and Halakhah keeping them hidden (Chapter Six). Nevertheless, an interesting finding shows that each one relies on its (opposite) attitude to values in order to reinforce judicial imperialism. Both the law and Halakhah proclaim the totality of their scope, aspire to implement this stance, and hint at their reluctance to ascribe any significant role in public life to the other system (Chapter Seven). This background clarifies some of the professional constructs of current Israeli law (such as expanded standing, judicial activism, involvement in areas pertinent to other authorities) and of Halakhah (such as monistic rulings, the lack of halakhic activism, rejecting the "new") (Chapter Eight). Lack of agreements among the communities making up Israeli Jewish society is too often translated into friction between competing normative orders that seek to regulate a given reality on the basis of different sources of authority and different value systems. Against their better interests, the law and Halakhah serve as the main ammunition in a *kulturkampf*.

This move carries a heavy price: waging this controversy in the normative arena vitiates the functioning of Israeli Jewish society. Exchanging a cultural discourse for a normative one leads to trivialization. The shift attempts to replace process with decision, inner experience with external dictates, public discourse with professional discourse, complexity with banality and dialogue with monologue. Israeli society as a whole must relinquish the delusion that normative answers to existential problems emerging from a diverse cultural reality are at all possible.[2] Cultural controversies cannot be settled through legal or halakhic discussions.[3] Instead, each of these communities should assume responsibility for developing genuine and relevant strategies for living with cultural duality. A rich repertoire of alternatives for contending with cultural variety is vital to Israel's existence as a Jewish and democratic state.

2. CULTURAL DUALITY

Jewish society in Israel is based mainly on two cultures: Western-liberal and Jewish-traditional. The two are clasped in a mutual embrace, and in many ways draw on each other and constitute an organic element of one another. Although presenting them as alternatives is to some extent artificial, I relate to them here as separate cultures for the purpose of the analysis. Public discourse tends to categorize Jewish society in Israel along a religious axis divided into four groups: secular, traditional, religious, and ultra-Orthodox.[4] A majority in each of these groups appears to identify, at various levels of internalization and awareness, with both cultures. They experience Western and Jewish cultures immanently and both are components of their identity, shaping their lifesyles and behavior.[5] Thus, for instance, many within the secular and the traditional groups (grouped together for purposes of this discussion) use certain symbolic and material products of Jewish culture, and even of Jewish religion.[6] For their part, members of the religious group have adopted central values of Western-liberal culture, such as equality, self-realization, freedom, a positive attitude toward science and the rule of law. Even members of the ultra-Orthodox community, who declare their rejection of anything "new" and conduct their lives "within bastions of holiness," internalize cultural duality at the personal level[7] (though not in their discourse with their community). The substantial majority of Jews living in Israel, then, fashion their lives out of the rich lodes of both cultures.

Theoretically, cultural duality (or multiplicity) involves a complex potential. On the one hand, it enables a diversification of cultural sources. In a pluralistic society, open to the possibility of validating the truth of the "other," duality can bring great blessing. Diversity allows every individual and every community to construct their identity from the dialogue between the two cultures. Diversity could also lead to growth and development within each culture, arising from the challenge posed by the other. On the other hand, duality could also be a catalyst for the growth of a lethal competition for budgetary primacy, ideological influence, and political power. Although this competition exists in pluralistic societies as well, its effects are particularly virulent in a monistic society, where it could focus on one purpose: silencing the other's voice. Furthermore, if truth zealots are not satisfied with a hierarchy of truths (our truth above the other's truth) but are also intolerant toward the other's truth, competition could slide into confrontation.

Which of these possible consequences of duality — from rewarding diversity to stifling confrontation and all the options in between — is implemented in Israel's Jewish society? If we accept the assumption that members of all its groups fashion their identity from the lodes of both cultures, we might expect that none of the segments of society — secular, religious, and ultra-Orthodox — would relate to either of these two cultures as an "other" to be gagged or restrained. In the absence of an "other," conditions appear ripe for an open discourse between the two cultures, marked by mutual respect. In practice, however, observers of current Israeli society do not sense the joy of diversity's blessing, but only the sorrow of multiplicity's curse. Agents of influence in both cultures tend to downplay the similarities and the interface between them, preferring to present them as mutually hostile alternatives deployed for an inevitable *kulturkampf*.[8] They market each culture as an exclusive socio-cultural product that "belongs" to one of the groups, concealing the inclusive dimension of cultural duality in the Israeli Jewish experience. They also shift the relationhip between the two cultures from a course of process to one of decision. They prefer a simplistic to a complex perception of reality and choose to engage in the cultural dispute on a monistic rather than on a pluralistic basis.[9]

Why this schizophrenia? Why, although every group is both "Western" and "Jewish," is Israel's public space daubed with the war paint of a cultural conflict? This critical question will not be the focus of the present discussion, although the discussion does occasionally touch upon it. My main concerns are not the causes of this state of affairs, but the description and analysis of its implications for the place of law and Halakhah in Israeli society.

3. AVAILABLE STRATEGIES FOR COPING WITH CULTURAL DUALITY

How is it possible to function in a reality of dual cultural loyalties[10] sometimes perceived as disharmonious? Although the question is not new, it has recurred more frequently and acrimoniously in recent years.[11] It is hurled with increasing force at all Israeli Jews. It touches, spiritually, the very essence of some of us, and practically, the cohesion of Israeli society and its ability to survive.

I will characterize three strategies of behavior adopted by three key groups facing this threatening duality. The common denominator of the three strategies is that none of them offers a substantive ideological option for grappling with the reality of existence in circumstances of cultural duality. None offers contemporary Israeli Jews the practical option of being "Jews" and "human beings" simultaneously. The existing strategies are concrete, practical coping options that a frantic reality has allowed to develop and survive over time, but which are obviously incapable of providing personal or national solace.

The religious-Zionist community (also called Orthodox) has adopted and perfected with exceptional success a technique of compartmentalization and evasiveness.[12] Dual loyalty is not harmonious.[13] The Orthodox person is made up of different drawers, each opening up at the appropriate time and place in order to be filled with contents and norms from one of the two cultures. When the Orthodox person is studying at a *yeshivah*, poring over a page of Talmud, involved in education, thinking of ideas or engaged by moral dilemmas and existential questions, s/he is loading the "Judaism drawer." When training for a profession, working, reading literature, having fun, consuming goods, and sustaining bourgeois life, s/he closes the first drawer, sometimes hermetically, and opens up the "liberal-Western drawer" to load it with other contents and norms.[14] The dresser (and its drawers) is both the private individual and the Orthodox community. Compartmentalization and evasiveness ensue from the partitions separating the drawers, precluding integration between the worlds.[15] As double security doors, with one programmed to open only after the other closes, so the world of the Orthodox, who beware of mingling the two parts of their identity.[16] Note that Orthodox ethos and ideology resort to a language of renaissance and renewal, intended to discover the modern facets latent in tradition. The actual attempt to cope with duality, however, both individually and communally, is based on compartmentalization and evasiveness. Rather than a harmonious solution, this is a technique of survival in a world of multiple identities perceived as contradictory.[17]

The strategy of the ultra-Orthodox [*haredi*] community is relatively easy to discover. Alienation replaces compartmentalization, and retreat supplants evasiveness. Faced with cultural duality, members of the *haredi* community adopt the mentality of the vanquished. They define their immediate surroundings as their "little piece of Heaven."[18] In despair, they renounce "*Klal Israel*" [the community of Israel], who have sinned, and mourn the cultural death of all other Jews. Having adopted this perspective, they can cooperate in civic matters, although cooperation is minimal and instrumental, not at the experiential level, and certainly not at the level of values.[19] The *haredi* strategy, therefore, does not promote shared responsibility.

What does the secular public do? Against compartmentalization and alienation, it endorses abdication.[20] Instead of evasiveness and retreat, we find oblivion. In fact, the secular public generally draws away from intimacy with its heritage.[21] Although a deliberate call for full abandonment of the Jewish heritage resonates at present only within limited (though prestigious) circles, this idea has gained a large and far broader concrete following among Israelis. First, replacing national identity with neutral individualism is a project attuned to the *zeitgeist*, which courts the idea of normalcy and integration in the family of nations. Second, and most significant for my argument, many are interested in a Jewish identity steeped in the historical legacy, but do not act upon their wishes. General Israeli culture — as manifest in the educational system, the arts and local creativity, philosophy, ethics, in the economy, the law, the language, the media, politics, symbols, and role models, and in the complex of life-cycle social practices — bears hardly any traces of the Jewish cultural legacy. Direct involvement in Jewish studies is also gradually decreasing.[22] This means renouncing current experiential applications of the wealth of knowledge, memory, and meaning of Jewish existence throughout the ages, as preserved in the cultural heritage.

The loss of cultural and national identity and the severance of historical continuity are easily evident in an area where Jewish culture was for long highly prominent, and will be the focus of my discussion in the rest of this paper: the law. When Knesset legislation did occasionally enable a meaningful use of elements of Jewish culture to interpret modern norms, the courts charged with the implementation and interpretation of this legislation chose to ignore this option. Examples are well-known: the section in the Foundations of the Law Statute, 1980, stating that the court will resort to "the principles of freedom, justice, equity, and peace of Israel's heritage" as complementary sources in cases of legal lacunae, remains a dead letter.[23] For over twenty years, the court has not sought inspiration in these principles of Jewish heritage. Even more significantly, when a Basic Law in the early 1990s coined the phrase "the values of the State of Israel as a Jewish and democratic state," it was suggested that those values be interpreted as values addressed at their level of universalist abstraction, suited to the democratic character of the state.[24] In other words, the values of a Jewish state will assume normative meaning in state law if they are compatible with the values of a democratic state, not necessarily Jewish.[25] The values of Judaism are subject to judicial review according to criteria set by democratic values. When cultural duality exposes an intractable discrepancy between these two cultural systems, the judge will decide according to the views of the "enlightened public."[26]

Judges making hermeneutical choices of this kind[27] are not adopting a personal judicial policy. They are conveying an attitude widespread in Israeli society, accepting Jewish outlooks when compatible with a general *weltanschauung* and renouncing deeper layers of traditional Jewish culture when they convey unique values and priorities incompatible with Western-liberal culture. This signals a renunciation of "Judaism" in its traditional-halakhic sense, as a relevant factor in a value decision unacceptable in the universal marketplace of ideas.

4. THE STRATEGIES COLLAPSE

These three strategies are presently collapsing. Compartmentalization, alienation, and abdication served each of the communities in Israeli Jewish society and enabled them to survive without dealing with the implications for the Israeli "whole" of the strategies adopted by the other communities. Their relative success in the first thirty years of the state reflected the priority that the young state of Israel ascribed to the preservation of a broad consensus among members of the various Jewish communities in the country. At the time, everyone was wary of pushing the other beyond the pale of the consensus that united all. Thus, for instance, David Ben-Gurion, who was personally alienated from religion, guided the political system to adopt a consociational model of democracy on matters of religion and state. He understood the national importance of agreeing upon a status quo on matters of religion, and was willing to pay the high price of the secular majority's relinquishing control over some of its ways of life.[28] Yet, the traditional consensus between the Jewish communities in Israel is now gradually collapsing, and the pressure on each of these three strategies is intensifying.

Many are concerned with the analysis of this breakdown, and with Israel's transition from a consociational democracy[29] to a democracy in crisis.[30] In the last decade, when many believed we were about to find a peaceful solution to the Israeli-Arab conflict, the perception of an attenuated security threat allowed us to focus on our cultural disagreements. Less obvious is the effect of the collapse of the prevalent hegemonies and of the reallocation of political, economic, and social resources, shifting from the old elites to peripheral forces.[31] In the future, we may have to pay attention to the effects of globalization on the ties binding Israelis together. As foreign cultures become more accessible and their marketing instruments more aggressive, and as the national unit becomes less important and is replaced by other forms of social organization (such as multinational or supra-national bodies),[32] Israeli individuals may become progressively estranged from their "Israeliness."[33] Consensus will then be threatened not only from the inside, by the inter-communal struggle for dominance in influencing Israeli identity, but also from the outside, by the global alternative.[34]

How do the decline of social and political consensus in Israel and the focus of the public discourse on internal cultural controversies affect the behavioral strategies of each of the three communities?

The Orthodox community, which has yet to develop practical alternatives to the compartmentalization of its identities, pays a heavy price every day. In the new reality of open contest between Israel's various cultures, the partitions between the drawers are being removed against its will. The Orthodox find it hard to persist in their compartmentalization while faced with an ongoing confrontation between the two components of their identity. Barring a strategy enabling the harmonious coexistence of both components, they are forced to choose between the available alternatives.[35] They can opt for the Jewish drawer and then, to push away the "other," incline toward ultra-Orthodoxy;[36] or they can opt for the liberal drawer and then, at times, feel they must shed the religious identity that ostensibly contradicts this option.

Statistics show that the religious-Zionist community faces considerable difficulties in keeping its youngsters within the ideological framework accepted by its adults.[37] In my view, the compartmentalization strategy is the built-in flaw, the faulty gene of religious-Zionism, which led to this result. Compartmentalization is not marketable, and cannot be bequeathed either, because it cannot function as a mechanism for coping with a reality torn by cultural conflict. The constitutive text offering the non-*haredi* Orthodox a harmonious, or at least dialectical, solution to the complex riddle of their existence between two cultures has yet to be written.

Neither does the *haredi* alienation strategy offer a real solution. An ideology that readily dispenses labels of good and evil according to rigid criteria enjoys the advantage of clear and sharp messages. But the cost of alienation has proven too high for *haredi* society. First, in the past, alienation offered an option for operative functioning because it had developed in a context that took consociational existence for granted. At present, when the shared web is tearing, alienation begins to pose a real threat to the possibility of a shared existence.

Second, *haredi* society is growing larger and so are its needs, forcing increasing recourse to political power. To use this power for its more natural and obvious needs, *haredi* society has taken over large segments of the government.[38] With power and government come responsibility, and with it cooperation. In the long range, however, cooperation and alienation cannot coexist since they represent a contradiction in terms.

Third, the economic pressures affecting *haredi* society[39] almost preclude the withdrawal option. In the new world, where capital, land, work power, and material resources make way for information as the major resource asset, *haredi* society must resort to non-traditional forms of knowledge, as news about intentions to establish a *haredi* university confirms. According to original *haredi* ideology, the very idea of a *haredi* university is absurd, but economic reality has its own laws. Education, power, and responsibility will necessarily lead to the collapse of the alienation and withdrawal strategy.

As for the secular strategy of abdication, there are initial signs of acknowledgement that "normal" existence, a desirable goal for part of the public, could emerge as a significant threat to Israeli culture because it would blur its uniqueness. In the wake of this acknowledgement, the thorny question of identity,[40] among others, has cropped up again. The "Jewish bookshelf" is of interest to secular Jews sensitive to identity issues. They are unwilling to surrender this shelf, since it could hold the most significant answer to the riddle of their national and cultural uniqueness.[41] I do not share the perception that this is a passing fad. In my view, this is the existential need of a culture seeking meaning in its sources,[42] possibly leading to the creation of a modern *midrash* that will pour unique and novel content into secular Jewish existence.[43] At present, however, this is essentially an avant-garde phenomenon in which most secular Jews take no part.

The analysis suggests that despite signs of change, all Jewish communities in Israel have difficulties coping with cultural duality, and none of them has adopted ideological models integrating both cultures. In the past, this was not enough to lead to an open identity crisis and to a confrontation between cultures because Israeli society functioned within a consociational framework. A practical arrangement, in a supportive political environment, provided a substitute for ideological confrontation with the tension resulting from cultural duality. Consensus created a reasonably firm and stable bulwark, which enabled joint survival while evading open discussion of fundamental questions of identity. Today, when Israel is a democracy in crisis, hidden strains have burst into the open. The primary impulse is no longer the search for a common denominator, for compromise or reconciliation, but a search for achievements, for the final truth, accentuating differences and stigmatizing the faults each finds in the other. Hence, the external defense line is now collapsing. The crisis paralyzes the ability to reach an "arrangement" through political and social mechanisms of tension release. The dispute over the question of identity is fully evident at the ideological level. Each community, exposed to pressures by the others, stands in the Israeli marketplace of ideas equipped with the strategy it had adopted for a life facing cultural duality — compartmentalization, alienation, or abdication. But these are flimsy props, since they have nothing to say to those seeking inclusiveness and integration of the two cultures. The collapse of past strategies brought about by the present crisis leaves key groups (and individuals) in Israeli Jewish society bereft of the ideological thinking patterns that had aided them to contend with the identity tension between Western and Jewish cultures. But, as King Solomon teaches: "Where there is no vision, the people become unruly."[44] In circumstances of ongoing crisis, the Israeli public agenda includes more and more items whose core is inter-cultural tension. The general ideological failure hinders the attainment of inclusive solutions to these problems, with the unfortunate result of pushing everyone into a power struggle. The common fabric of Israeli society is stretched to the breaking point. The two cultures face each other as though deployed for war, each viewing the implementation of its platform as a deterministic need. Not only interests are at stake, although they are certainly at play, but also elements that, subjectively, constitute and explain reality.[45]

5. FROM CULTURAL DUALITY TO NORMATIVE DUALITY

The increasing dominance of the law and of the legal system in Israeli society[46] (and in other democratic societies as well, although on a smaller scale)[47] has been explained in various ways. The literature offers cultural-liberal explanations (the growing strength of liberal sentiment in Israeli culture, including the expansion of individual rights and the protection of individuals vis-à-vis the government, requires greater intervention of the Supreme Court as the protector of these values); arguments focusing on the institutional character of the courts and on the political context of their functioning (courts fill the vacuum created by the weakness of the Israeli political system and the difficulties in functioning that beset the legislative and executive branches); neo-realistic cultural approaches (the law and its systems are perceived as having objective and professional powers of persuasion), and so forth.[48] Besides these explanations, which I do not discuss here,[49] I argue that the increasing recourse of Israeli society to judicial decisions on issues involving inter-cultural friction can be ascribed, *inter alia*, to the failure of the existing strategies for coping with cultural duality.[50] Due to the collapse of these three strategies, Israelis are now suffering from an identity malaise that leads them to translate intercultural discourse into a discourse between legal systems: state law and halakhic law.

The identity malaise is evident on several levels, and is primarily an intrapersonal problem. In this context, unsolved identity questions do not have social implications linked to the subject being discussed here. But this identity malaise is also an interpersonal problem and, as such, entails social implications with a direct bearing on the status of law in society. It poses problems for each of the three groups seeking to define their inner identity but now unable to cope with the problem due to the collapse of the traditional strategy that had guided them thus far. The intra-group ideological failure projects further, to inter-group relationships. How? Were each group to succeed in easing its inner identity tension by integrating both cultures, a shared language of values would emerge between the secular, religious, and ultra-Orthodox, enhancing the chances of settling group differences through persuasion or negotiation. A shared language does not mean agreement on the content of identity, but only acknowledgement of the legitimacy and validity of a dual cultural presence in the identity of every group. This acknowledgement could be an excellent foundation for a fruitful interpersonal dialogue that would not need to resort to judicial decisions at every step.[51] The strategies of compartmentalization, alienation, and abdication, which do not present genuine options for a full life within normative duality, have restricted the shared public space required for inter-group dialogue, leaving us bereft of ideological goods to cope with the other.[52] This reinforces the urge to attain cultural victory over the "other" through judicial rulings. Furthermore: let us assume that each group develops a clear identity doctrine vis-à-vis cultural duality, and that this doctrine can answer the needs of group members yearning for an integrated identity. When formulating their attitudes to questions evoked by cultural duality, group members will then probably follow the thinkers who developed the group identity doctrine, the people charged with disseminating it, marketing it, and educating in its light, and those who are elected on the basis of its platform. These individuals would eventually coalesce into the ideological leadership of each group, and negotiations between the groups would then be conducted between these ideological leaders. Unfortunately, the inner ideological failure within each group has lowered our expectations of organizations and individuals involved in thinking, education, or the dissemination of ideas. Instead, they seek the help of legal institutions. Overstating the case, one could argue that we choose the leaders of the competing legal systems as the leaders of each culture. We marked the borders of the competing cultural territories by defining the limits of the competing legal systems.

What is the motivation for this process of "lawlization" and "halakhization" in Israeli society? Turning to the law appears to enable adversaries in all camps to achieve a complex goal: twisting the arm of the cultural "other" while exempting themselves of all responsibility for the intolerant and aggressive implication of this act: waging a *Kulturkampf* while preserving their self-image untainted.

Arm-twisting in what way? Courts, secular and religious, serve as ammunition because the judicial product, by definition, sharpens the decision. The judicial ruling acts as a guillotine, encouraging a discourse of victors and vanquished. The judicial procedure fits an environment of strife because it unfolds within a drama of competition and of decision-making, and because it sometimes results in the demonization of the other.[53]

Exemption from responsibility in what way? Turning to the courts does not tarnish the self-perception of litigants, who do not consider themselves as having adopted an aggressive attitude. In their view, the judicial procedure is bound by an inner, "pristine" system of rules, autonomous and universal, projecting "professional immaculacy," objectivity, neutrality free of political bias, sterility untarnished by external considerations, expertise and authority.[54] The same is true of those turning to Halakhah, with an a fortiori addition: if law, a human creation, is viewed as acting within an autonomous space unaffected by the power struggles of a particular society, all the more so Halakhah, which is perceived by the religiously observant public to be the "true Torah," originating in a unique divine revelation whose validity and persuasive powers are unquestionable. Furthermore, as the public discourse tends to present judges as loyal only to the law and never suspect of promoting their personal values, so does intra-religious discourse present halakhists as implementing "*da'at Torah*" [Torah wisdom]. "*Da'at Torah*" is purported to be external to halakhic judges and uninfluenced by their personal values, hence all are commanded to comply with their rulings due to an unconditional "faith in the sages."

Each group, then, is characterized by an unresolved inner identity tension that has deleterious effects on the possibility of dialogue, pushing groups toward confrontation and an ambiance of *kulturkampf*. The increasing recourse to law and Halakhah was intended to gain validity for the inner identity of each group. The law and Halakhah provide a clean field for this war, which enhances their social status.

Translating cultural duality into normative duality could create several cumulative effects. A judicial decision is liable to lead to the banalization of the dispute, and to blithe disregard of the complexity of cultural duality.[55] It intensifies and sharpens the alienation prevailing between various segments of Israeli society; it escalates differences and entrenches the parties behind defense lines formulated in binary terms — rights and duties, commandments and transgressions, forbidden and allowed. It hinders the development of moderate, complex, experiential, or ongoing educational possibilities. It fences in the camps and undermines the possibility of broadening the common denominator uniting different communities. It compels an essentially monological rights discourse, which effaces the "other" and relates to him instrumentally, on an essentially dialogical identity discourse.[56] It paralyzes the marketplace of ideas, dilutes the social importance of the political procedure, and, ultimately, could considerably erode the trust that large segments of the public place in the judiciary.[57]

6. NORMATIVE DUALITY AND VALUES

Court rulings, and particularly Supreme Court rulings, have undergone significant changes over the past few decades. Until the 1980s, the legal narrative was distinctly formalistic: the legal realm was perceived as an autonomous professional system with a domain and a language of its own. It was believed that the aim of judicial procedure is to impose on any given conflict the normative answer available in the law and, in a sense, it is a clarification of a technical nature. The judge is a professional, a state employee, whose role is to find the specific norm relevant to the conflict, reveal it, and proclaim it.

Menachem Mautner outlined the change that the Israeli Court underwent during the 1980s, shifting the emphasis from the formal dimension to the value dimension.[58] Court rulings externalized the fact that every judicial ruling, even those considered technical, involves a value choice. Rather than being impersonal, the normative answer depends on the value preferences of the judge, who is the final arbiter. Indeed, a word frequently found in Supreme Court rulings of the last twenty years is "balance."[59] The court decides after weighing several values — one against the other — that sometimes lead to contradictory outcomes. The very recourse to the term "balance" indicates that the façade of one mandatory answer to every given question has been relinquished. In the process of objective balance, judges obviously rule according to their best understanding, in line with the relative weight they feel should be assigned to conflicting values and interests at a given time and place. In a process resembling legislation, they thereby carve out the legal result from within themselves, by exercising judicial discretion.[60]

A contrary process takes place in halakhic law. Avi Sagi has exposed the centrality of the pluralistic approach within Halakhah.[61] Whereas a monistic halakhic approach holds that every dilemma has only one halakhic solution, a pluralistic view holds that the response may be found among a range of options, all legitimate. From the spectrum of legitimate responses that fill halakhic discourse, all equally close to the truth, the halakhist must choose the one he considers most plausible. According to the pluralistic perception, which has been widely accepted throughout the history of Halakhah, the halakhist is not only a legal expert who knows how to disclose the "truth" latent in the halakhic code. Rather, the halakhist creates a Halakhah imbued with personal characteristics,[62] expressing the values and social considerations to be taken into account.[63] After the halakhist rules out those options beyond the realm of halakhic legitimacy, he must ask himself what would be a worthy ruling in the specific case.[64] According to this approach, halakhic activity — as opposed, for instance, to scientific activity — is not meant to describe or expose reality, its structure or its characteristics, but to determine it. Halakhah is a product of human activity and, therefore, reflects human consciousness in its multifaceted and changing dimensions.[65]

At present, however, the monistic perception of Halakhah[66] has clearly gained ground, and halakhic pluralism has become increasingly restricted.

Halakhic rulings are now envisaged as an act taking place without human intervention. The consumers of Halakhah expect the halakhist to proclaim the legal result they deem necessary, as the only possible one, handed down to Moses at Sinai.[67] The common assumption is that halakhic rulings, rather than creating the response and thus being constitutive, only discover it and proclaim it, thus being merely declarative. According to this view, Halakhah is not affected by extra-halakhic factors either, be they the halakhist's personality[68] or his ethical philosophy.[69] The values of the halakhist and his personal preferences are irrelevant to his legal conclusion.

In sum, the two legal systems relate to values in opposite ways: state law now chooses to externalize the realm of values underlying the law, while contemporary Halakhah emphasizes the formal-technical-logical aspect of judicial rulings, as if they were devoid of value choices and personal discretion.

7. JUDICIAL IMPERIALISM

The fascinating finding is that, despite their diametrical approach to values, the attitude of both systems to their place and role in Israeli reality is almost identical: both endorse an unmistakable rhetoric of judicial imperialism. This trend creates problems for consumers of both systems, and is a unique and major source of distress for people who personally experience normative duality. This dual judicial imperialism narrows the range of options available to a public wishing to resort to the norms of both systems.

First, each system maintains, at least at the rhetorical level, that its scope is total. Some religious sayings (which are admittedly philosophical declarations rather than halakhic injunctions) claim, "Turn it [the Torah] and turn it, for everything is in it,"[70] and "nothing exists that was not intimated in the Torah." At the same time, in a conceptualization borrowed from the religious domain, Chief Justice Barak holds that "the law fills the earth."[71] Both legal systems, then, pretend to regulate all aspects of reality, leaving nothing uncovered.[72]

Second, is the totality of law at the theoretical-philosophical level expected to be concretized in reality? Does the legal policy of these competing systems direct judges to actually decide on every question placed on the public agenda? Here too, both systems give similar answers. Chief Justice Barak states, as a policy matter, that the Court is required to refrain from ruling only in a small number of cases, because "without the judge, no law is kept."[73] Halakhah has also shown a tendency to expand its scope over the last decades through a novel use of the notion of "*da'at Torah*." "*Da'at Torah*" was once perceived as the pronouncement of the community's sage, the learned rabbi. Its power stemmed from the rabbi's relative advantage as an educated man.[74] Later, "*da'at Torah*" came to be accepted as a kind of divine inspiration, requiring the public to grant it special meaning. Recently, we have seen the concept develop in a legally binding direction: "*da'at Torah*" is sometimes placed beside "halakhic ruling" as an alternative normative product, equally important,[75] or perhaps even more so.[76] The problem, however, is that the topics and issues on which "*da'at Torah*" is demanded and supplied are not at all defined (in striking contrast to the restriction and limitation of the content of issues included in the classic halakhic code, the *Shulkhan Arukh*).[77]

Third, the imperialism characterizing both legal systems is also manifest in their attitudes toward one another. Some of Halakhah's consumers question the binding validity of Israeli state law. The religiously observant sometimes publicly verbalize their contempt for state courts and their incumbents, and contemporary halakhists tend to support the view that recourse to state courts should be forbidden.[78] Many, whether ultra-Orthodox or religious-Zionists, hold that the courts of the Jewish state should be viewed as "Gentile courts."[79] The halakhic and cognitive implications[80] of these statements create profound discord with the surrounding reality for most observant Jews. This pertains not only to religious judges, lawyers, and jurists, but also to the wider public of religious and ultra-Orthodox Jews, including their rabbis, who all routinely resort to Israeli courts. Nor do rulings of state courts recognize the value of Halakhah as a vibrant legal system in a multicultural state.[81] Claims have been voiced stating that the legal system seeks to restrict the influence of halakhic norms on Israeli reality.[82] Both systems claim exclusivity in the regulation of reality, thereby hinting at the illegitimacy of the other.

8. JUDICIAL REALITY

The preceding analysis could provide an explanation — which I postulate but do not prove here — for some of the constructs of professional activity adopted by both state law and Halakhah. I begin with state law.

First, the expansion of standing.[83] In the past, the court was wary of opening its doors to all who might be interested in litigation. Petitioners had to prove a personal link to the issue in question. Selectivity was meant to ensure that only "relevant parties" would seek remedy through legal procedures, and that these would not be exploited for unworthy purposes. At present, standing is almost unrestricted, and the Court is willing to consider a conflict without ascribing too much importance to the identity and to the interest of the petitioner.[84] The increasing accessibility of legal services may reflect the general responsibility assumed by the courts in regulating values in Israeli society.[85] If the Court holds that its task is not only to solve a specific dispute but also to formulate a set of values for Israeli society in general, no great importance should be ascribed to the somewhat technical question of the petitioner's identity. In a rough generalization, the question of standing determines only the identity of the specific peg on which to hang a trailblazing ruling, which will serve society as a whole.

Second, judicial activism, according to one of its definitions,[86] prevails when the Court, out of all the possibilities at its disposal for ruling on a dilemma, chooses the one furthest removed from the law as heretofore practiced. An activist Court is more willing than other courts to change existing law through interpretive means. Changing the law is a means enabling the Court to bridge the gap that sometimes emerges between the law and reality. A legal system is by nature conservative and committed to custom and precedent. By contrast, the reality of our lives is dynamic, and raises new questions requiring decisions. New ideological currents change conventional thinking patterns concerning old questions. These general remarks are particularly true concerning Israel, which in recent years has been through several shakeups in values, which have been both the cause and the effect of its present plight as a society in crisis. Changing value preferences, reflecting the spirit of Israeli society and its time-related needs, are supposed to affect the judicial outcome for which an involved judge, sensitive and socially responsible, would wish. Not surprisingly, then, the Court assumes responsibility for reforming the law through its rulings.[87] Indeed, the more judges and their surroundings are aware of this commitment, the greater the judge's legitimacy and daring when relying on interpretation to change the law through adjudication.[88]

Third, judicial activism in its other sense — the Court's growing involvement in issues usually appertaining to other branches of government — is also related to the leading role assumed by the Court concerning values. Some hold that the response expected from a Court attentive to social values concerning social needs cannot wait until clumsy legislative procedures mature. Furthermore, the legislative branch, partly because of its representative character and its sectarian fragmentation, is sometimes tainted by obstructive interests, and even by the suspicion of misuse of power. The executive branch also wields wide-ranging powers in

Israel (anachronistically anchored in the relationship between the British Empire and its colonies, and presently justified by a longstanding state of emergency), incompatible with the present preferences of democratic Israel. Hence, in order for the Court to fulfill its role in influencing society's ways of life and shaping them so that they reflect the public's current choices, it must cast a wide net and enlarge the scope of "justiciability"[89] by including issues more germane to the legislative or executive branches. Not only ordinary citizens[90] but even members of the legislature tend to seek the Court's assistance to implement their own value preferences,[91] in a move seemingly puzzling in theory[92] but easily explained in practice.[93] Thus, as the value infrastructure of judicial activity is externalized, the justification for strengthening the status of the courts vis-à-vis other branches of government becomes clearer.[94]

Fourth, similarly, we can understand the tendency of the Supreme Court to formulate its rulings, sometimes at great length, as part of a comprehensive and systematic doctrine even when this is not required by the case in point.[95] Quite simply: if the Court envisages its task as providing a broad social service while solving a private conflict, it must present in its ruling the entire panorama of values. Only a full perspective will enable us to determine a hierarchy of values and a solid order of priorities that will stand the test of criticism. Therefore, when the conflict between the parties arguing before the Court does not bring to light the full complexity of the underlying principle in the case in point, the Court takes the liberty of expanding the range and suggesting a broad solution, even if it thereby exceeds the boundaries of the specific legal dispute.

In sum, the externalized value dimension in the Court's rulings is the bridge across which march the imperialist forces of the law in Israeli society.[96]

What about Halakhah? Although the end result is similar, it is attained through opposite means: the concealment of the value dimension in halakhic rulings is what enables its expanded influence.

As noted, a halakhic ruling, like any judicial ruling,[97] relies on a value choice.[98] The current monistic perception of Halakhah, however, tries to conceal this.[99] This strategy emerges as a *sine qua non* element for contemporary halakhists: were a value language evident in their rulings, Halakhah would be forced to adopt a direct attitude toward "modern" values, which on the one hand are generally accepted by Halakhah's present consumers and, on the other, is one "your fathers dreaded not" (Deuteronomy 32:17).

Emphasizing the discourse of values underlying halakhic rulings would force halakhists to bring to the surface their own attitudes towards liberal culture and its values to the surface. They would be forced to choose between a clear and explicit rejection of liberal values and the endorsement and legitimization of these values, internalizing them into the halakhic discourse.[100] Both these options, however, are bad for halakhists. If they reject liberal values they might alienate their listeners who, as noted, experience cultural duality in their daily lives and have therefore internalized many dimensions of the liberal worldview. If they endorse them, their halakhic rulings would reflect this, and they would be functioning as judicial activists.[101] Contemporary halakhists find it hard, for reasons I will not discuss here, to become halakhic activists, although this is an acceptable option in halakhic history (through decrees, interpretation, or midrash, as well as through legislative means, such as ordinances).[102] Hence, halakhists prefer to expunge value references from halakhic language. When Halakhah is monistic, a "mandatory" outcome of the Torah given to Moses on Mount Sinai, halakhists need not, and perhaps are even forbidden to, discuss the value basis of their ruling. This enables compartmentalization (to the modern Orthodox) and alienation (to the ultra-Orthodox) — Halakhah and reality do not meet.

Concealing the values in halakhic rulings extracts a heavy price: a "value-laden" Halakhah could have been more spiritual, more intellectual, and more relevant. It could have expanded the meaning of contemporary religious existence because it would have narrowed the gap between Halakhah and reality. Instead, some contemporary halakhists incline toward entrenchment within the walls: "the Torah forbids the new."[103] Unfortunately, the new refuses to disappear and increasingly threatens the old.[104] An entrenched, immutable Halakhah must defend itself. It endorses an imperialist policy — "Turn it and turn it, for everything is in it" — and proclaims exclusivity in the regulation of reality. Halakhah thereby enables the compartmentalized and alienated existence of the halakhic individual in a world of dynamic values.

The picture that emerges, then, is one of a struggle between two cultures that is manifest in both legal systems: halakhic law conceals the place of values out of weakness, and state law flaunts the place of values out of a position of strength. The common denominator is that their — opposite — attitude towards values encourages them to endorse judicial imperialism. Furthermore, on the one hand, some contemporary halakhic mediators fail to internalize the full complexity of democratic values into Jewish-religious discourse, and feel threatened by them. On the other, state law has difficulty internalizing a perception of Jewish tradition, including its philosophy and its norms, as potentially contributing to shaping Israeli identity. This reality of growing disharmony between two imperialistic legal systems places individuals experiencing normative duality and multiple commitments in an impossible situation: they are required by both systems to choose between the yoke of the Heavenly Kingdom and the yoke of the world of law.

9. SUMMARY

All the main Jewish communities in Israel find it difficult to deal with the complexity of cultural duality. Barring an inclusive ideological model, and faced with the reality of a democracy in crisis requiring decisions, all are dragged into a *kulturkampf*. Hence the mutual choice of both religious and secular camps to conduct most of their discourse in a normative language. Normative systems are perceived as effective instruments for reaching a clean decision and a professional, untainted victory over the "other."

The primary responsibility for the overstated centrality of the law when determining cultural decisions lies with Israeli society rather than with the judiciary. Judges do not choose the issues brought before them and are dragged into involvement in cultural disputes by parties seeking rulings in particular cases. They are forced, by definition of their roles, to answer such questions as: Is the conversion valid? Can the street be closed on the Sabbath? Does a same sex partner have rights? The demand of legal restraint in settling cultural questions, therefore, should be directed towards society in general. Legal restraint can be promoted in a society that adopts a culture of open discourse; that has effective institutions for settling conflicts in extra-legal ways at the local and national levels; that is highly consensual, offers political rewards for easing tensions, and so forth. Having said that, judicial systems should not be exempted from responsibility for exacerbating cultural controversy through their rulings. This is a serious responsibility, which courts and halakhists do not always discharge successfully.[105]

In my view, leaders in both normative systems are not sufficiently cautious regarding the ways in which they allow others to use them in order to reach cultural decisions. They emphasize theoretical positions about the totality of the law and of Halakhah that could prove extremely harmful since the other side, for whom the norm is crucial, might infer from these pronouncements an intention to deny it a role in Israeli culture.[106] Moreover, people involved in law and Halakhah must, by the very nature of their activity, make value choices. Although the law and Halakhah relate to this necessary feature of judicial work in different ways (the law emphasizes it and Halakhah conceals it), both use it to achieve the same aim: the creation of an intellectual environment that will enable them to endorse imperialistic patterns of activity and will legitimize their assumption of exclusive responsibility for molding social reality.

The consequences of translating cultural duality into normative duality, and of reducing the former to the latter, are problematic. Everyone must be aware of the limitations inherent in the law, its language, and its frameworks: a legal decision, whether religious or secular, is contingent and haphazard (according to the factual limitations of the case in point), artificial (because it cannot always include macro considerations), and also unprofessional (since the deciding agent lacks relevant training).[107] Settling essential, fundamental conflicts between two dominant cultures in a given society is an unusually complex task. It cannot be attained by reaching a "correct" decision, and no extant institution can offer "professional" solutions. The anticipated consensus cannot emerge from the application of an external criterion to the experience of those involved in the process.

From this perspective, the task that Israeli society imposes on the law and on Halakhah is far too heavy. It tends to view them as a decisive weapon in the intercultural struggle; it resorts to them as gurus, oracles yielding true answers in a complicated reality. The intensive and inflated use of normative systems interferes with the ability of each community to speak with itself, internally, and with the other, externally. As many in Israeli society have now sobered up from the illusion that power could be the main instrument for tackling problems of security and foreign policy, they must also sober up from the delusion that the law could be the main tool for solving social problems.[108] Just as power is a vital component of foreign policy, so is a strong and independent judiciary vital for the relationships between the tribes that make up Israeli society, and so is a halakhic system that is autonomous (but engaged in a dialogue with "life") vital for preserving the unique character of the religious way of life. Use of state law and of Halakhah, however, must be conscious and responsive to the limitations noted above and, like power, should be viewed as a last resort in the molding of society. Overuse of the law and of Halakhah erodes the authority of the institutions and the personalities implementing both normative systems. It mars the rule of law as well as the authority of Halakhah and, above all, it activates forces that shred the web of shared existence within cultural duality.

This analysis indicates the need to restrict the role of the law and of Halakhah as the bellwethers in the controversy over the character of Israeli society. The discourse between the two cultures requires a change of venue. Social regulation will not be attained in the courts, but in social and political settings. Normative decisions will not heal society nor daunt the opponents. Over the past two decades, decision-making in Israeli society has slipped from ideological systems, through political arrangements, into legal structures. The slide needs to be reversed.

The real chance of stabilizing Jewish society in Israel — however colorful, multifaceted, and sectarian it may be — lies in the ability of each community to reshape its inner attitude toward the two fundamental cultures of Israeli life. As the analysis shows, the three strategies for coping with cultural duality — compartmentalization, alienation, and abdication — share a common denominator that is the main reason for their failure: they deny the very confrontation with the meanings of life within cultural duality. Neither of the communities offers its members a texture of identity that is both existentially and spiritually satisfactory and coherent with the community's fundamental principles. The ideological credo of each community as conveyed, for instance, in its models of leadership or in its cultural products, is detached from the basic needs of community members, who experience the complexity of cultural duality.

It is in the distinct interest of each community, therefore, to clarify its own relationship toward cultural duality. Continuing the present pattern, impervious to the basic questions troubling the community's members, may eventually harm the very ability of each community to preserve itself as an alternative relevant to future generations. I do not place my trust in an increased sense of national responsibility or a preference for mutual responsibility over particularistic interests.[109] Rather, the particularistic interests of each community are those imposing a need for examining the options it can offer its members concerning ways of coping with cultural duality. Communities anxious to survive must react to the collapse of the strategies that had served them in the past. They must engage in an authentic ideological renewal that will seek real and experientially persuasive solutions toward a harmonious, or at least dialectical, existence in a reality of cultural diversity.

The trivialization of the cultural discourse and its reduction to a normative discourse were part of an attempt to force determination. But cultural duality does not need a determination. Quite the contrary. All parties can actually yield vast benefits from the existence of a cultural other. On the one hand, secular Jewish society in Israel is looking for its own uniqueness vis-à-vis global trends toward uniformity; on the other, religious and ultra-Orthodox society needs renewal to cope with hitherto unknown phenomena, such as Jewish sovereignty, secularism, and the demotion of halakhic law from its position of dominance. These overall trends signal the latent advantages of developing and deepening the discourse between the two basic cultures shaping Jewish society in Israel. Each culture must internalize that living its life within a closed, autarchic system is unworthy (and actually impossible). Instead, they must assume their place as partners in a dynamic intercultural discourse where each will shape the other and be shaped by it.[110] Diversity, then, rather than a dubious blessing, will turn out to be a hidden treasure, for the benefit of all.

NOTES

The Hebrew version of this paper was published in *Alpayim* 23 (2002), and in *Mehkarei Mishpat* 18 (2002). Thanks to Shuki Friedman, who was a superb research assistant. Thanks to my colleagues Yitzhak Brand, Yaron Ezrahi, Menachem Fisch, Ruth Gavison, Moshe Halbertal, Charles Liebman, Aryieh Naor, Avi Ravitzky, Amihai Redziner, Avi Sagi, Ronen Shamir, Ron Shapira, Yosef Shilhav, and Daniel Statman for their comments.

This article was translated by Batya Stein.

[1] The freedom to observe religious commandments, derived from the basic protection of human dignity, is generally guaranteed by Israeli law, as is the protection of religious feelings. Yet, this freedom is not absolute. See, for instance HCJ 292/83, *Temple Mount Faithful v. Jerusalem Police Commissioner*, PD 38(2) 449, 455; see also HCJ 7128/96 *Temple Mount Faithful v. the Government of Israel*, PD 51(2) 509, 521. Situations might be possible in which the relative balance between conflicting values could result in an affront to religious feelings, or even in an infringement of religious freedom. See for example, CA 6024/97, *Frederica Shavit v. the Rishon le-Zion Burial and Benevolence Society* PD 53(3) 600.

[2] In the title as well as in the discussion, I relate to Israeli society, although this article deals only with Israeli Jewish society. Readers are invited to consider the relevance of the present analysis, with the necessary adjustments, to the context of Jewish-Arab relationships.

[3] Note that the call for reducing the role of the law in cultural decisions is addressed, above all, to Israeli society in general and not only to the judiciary. See ch. 9 below.

[4] An up-to-date survey found that 6% of Israeli Jews define themselves as ultra-Orthodox; 9% as religious; 34% as traditional, and 51% as secular. See Uryiah Shavit, "Playing it Safe" [Hebrew] *Haaretz*, 6/10/2000, Weekend Supplement.

[5] See Avigdor Levontin, "A Riddle of Twin Worlds" [Hebrew], *Bar-Ilan Law Studies* 16 (2001): 7, 12, 13, 15.

[6] According to a survey of the Guttman Institute, about 80% of the Jewish population in Israel has some connection to Jewish religion and its commandments. See Shlomit Levi, Hanna Levinson and Elihu Katz, *Beliefs, Observance, and Social Relationships among Israeli Jews* [Hebrew] (Jerusalem: Guttman Institute for Applied Social

Research, 1993). For an interpretation of the findings of this report see Charles S. Liebman and Elihu Katz, eds., *The Jewishness of Israelis: Responses to the Guttman Report* (Albany: SUNY, 1997). See also Baruch Kimmerling, "Religion, Nationalism and Democracy in Israel" [Hebrew], *Zmanim: A Historical Quarterly* 13 (1994): 116, 129, and Eliezer Don Yehiyah and Charles S. Liebman, "The Dilemma of Reconciling Traditional Culture and Political Needs: Civil Religion in Israel" [Hebrew], *Megamot* 28 (1984): 461.

7   Breakthroughs in "the bastions of holiness" can be identified in several areas, such as the political realm (with ultra-Orthodox elements assuming increasing responsibility at the national level) and the geographical realm (with ultra-Orthodox elements leaving their traditional dwelling areas and settling in mixed cities). See Yosef Shilhav, *Ultra-Orthodoxy in Urban Governance in Israel* (Jerusalem: Floersheimer Institute for Policy Studies, 1998), p. 90.

8   Among the religious and the ultra-Orthodox, many tend to relate to theological dimensions in Jewish culture as a self-sustaining whole that fully explains reality. Hence, they sometimes perceive the very possibility of liberal-Western culture playing a significant role in the lives of Jews as a threat. By contrast, the secular public tends to relate to the two cultures as hierarchically ranked: Jewish culture, as embodied in Jewish tradition, is an earlier stage, meant to be superseded by liberal-Western culture. Due to the rebellion against tradition, this replacement is viewed as a necessary stage in an evolutionary process. In line with this analysis, the threat of a *kulturkampf* reflects the problem the religious public faces when required to give up the notion of wholeness, and the problem the secular public faces when required to give up the notion of rebelling against tradition.

9   Even in a pluralistic culture with an open marketplace of ideas, each culture could obviously consecrate a separate system of authority; champion unique values and priorities, uphold a separate ethos as well as different symbols and myths, and promote autonomous systems of meaning. Yet, it could do so in a non-imperialistic mode, assuming room for another "good" beside it.

10   For a general discussion of various aspects of double loyalty, see Ruth Gavison, *Can Israel Be Both Jewish and Democratic?: Tensions and Prospects* [Hebrew] (Jerusalem and Tel-Aviv: Van Leer Institute and Hakibbutz Hameuhad, 1999), pp. 21–45; Gershon Weiler, *Jewish Theocracy* [Hebrew] (Tel-Aviv: Am Oved, 1976); Ariel Rosen-Zvi, "'A Jewish and Democratic State': Spiritual Parenthood, Alienation, and Symbiosis — Can We Square the Circle?" [Hebrew], *Tel Aviv University Law Review* 19 (1995): 479; Uzzi Ornan, *Asmodeus' Claws: Eight Chapters on Secularism* [Hebrew] (Kiryiat Tiv'on: Einam, 1999); Levontin, "A Riddle of Twin Worlds."

11   Thus, for instance, the issue of double loyalties among the religious (and in recent years among the ultra-Orthodox as well) assumes specific meanings in the context of the controversy over the peace process. For example, halakhic rulings issued at the time of the Oslo Accords, forbidding territorial concessions and stating an obligation to disobey orders to vacate IDF bases in Judea and Samaria, sharpened the question of double loyalties.

12   For an up to date description of religious-Zionist society see Yair Sheleg, *The New Religious Jews: Recent Developments Among Observant Jews in Israel* [Hebrew] (Jerusalem: Keter, 2000), Part 1.

13   The tension between tradition and modernity is a primary experience and an existential challenge for the religious-Zionist public. Many rabbis presently leading this public are clearly inclined towards an anti-modernist stance. Some of them adopt the ultra-Orthodox model, which negates modernity in principle. These findings are surprising, given the vast philosophical and educational efforts that the spiritual historical leadership of neo-Orthodoxy invested in the intellectual and spiritual integration of tradition and modernity. The three outstanding thinkers in this area are Samson Raphael Hirsch, founder of the *Torah im Derekh Eretz* movement in nineteenth century Germany (see, for instance Eliezer Stern, *The Educational Ideal of Torah Im Derekh-Eretz* [Hebrew] [Ramat Gan: Bar Ilan University Press, 1987]); Abraham Yitzhak Kook, the first Chief Rabbi in the land of Israel (see, for instance, Nachum Arieli, "Integration in the Philosophy of Rav Kook," in *The World of Rav Kook's Thought*, ed. Benjamin-Ish-Shalom and Shalom Rosenberg, trans. Shalom Carmy and Bernard Casper [New York: Avi Chai, 1991], pp. 156–186), and Joseph Dov Soloveitchik, who was the spiritual inspiration and the leader of twentieth century North-American Orthodoxy (see, for instance, Avi Sagi, ed., *Faith in Changing Times: On the Doctrine of R. Joseph Dov Soloveitchik* [Hebrew] [Jerusalem: WZO, 1996], particularly Part 4). My concern here is not with the reasons for this failure, but only with its detection.

14   See Yoav Shorek (Schlesinger), "The Unbearable Irrelevance of the Torah" [Hebrew], *Tkhelet: A Journal of Israeli Thought* 2 (1997): 56, 78.

15   Sociologists of religious societies have recognized and analyzed the phenomenon of compartmentalization. See, generally, Peter L. Berger, *The Heretical Imperative* (Garden City, N. Y.: Anchor Press, 1979). For the phenomenon of compartmentalization in Jewish religious society, see for example, Charles S. Liebman and Eliezer Don-Yehiya, *Civil Religion in Israel* (Berkeley and Los Angeles, California: University of California Press, 1983), pp. 191–194 and Charles S. Liebman, "The Rise of Neo-Traditionalism Among Moderate Religious Circles in Israel" [Hebrew], *Megamot* 27 (1982): 231, 234–235. Some scholars locate the roots of the compartmentalization strategy in the Orthodox community in Germany at the end of the nineteenth-century, led by Samson Raphael Hirsch. See Ismar Schorsch, *Jewish Reactions to German Anti-Semitism 1870–1914* (New York: Columbia University Press, 1972), p. 10.

16   But see Yeshayahu Leibowitz's early thinking in Aryei Fishman, "The Search for Existential-Religious Unity: The Early Writings of Yeshayahu Leibowitz" [Hebrew], in *Yeshayahu Leibowitz: His World and Philosophy*, ed. Avi Sagi (Jerusalem: Keter, 1995), p. 121.

17   Compartmentalization is certainly not the only technique. For instance, religious-Zionism successfully resorted to hermeneutical mechanisms to deal with the cognitive dissonance resulting from the gap between the ethos and consciousness of religious-Zionism, which are traditional, and the ways of life of religious-Zionism, which are modern. See Avi Sagi, "Religious-Zionism: Between Closure and Openness" [Hebrew], in *Judaism: A Dialogue Between Cultures*, ed. Avi Sagi, Dudi Schwartz, and Yedidia Z. Stern (Jerusalem: Magnes Press, 1999), p. 124.

18   On this issue, see Menachem Friedman, *The Haredi (Ultra-Orthodox) Society: Sources, Trends and Processes* (Jerusalem: The Jerusalem Institute for Israel Studies, 1991), pp. 144–161.

19 See Eliezer Schweid, "Is Judaism a 'Separate Domain' or a Culture?" [Hebrew], in *Judaism: A Dialogue Between Cultures*, p. 407.

20 Defining their identity through a conscious renunciation of the legacy of Judaism is not widespread among secularists. The usual stance is that Jewish secularism "has been nurtured by Hebrew and Jewish culture throughout Jewish history. It includes the Hebrew language, its culture and literature –its sacred as well as its lay literature, which has been part of our literature since its inception. Secular Jewish culture also includes the principles of Jewish faith as one of Judaism's crucial values, the Jewish way of life, including the rich religious literature, Jewish philosophy through the ages, religious and non-religious, and the Jewish culture that has emerged over the last generations and is still unfolding at present, in Hebrew and in other languages. All these and many others belong to our national culture, on which we base our Jewish identity. Our vast cultural legacy is the foundation of our Jewish identity." See Yedidia Yitzhaki, *Principles of Jewish Secularity* [Hebrew] (Haifa: Haifa University Press and Zmora-Bitan, 1999); Yaron London, "Religious and Freethinkers" [Hebrew], in *We Secular Jews*, ed. Dedi Zucker (Tel-Aviv: Yediot Aharonot, 1999), pp. 23, 30; Yaakov Malkin, *What do Secular Jews Believe* [Hebrew] (Tel-Aviv: Sifriat Poalim, 2000); Weiler, *Jewish Theocracy*; Abraham B. Yehoshua, *Between Right and Right* [Hebrew] (Tel-Aviv: Schocken, 1980); Joseph Agassi, *Religion and Nationality: Towards an Israel National Identity* [Hebrew] (Tel-Aviv: Papyrus, 1984); "Pratt" (Avigdor Levontin) *Dawn and Dusk* [Hebrew] (Jerusalem: Shashar, 1991). At the end of the spectrum is a view holding that Israeli culture must be detached from any link to Judaism and its heritage: "There is a need to move ahead to a more Western, more pluralistic, less 'ideological' form of patriotism and citizenship. One looks with envy at the United States, where patriotism is centered on the Constitution; naturalization is conferred by a judge in a court of law; identity is defined politically and is based on law, not on history, culture, race, religion, nationality or language." Amos Elon, "Israel and the End of Zionism," *The New York Review of Books*, 19 December 1966, pp. 27–28.

21 Eliezer Schweid analyzes the concern surrounding the place of religious contents in Israeli secular culture in *Judaism and Secular Culture* [Hebrew] (Tel-Aviv: Hakibbutz Hameuhad, 1981), pp. 221–222.

22 See Yosef Dan, "The Liberation of Ultra-Orthodoxy: A Product of Secular Israel" [Hebrew], *Alpayim* 15 (1998): 234, 236–237.

23 This legislation was accompanied by great controversy. See, for example, Aaron Kirschenbaum, "The Foundations of Law, 1980: Today and Tomorrow" [Hebrew], *Tel-Aviv University Law Review* 2 (1985): 117–126; Menachem Elon, "More About the Foundations of Law Act" [Hebrew], *Shenaton ha-Mishpat ha-Ivri* 13 (1987): 227–256; Aharon Barak, "The Foundations of Law Act and the Heritage of Israel" [Hebrew], *Shenaton ha-Mishpat ha-Ivri* 13 (1987): 265–284.

24 See Aharon Barak, "The Constitutional Revolution: Protected Basic Rights" [Hebrew], *Mishpat u-Mimshal* 1 (1992–1993): 9, 31.

25 Elon criticizes this approach based on the discriminatory approach he identifies in Barak's treatment of the twin concepts of a "democratic state" and a "Jewish state." See Menachem Elon, "The Values of a Jewish Democratic State in Light of

the Basic Law: Human Liberty and Dignity" [Hebrew], *Tel-Aviv University Law Review* 17 (1993): 659, 686. Barak rejects this interpretation of his outlook. See Aharon Barak, *Constitutional Interpretation* [Hebrew], vol. 3 of *Interpretation in Law* (Jerusalem: Nevo, 1994), pp. 343–344.

26 Ibid., pp. 345–347.

27 One of the more enraged responses to this approach came from the Shas party, in a document that Attorney Yaakov Weinrot submitted on 28 December 1992 to Minister of Justice David Libai, entitled *The Position of Shas on the Basic Law: Basic Human Rights*.

28 See Zvi Zameret "Judaism in Israel: Ben-Gurion's Private Beliefs and Public Policy" *Israel Studies* 4 (1999): 64. See also Zvi Zameret, "Yes to a Jewish State, No to a Clericalist State: The Mapai Leadership and its Attitude to Religion and Religious Jews" [Hebrew], in *On Both Sides Of The Bridge: Religion and State in the Early Years of Israel* , ed. Mordechai Bar-On and Zvi Zameret (Jerusalem: Yad Ben Zvi Press, 2002).

29 The model of consociational democracy was suggested by Arendt Lijphart, *The Politics of Accommodation* (Berkeley: University of California Press, 1968); Arendt Lijphart, *Democracies* (New Haven and London: Yale University Press, 1984). In Israel, the concept was used to understand the organization of the Jewish political community during the British Mandate (Dan Horowitz and Moshe Lisak, *Origins of the Israeli Polity: Palestine Under the Mandate*, trans. Charles Hoffman [Chicago: University of Chicago Press, 1978]); as a key for understanding the relationships between religious and secularists after the establishment of the state (Dan Horowitz and Moshe Lisak, *Trouble in Utopia: The Overburdened Polity of Israel* [Albany, N.Y.: State University of New York Press, 1989], pp. 16–17), and to deal with various aspects of the religion and state relationship (Eliezer Don-Yehyiah, *Cooperation and Conflict Between Political Camps: The Religious Camp and the Labor Movement and the Education Crisis in Israel* [Ph. D. diss., Hebrew University of Jerusalem, 1977]).

30 Asher Cohen and Bernard Susser, "Changes in the Relationship between Religion and State: Between Consociationalism and Resolution" [Hebrew], in *Multiculturalism in a Democratic and Jewish State: Memorial Volume for Ariel Rosen-Zvi*, ed. Menachem Mautner, Avi Sagi and Ronen Shamir (Tel-Aviv: Ramot, 1998), p. 675.

31 Menachem Mautner, "Israeli Law in a Multicultural Society" [Hebrew], in *The Rule of Law in a Polarized Society: Legal, Social, and Cultural Aspects*, ed. Aeyal Yinon (Jerusalem: The Israel Democracy Institute, 1999), p. 27.

32 Peter Ferdinand Drucker, *Post-Capitalist Society* (New York: Harper Business, 1993), Part 2.

33 The process of estrangement extends to several elements of the sense of belonging, such as the attitude of Israelis to their surroundings (Joshua Meyrowitz, *No Sense of Place: The Impact of Electronic Media on Social Behavior* [New York: Oxford University Press, 1985]); their attitude toward sovereignty and the political unit (Joseph A. Camilleri and Jim Falk, *The End of Sovereignty: The Politics of a Shrinking and Fragmenting World* [Aldershot, UK: Edward Elgar, 1992]); their mutual relationship with the local society and economy (Thomas L. Friedman, *The Lexus and the Olive Tree* [New York: Anchor Books, 2000]).

34 See Charles S. Liebman, "Secular Judaism and its Prospects" [Hebrew], *Alpayim* 14 (1997): 97; Samuel Avigdor Ben-Sasson, "The Ascent of Man and the Absence of God: Notes on the Question of Our National Identity" [Hebrew], *Alpayim* 14 (1997): 117.

35 Many do not make clear-cut and unequivocal choices concerning their preferred drawers. Were it otherwise, the Orthodox community would become an empty cell. Indeed, many in this community go on shaping their ways of life in some kind of compromise, despite the difficulties, although they too are influenced by the social and cultural processes that Israeli society is undergoing.

36 Charles Liebman, who analyzed this phenomenon about twenty five years ago, enumerated five elements defining the decline of non-*haredi* Orthodoxy in Israel. See Liebman, "The Rise of Neo-Traditionalism," pp. 237–240. These trends have definitely expanded over the last two decades, as evident in the significant numbers of non-*haredi* Orthodox youngsters studying at private institutions that are not part of the state-religious educational system. Additional signs are the preference of many religious-Zionists for residence in homogeneous surroundings, their recourse to separate social and communal agencies, different from those dealing with the rest of the population; a dress code that sets them apart through special and conspicuous features ; increasing recourse to rabbinical authority on everyday matters, and so forth.

37 For empirical studies of religiosity levels among students and graduates of the state-religious system, see Abraham Laslevi and Mordechai Bar-Lev, *The Religious World of State Religious Education Graduates* [Hebrew] (Ramat Gan: Bar-Ilan University, 1993).

38 For a description of the mutual relationships between the perception of democracy by the Israeli public and by the *haredi* public see Shilhav, *Ultra-Orthodoxy in Urban Governance*, pp. 103–105. On the ideological aspects of ultra-Orthodox attitudes toward the state, see Aryeh Naor, "The Sovereignty of the State of Israel in Orthodox Religious Thought" [Hebrew], *Politika* 2 (1998): 71, 77–80.

39 Bnei Berak and Jerusalem are among the poorest cities in Israel. For extensive information on Jerusalem's ultra-Orthodox population see Momi Dahan, *Ultra-Orthodox Jews and the Municipal Authorities* (Jerusalem: Jerusalem Institute for Israel Studies, 1998).

40 See Uriel Simon, "Religious-Secular Cooperation in the Building of a 'Jewish Democratic State'" [Hebrew], *Alpayim* 13 (1997): 154, 158.

41 On the burgeoning of study settings for an open discussion of Jewish sources, now numbering over one hundred and intended also for secular Jews, see Tamar Rotem, "Each one will choose whatever he wants from Judaism" [Hebrew], *Haaretz*, 13/10/2000, B12 and Micha Oddenheimer, "In the Backyards" [Hebrew], *Eretz Aheret* 1 (2000):10.

42 I have no data on the success of the Conservative and Reform movements in spreading their message in Israel. The general sense is that Israelis are showing growing interest in the cultural and religious options that these movements offer, and that rates of membership in their communities have largely increased over the past decade. In my view, this success, though still small in absolute numbers, should be ascribed to the search of the secular public for links to their Jewish heritage.

43 See Ruth Gavison, "A Jewish Democratic State: Political Identity, Ideology, and Law" [Hebrew], in *A Jewish Democratic State*, ed. Daphne Barak-Erez (Tel-Aviv: Ramot, 1996), pp. 169, 216, and Liebman, "Secular Judaism and its Prospects," pp. 113–116.

44 Proverbs 29:18.

45 An unfortunate instance of this is the political move known as the civic-secular revolution adopted by Ehud Barak's government. The very idea of dealing with such acutely sensitive issues through one blunt stroke devised by a random political constellation is evidence of the crisis affecting Israeli society and of its leaders' immaturity. A decision that favors one side in a *kulturkampf* setting is a proven recipe for disaster. When each side becomes entrenched in one cultural truth, the realization of one's dream is possible only at the cost of the other's nightmare. In my view, both contradictory views about the meaning of the civic-secular revolution are to some extent true. Barring a philosophy or ways of thinking that leave place for the values of both cultures to coexist, however, we will forever be forced to choose between them. The inevitable consequence will be the losing side's unyielding refusal to accept the result.

46 Amnon Rubinstein preceded others in pointing to the "lawlization of Israel" in a series of three articles with this title, which he published in *Haaretz* in June 1987.

47 Indeed, legal imperialism is not exclusive to Israel or to countries characterized by cultural duality or identity problems. Hence, my remarks on this question are not meant as the sole explanation of a local phenomenon. Thus, for instance, some see the law as a meta-narrative serving to anchor contemporary post-modern culture. See Peter Goodrich, *Languages of Law: From Logics of Memory to Nomadic Masks* (London: Weidenfeld and Nicholson, 1990). On the central role of the law in current American culture and on different perspectives on this topic, see Paul F. Campos, *Jurismania: American Culture and the Madness of Law* (New York: Oxford University Press, 1998); Lawrence Meir Friedman, *Total Justice* (New York: Russell Sage, 1985); Walter K. Olson, *The Litigation Explosion: What Happened When America Unleashed the Lawsuit* (New York: Truman Talley, 1991). The law also plays a special role as a by-product of the globalization process, affecting economic and social aspects. Nevertheless, the current legal and halakhic imperialism in Israel is still uniquely prominent by comparison with other places.

48 For the various approaches and for references, see Gad Barzilai, "Judicial Hegemony, Sectarian Polarization, and Social Change" [Hebrew], *Politika* 2 (1998): 31, 32–35.

49 Note, however, that all the explanations so far refer only to the dominance of state law. They do not contribute to an understanding of the parallel phenomenon concerning the dominance of Halakhah. By contrast, in this discussion I seek an overall explanation for the reliance on both these legal systems.

50 I do not claim that this is the sole explanation. Findings reveal increasing recourse to litigation in Israel on issues not directly related to the inter-cultural strife, as is also true of societies that are not characterized by identity conflicts. See the text above and note 47.

51 The literature acknowledges the link between social cohesiveness and extra-legal social regulation. As social cohesiveness breaks down, the power of social authority and of extra-legal normative systems is weakened, intensifying the need for

authoritative legal rulings. See, for instance, Robert C. Ellickson, *Order Without Law: How Neighbors Settle Disputes* (Cambridge, Mass.: Harvard University Press, 1991); Jonathan R. Macey "Public and Private Ordering and the Production of Legitimate and Illegitimate Legal Rules," *Cornell Law Review* 82 (1997): 1123.

52   Thus, for instance, a common denominator between ultra-Orthodox who choose exclusion from Western culture and secular Jews who have actually relinquished the option of significant links with Jewish culture and are oblivious to its values, is hard to find. If each of these two groups were to develop, separately, ideological models that leave room for both cultures within their own (different) worldviews, they could probably discuss their disputes in more leisurely, empathetic, and trusting terms, striving for an arrangement. Furthermore, if each group could preserve its traditional strategy of action vis-à-vis cultural duality, across-the-board normative decisions to regulate the relationships between them would probably not be required.

53   See Ronen Shamir, "The Politics of Reasonableness: Reasonableness and Judicial Power at Israel's Supreme Court" [Hebrew], *Theory and Criticism* 5 (1994): 7, 19.

54   See, for instance, Baruch Kimmerling, "Legislation and Jurisprudence in a Settler-Immigrant Society" [Hebrew], *Bar-Ilan Law Studies* 16 (2001): 17, 18; Shamir, "The Politics of Reasonableness," p. 19.

55   In the introduction to his ruling concerning the Bar-Ilan road, Chief Justice Barak appears to be aware of this: "In Israel's public discourse, Bar-Ilan is no longer a road and has become a social concept. It signals a deep political controversy between ultra-Orthodox and secularists...Our concern is not the social dispute, our considerations are not political. Our interest is the legal controversy; our considerations are normative. We do not deal with the relationship between ultra-Orthodox and secularists in Israel; ...Our interest is simply the Bar-Ilan Road; our interest is the mandate of the Central Signposting Authority and the latitude of its discretion. Our concern is the relationship between freedom of movement on the one hand, and hurting religious feelings and a religious way of life on the other hand." HCJ 5016/96, *Lior Horev v. The Minister of Transport*, PD 51(4) 1, 15. This is an instance of the Supreme Court's awareness of the limitations of legal discourse: the Court is required, against its better interests, to cope with cultural duality.

56   In his article in this volume, "Society and Law in Israel," Avi Sagi develops an important conceptual distinction. The rights discourse resorts to the legal system and to arguments drawn from legal language. This is a discourse between plaintiffs and defendants, in which the meeting with the other touches on a conflict of interests, and the relationships between the parties are hierarchical and asymmetrical. By contrast, an identity discourse evolves between individuals who do not ascribe characteristics and do not apply categories to the other, allowing the self and the other to meet in their "concrete fullness." In this discourse, people talk, listen, confess, and tell.

57   In the past, Israeli society had evinced considerable trust in its Supreme Court. See Gad Barzilai, Ephraim Yaar-Yuchtman and Zeev Segal, *The Israeli Supreme Court and the Israeli Public* [Hebrew] (Tel-Aviv: Papyrus, 1994). Over the past few years, the public, the media, and the professional community have intensified their attacks against the Court.

58   Menachem Mautner, *The Decline of Formalism and the Rise of Values in Israeli Law* [Hebrew] (Tel-Aviv: Ma'agalei Da'at, 1993). Ruth Gavison offers another description of the changes affecting the Court. See Ruth Gavison, Mordechai Kremnitzer and Yoav Dotan, *Judicial Activism — For and Against: The Role of the High Court of Justice in Israeli Society* [Hebrew] (Jerusalem: Magnes Press, 2000), pp. 74–91.

59   On Justice Barak's perception of balance, see Barak, *Constitutional Interpretation*, pp. 215-227.

60   Although judges exercise personal discretion when ruling, they cannot decide arbitrarily. According to Barak's theory of judicial interpretation, the balancing task must fit criteria of reasonableness. Reasonableness refers to the appropriate weight to be assigned to clashing interests and values. The criterion for determining the relative importance of a value or an interest depends, *inter alia*, on the views endorsed by the enlightened public. Thereby, the judge's personal interpretive task acquires its objective dimension. See Barak, *Constitutional Interpretation*, pp. 227–241. Justice Elon holds that "the concept of an 'enlightened' public or individual is indeterminate and altogether lacking in any content." See CA 506/88 *Shefer v. the Government of Israel*, PD 48(1) 87. Barak rejects this critique, although he himself admits that the potential guidelines that can be drawn from the worldview of the Israeli enlightened public are vague. Yet, although "it does not provide the judge with a road map … it does provide a compass concerning the correct direction of the judicial ruling." Barak, *Constitutional Interpretation*, p. 240. It appears that the gap between the general guideline providing direction and the precise navigation of the judicial decision toward a safe haven in every specific case, must be bridged by the judges through their personal interpretation of reality. Judges must function within consensual value settings but, beyond this general directive, they cannot apply any objective truth and must resort to their personal scale of values.

61   Avi Sagi, *The Open Canon: On the Meaning of Halakhic Discourse*, trans. Batya Stein (London: Continuum, 2007), Part 2.

62   Thus, for instance, many scholars have tried to disclose the theoretical foundation underlying many famous disputes between the House of Shammai and the House of Hillel. For an extensive review of the pertinent literature, see Haim Shapira and Menachem Fisch "The Debates Between the Houses of Shammai and Hillel: The Meta-Halakhic Issue" [Hebrew], *Tel-Aviv University Law Review* 22 (1999): 461, 463–468.

63   These two views on the character of Halakhah are illustrated in the controversy between Haim Soloveitchik and David Hartman on the appropriate classification of Maimonides' *Epistle on Martyrdom*. See Haim Soloveitchik, "Maimonides' *Iggeret Ha-Shemad*: Law and Rhetoric," in *Rabbi Joseph H. Lookstein Volume*, ed. Leo Landman (New York: Ktav, 1980), pp. 281–318; David Hartman, "Maimonides' *Epistle on Martyrdom*" [Hebrew], *Jerusalem Studies in Jewish Thought* 2 (1982–1983): 362. For the description of the dispute see Yair Lorberbaum and Haim Shapira, "Maimonides' 'Epistle on Martyrdom': The Hartman-Soloveitchik Controversy in Light of the Philosophy of Law" [Hebrew], in *Renewing Jewish Commitment: The Work and Thought of David Hartman*, ed. Avi Sagi and Zvi Zohar (Jerusalem and Tel-Aviv: Shalom Hartman Institute and Hakibbutz Hameuhad, 2001), pp. 1: 345–373.

64   The process whereby halakhists exercise discretion is complex. For a discussion of this issue see Avi Sagi, "Halakhah, Discretion, Responsibility, and Religious-Zionism" [Hebrew], in *Between Authority and Autonomy in Jewish Tradition*, ed. Avi Sagi and Zeev Safrai (Tel-Aviv: Hakibbutz Hameuhad, 1997), p. 195.

65   Sagi, *The Open Canon*, pp. 88–99.

66   See, for instance, Pinhas Shiffman's formulation in "Halakhic Man is Sentenced to Freedom" [Hebrew], in *Between Authority and Autonomy*, p. 244.

67   The problem is that the methodology of the halakhic ruling may expose it to substantive rebuttals. Discussion and controversy encourage halakhic pluralism. Some hold that this is the background for the increasingly widespread use of the "*da'at Torah*" notion in recent times. By diverting the decision from the "halakhic ruling" context to the *da'at Torah* context, the halakhist can express his view as an authentic Torah outlook that does not require discussion, analysis, and clarification, and does not require the exposure immanent in the methodology of halakhic rulings. See Lawrence Kaplan, "*Daas Torah*: A Modern Conception of Rabbinic Authority," in *Rabbinic Authority and Personal Autonomy*, ed. Moshe Sokol (Northvale, N.J.: Jason Aronson, 1992), p. 1.

68   See Soloveitchik's description of the way endorsed by his grandfather, R. Haim from Brisk, concerning halakhic debate in Joseph Dov Soloveitchik, *Divrei Hagut ve-Ha'arakha* [Hebrew] (Jerusalem: WZO, 1981), pp. 76–77.

69   Thus, for instance, Abraham Yeshayahu Karelitz (known as *Hazon Ish*) claims that morality is not personal but derives from Halakhah. See *Sefer Hazon Ish: Emunah u-Bitahon* (Tel-Aviv: Sifryiati, 1984), p. 21. When individuals face a moral decision, their only criterion for choice is the halakhic ruling rather than their personal moral stance. For a systematic analysis of whether Jewish tradition acknowledges the existence of a morality independent of God's command see Avi Sagi, *Judaism: Between Religion and Morality* [Hebrew] (Tel-Aviv: Hakibbutz Hameuhad, 1998).

70   Mishnah Avot 5:22, and Avot de-Rabbi Nathan, Version B, ch. 27, s.v. *u-mah-hu*.

71   Aharon Barak, "Judicial Philosophy and Judicial Activism" [Hebrew], *Tel-Aviv University Law Review* 17 (1993): 475, 477.

72   See the opinions of Justices Aharon Barak and Menachem Elon in HCJ 1635/90, *Zerzevski v. the Prime Minister et al.* PD 45(1)749. For an extensive discussion of questions bearing on the scope of both legal systems see Yedidia Z. Stern, "The Halakhic Approach on Political Affairs" [Hebrew], *Mishpat Umimshal* 4 (1997): 215, 217–229. In a private conversation, Justice Elon clarified he had not intended to support the totality of Halakhah, but only to state that the scope of Halakhah is broader than that of state law.

73   HCJ 1635/90, *Zerzevski v. the Prime Minister et al.*, at 773.

74   In this context, see Gershon C. Bacon, "*Da'at Torah* and Birthpangs of the Messiah" [Hebrew]," *Tarbiz* 52 (1983): 497.

75   See, for instance, Shalom Dov Wolpo, *Da'at Torah: On the Situation in the Holy Land* [Hebrew] (Kiryiat Gat: n.p., 1981), based on conversations with the late leader of the Habad movement, R. Menachem Mendel Schneersohn of Lubawitz. Throughout the book, the terms "*da'at Torah*" and "halakhic ruling" are used interchangeably.

[76] Concerning the halakhic ruling issued by rabbis identified with religious-Zionism, which called IDF soldiers to refuse orders if required to retreat from occupied territories in Judea and Samaria, see R. Israel Rosen statement in Israel Rosen, *"Da'at Torah* is above a ruling" [Hebrew], *Hatsofeh*, 20/05/1994.

[77] Jacob Katz holds that the term *da'at Torah* "is meant to confer legitimacy on the halakhist's role, beyond the usual domain of halakhic procedure." He illustrates this through historical examples of the halakhist's new functions beyond the halakhic realm. See Jacob Katz, "Da'at Torah: The Unqualified Authority Claimed by Halakhists," in Sagi and Safrai, *Between Authority and Autonomy*, p. 95.

[78] See Eliav Shochetman, "The Halakhic Status of Israeli Courts" [Hebrew], *Tehumin* 13 (1992–1993): 337, 346.

[79] Yaakov Ariel, the Chief Rabbi of Ramat-Gan and a religious-Zionist leader, writes as follows: "All halakhists, including religious-Zionist ones, view it [the judicial system and all its components — Y. Z. S.] as *arka'ot* [Gentile courts], which Halakhah strictly forbids." See Yaakov Ariel, "Not at a Crossroads: 'The Beginning of our Redemption' Through the Test of Time" (Hebrew), *Tsohar* 5 (2001): 95, 108 (note 15).

[80] The late Justice Haim Cohen related to a directive published at the time by then Chief Rabbi Ovadia Yosef concerning the prohibition of turning to the courts in "Gentile Courts and Jewish Values," *Mishpat Umimshal* 4 (1997): 299, 300.

[81] As noted in ch. 3 above, cases wherein the judiciary chose to fill statutory lacunae by recourse to the "principles of Israel's heritage" are hard to find. Chief Justice Barak stated that, in principle, the halakhic dimension is one of the two main features of the state of Israel as a Jewish state (the other being the Zionist dimension). This statement may prove important in changing the feeling now prevalent among both religious and secularists, that state law does not recognize Halakhah, but this interpretation has yet to be concretized in a significant yield of legal rulings. See Barak, *Constitutional Law*, pp. 330–331.

[82] As is the case, for instance, in the context of court rulings seeking to limit the authority of the rabbinical court. The deeper layers of this controversy emerge, in fascinating ways, in HCJ 3269/95, *Yosef Katz v. The Regional Rabbinical Court in Jerusalem*, PD 50(4) 590.

[83] For a general discussion, see Zeev Segal, *Standing Before the Supreme Court* [Hebrew] second edition (Tel-Aviv: Papyrus, 1993).

[84] Indeed, the expansion of standing rights, at least so far, extends only to public law. For an explanation of the distinction consult Aharon Barak, "The Idea of Judicial Activism: Judicial Philosophy and Judicial Activism" [Hebrew], *Tel-Aviv University Law Review* 17 (1993): 475, 488.

[85] "The judge's approach to rules of standing conveys his view of the role of the court in a democratic society and of its standing vis-à-vis other branches of government." Ibid.

[86] For this definition, see Aharon Barak, *Judicial Discretion*, trans. Yadin Kaufmann (New Haven: Yale University Press, 1989), p. 113.

[87] See Yitzhak Zamir, "Judicial Activism: The Decision to Decide" [Hebrew], *Tel-Aviv University Law Review* 17 (1993): 649.

88 Since these value changes are taking place in a society in crisis, considerable sections of the public will indeed identify in the value decisions of the Supreme Court a concrete threat to their own values. Activism, in the sense of changing the law, alienates segments of the public not only from the specific ruling but also from the institution that creates it — the Supreme Court.

89 See, for instance Ariel Bendor, "Justiciability in the High Court of Justice" [Hebrew], *Mishpatim* 17 (1987): 592.

90 See, for instance, Dan Maler, "The High Court of Justice: The Secular Israelis' Option in the Fight Against Religious Coercion" [Hebrew], *Free Judaism* 14 (1999).

91 "The civil judicial system is now viewed by a considerable portion of the Israeli population as an active participant in a political debate, an actor identified with the secular liberal segment of Israeli society." See Menachem Hofnung "The Unintended Consequences of Unplanned Constitutional Reform: Constitutional Politics in Israel," *American Journal of Comparative Law* 44 (1996): 585, 602. Yet, the Court's tendency to assume a responsibility incumbent on other branches of government extracts a heavy price. Part of the public identifies this tendency as a deliberate effort by an elite, entrenched in the legal system, to impose its scale of values without testing them in the political marketplace of ideas. They view this as a power struggle between the Knesset, which is a representative system, and the Court, which is not. Critics do not accept the claim that judicial decisions are professional (so that the Court need not be representative), and that the judicial effort seeks to arrive at a result that will objectively reflect the values accepted in Israeli society. They describe Knesset members petitioning the Court as "bypassing the Knesset," seeking assistance among ideological allies and bypassing the democratic procedure that should purportedly come to the fore in the Knesset's political negotiations. Objections are voiced not only by political and cultural representatives of special minority groups in Israeli society (the ultra-Orthodox, modern Orthodox or Arab constituencies) or by interested parties, but also resonate increasingly in the media, in academia, and in various professional groups, including the legal community.

92 The politicians' obvious interest is to prevent the seepage of decision-making powers from the political into the judiciary realm and to protect, as far as possible, the autonomy of the game and of the rules of the game in which they all participate. Quite obviously, although the two systems coexist, they also compete.

93 See Menachem Hofnung and Yoav Dotan, *Litigating Legislators: Political Parties in Courts* (unpublished manuscript).

94 See Mautner, *The Decline of Formalism*, p. 108.

95 This procedure involves high costs. See Ruth Gavison, "The Public Involvement of the High Court of Justice: A Critical Perspective" [Hebrew], in Gavison et al., *Judicial Activism*, pp. 76–79.

96 Through this formulation, I am not trying to contend with the complex judicial rhetoric used to explain the law's professional constructs. My main focus is precisely on an outsider's analysis of the judicial reality.

97 One could claim that the decisions of a secular judicial system, interpreting a human law, are not comparable to the decisions of a religious judicial system, interpreting

norms that originate (according to some views) in a divine revelation documented in sacred texts. This difference, however, is irrelevant to the present discussion, since all normative decisions, even one originating in revelation, necessarily rest on a value foundation.

98 Moshe Halbertal submits that the history of Halakhah should be explained as a series of interpretive moves. See Moshe Halbertal, *Interpretive Revolutions in the Making: Values as Interpretative Considerations in Midrashei Halakhah* [Hebrew] (Jerusalem: Magnes Press, 1997).

99 In this context, we should understand the decline in the value of Agaddah study in our time. It could be that, precisely because of the abundance of value considerations explicitly manifest in aggadic discourse, Aggadah became less attractive to contemporary scholars, to *yeshiva* students, and to halakhic authorities. On the relationship between Aggadah and Halakhah see, for instance, Yair Lorberbaum, *Imago Dei: Halakhah and Aggadah* [Hebrew] (Jerusalem: Schocken, 2004); Zipora Kagan, *Halakhah and Aggadah as a Code of Literature* [Hebrew] (Jerusalem: Bialik Institute, 1988); Shulamit Almog, "Law and Literature, *Halakhah* and *Aggadah*" [Hebrew], *Bar-Ilan Law Studies* 13 (1996): 432–435.

100 In the halakhic homilies that Halbertal discusses, the sages reveal great awareness of their own value choices. See Halbertal, *Interpretive Revolutions*, pp. 171–183.

101 Halbertal proves that, in the issues he discusses, the rabbis' value preferences change the contents of their halakhic rulings. Ibid., p. 172.

102 See Menachem Elon, *Jewish Law: History, Sources, Principles*, trans. Bernard Auerbach and Melvin J. Sykes (Philadelphia and Jerusalem: Jewish Publication Society, 1994), Part 2.

103 R. Moshe Sofer, known as *Hatam Sofer*, was the first to use a defined halakhic injunction (forbidding the "new") to formulate a general ruling objecting to innovation *per se*. See, for instance, *Responsa Hatam Sofer*, Part 1 (Orah Hayyim), # 181.

104 For a definition of the threat that the "new" poses to Jewish tradition, see Aviezer Ravitzky, *Freedom Inscribed: Diverse Voices in Jewish Religious Thought* [Hebrew] (Tel-Aviv: Am Oved, 1999), pp. 166–167.

105 Furthermore, judicial systems can refrain from issuing rulings on questions they categorize as non-justiciable. Obviously, this option entails a significant cost: by relinquishing the regulation of specific issues, the law may leave them open to be regulated by other agencies, free of supervision.

106 Whatever the conceptual view one endorses concerning the totality of the law or of Halakhah, any emphasis on theoretical approaches should be discouraged. Now that normative duality threatens social integrity, airing these conceptual views could have substantive damaging effects. A more cautious formulation, even if not fully suited to the jurisprudence of the halakhic philosophy some may embrace, would be willing to recognize that the law and Halakhah do not necessarily uphold a normative perception concerning every human situation. In reality, a gap prevails between (maximalistic) declarations concerning the scope of law and Halakhah and their (qualified) implementation in both legal systems. The substantive concession required from each system is not unbearable, nor can it undermine either of them. State law and Halakhah should both show each other, and together to the public,

a "smiling face," which leaves a human space without normative regulation. Such a space does exist in practice, and should be acknowledged.

[107] Questioning the suitability of the judge's or the halakhist's training for decisions on matters of principle arising from cultural duality is not meant to undermine their authority or their formal qualifications. Rather, the purpose is to call attention to the substantive gap between the formal legal training (or, in the case of a halakhic sage, the knowledge required for rabbinic ordination) of the person in authority, and the background that is relevant for making this decision. This gap is a necessary outcome of the decision of human societies to entrust the power to settle conflicts between social groups to judges, who are service providers specializing in decision-making (as opposed to specialists on the matter at stake in the conflict). This gap cannot be closed but we must not ignore its very existence. When we develop expectations from normative decisions, we should be fully aware of the substantive limitations that the educational training of both judges and halakhists impose on this process.

[108] The deceit entailed by the reliance on normative solutions as a tool for shaping Israeli society has become increasingly obvious. Irresponsible attempts seeking a breakthrough or a *coup de grâce* in the social arena by resorting to a normative weapon may still lie ahead. Both might initiate it. Secularists still brandish the ultimate Armaggedon weapon: a unilateral constitution, broad and ironclad, to be imposed on future generations by a random Knesset majority. The religious side is still involved in rearguard battles, meant to observe modern reality and determine the attitude toward it solely through the limited prism of a narrow and preset inventory of halakhic categories as interpreted in previous generations. A wider understanding, however, seems to be ripening concerning the hopelessness of the endeavor to stretch the cover of the normative bubble far beyond its logical borders.

[109] Although responsibility for the whole is supposedly incumbent on all its parts, I do not believe that in the Israeli reality we can expect any of these communities to withdraw from its position out of consideration for the common interest. Furthermore, the very search for a compromise, as opposed to an agreement, is inappropriate, since it may be opposed to the basic integrity of each community's inner outlook.

[110] On this question, see Sagi et al., *Judaism: A Dialogue Between Cultures*, pp. 1–4.

SOCIETY AND LAW IN ISRAEL BETWEEN A RIGHTS DISCOURSE AND AN IDENTITY DISCOURSE

AVI SAGI

1. Introduction

Israeli society has long been engaged in a serious discourse about issues touching on the relationship between its various components. This article will examine this exchange by introducing two key concepts — the discourse of rights and the discourse of identity — that reflect and also determine different types of relationships between the parties. Patterns of internal discourse in a society have proved highly revealing concerning its character, and my central claim here is that Israeli society speaks mainly through a discourse of rights, as evident in its frequent recourse to the legal system and to arguments from legal language.

My discussion opens with an analysis of a ruling issued by Chief Justice Aharon Barak.[1] Justice Barak implicitly acknowledges in this ruling a distinction between these two types of discourse by pointing out the limitations of legal discourse that, as shown below, epitomizes the discourse of rights. He states:

> In Israel's public discourse, Bar-Ilan is no longer a road and has become a social concept. It signals a deep political controversy between ultra-Orthodox and secularists. It is not merely a conflict about freedom of movement on the Sabbath. Fundamentally, it is a harsh conflict about the relationship between religion and state in Israel, a glaring dispute about the character of Israel as a Jewish or democratic state. This conflict has now turned up at the Court and we must decide on it, despite the political consequences.[2]

According to Justice Barak, at play in *Bar-Ilan Road* are a political-social context and a legal context. Whereas the political-social context reflects the fundamental controversy between ultra-Orthodox and secular Jews concerning the character of the State of the Israel, the legal context touches on the issue of freedom of movement on the Sabbath. Following this distinction, Justice Barak states:

> Our concern is not the social dispute, our considerations are not political. Our interest is the legal controversy; our considerations are normative. We do not deal with the relationship between ultra-Orthodox and secularists in Israel; the issue for us is not the relationship between religion and state in Israel... Our interest is simply the Bar-Ilan Road, the mandate of the Central Signposting Authority, and the latitude of its discretion. Our concern is the relationship between freedom of movement on the one hand, and hurting religious feelings and a religious way of life on the other.[3]

Justice Barak is aware of apprehensions lest the role of the legal system in the context of the political-social discourse be misunderstood, given that legal issues are only one aspect of the broader public context. He therefore adds:

> Many are concerned that the court might be viewed as if it had abandoned its proper place and descended into the arena of public controversy... In this sense I see myself here, compelled as I am by law to rule on all issues brought before the Court, as working under an imposition, well knowing that the public will not pay attention to the legal rationale but only to the final conclusion, and the Court's standing as an institution that is above publicly divisive matters might be hurt. What can we do, however, when this is our role and our obligation as judges?[4]

Relying on this analysis, Justice Barak then argues that the Court is not a suitable venue for dealing with this confrontation, which should instead be returned to its natural context — the public-social arena where it originated. He recommends "reaching social consensus between the various segments of the public in all that concerns transportation during the Sabbath."[5] Justice Barak even outlines the suitable parameters of such a consensus, claiming it should be based on extensive discussion and should develop mechanisms for interpersonal dialogue. In his formulation, "this consensus will be based on mutual patience and tolerance" and will have to offer solutions for the specific problem on the public agenda as well as examine its broader context. Hence, "not only will it focus on the question of whether the Bar-Ilan road should be closed to traffic on the Sabbath, but will also deal with the projected social dynamic and with its influence on secular-religious relationships in Jerusalem in coming years."[6]

This analysis, then, assumes that the legal context is essentially different from the public socio-political context, since legal procedures are confined to the specific problem presented to the court by plaintiffs and defendants. The judicial decision determines who won and who lost the lawsuit. It is not interested in the parties' interpersonal relations or in the future of the relationships between the social groups to which they belong.

In these statements, Justice Barak implicitly acknowledges the existence of two different types of discourse in Israeli society: a rights discourse and an identity discourse. In terms of this conceptual framework, Justice Barak is claiming that the rights discourse cannot replace the identity discourse. The constant transposition of the identity discourse to a key of rights may actually distort its meaning and, thereby, its broader social context. A systematic analysis of the phenomenology that characterizes these two types of discourse is my concern in the following sections.

2. THE RIGHTS DISCOURSE

In a discourse of rights, a negotiation process unfolds between two parties: the plaintiffs, who demand their rights, and the defendants, who are the object of a claim imposing on them matching obligations. This discourse may, but need not, take place within a court of law. A discourse of rights prevails wherever its features prevail and, for instance, the relationship between a client and a bank clerk also belongs in this category. The distinguishing feature of a rights discourse, then, is not its location but the identification of the parties as plaintiffs and defendants.

Let us consider the concept of right, which underlies this discourse. A detailed analysis of the meaning of this concept and of the logical relationships between rights and obligations exceeds the scope of this paper. Note, however, the two types of theories attempting to explain the meaning and the role of the concept of right: theories of interest and theories of will.[7] Theories of interest, linked to the philosophical tradition of utilitarianism, assume that the role of rights is to promote individual or group interests, whereas theories of will, linked to the Kantian philosophical tradition, assume that the role of rights is to promote individual or group autonomy.

For the purposes of this discussion, I endorse the theory of interest that Joseph Raz proposes for the concept of right.[8] Raz points to the role of this concept in practical thinking: claiming that an individual or a group have a right usually implies that the interest of the individual or the group is a sufficient reason for claiming that others are under an obligation.

Obviously, not every individual or group interest turns automatically into a right; only a sufficiently valuable and important interest imposes a matching obligation on the other.

In this definition, however, the concept of right assumes an additional dimension, which conditions the very possibility of a rights discourse. If a right is a demand from the other, this implies the existence of some legal system — judicial, moral, or other — agreed upon by the parties to the discourse. In the absence of a shared legal system, to speak of a right as a demand from the other is meaningless.

Although a rights discourse does involve interaction, it is not a dialogue. First, interaction in a rights discourse hinges on particular interests, and the meeting takes place only in their perspective. In a dialogue, two individuals meet in the fullness of their human existence. In the terms of Emannuel Lévinas, human beings in a dialogue meet each other's "face," whereas parties to a rights discourse meet their own needs and interests, namely, themselves. In the perspective of a rights discourse, the other is either plaintiff or defendant.

Second, constitutive relationships in a rights discourse are hierarchical rather than symmetrical, whereas parties to a dialogue face each other in their full concreteness as equal creatures. This difference reflects a difference in their basic situation: while a dialogue involves direct address, a rights discourse uses the language of law and thus incorporates the law's fundamental characteristics.

The law, in Aristotle's terms, is meant to establish legal justice, which is basically conveyed through the generality of the law, namely, the possibility of applying the law equally to all those bound by it.[9] As Aristotle had already noted, however, generality entails limitations, insofar as it hinders special consideration of individual cases, thus possibly leading to injustice. Aristotle argued that we might overcome this limitation through equity. The equitable man, argued Aristotle, is one who "does not stand on his rights unduly, but is content to receive a smaller share although he has the law on his side."[10]

If we translate Aristotle's position into the conceptual terms of the rights discourse, we could argue that a rights discourse, which is based on the generality of the law, cannot exhaust the complexity of human reality and should not be the sole language of human discourse. Aristotle sought to correct generality — or, in my terms, the rights discourse — by resorting to equity, which reflects a disposition different from justice. A rights discourse, as a discourse of legal justice, erases the other's face. It views others through concepts of rights and obligations, unlike equity, which sees them in their full concreteness. According to Lévinas, equity responds to the basic obligation under which I am placed by the other's face.

Equity does not require entering into a dialogue with the other, but makes dialogue possible even within a legal rights discourse. Fostering this disposition enables the individual to develop a perception of the other as worthy of respect and attention, and can even lead to a limitation of the self in order to make room for the other. A dialogue defined as turning to the other's face involves great danger, as Hegel, Jaspers, Ricoeur, and others have pointed out. When we open up to the world of the other, we may jeopardize our own world and identity. Partners to a dialogue know how they enter it but, if the dialogue is genuine, they do not know how they will leave it. A dialogue, in Hegel's terms, is a "life and death struggle," since the likelihood of something dying equals the likelihood of something being born.

Dialogue, then, is the antithesis of a rights discourse. In a rights discourse, the parties address each other obliquely and entrench themselves in their own territory, through the law, only to protect themselves from possible harm. In a dialogue, however, this territory is precisely what is encroached upon. A discourse of rights protects what Isaiah Berlin called the individual's negative liberty, the domain where individuals will not be disturbed and will be autonomous to do as they please.[11] A rights discourse is meant to protect "our castle," our concrete and spiritual home, preserving the surrounding walls in line with the legal constraints. In a dialogue, borders are breached, walls are cracked open, and the protected territory becomes the main topic of the dialogical "struggle." Dialogue, by definition, is a struggle over the very meaning of identity. A rights discourse is thus meant to preserve the personal, biographical, cultural, and economic identity of individuals and of society, whereas a dialogical relationship tears this identity apart.

One remarkable outcome emerges from this analysis: the two main theories of right noted above share a model of right as a fundamental concept, involving recognition of the value and identity of human beings. According to the theory of interest, the concept of right recognizes human beings as persons with interests worth protecting. The concept of right thus recognizes the value of human beings as holding interests that, by definition, will differ for various individuals or groups. The recognition of interests as rights thus assumes that the unique identity of those holding interests is a value deserving normative protection.

The concept of right in the theory of will also recognizes the autonomy of individuals or groups as a value worth protecting. In a Kantian sense, the concept of right conveys the recognition that "man...exists as an end in itself, and not merely as a means to be arbitrarily used by this or that will."[12] The concept of right expresses the notion that human beings are unique persons worthy of respect. In Kant's formulation, human beings are "persons inasmuch as their nature already marks them out as ends in themselves, i.e., as something which is not to be used merely as means, and there is imposed thereby a limit on all arbitrary use of such beings, which are thus objects of respect."[13] Right protects the person, and in the name of protecting the right of one, it sets limitations on the realization of another's will.

Both theories of the concept of right, then, affirm the value of human beings. Moreover, both affirm the value of particular identity: the theory of interest does so directly, since the interest is an expression of this identity, and the theory of will does so indirectly, since protecting autonomy enables the space required for particular identities to grow and thrive. The concept of right thus sets the foundation for the growth of identity.

The symmetry between rights and obligations also reflects this notion. A right usually imposes a parallel obligation. In James Nickel's words: "Rights have assignable addresses, people or agencies who bear normative burdens such as duties, liabilities, and disabilities."[14] As Nickel notes, this is the presumption underlying the ubiquitous question concerning human rights: who is responsible for realizing them? The standard answer to this question is that this responsibility is incumbent on states, but although this answer is correct in some cases, it fails to give the full picture. Nickel shows that many rights in the 1948 UN Declaration of Human Rights impose an obligation on individuals as well and not necessarily on the state. This is true concerning Section 4, for instance, which forbids slavery or slave trading. Slave traders or slave owners are individuals, so that the right to freedom from slavery imposes an obligation not only on governments but also on individuals.[15]

The acknowledgement of an obligation and a responsibility toward the other derived from the concept of right is an act involving self-restraint on the one hand and, on the other, the performance of concrete activities for the other's sake. In this sense, the right presumes the space wherein people grow and prosper as particular creatures. The rights discourse thus lays the foundation for an identity discourse through the very act of protecting it. Jeremy Waldron explicitly formulates these insights when pointing out that rights do not establish social life, but do set the foundation on which human beings will establish social life:

> The structure of impersonal rules and rights not only provides a background guarantee; it also furnishes a basis on which people can initiate new relations with other people even from a position of alienation from the affective bonds of existing attachments and community. Impersonal rules and rights provide a basis for new beginnings and for moral initiatives which challenge existing affections.[16]

Waldron thus claims, accurately in my view, that the power of the rights framework is precisely in its detachment from the immediate social context, a detachment ensuring that basic human existence, regardless of internal social changes, is safe and secure.[17]

But when the public discourse is confined to a rights discourse, when a rights discourse is not the scaffold of interpersonal discourse but its most thorough expression, it erodes, hinders, and harms the identity discourse. In this type of rights discourse, human beings perceive each other only in instrumental terms, from an egoistic perspective and without undue care for the other.[18] Waldron sums this up succinctly: "To stand on one's rights is to distance oneself from those to whom the claim is made; it is to announce, so to speak, an opening of hostilities, and it is to acknowledge that other warmer bonds of kinship, affection and intimacy can no longer hold."[19]

Relying on this analysis, my central claim is that the status of the rights discourse in any given culture is the litmus test of its internal social discourse, and of the relationship between self and other. The greater the dominance of a rights discourse mode in the public, internal social discourse, the less vital the interpersonal cultural dialogue. When the rights discourse becomes the only one prevailing in a given society, it leads to rigid borders between its various elements and to relationships of mutual alienation and self-seclusion. It also makes true dialogue in an identity discourse impossible.

3. THE IDENTITY DISCOURSE

In an identity discourse, individuals meet one another in the fullness of their existence. An identity discourse involves an encounter where the core of the parties' identity is at the center, as opposed to another, more prevalent mode of encounter, where we perceive them as "entities" endowed with certain qualities and characterized by certain modes of functioning. In these processes of objectification, the other, be it an individual or a society, is fixed within pre-set molds. The other is a "bank clerk," a "doctor," or a "police officer," "secular" or "religious." When objectifying others in this fashion, we tend to perceive their wholeness through one or several constitutive traits.[20] As soon as we have identified these traits in the other, we ascribe to them additional secondary traits, which we usually tend to link to the main ones. A secular person will be someone to whom freedom is important, for whom self-realization is decisive, and so forth. A religious person will be an obedient, compliant individual, for whom self-realization is less significant.

The complement to this objectification of the other is the objectification and rigidity of the self, which is now interpreted through categories and traits to be contrasted with the other. The subject-object relationship is not unidirectional and unilateral. People who turn others into pre-set objects will also perceive themselves in similar fashion. If I perceive the other "as," or "being like" something specific, this is how I will perceive myself. In a society where I perceive others through this type of conceptual frameworks, we can expect others to answer in kind. But although subject-object relationships are naturally hierarchical and asymmetrical, they are not synonymous with those prevailing in a rights discourse. In a rights discourse, hierarchical and asymmetrical relationships move in one direction, from plaintiff to defendant, whereas interpersonal relationships mediated by subject-object relationships are characterized by a mutual activation of hierarchy and asymmetry. This type of discourse, then, as Hegel describes it in the "dialectic of master and slave,"[21] is a process that largely deprives the parties of their very essence as free, full human creatures. In Hegelian terms, this is a process where each one kills the other.

The contrary process unfolds in an identity discourse, which is liberated from mutual objectification and from the ascription of specific traits or categories to the other. In an identity discourse, self and other meet in their concrete fullness. Although it might include aspects of objectification, the uniqueness of this discourse lies in the parties' ability to release each other from them and, in Hegelian terms, to struggle for mutual life rather than mutual death.[22] This discourse is communicative rather than epistemological — the parties talk to one another rather than about each other. It unfolds through confession and narrative as well as by listening to the other's "voice," and includes an ongoing process of correcting mutual preconceptions. An identity discourse is *ipso facto* particular, since identity differentiates and draws distinctions between individuals and groups. It addresses the unique and, in many ways, it is therefore a process of shattering stigmas, generalizations, and stereotypes.

4. The Concept of Identity in a Rights Discourse and in an Identity Discourse

The concept of identity emerges as significantly different in these two types of discourse. The rights discourse recognizes the intrinsic value of all human beings. All human beings are entitled to equal recognition since all represent universal human nature or the universal human identity. The rights discourse thus provides the space required for the growth of human identities that are essentially particular, but does so as an application of a universal concept rather than as part of a genuine identity discourse:

> All human beings as the bearers of a universal human nature as persons — are of equal value from the democratic perspective, and all people as persons deserve equal respect and equal opportunity for self-realization. In other words, from the liberal-democratic point of view, a person has a right to claim equal recognition first and foremost on the basis of his or her universal human identity and potential, not primarily on the basis of an ethnic identity.[23]

The recognition that human beings have rights rests on this universal human identity. This recognition applies equally to the universal rights that all human beings share and to the particular rights of individuals or of groups. From a rights discourse perspective, the recognition of particular aspects worthy of protection is a clear expression of a universal human foundation: the general human capability to mold individual patterns of identity.[24]

Hence, even if the rights discourse focuses on a particular right of individuals or of specific groups, it does not represent a concern with these particular aspects *per se*. A discourse of rights concerned with particular rights does not address the fullness and concreteness of the specific individual or group whose rights it means to protect. It acknowledges that each one has a personality with unique features, but is not truly concerned with these features and with this personal identity.

This distinction between a rights discourse and a genuine interest in the other is well illustrated in two fundamental issues: the prevalent defenses of the right to culture on the one hand, and of pluralism on the other.

Will Kymlicka adduces one of the better-known arguments for the right to culture, based on the recognition of a universal right to freedom. In his view, the right to culture expresses this fundamental right because an essential component of the potential to realize the right to freedom is contingent on the ability of human beings to examine and evaluate their ends and values, and change them if they feel them to be mistaken. The spectrum of cultural possibilities provides the options, from which individuals will choose those that suit them.[25] Cultural particularism for Kymlicka, then, is merely a necessary condition for realizing the universal value of freedom rather than an intrinsically valuable feature.

Kymlicka's critics too, such as Avishai Margalit and Moshe Halbertal, who propose a defense of the right to culture that links it to a personal particular identity, resort to a perspective typical of the rights discourse: lack of genuine interest in the other as a particular "entity":

> The individual's right to culture stems from the fact that every person has an overriding interest in his personality identity — that is, in preserving his way of life and the traits that are central identity components for him and the other members of his cultural group. Mainly, we consider the best formulation of the right to culture to be internal to the viewpoint of the members of a particular culture.[26]

This defense of the right to culture, contrary to the defense proposed by Kymlicka, takes into account the internal perspective of the specific group — what its members consider important and valuable. Kymlicka had assumed that the supreme value justifying the right to culture is freedom, but freedom is not a value that every cultural community endorses. Margalit and Halbertal, who reject Kymlicka's argument, wish to make the internal perspective of the identity bearers the basis of the defense of the right to culture.

This approach does represent an important shift from Kymlicka's liberal position since it relates seriously to the variety of human identities and acknowledges that identity is the core of the right to culture. Such an approach could represent a change in the disposition toward the other because, by nature, it begins by directing attention to the other. And yet, this need not be the case. This defense of the right to culture rests on the recognition that human beings shape particular cultures, which endow their lives with meaning. Interest in the other, however, is not a necessary sequel. The necessary assumption of this defense is that the bearers of a particular culture have an interest in it, and that this interest suffices to justify this defense. But this assumption does not inevitably lead to the conclusion that the defenders of this right are also interested in the specific identity embodied in a particular culture. In other words, this defense of the right to culture recognizes the ability of human beings to shape private identities, which are then materialized in specific cultures. It does not necessarily denote a transition to an identity discourse.

The second issue allowing us to infer that a rights discourse is not identical with a genuine interest in the other concerns, as noted, the prevalent defenses of pluralism. Pluralism is an approach that recognizes and affirms the intrinsic value of different views.[27] Ostensibly, the obvious conclusion is that a pluralist is a person interested in the other since the other represents an intrinsically valuable fullness. But the more common defenses of pluralism show no necessary link between pluralism and its implications for both a rights discourse and for the acknowledgement of the other's value as a constitutive element of identity. In other words, pluralists are not compelled to enter into an identity discourse by virtue of their pluralistic stance.

There are two prominent defenses of pluralism. According to one, advocated by John Stuart Mill and later by Berlin, pluralism denotes recognition of the value of individualism that, as Mill notes, comes to the fore in human differences: "It is not by wearing down into uniformity all that is individual in themselves ... that human beings become a noble and beautiful object of contemplation."[28] Human differences, then, create variety and diversity between various lifestyles, all equally valuable. Similarly, Berlin argues that pluralism is "the conception that there are many different ends that men may seek."[29] The acknowledgement of human diversity is a descriptive statement but also a prescriptive one, and assumes that individuality can only develop and grow within a pluralistic worldview. At the same time, however, this view of pluralism assumes that personal or group identity is static and distinct; in fact, the recognition of sharply marked differences is the very hallmark of this view. Pluralists, then, do not necessarily engage in a genuine identity discourse since they need not show any interest in the other. The other does not represent possibilities that might ever become personally relevant. Nor do pluralists require the other in order to become aware of their own uniqueness. This type of pluralism conveys nothing more than recognition of the universal human potential to shape particular identities.

Raz suggests another defense of pluralism. In his view, pluralism is a necessary condition of human autonomy. Autonomous individuals are those who shape their lives and control their destiny as far as possible, as expressed in their choices. But freedom of choice, argues Raz, is not sufficient for an individual to be truly autonomous. Individuals must choose between different and contradictory options, and no "autonomy" to speak of is possible in the absence of options to choose from. The selection cannot be limited to a choice between good and evil, and must be a choice between several good options that are nevertheless different.[30]

But this approach does not require entering into a genuine identity discourse either since the other plays an instrumental role here, and provides various options serving to expand autonomy. Both Raz and Kymlicka view concrete cultures and identities as means for self-realization and for enhancing freedom. A pluralistic worldview, then, can coexist with disinterest in the other as such, since pluralism is either a conclusion derived from an overall universal principle — the human ability to shape individual identities — or no more than a means to the end of individual freedom.

By contrast, in an identity discourse, the particularistic aspect as such — the other's full face — is the subject of the discourse. An identity discourse, therefore, does not focus on the question of rights but on the dialogue with the other. "The other," in Mead's terms, is a "significant other," who makes a crucial contribution to shaping the identity of the self.[31]

Individuals and groups meeting in a discourse of identity are interested in the other for one of the following two reasons: (1) Because the other represents existential possibilities that could become relevant to their own existence.[32] The other, then, plays a decisive existential role in the development of their own identity that, through the encounter, will evolve in a ceaseless process affecting its most basic patterns.

(2) Because, through the encounter with the other, individuals or groups become aware of the real limits of their own identity.[33] In other words, their self-awareness is mediated through their awareness of the other.

The identity discourse, then, focuses on the other's particular identity, in a mutual process that Karl Jaspers succinctly defines as follows:

> I cannot be sure of myself unless I am sure of him. In communication I feel responsible not only for myself but for the other .... I do not reach the point of communication by my own action alone; the other's action must match it. An agonizingly, externally inadequate relationship becomes inevitable at the moment when the other, instead of coming to meet me, turns himself into my object... Only mutual recognition allows both of us to rise as ourselves. Only together can we reach the goal each one is aiming at.[34]

The relationship between a rights discourse and an identity discourse can now be formulated more clearly. The rights discourse is the ground floor of the identity discourse, since it assumes both a universal and an individual identity, even if not at its focus. The rights discourse is not concerned with identity as such but with the rights derived from it, and identity remains in it as an abstract particularity, meaning that the identity and those of its features relevant to the rights discourse are acknowledged, but without dealing with it directly.

Even when the discourse is one of identity, however, it still entails implications for the discourse of rights discourse because the particularistic identity discourse brings the issue of rights to the fore. When the identity discourse reveals that the differences between the parties are so profound that they feel threatened, the protection of diversity is translated in the public political arena into a discourse of rights. Since the identities are different, so are the interests, and the rights are the normative formulation of these interests.

The social and interpersonal dynamic that develops in a public discourse confined to a context of rights is strikingly different from that evolving in a discourse whose basic context is one of identity. A society or an interpersonal relationship based on a discourse of rights indicates that the society or the parties to the discourse have lost their sense of solidarity and of personal attachment. The rights discourse is evidence of self-seclusion and perhaps alienation. The law predicated on this discourse is the product of a balance of power. It cannot provide a basis for social solidarity nor can it replace the intricate web of personal relationships. Hence, a society whose members communicate exclusively through a discourse of rights comes perilously close to losing its connecting bonds. A discourse of rights as the sole form of discourse attests to these circumstances and also accelerates the centrifugal processes of closure and social collapse.

By contrast, when the public discourse develops mainly in an identity context, it is characterized by mutual attention and openness, by the overpowering of self-seclusion and alienation. When a rights discourse takes place in this setting, it undergoes modification. Even when there are plaintiffs and defendants, the aim of the discourse is to find the way to a social agreement that balances the interests and rights of the parties to the identity discourse. A rights discourse in this context does not seek victory over the other, but rather the protection of both plaintiff and defendant. Hence, if the natural locale of the rights discourse is the court, the rights discourse typical of the identity discourse will find its home in public consensus.

5. Israeli Society: Between an Identity Discourse and a Rights Discourse

The description so far has outlined the contexts of the two types of discourse. A unique situation emerges, however, when one party engages in an identity discourse and the other in a rights discourse. Richard Rorty refers to this situation as an "abnormal discourse,"[35] or a discourse without agreed rules that turns into a kind of monologue.

A telling instance of this type of discourse is the *Bar-Ilan Road* ruling. According to Justice Barak, the issues at stake in this case are freedom of movement on the one hand, and "hurting religious feelings and a religious way of life" on the other. Justice Barak qualifies this statement by pointing out that this description reflects the legal context of the discussion, but why not assume that this is also the definition of the public problem? Freedom of movement is a concept taken from the rights discourse, and "hurting feelings" or "hurting a religious way of life" are concepts taken from an identity discourse. The controversy between the parties is thus unfolding in two different domains — the secular public is struggling for its right to freedom of movement, whereas the ultra-Orthodox public is struggling to preserve its religious way of life. In their view, traveling through their neighborhood on the Sabbath strikes at the very heart of their Jewish identity and requires that travel be stopped.

Justice Barak also raised this issue, although favoring a rhetoric of hurt feelings:[36]

> A religious community expects the Sabbath rest not to be confined to the individual domain of its members, but to envelop and inspire the public domain.... A street through the heart of the neighborhood involving a significant volume of traffic, the din of horns and the noise of engines, are definitely in sharp contrasts with the Sabbath atmosphere envisioned by its residents.[37]

Although this would appear to be a classic case of abnormal discourse — one side concerned with the protection of its rights and the other with the protection of its identity — the picture is more complex. For many secularists, protecting their *right* to freedom of movement is an indirect way of protecting their secular *identity*. They use the language of rights to protect their secular identity since for them, as well as for many ultra-Orthodox, forbidding travel on the Sabbath implies disregard for the secular Jewish option. Forbidding travel on the Sabbath would suggest that the religious-traditional version of Judaism is acceptable and the secular version is not.

The problem cannot remain solely within the bounds of an identity discourse from an ultra-Orthodox perspective either because, once identity is threatened, the protection of the identity's vital interests translates into a rights discourse.

Since it simultaneously involves dimensions of rights and identity, then, this is indeed an "abnormal discourse." Nevertheless, it could be translated into either one of these two dimensions. Returning to Justice Barak's legal description of this clash as a conflict between the right to freedom of movement and hurting the feelings of the religious public is thus uncalled for.

6. ISRAELI PUBLIC DISCOURSE AS A MONOLOGUE: REFLECTIONS AND CONCLUSIONS

The characterization of Israeli public discourse as abnormal implies that it is fundamentally monological. This concept seems paradoxical at first glance, since monologue is the antithesis of a discourse involving several parties. Hence, monological discourse would be better characterized as an "apparent discourse," since each side talks to itself rather than to the other. Although it assumes a dialogical garb, it casts doubt on the very possibility of dialogue. In order to clarify this point, some basic differences between dialogue and monologue will be discussed below.

In a monologue, the speaking party is interested in its own story and its own perceptions. The other is not present or, at most, serves as a passive "entity" meant to absorb and internalize the speaker's world. A monologue is based on an unambiguous hierarchy: one speaks and the other listens. The speaking party assumes that its narrative, its truth, have absolute value and must therefore be told, and is not genuinely interested in the listener's account. The face and the world of the other are erased, as it were, because they do not sustain a meaningful world holding any interest to the speaking party. A monological world is predicated on one certainty, the speaker's, and on a monistic perception of values.

One of the main tasks of monological discourse, then, is to convince the listener to accept the one and only truth the speaker believes in and also to persuade the speaker anew, reaffirming the absolute value of his or her world. The monologue, then, dismisses the fullness of the other: if the speaker's truth is equally valid for everyone, no special validity attaches to this particular person, with a unique face and a specific culture and personality. All the listeners have the same face, all have been flattened into uniformity and equality, their uniqueness stamped out. To use Hegel's aphorism, "at night all cows are black." The monologue is the night that makes the other's world invisible.

A dialogue represents the exact antithesis. As noted in Section 2, parties to a dialogue meet each other in the fullness of their unique personalities.

They want to hear the voice of the other and absorb all the other's features. A dialogue is an effort to return to human beings their face, their world, and their unique value. In a dialogue, there is speech and also attention and silence. Through them, each of the parties to the dialogue becomes passive in turn, limiting themselves and making room for the other. Each party goes through the dual experience of control and passivity, of speech and attentive silence.

Monological time is, in truth, only apparent time, since no change process is taking place and people leave it as they entered it. Monological discourse becomes a means for transmitting contents whose value is beyond time and beyond the monologue situation. The monologue is supposed to eliminate itself, since its content is not contingent on speech and its value is eternal. By contrast, time in the dialogue is compressed, dramatic, each moment bearing a unique fullness. The true dialogical event changes the parties' lives, and each one absorbs something from the other. This absorption may subvert something in their previous being and identity, just as it may sharpen and clarify the differences between them. Dialogical time, then, is unique.

In a dialogue, experience is based on an acknowledgement of the other's intrinsic worth. Each of the parties is a creature that deserves respect, since each bears a fullness, an individuality, and a valuable world. In other words, true dialogue assumes one or another version of pluralism rather than of monism.

Pluralistic dialogical discourse, as noted in Section 4, can be predicated on two dissimilar and even contradictory assumptions. The first assumption acknowledges that the other portrays a full and meaningful world, which could also be a relevant option for the partner to the dialogue. The world of the other, then, is an open possibility. The second assumption, in many ways antithetical, is that through the dialogical discourse individuals learn about the differences between themselves and others — their own world becomes clearer and sharper. One assumption, then, views dialogical discourse as opening up new possibilities; according to the other, dialogue leads to self-awareness. Individuals learn about the constitutive elements of their personality and their being by understanding the differences between themselves and their partners to the dialogue. According to this option, we learn about our world and our identity in indirect ways — by learning about the world of the other.

In either case, dialogical discourse invariably acknowledges the intrinsic value of the other's inner world, the importance of the encounter with the other for constituting and sharpening one's own identity. Monological discourse, however, sees no special value in it, since it is based on the expectation of the other's acquiescent silence at the end of the discourse.

Monologue is a crucial element of Israel's public discourse, as evident in its growing recourse to persuasive means and to a rhetoric lacking openness and attentiveness. The background of this process are the deep cleavages between various elements of Israeli society. No wonder, then, that this monological discourse is gradually transformed into a rights discourse, which equips the monologue with a tool for action in the public-political field. The monologue, seeking to impose one narrative, is translated into a formal language of rights bearing no trace of the concrete identity that engendered it. On the surface, a discourse of rights makes it possible to mask the clash between the various cultural identities making up Israel's social web. A discourse of rights appears to confirm the monological discourse, thus reaffirming the intrinsic value of the speaker's identity.

Against a background of diverse identities, however, the framework enabling the rights discourse is itself threatened. Some segments of Israeli society question the legitimacy of the legal framework that constitutes the basis of the rights discourse, precisely because they negate the identities that the rights discourse seeks to protect.

A negotiating process exclusively based on a discourse of rights could lead to growing alienation, given the basic nature of this discourse and the status of the parties involved. Then again, a negotiating process taking place within an identity discourse may be harder and more painful at the start, since the various identities question and threaten each other. A true identity discourse, however, relies on and fosters dispositions of mutual attentiveness and openness; when these are applied to the organization of a shared public life, they could evolve into a rights discourse conducted out of respect for the other rather than as an imposition.

The Israeli preference for a rights discourse is particularly evident in the making of the courts the arena for deciding the most vital issues of public life. But even concerning public matters discussed outside the confines of the court, we have recently witnessed renewed attempts to organize public life by formulating fixed social contracts, seeking remedy through the panacea of social agreement.

Social agreements and contracts are by nature another form of the rights discourse. They freeze contractual parties in set, fixed frames. They balance the interests of various parties. Furthermore, social contracts are a game in which various political participants claim to be the true "voice" of the different constituencies they supposedly represent, while they actually represent mainly power, influence, and control of resources. The garb of "pastoral" (a term coined by Michel Foucalt) power, which politicians and public opinion leaders sometimes choose to wear, is a screen often hiding political interests and far more brutal aspects. Awareness of the brutal dimension of the political field was purportedly meant to lead to a deep-seated aversion to political involvement. In Israel, however, pastoral political discourse is an acceptable alternative to genuine identity discourse. The Israeli public still prefers to meet the other in what Ariel Rosen-Zvi called "an encounter at the level of results,"[38] implying a negotiation at the level of the rights discourse that relinquishes the other's "face," the living dialogue with other, intrinsically full worlds. A political discourse centered on social contracts clearly suits this model.

These processes enable normal life to proceed for a limited period, but they cannot replace the discourse of identity. Indeed, since they actually threaten it, these processes incur painful costs — growing estrangement, the stoking of mutual frustrations, and the loosening of solidarity bonds.

Public discourse in Israel resorts to a rights discourse chiefly in order to evade the problematic entailed by an identity discourse, which is conducted mainly along lines involving the other's total denial. The other is not only the one who is not I, whose identity differs from mine, through whom I can learn about the actual limits of my own identity. The other is the one whose identity casts doubts on mine, and who must therefore be totally denied so that I may affirm my own. This description is true whether the other is a Jew or an Arab, secular, religious, or ultra-Orthodox.[39]

In this backdrop of conflicting identities, however, when the framework that enables the discourse of rights is itself in jeopardy, Israeli society cannot circumvent the identity discourse much longer without risking ominous consequences. This is particularly true at present, when the various communities making up Israeli society have become increasingly self-assured about the fullness of their own identity. A paradoxical result might obtain in these circumstances: a rights discourse designed to protect the various identities could emerge as the force that will crush the solidarity bonds tying these communities together. Barring a profound change in the way Israeli society thinks about itself, the seams that hold its web together may not hold. The rights discourse that had protected this web in the past is no longer viable and must now give way to the identity discourse.

What will an identity discourse in Israeli society look like? This question must remain open because in an identity discourse, unlike a rights discourse, the borders and modes of discussion are not pre-defined and will be decided by the participants.

Despite this immanent opacity, the character of this identity discourse will largely be defined by the dispositions of the parties concerning the relationship between the shaping of the self and of the other. Increasing awareness of this relationship brings the identity discourse closer to an attentive dialogue while, as this awareness lessens, the identity discourse turns into a monologue gradually dwindling into a perilous discourse of rights.

Israeli society stands at a crucial crossroads. On the one hand, it appears to have exhausted the rights discourse without having shaped a suitable alternative. On the other, the tapering of a dominant cultural hegemony and the increasing awareness of Israel as a multicultural society compel the adoption of new modes of discourse, lest Israeli multiculturalism comes down to a struggle between cultures and a growing negation of solidarity between society's various elements.

Will Israeli society succeed in developing a new discourse, richer and more fruitful, capable of dealing with questions of identity? Will the emerging identity discourse avoid a return to monological discourse? How will the new identity discourse unfold? I cannot answer these questions within an analytical, philosophical outline. Responses to these questions may emerge, if at all, in the concrete experiences of the real world, confronting obstacles and challenges.

NOTES

Thanks to Eliezer Goldman, Dror Yinon, and Menachem Mautner, who read several versions of this article. I am grateful for their useful and fruitful comments. Special thanks to Batya Stein who translated this article from the Hebrew.

[1]   *Lior Horev v. The Ministry of Transport*, Supreme Court of Justice 5016/96, PD 51(4) 1 (henceforth *Bar-Ilan Road*).

[2]   Ibid., p. 15.

[3]   Ibid.

[4]   Ibid.

[5]   Ibid., p. 25.

[6]   Ibid.

[7]   The discussion that follows is based on the analysis outlined by James W. Nickel, *Making Sense of Human Rights: Philosophical Reflections on the Universal Declaration of Human Rights* (Berkeley, CA: University of California Press, 1987). See, in particular, pp. 19–23.

[8]   Joseph Raz, "On the Nature of Rights," *Mind* 93 (1984): 94.

9   Aristotle, *The Nichomachean Ethics*, trans. Harris Rackham (Hertfordshire, England: Wordsworth, 1996), 5:x, pp. 133–134. For further discussion, see Chaim Perelman, *Justice, Law, and Argument: Essays on Moral and Legal Reasoning* (Dordrecht, Holland: Reidel, 1980).

10   Ibid., p. 134.

11   Isaiah Berlin, *Four Essays on Liberty* (Oxford: Oxford University Press, 1969), pp. 118–172.

12   Immanuel Kant, *Groundings for the Metaphysics of Morals*, trans. William Ellington (Indianapolis, IN: Hackett, 1981), p. 35.

13   Ibid., p. 36.

14   Nickel, *Making Sense of Human Rights*, p. 41.

15   Ibid., p. 42.

16   Jeremy Waldron, *Liberal Rights: Collected Papers 1981–1991* (Cambridge: Cambridge University Press, 1993), p. 376. See, in particular, ch. 15.

17   Ibid., p. 379.

18   *Cf.* Jeffrey C. Alexander, "The Paradoxes of Civil Society," *International Sociology* 12 (1997): 115–133.

19   Waldron, *Liberal Rights*, p. 373. Waldron relies here on Hegel.

20   On the distinction between central and secondary status features, see Everett C. Hughes, "Dilemmas and Contradictions of Status," *American Journal of Sociology* 4 (1945): 353–359.

21   Georg Wilhelm Hegel, *Phenomenology of Spirit* (Oxford: Clarendon Press, 1979), pp. 111–119. For an exceptionally brilliant analysis of Hegel's text, see Yitzhak Klein, *The Dialectic of Master and Slave* [Hebrew] (Tel-Aviv: Am Oved, 1978).

22   My interpretation of Hegel here is based largely on Klein's analysis (ibid.).

23   Steven C. Rockefeller, "Comment," in Charles Taylor, *Multiculturalism: Examining the Politics of Recognition*, ed. Amy Gutmann (Princeton: Princeton University Press, 1994), p. 88.

24   Ibid. In the same volume, see also Charles Taylor, "The Politics of Recognition," p. 42.

25   See Will Kymlicka, *Liberalism, Community, and Culture* (Oxford: Clarendon Press, 1989), ch. 8.

26   Avishai Margalit and Moshe Halbertal, "Liberalism and the Right to Culture," *Social Research* 61 (1994): 505.

27   See Avi Sagi, *Jewish Religion after Theology*, trans. Batya Stein (Boston: Academic Studies Press, 2009), ch. 1.

28   John Stuart Mill, *On Liberty* (Harmondsworth: Penguin Books, 1982), p. 127.

29   Isaiah Berlin, *The Crooked Timber of Humanity: Chapters in the History of Ideas* (London: John Murray, 1990), p. 11. See also pp. 78–92. Robert Nozick has a similar view of pluralism, claiming that no one idea of the good life is equally suitable for all, and

an utopian society is one in which individuals can realize a way of life as long as they respect the rights of others. See Robert Nozick, *Anarchy, State, and Utopia* (New York: Basic Books, 1974).

30   See Joseph Raz, "Autonomy, Toleration, and the Harm Principle," in *Justifying Toleration: Conceptual and Historical Perspectives*, ed. Susan Mendus (New York: Cambridge University Press, 1988), pp. 156–157. *Cf.* S. I. Benn, "Freedom and the Concept of a Person," *Proceedings of the Aristotelian Society* 76 (1975–1976): 123–128.

31   See George Herbert Mead, *Mind, Self and Society: From the Standpoint of a Social Behaviorist* (Chicago: University of Chicago Press, 1934). For an analysis of Mead's approach, see Paul E. Pfuetze, *Self, Society, Existence: Human Nature and Dialogue in the Thought of George Herbert Mead and Martin Buber* (New York: Harpers Brothers, 1954).

32   Supporters of this approach include Søren Kierkegaard, Karl Jaspers, and Charles Taylor. See Avi Sagi, *Kierkegaard, Religion, and Existence: The Voyage of the Self*, trans. Batya Stein (Amsterdam and Atlanta, GA: Rodopi, 2000), pp. 61–62; Taylor, "The Politics of Recognition."

33   William Dilthey, *Descriptive Psychology and Historical Understanding*, trans. Richard M. Zaner and Kenneth L. Heiges (The Hague: Martinus Nijhoff, 1977), p. 134.

34   Karl Jaspers, *Philosophy*, trans. E. B. Ashton, vol. 2 (Chicago: University of Chicago Press, 1969), p. 53.

35   Richard Rorty, *Philosophy and the Mirror of Nature* (Princeton, NJ: Princeton University Press, 1979), p. 320.

36   For an analytical critique of the concept of "hurting religious feelings," and for the use of this concept in *Bar-Ilan Road*, see Daniel Statman, "Hurting Religious Feelings" [Hebrew], in *Multiculturalism in a Democratic and Jewish State*, ed. Menachem Mautner, Avi Sagi, and Ronen Shamir (Tel-Aviv: Ramot, 1998), pp. 133–188. For an analysis of the *Bar-Ilan Road* ruling, see p. 159, note 51, pp. 161–162.

37   *Bar-Ilan Road*, p. 64.

38   See Ariel Rosen-Zvi, "'A Jewish Democratic State': Spiritual Paternity, Alienation, and Symbiosis" [Hebrew], in *A Jewish Democratic State: An Anthology*, ed. Daphne Barak-Erez (Tel-Aviv: Ramot, 1996), p. 51.

39   Compare Yosef Hayim Yerushalmi, *Zakhor: Jewish History and Jewish Memory* (Seattle: University of Washington Press, 1982), ch. 4.

TRANSCENDING THE 'SECULARIZATION VS. TRADITIONALIZATION' DISCOURSE: JEWISH-ISRAELI TRADITIONISTS, THE POST-SECULAR, AND THE POSSIBILITIES OF MULTICULTURALISM

YAACOV YADGAR

1. INTRODUCTION

One of the major impediments on the maturation of viable multiculturalism has been the predominance of binary, dichotomous distinctions, which divide the world into allegedly 'coherent' and 'systematic' constructs of polar opposites. These opposites — defined by their extreme formulation of this or that sociocultural dilemma — are often taken to be marking the boundaries of the social world, hence as defining the (im)possibilities of maintaining structures of identity and culture which are not 'fully consistent' with either pole of the dominant opposition.

As critics have pointed out, such polar opposites are artificial constructs, the merit of which is limited mostly to the social-scientific world, which is preoccupied with formulating theories that would be universally applicable. Indeed, their 'scientific' value is rather obvious, as they allow for the conceptualization and pigeonholing of social — that is real — life into neat, systematic categories, and allow for the comparison of diverging cultures along a 'methodic' and 'universal' criteria. Moreover, a minority of people sometimes do find it comfortable to self-identify along these categories. However, most people are uncomfortable with such polar-opposites: their life is too complex and too 'inconsistent' (that is, combining different sets of sociocultural criteria, which are often incompatible with each other) — in short: too humane — to fit neatly into one binary opposite or another. Hence, the merit of overcoming the predominance of such dichotomies as the guiding coordinates for interpreting the sociocultural world for the development of a viable multicultural atmosphere is rather obvious. A more nuanced, tolerant approach that allows for the existence of complex, multilayered and often self-contradictory constructs of identity is essential in order for multiculturalism to truly take hold.

One of the major dichotomies to function as such a field- and possibilities- defining matrix has been the theory of secularization. This theory, which has advanced closest to becoming the guiding paradigm of the social sciences, constructs a complex worldview of a self-enforcing web of binary, dichotomous polar opposites, such as 'modern vs. traditional' (or 'primitive' in pre-politically-correct discourse), 'rational vs. irrational,' 'particular vs. universal,' 'progressive vs. backward,' and — most central of all — the 'religious vs. secular' distinction.

In what follows I wish to discuss both the predicament of maintaining such an identity that does not fit into either pole of a predominant dichotomous distinction, and the possibilities if offers for the (re)construction of a more tolerant, multicultural mindset. The dichotomy at hand, as the title of this paper suggests, is the one devised by the secularization and modernization thesis; and the alternative to be discussed here is what has come to be identified in Jewish-Israeli discourse as 'traditionism.' (This neologism, I shall contend, is the proper English translation to the Hebrew noun *masortiyut*; indeed, this very neologism stems from an attempt to overcome the unidimensional grid of secularism vs. traditio*nalism*, which is the product of the secularization discourse. More on this below.) I open with a discussion of the sociocultural phenomenon at hand, as well as a short presentation of the ways in which the secularization paradigm misrepresented and misinterpreted this phenomenon. This section also discusses the post-secular turn in the social-sciences as a possible fruitful alternative to the secularization thesis. The second part of the paper offers an alternative interpretation of several of the main components of traditionist identity, and discusses the possibilities suggested by it in regard to transcending the dichotomous worldview at hand.

2. Jewish Israeli Traditionism: A Short Introduction

People who identify as '*masorti*' (at least when asked to label their Jewish identity) constitute about one third of the Jewish-Israeli population. By comparison, fewer than 20 percent of Israeli Jews define themselves as either '*dati*' (i.e. 'religious', which is also a synonym for 'orthodox' in the Israeli context) or '*haredi*' ('ultra-orthodox'), while the remaining Israeli Jews define themselves as '*hiloni*' (secular).[1]

The meaning of these categories (which function as the basic outline for most studies of Jewish-Israeli society) and the differences between the categories are not entirely clear, and the category '*masorti*' (pl. *masortim*, deriving from *masoret*, Hebrew for 'tradition')[2] seems to have been the most enigmatic. Indeed, the very issue of the proper translation (hence understanding and interpretation) of the term '*masorti*' captures this *problematique* in whole. As I suggested above (and will elaborate below), I believe the proper way of approaching the issue is by overcoming the binary construct — which contrasts 'secularism' and 'tradition*alism*' as its two constitutive opposites — and translating *masorti* as traditio*nist*. This English neologism is aimed at distinguishing the *masorti* construct of identity from orthodox conservatism, which is often labeled as 'tradition*alism*.'[3] Edward Shils was probably the first to explicitly note the need to distinguish the traditionalist/orthodox stance from other forms of adherence to tradition (although he did not offer a label for this alternative option).[4] However, this notion is also implicit in several other major discussions regarding tradition.[5] Traditionism would thus denote an adherent stance toward tradition, which at the same time is non-orthodox, refusing to sanctify tradition in a conservative, traditio*nalist* manner.[6] I shall further discuss the issue below.

In any event, even among those who have stressed the demographic importance of this category among Israeli Jews, many have dismissed traditionism as no more than an inconsistent cocktail of beliefs and practices characterized by its lack of clarity. Oftentimes, it is used as a kind of intermediate category between the 'completely secular' and the 'really religious,' hence marked as a questionable form of identity of those who are 'both religious and secular' and hence neither of the two supposedly distinct categories. This use of the term renders traditionism or traditionist identity a kind of artificial or residual category located between two ideal types and lacking any meaning independent of these two other categories.

Viewed through the prism of the modernization and secularization paradigm, traditionism — which is a distinctly Mizrahi phenomenon[7] — has been usually described (or 'explained') as a transient by-product of the encounter between Jews who immigrated to Israel from 'pre-modern' (mostly Muslim) countries and the (allegedly) European-like, modern, secular nation-state. Thusly, traditionism has also been expected to dissolve and lose its demographic importance once Mizrahi Jews necessarily realign with the predominant (modern) axis of religious identities, becoming either 'secular' or 'religious.'[8]

Moreover, the predominance of the secularization and modernization discourse has led researchers to predict that traditionism's chances of survival are poor. But that forecast is not at all supported by an analysis of available data. According to the most updated surveys, even at the onset of the 21st century, a third of Israeli Jews still define themselves as traditionists — notwithstanding the rather intense processes of modernization and secularization that have taken place in the setting of the modern Israeli nation-state over the past sixty years. (Note that this figure does not include those who define themselves as secular and conduct, or rather observe, a lifestyle that is more than just close to traditionist practice). Nevertheless, from the point of view of both sociopolitical and academic discourses, traditionists' unique mixture of the supposedly mutually exclusive categories of traditional or tradition*alist* religiosity (usually understood in the Jewish-Israeli context as referring to observant adherence to the orthodox interpretation of Jewish Law) and modern secularism (correspondently understood as alluding to the total negation of- or indifference towards- these orthodox dictates) has rendered traditionist lifestyle allegedly 'inconsistent' and incomprehensible — hence neglectable and unworthy of proper representation in the public sphere.

Although traditionists have not 'disappeared' or 'dissolved' into the polar categories of Jewish identity, and although traditionists constitute a demographically significant minority, the traditionist voice has been rarely heard in the Israeli public sphere, even when it is manifestly relevant, as in the case of highly-charged and important debates (be they conducted in the popular-political arena or in academic circles) on the Jewish identity of Israelis, the Jewish nature of the Israeli public sphere and other issues associated with religion and politics in Israel. Needless to say, in the Israeli context, these issues constitute a fundamental part of any potential multicultural setting.

Contrary to this dismissive use and understanding of the term, when studied more closely, empathically yet critically, traditionism appears to be a uniquely modern phenomenon. It thus offers a fruitful alternative to the 'religious-secular' dichotomy, presenting a model of modernity that is not necessarily accompanied by secularization. Traditionism appears to be providing a different path through which modern Jewish identity can be preserved, updated and maintained. This alternative allows us to re-focus our attention on some cultural themes regarding Israeli identity that seem to have been neglected or overlooked by those scholars who have adhered to the modernization and secularization thesis. Furthermore, this perspective also sheds some new light on the complicated relation between Jewish identity, ethnicity and Israeli nationalism, hence enabling a novel critical view of Israeli secularism, opening up the discussion regarding multiculturalism in Israeli society.[9]

3. SOME THEORETICAL CONSIDERATIONS:
A POST-SECULAR PERSPECTIVE OF A 'SECULAR AGE'

The main characteristic of most (failed) attempts at understanding traditionist identity and practice has been the predominance of the secularization thesis as a guiding paradigm. This paradigm — or rather, as proposed by several students of secularism, this (meta-) narrative[10] — tends to construct a web of dichotomous distinctions, contrasting the modern, progressive, rational, and universal (that is, the 'secular') with the traditional (or 'primitive'), backward, irrational, and parochial (i.e. the 'religious'). Notably, this narrative tends to equate modernity with secularity, predicting (and expecting) that with the advent of modernization, religion is to be 'privatized' (that is, excluded from the public sphere). It also predicts that religious belief and practice are bound to decline in light of progressive, enlightened, and scientific modernity.[11]

Inside the domain of this paradigm (William Keenan suggests that we label secularism a 'big idea'[12]), traditionism is indeed an anomaly, refusing to fall into either of the 'systematic' categories constructed by the secularization narrative: 'complete' religiosity or 'total' secularity. Moreover, it also disrupts the binary distinction between modernity and tradition, presenting an obvious modern sense of choosing a (non-secularist) identity, which at the same time sees itself as bound by tradition — but refuses to be labeled as 'orthodox' or 'religious.'[13]

It seems that the solution to this theoretical conundrum arises from the emergence of a post-secular perspective that has been gaining momentum during the last two decades. This perspective offers a 'revisionist' reconsideration of the 'orthodox' narrative of secularization. The revisionism at hand involves practically all of the narrative's components, questioning not only the descriptive-analytical merit of the secularization thesis, but also its political and philosophical implications. Critics have pointed, among other things, to the thesis' misevaluation of the role of religion — as an institution — in the modern world,[14] its misunderstanding of the role of religious belief and practice in the modern, 'secular age,'[15] and its orientalist sense of the 'universalism' of the European-Protestant case.[16] As one prominent and heavily influential formulation of this revisionism argues, the secularization thesis is so deficient and lacking — whether in its historical assessment of the role of religion in times past or in its sociological (mis-)understanding of the role or religion today — that it is time to 'lay it to rest.'[17] Eventually, this criticism amounts to a recognition of the label 'post-secular' as adequate not only to describe the shape of the sociology of religion today, but also to identify the (post-) modern experience as a whole.[18]

Most importantly for the purpose of the current discussion, the revisionist, post-secular perspective also argues against the secularization narrative's insensitive imposition of dichotomous, categorical distinctions on the ambivalent, complex and ambiguous modern (be it 'late modern,' 'high modern,'[19] 'postmodern,'[20] or 'liquid modernity'[21]) 'project' of maintaining personal and collective identities.[22] As lucidly interpreted and narrated by Charles Taylor, although some individuals do find themselves comfortable identifying with one 'side' or the other (let them be called 'secularity' and 'religiosity'), most people do not identify with either pole, and choose to conduct themselves somewhere along the continuum suggested by these poles; "[P]eople take up a stance of this kind in a field which is polarized by the two extreme perspectives; they define themselves in relation to the polar opposites, whereas the people in the polar opposition don't return the favour, but usually define themselves in relation to each other, ignoring the middle (or abusively assimilating it to the other side). It is in this sense that the two extreme perspectives define the field."[23]

As argued persuasively by William Connolly, this abusive insensitivity, which tends to centralize political discourse around the religious-secular dichotomy, is critically lacking.[24] Hence, there is an acute need for an authentic de-centralized perspective that transcends secularism's 'endlessly circular chain of reference.'[25] José Casanova's denunciation of the secularization's perspective in America seems to capture this sentiment rather straightforwardly: "We may say with some confidence that currently, at least in America, both religious 'fundamentalist' and fundamentalist 'secular humanists' are cognitive minorities, that the majority of Americans tend to be humanists, who are simultaneously religious and secular. The theory of secularization should be reformulated is such a way that this empirical reality ceases to be a paradox."[26]

It is in this sense that the (Jewish-Israeli) traditionist perspective emerges as essentially post-secular, offering a practical-logical (although not always explicitly ideological and/or philosophical) exemplification of the possibility to transcend and decentralize the dichotomous worldview professed by the secularization thesis. Being both and at the same time 'modern' and 'traditional,' actively choosing an independent identity that sees itself as bound by tradition while at the same time refusing to sanctify tradition in an orthodox manner — in short, constructing a viable alternative that does not fit into either of the polarizing alternatives of 'pure religiosity' vs. 'complete secularity' — traditionists can be seen as offering a viable post-secular alternative of preserving religious practice and belief in this 'secular age.'[27]

I wish to discuss here several of the major implications of this overcoming of the polarizing worldview of the secularization paradigm. Mainly, I wish to answer the question: How do people who decentralize the monolithic identity structure of 'either' (secular) 'or' (religious) manage the apparent conflict between the different constituents of their 'identity project' (to paraphrase Bauman[28]) and maintain the ambivalence that necessarily arises? And what does this say about the possibilities of multiculturalism?

4. TOWARDS A DEFINITION OF TRADITIONISM

Defining traditionism has been a complex and difficult endeavor, and one that still awaits a proper solution at that. The most widely used approach has been to define traditionism and traditionists by reference to other binary distinctions and dichotomies. Of these, the most common views traditionism as an expression of 'folk' or 'popular' religion, which is contrasted with rabbinical-religious (orthodox) 'elite' religion.[29] However, this distinction — which nurtures on the same dichotomous worldview of the secularist credo — is also problematic, and fails to contribute much to an understanding of the phenomenon at hand. A possible solution to this problem is to define traditionism by its relation to the dominant, opposite poles, which define the parameters of the secular-religious dichotomy; for, example, contrasting traditionism with traditio*nalism* (or, in other words, extreme and reclusive religious conservatism). Such a comparison could highlight a list of unique characteristics of traditionism's.[30]

However, as should be apparent by now, I am reluctant to formulate a clear-cut definition of traditionism. Such rigid definitions of social phenomena, I suspect, tend to constrain the interpretive look, and infringe upon the deep understanding of the phenomenon at hand. Instead, such understanding calls for a continuous, circular interpretation, that moves back and forth between an ideal typical notion of the phenomenon, and the specific case study.[31]

As suggested above, the current interpretive circle might begin with the common division of Israeli Jews into those three major categories of Jewish identity: secular, religious, and traditionist. Although the meaning of these categories is far from clear, most Israeli Jews are used to being labeled — and indeed, to label themselves — along this categorization. Moreover, this classification has nurtured a vast political as well as academic discourse concerning the 'religious-secular cleavage,' which allegedly divides Jewish-Israeli society into two conflicting sub-cultures.[32] As this image suggests, the dominant discourse views the two opposite poles composing this cleavage (i.e. 'religiosity' and 'secularity') as also setting the coordinates for Jewish identity among Israelis in general. This is the context in which traditionism emerges as an immanently residual category of 'neither this nor that.' However, as discussed above, as time progressed and generations shifted (and traditionism, refuting sociologists' prediction, did not dissolve into one of the polar opposites), the term has gained a different, renewed meaning, defining itself — to borrow from Taylor — in relation to these polar opposites, but not by them.[33] As aforementioned, this (re-) definition involves a reference to an adamant adherence to tradition, which at the same time is distinctly not 'religious,' 'traditionalist,' or 'extreme,' refusing to sanctify religion in an orthodox manner.

This formula gives birth to a rather complex attitude toward religious Jewish practice: somewhat independent from the orthodox interpretation of Jewish Law while at the same time distant from the secularist indifference (or even disdain) toward this Law. The fact that traditionism lacks a coherent textual formulation (it is essentially practical, oftentimes refusing to be textually inscribed and thus legitimized) only further complicates the picture.

The current paper offers a continuation of this circular interpretation of traditionism, aiming to present a discussion of several of the main components of the phenomenology of traditionism.[34] Naturally, given the limited space, this discussion shall be rather introductory, leaving much to be further elaborated in future discussions.[35]

5. Traditionism: Some Phenomenological Notes

Traditionism, Practice, and Method

One of the most prominent dilemmas concerning traditionist identity has been the issue of the method — or rather, the apparent lack of method — guiding traditionist Jewish practice. As aforementioned, traditionists' unique mixture of adhering to several traditional dictates (such as fasting on Yom-Kippur) while overlooking others, which are deemed by orthodox Jews as not less essential to the preservation of an authentic Jewish identity (such as using electricity during the Sabbath) seems to render their practice 'unmethodical' if not simply 'funny.'

In this context, academic efforts at understanding traditionist practice and traditionist identity seem to have been thwarted by the complexity of the phenomena at hand. In fact, students of traditionism are often better served by the rather critical, it not derogatory, popular image of a Jewish-Israeli traditionist, as a person who 'prays in the synagogue on the Sabbath and then travels by car to the beach' (or to watch a soccer game). This image captures both the complexity of traditionist practice and the 'unease' it generates among the 'secular' and 'religious' Jewish-Israeli identity groups, who enjoy an image of 'consistency' and play a dominant cultural role by setting down the parameters in accordance with which Jewish identity discourse is conducted in Israel. This image does capture the fact that traditionist practice presents a unique understanding and application of Jewish law, one that does not always follow the orthodox interpretation of this law.

In this vein, traditionists have been accused of failing to observe the demanding orthodox code, while nevertheless hoping to be seen as loyal to the Jewish identity built upon it. This view, which can also be found among traditionists themselves, functions as a potential feed to a predominant sense of ambivalence and guilt. It stresses that traditionists, even though they believe in the fundamental truthfulness of orthodox religiosity, are not willing to make the sacrifices it demands. As two interviewees explained:

> The traditionist observes the easy, comfortable parts of Jewish religion. It is a matter of comfortableness (Liav); the choice [regarding which practices are observed and which are not] derives from considerations of comfortableness … It is important to observe values and tradition. I wish I could observe more than I do now … God forgive me, but out of considerations for my comfort (Dalia).

Traditionist lifestyle would thus seem as if it is guided by a selfish selectiveness of religious practices, therefore lacking a truly 'consistent' and 'systematic' ideological guideline. It clearly appears to be lacking a lucid 'method' that would solve this ambivalence by explaining — both to traditionists themselves and to those who observe them — which religious practices traditionists choose to adhere to and which they choose to ignore.

Against this background I would content that traditionists' discussions regarding their practice can be used to reconstruct a rather clear and comprehensible picture of the logic, or code, guiding traditionist lifestyle and practice. This logic is focused on the preservation of a valid, 'thick' sense of ethno-national (Jewish) identification. The 'selectiveness' in adherence to orthodox dictates is not based on considerations of comfortableness, but rather on the identification of a strict list of religious practices as essential for the reaffirmation of a modern Jewish identity: Traditionists observe — in a rather strict manner — those practices that they deem 'essential' for their self-identification as Jews. On the other hand, those practices that are seen as mere 'additives' to that 'core practice' are dismissed as 'non-essential.' Although traditionists do not cancel out the relevance of these 'additional' practices, they nevertheless do not feel that their Jewish authenticity is hurt by their failure to observe these practices. These discussions would thus retrace the ways in which traditionists maintain the ambivalence between a (traditional) 'religious' ideal and a (modern) 'secular' lifestyle, without necessarily solving it.

The notion of a 'necessary minimum' has been repeatedly evoked in the interviews to describe this selctivness. According to this formulation, traditionists observe only the 'crucial', most important Jewish practices. Failing to observe these practices amount to breaching those 'red lines' of Jewishness: "Jews have to observe this minimum, even if only for the sake of distinguishing us from the gentiles" (Dalia).

The practical content of this minimal core is not fixed, and it appears to be a rather 'thick' and inclusive 'minimal' set of practices; after all, "the traditionist's minimum is to preserve some connection to tradition" (Tamar), which is viewed as a rather wide array of behavioral precepts:

> The traditionist should practice the religious minimum. And this means celebrating Rosh Hashanah the proper way, and celebrating Sukkoth the proper way, and Passover—the proper way, and to have a special Sabbath dinner (Ronen); Judaism has a basic code…The Sabbath is important to Judaism. The very celebration of the Sabbath… A certain degree of *Kashrut*, celebration of certain holidays, circumcision, Bar-Mitzvah—those phases in life. This is traditionism. (Tehila)

This necessary minimum is the realm in which compromise and preference of 'comfortableness' are irrelevant, as they give way to the adamant preservation of the essential core of Jewish identity. It seems that the traditionist 'flexibility' disappears in this realm:

> Like in everything else in life, there are certain minimal things that everyone agrees on. *Kashrut*, family life, Yom Kippur, the Jewish holidays…I don't compromise on the necessary minimum…Because you can't do without it. (Revital)

The term 'minimum' can thus be misleading, since, as the interviewees made quite clear, it alludes to a rather wide array of practices. Accordingly, a somewhat more complicated formulation of the same principle presents traditionist practice as observance of the 'minimal maximum'. Thus, when one interviewee contemplated whether she should be described as observing the necessary minimum, she noted:

> We are observing the maximum in these things. We observe what's essential, but we practice it unwaveringly. Extremely committed. You should not compromise [on those 'essential' practices]. (Vered)

In this regard, one of the distinguishing characteristics of traditionism seems to lie in the uniqueness of traditionists' solution to the apparent tension between 'traditional' religion and modernity. Unlike orthodox/ religious Israeli-Jews, who insist that all of life is governed by religious law, in a sense sacralizing every aspect of life, and unlike secular Israeli-Jews, who (at least nominally) widely reject what is considered to be traditionally sacred, traditionists incorporate that which they consider religious or holy into the regular pattern of their otherwise modern ('secular') lives. Traditionists also draw a rather sharp distinction between the public and the private domains: a significant gap separates traditionists' degree of religious observance within their homes from the latitude that they allow themselves outside its confines.

Public Silence and Cross Pressures

Traditionist identity also suffers from a dearth of major socialization agents and institutions — other than the family and close circle of friends — which could serve as support groups that bolster and encourage traditionist identity. Moreover, the Israeli media and popular culture seem to ignore the traditionist lifestyle, and do not represent it adequately.[36] Most importantly, the Israeli public sphere lacks schools that cater for traditionist identity.

One of the important consequences of this public under-representation, combined with the complex and 'problematic' nature of traditionist practice and identity, is that traditionists live under a set of constant cross-pressures, and enjoy no external support other than that of the family and close (traditionist) friends. Thus, one of the prominent characteristics of traditionist identity is the individual's sense of loneliness. In the context of a dominant 'secular-religious cleavage' discourse — that is, in a context where Israeli secularism is associated and identified with progress, liberty, 'normal' life, self-fulfillment, and other contemporary liberal-Western images, while the religious (orthodox) are identified with 'authentic' Jewish identity — Jewish-Israeli traditionists constantly find themselves in multiple cultural, social, and political settings in which they constitute a peripheral minority group. Traditionists seem to be always close to the dominant circle, but never really a part of it. Whether in the company of friends in the pub or the fashionable café, or whether surrounded by fellow worshipers in the (orthodox) synagogue on Friday nights, the traditionist constantly finds him/her self in an 'inferior' position, a state of estrangement that characterizes those who do not fully and wholeheartedly adopt the dominant group's culture. The frequency in which my respondents referred to this experience of living under cross pressures, and the intensity with which these references where instilled clearly marks this experience as one of the constitutive, forming experiences of the Jewish-Israeli traditionist phenomenon. See, for example, how one interviewee framed the issue.

> [As a traditionist], you live between two worlds... You reach a point in life where you are captured between these two worlds. Here in Israel, people don't like compromises. They prefer either white or black. There is no room for traditionists. In Israel, there's no sense of the middle ground—people like either left or right... My brother had been observing the Sabbath for many years. He tells me: 'The seculars don't accept me, and the religious society doesn't accept me. If I lived somewhere else, it might have been easier on me'. (Haim)

It is thus not surprising that amongst the three categories of Israeli Jews grouped by religious identity (that is, religious, secular and traditionist) only the percentage of traditionists declined (by seven points) between 1990 and 1999. The proportion of the other two groups within the Jewish population remained constant or grew.[37] The influx of immigrants from the former Soviet Union is a partial explanation for the decline in the proportion of traditionist (the category of traditionism is practically non-existent among these immigrants) but I suspect that the major explanation for this decline is the absence of socializing agents, combined with the cross pressures applied on traditionists.

The identity problems of the traditionists are compounded by the sense many of them have that the manner in which they conduct their religious life is almost unique. That is, one of the problems in sustaining a traditionist identity is the sense that one is 'peculiar' and different. The religious Jew easily identifies others who self-identify as religious. Since orthodox Jews tend to live in orthodox neighborhoods their religious identity is reinforced by those they see around them. The same is true of secular Jews. Religious and secular Israeli-Jews readily recognize one another by their public mannerisms but especially by their dress. Traditionists, however, who dress like secular Jews and who practice their Judaism in the confines of the home and family do not readily identify with one another. Some of my respondents were shocked when told that traditionists constituted over thirty percent of the Jewish population of Israel. They live with the sense that they alone are making the temptations to join the ranks of either the secular or the religious that much more pronounced.

The major source of pressures on traditionists is the demand for coherence and consistency. In the eyes of religious and secular Israeli Jews, the behavior of the traditionist is inconsistent if not hypocritical. It should be noted that this pressure comes not only from orthodox Jews. Jewish Israeli secularists, at least by implication but sometimes explicitly, also demand that the traditionist decide to which side s/he belongs and to act accordingly.

The cultural context of Israeli life plays an important role in this regard. The demand of both sides that the traditionist chooses where s/he belongs is a demand to leave that liminal state of 'neither here nor there.' Choosing one of the two sides requires the traditionist to identify the other side as 'other' and to structure his/her behavior in opposition to this 'other'. One interviewee described this mindset as a "brainwash":

> This is the brainwashing to which we are subjected in this country: That there is secular, and there is religious. Nothing in the middle. No middle ground. Nothing else. There is no definition of anything else. There are secular parties and religious parties; so the traditionist carries a sense of guilt—I'm neither here nor there... This is one of the most horrible things they are doing to the traditionists. (Gil)

As alluded to above, from the orthodox point of view, traditionist practice is simply flawed. It reflects a weakness of character if not a choice of sin rather than religious compliance. Traditionism is seen in this context as partial heresy. Rabbis sometimes play a word game with the etymology of the term traditionist *(masorti)* in order to deny its legitimacy. *Masorti*, they say, comes from the word *masor* (saw) and *nisur* (sawing) and not from the words *masoret* (tradition) and *mesira* (handing over). The *traditionist* 'saws off' a piece of Judaism for himself, chooses what is easy for him and throws away that which denies him the pleasures which secular culture offers.[38] From this critical point of view, traditionism is not an error stemming, for example, from ignorance but rather a self-conscious transgression stemming from weak spirit, from a search for personal comfort at the expense of religious truth. This attitude is also found in most religious schools, whether they are schools run by ultra-orthodox or religious Zionists.

A central component in these pressures is the conception of the secular in the eyes of the rabbis. Orthodox spokesmen tend to portray secular Israeli Jews as the opposite of all that is good and proper. The secular is vacuous, irresponsible, and immoral. Even when they show an understanding toward the traditionist and try to draw her/him closer to them, the orthodox continue to voice their total rejection of 'modern' life, which they often identify with democracy. The traditionist, even when s/he escapes this criticism is as it were infected with the disease of secularism.

The demand for 'consistency' also comes from the secular side. However, in this case the rhetoric is less one-sided. The secular demands that the traditionist 'make her/himself clear'; that s/he chooses one of two coherent paths: secularism *or* religion. Secular Israeli Jews often stress the right of the individual to live as s/he chooses. But this choice is more often than not limited to the two end points of the alleged continuum.

It is also worth recalling the distinction, at least within academic circles, between the traditional and the modern. One of the characteristics of the non-modern ('primitive' in the pre-politically correct era) is religion, or religiousness. This distinction between the modern and traditional (which also guided social and educational policy) demanded that the traditionist modernize. The need was felt to de-socialize the Mizrahi traditionists (i.e., undermine traditional society) and then re-socialize them into modern Israeli society.[39] A major component in modernization was abandoning religion. That was the demand implied in the political and academic establishment's insistence on consistency and coherence, for locating oneself in one of the two dichotomous categories and abandoning the 'primitive' traditionism for the sake of modernity.[40]

Traditionism seems to 'bother' both extreme positions — secularism on the one hand and religion on the other. It provides a living example of the possibility that there is an alternative to rejecting either modernity or religion. This is true of Reform and Conservative Judaism as well but their presence in Israel is too weak for them to constitute a threat. The dichotomy of secular vs. orthodox builds the identity of each side. Each benefits from this binary image. The religious camp is crowned with a monopoly on the definition of the Jewish religion, the secular on the definition of freedom and progress. Recognition of the presence of the traditionist undermines all this.

Traditionism and Modernity

As I have mentioned earlier, an empathic regard for- or attentiveness to-traditionist identity immediately brings to the surface the major weakness of the modernization-secularization paradigm as a tool for understanding and analyzing traditionalist identity: this paradigm has prevented researchers from seeing that traditionist identity is, simply put, a modern phenomenon.

The most important respect in which traditionism constitutes a decidedly modern phenomenon is that the traditionist consciously chooses to be identified as such, and labors to preserve her/his traditionist identity. Traditionism is not forced upon the individual, nor is it simply 'passed on' to her/him by the very inertia of tradition. Rather, it is an obvious example of what Zygmunt Bauman describes as the major characteristic of (late) modern life, that is the necessity to constantly choose, reaffirm and maintain one's identity, which is no longer a simple, 'obvious given.'[41]

Considering the countervailing pressures emanating from both the secularists and the religious (orthodox) poles, neither by any stretch of the imagination can traditionism be taken for granted. The traditionist is quite familiar with the other, culturally dominant alternatives. S/he hears their demands, is aware of their system of values, and is conscious of the fact that both secularism and orthodoxy offer what seems to be a consistent way of life which imbues the follower with a sense of confidence in his/her own identity — a quality that many of the traditionists with whom I have spoken admit they lack. Nonetheless, traditionists choose to be traditionist. They are conscious of their identity, of its special character and of its advantages (as he/she sees them, of course), and of its unique place in the map of socio-political identities in Israel.

The importance of this element of choice should not be underestimated. It reflects not only the traditionists' sensitivity to the presence of alternative, dominant identities, but also their sense that their identity is not taken for granted. This, in fact, is traditionism's most blatantly modern characteristic: it constitutes a compound of both an awareness of its own complexity (as well as that of other identities) and an understanding that the components of one's personality are not 'a given' or 'taken for granted,' but rather an outcome of a continuous and dynamic process of choosing, preferring, and identifying.

The 'Essence' of Identity and the Limits of Toleration

Against this background, contemporary academic discourse might well be inclined to label traditionist identity as a 'post-modern' rather than a 'modern' phenomenon. Indeed, it is not difficult to see the 'super-market' character of traditionist identity. After all, traditionists do not hesitate to describe themselves as choosing to be loyal to some elements of their Jewish and/or modern-secular identity, while adopting a lenient, even permissive approach to others. In this regard, traditionists could be described as manifesting yet another expression of a tolerant, self-interpreting, multicultural carnival of identities. However, it is important to stress that in most cases traditionists do not accept the value-relativism that is usually associated with such understanding of post-modernity. As already noted, the traditionist 'method' is based on identifying what can be called 'a core of Jewish authenticity': a minimum of practice, values and beliefs, without which one's identity is not 'really Jewish.'

One venue for the articulation of such a judgmental (and hence not exactly 'post-modern,' and somewhat challenging from a multicultural perspective) approach can be located in the traditionists' attitude towards the (American) denominational group that is closest to them in terms of practice: Conservative Judaism. Much has been said and written on the apparent proximity and similarities between the two groups, especially in terms of practice. Frequently, Israeli traditionists are said to comprise 'in theory' the Conservative movement's most significant 'natural' constituency, since they embody the extraordinary (and unrealized) potential of Conservative Judaism to become one of the dominant denominations in Israel. This is not the place to explain why this supposed potential has not been realized. Rather, within the present context attention will be focused on the judgmental and critical attitude of traditionists toward Conservative Jews.[42]

Traditionists' most important criticism against Conservative Judaism is that Conservatives 'parody religion' by giving allegedly *halachic* legitimization to their (and the traditionists') religious behavior, which from an orthodox-Jewish point of view is both lenient and permissive. Traditionists thus adopt the orthodox point of view on religion (at least as an ideal to aspire to) and accept the orthodox interpretation of Jewish law as '*religiously* authentic Judaism.' This does not mean that traditionists do not view themselves as authentically Jewish, but they surely believe that someone who wants to be truly whole as a religious Jew has to observe all of dictates, in accordance with their orthodox interpretation. Attempts at presenting new, non-orthodox interpretation of the religious tradition are thus deemed inappropriate. Many interviewees find such new interpretations to be simply funny. See, for example, Sigal's judgment of Conservative Judaism:

> I don't find it attractive at all. It makes me lough... Their inventions make me lough... You don't want to observe something? Go ahead. But why should you invent something new on top of this? In my view, excuse me for saying this, it is like a whole different religion. Why do you call this Judaism? You should invent another religion, like Christianity.

In this vein, the clearest distinction between traditionists' self-image and their image of Conservatives (and Reform) Judaism is what traditionist see as their attitude toward the breaching of (orthodox) *halacha*: Traditionists, like both Reform and Conservative Jews, knowingly disobey some of the *halachic* dictations. But, unlike those non-orthodox movements, traditionsits do not seek to legitimize this behavior. The important aspect here is the traditionist self-awarnece that emerges from this distinction. For one interviewee, this distinction is what forms her identity as traditionist:

> I find phenomena like Reform Judaism to be outrageous. I don't like them. They cause me uneasiness. Women donning *tefilin* or are called up [in the synagogue] to read the Torah, changing portions of the prayer book, etc. So then one must ask: In what am I different from them? They decide for themselves what to observe and what not to, and so do I, basically. So I believe the most accurate way to define to myself what is a traditionist, is that traditionist is someone who does not observe the whole system of *mitzvot* (*halachic* dictations), but knows it is wrong to do so. (Roni).

Traditionists, in other words, are unwilling to legitimize and generalize their own 'forgiveness' towards themselves. They choose not to fully observe all of the religious commandments, and are usually happy with their non-orthodox lifestyle, even when they know (and admit) that from an orthodox point of view they are behaving improperly. But this does not mean that they would support the formal legitimization of their behavior as '*halachicly* correct.'

Traditionism and Gender

An even more complex component in this regard is traditionists' attitudes toward issues of gender equality. As I have argued elsewhere,[43] formal institutional-organizational aspects of gender equality do not occupy a significant place in the worldview and feminine or feminist identity of traditionist women. Moreover, a study of the interaction between the varying components of traditionist women's identity reveals a complex and intriguing picture of a proud, continuous and dynamic personal struggle for a free and egalitarian Jewish self-identification, accompanied by explicit and sometimes scathing disagreements with what many traditionist women see as radical feminism. Indeed, this fascinating amalgam highlights the importance of differentiating between the public and the private as well as between the formal and the practical in the lives of traditionists.

In the context of the current discussion of traditionists' and especially traditionist women's attitude towards Reform and Conservative Judaism, issues of gender seem to capture a core characteristic in this complicated relationship. Traditionist women, who report on having had an opportunity to attend Conservative or Reform services (usually, it is interesting to note, whilst on a visit to the United States), and also report that they found the egalitarian element in these services to be positive and flattering, usually reject the option of joining a Conservative or Reform congregation in Israel, precisely because of the progressive attitudes toward issues of gender displayed by the Conservatism and Reform movements. At the most basic level, they believe these egalitarian services to be 'Jewishly wrong'. As one interviewee summed up her encounter with such non-orthodox services:

> I had a shocking encounter with this... Reform and Conservative Jews... I was simply shocked. I saw a women being called up to read the torah. I am a feminist woman, but I still found this very difficult to swallow. It bothered me. (Tehila)

Traditionism, Rabbinic (Orthodox) Authority, and Halachic Reform

An important component in traditionist identity in this regard is the acceptance of the orthodox rabbinate as the sole Jewish-religious authority. This is true also when traditionists (and especially traditionist women) dismiss the monopolistic institutional body of Israel's Chief Rabbinate, harshly criticizing its alleged corruption and fraudulence. Even though traditionist women furthermore report strongly negative feelings towards the Rabbinate and its arrogant behavior, they nevertheless stop short of denying the rabbis' religious authority. On the contrary: their criticism stems from their basic demand that the rabbi act as a model of Jewish-religious life, a model or ideal that should be on a higher level than that attained by other Jews.

Much attention has been lavished on the special role of rabbis in the world of Mizrahi traditionists.[44] However, these discussions, which have tended to focus on rabbinic authority (oftentimes from a point of view that considers rabbis and rabbinic authority as impediments to the process of modernization and secularization), seem to have failed to identify what is most unique about the traditionist attitude toward rabbis. In fact, that attitude is a compound. It acknowledges and even asserts the rabbi's authority. At the same time, however, it presents the rabbi with an uncompromising demand that he 'knows how to behave,' — which is another way of saying that he ought to sensibly limit the scope of his authority and be patient (even if passively) toward the somewhat lenient observance of the traditionist. This is not a demand to make kosher that which is inherently profane (the traditionist criticism against Reform and Conservative Jews is that this is exactly what they do), but rather to present a firm, almost pure model of authentic and precise religious Judaism. Part of this precision is indeed manifested in being tolerant toward those who do not obey the model in a strict manner. The rabbi, in other words, should set an example, but also be wary of imposing it on his audience:

> For many people, the rabbi is a role model … You are a rabbi, and you have an influence on people's lives … There are people who listen to what rabbis say, and do what they say, trying to imitate their lifestyle. You [as a rabbi] are occupying an influential post, influencing the lives of communities, so you have to be a role model. (Ziva)

The traditionists' attitude towards rabbis is closely linked to their stance in regard to religious reform. It is rather obvious that traditionists view some *halachic*-rabbinic prohibitions and restrictions as anachronistic and out of place in the contemporary, modern age. This conception is what gives them the implicit (self-granted) liberty to ignore such prohibitions and still feel themselves to be authentically Jewish. It is not uncommon to hear traditionists explicitly criticizing anachronistic commandments that have accumulated during the long years of Jewish history and argue that the time has come to amend the *halachic* stance in regard to certain issues. (The prohibition against turning on and off an electric light during the Sabbath is one of the most outstanding examples in this regard.) However — and this is where the important qualification lies — the only authority that a traditionist would accept as legitimate for the introduction of such *halachic* reforms is the orthodox rabbinate itself.

Religion and Morality: The Traditionist Perspective

Traditionists' attitudes toward rabbinic authority appear to be closely tied to the question of the relation between morality and religion. This issue was raised during my interviews with Jewish-Israeli traditionists under the (admittedly misleading) questions of 'who is a good Jew?' and 'what makes a good person?' The vast majority of my respondents denied emphatically that a Jew who observed religious law punctiliously was a better Jew or a better person. Instead they defined morality, ethics and humanitarianism as the criteria by which to judge who is a good person as well as a good Jew. In other words, my interviewees refused to identify religiosity with morality. As summed up by one interviewee:

> This [the connection between religiosity and morality] is something that exists because that's what society and norm demand, but I don't think it is true as a general rule. Every case is a different story ... Being a good person is not something that is connected to being traditional or observing the religious commandments. A good person is someone who is honest with herself or himself, that doesn't feel a need to harm her/his surrounding ... For me, this is not connected to religion, although there are, among other myths and stigmas, the belief that traditionist are good-hearted people. (Ziva)

My respondents described what they call a good person. That good person is someone who cares for and helps others without regard to who those other persons are. My respondents claimed that they strive to be such people, that such people rank very highly in their eyes. However, they denied that there is a connection between being such a good person and being a religious Jew or fulfilling one's religious obligations. Indeed, my respondents have repeatedly mentioned that Judaism does demand of one the qualities that make for a good person. Moreover, in principle, they have repeatedly said, Jewish Law should enhance one's ability to conduct a moral life; for many, this is the real aim of Jewish practice. But intuitive sense, as well as experience, teaches them a different lesson. Their intuitive sense is that religion has to do with punctiliously fulfilling ritual demands and acquiring knowledge of sacred text. They know too many rabbis and have too many acquaintances that meet the requirements necessary to call oneself ortho-dox who are not good people. On the other hand they have acquaintances who are good people but clearly aren't religious.

Nevertheless, the 'principle' identification of religiosity and morality should not be discounted. It seems to nurture an ideal typical notion of

Judaism as the ultimate guarantor of moral conduct. In this regard, they view religious Jews who do not stand up to this ideal image as betraying their commitment to represent authentic Judaism in the best possible way. (The issue of whether such representation is the original intention of the religious Jew is irrelevant; such representation of authentic Judaism is what traditionists assign the image of 'the real religious Jew' with.) One interviewee explained why others expect such a high ethical standard from religious Jews: "It is because religiosity is supposed to instill you with values, which in their basis are values of respect to other human beings, respect toward God; and as a basis, it makes you a better person" (Limore). Indeed, on a number of occasions the passion with which my respondents insisted that there is no necessary relationship between how religious a person was and whether s/he was a good person — that they know for a fact that there are 'extremely religious' Jews who at the same time conducted their life immorally — reflected an opposite position. They expressed disappointment when they found fully observing Jews wanting from a moral point of view. In other words, traditionists seem to anticipate that the religious Jew would act in a more ethical and humane manner than others. But the expectation that the religious Jew would serve as a kind of exemplary model for Judaism, for the Jewish way of life was often met with disappointment.

Traditionists' Image of 'the Religious' and 'the Secular'

One prominent way in which the dominance of the binary construct of 'secularism vs. traditionalism (or religiosity)' influences traditionist self-understanding can be derived from Charles Taylor's above mentioned argument, that while most people do not identify *with* or *by* those polar opposite, they nevertheless self-identify *in relation* to them.[45] These extreme identity-formulations function as major benchmarks, against which self- and collective- identity is being formed and maintained. Such 'identification in relation' seems to play a major role in traditionists' self-understanding: the images of 'the religious' and 'the secular' have been repeatedly invoked in my conversations with traditionists, who were grappling with the meaning of their own identity qua traditionists, as relevant for their self-understanding.

The abovementioned (sometimes implicit) identification between religiosity and morality emerges as one major component of traditionist image of 'the religious'. In more general terms, the image of 'the religious' seems to represent for the traditionist an absolute — fundamental, in the literal sense — but also extreme and impossible expression of authentic Judaism. This does not mean that traditionists see themselves as 'less Jewish' than religious Jews. Nevertheless, they do tend to view orthodox Jews as embodying (or, to be percise: as those who *should* embody) an ideal, absolute role model, towards which the traditionist should aspire. This allows for a wide space for criticism of orthodox Judaism by traditionists. See, for example, Meir's conclusion in this matter:

> I expect him [the religious Jew] to be moral. I expect of him to present higher moral standards. Secular Jews aren't committed to such moral standards … I expect from someone who wears a *kippa* [thus marking himself to be a religious Jew, at least in the Israeli context] not to be a liar … I think that someone who takes it upon himself and declares publicly, by putting on all sorts of external signs, like the *kippa*, that he is religious — I expect that he takes upon himself a moral obligation, too.

In one, major sense, then, traditionists view orthodoxy (and especially its religious-Zionist variant) as an ideal model of Jewish-Israeli identity. Orthodoxy is seen here as representing a value-laden lifestyle, unselfishly committed to the common, collective good. One's personal life, it thus emerges, is simply better if one lives by the religious code.

However, a closer look at the ways in which traditionists construct the image of 'the religious' reveals a much more complex, ambivalent picture. Traditionists' relative proximity to the religious pole (at least when traditionism is compared with the other, secular pole) seems to both threaten traditionists and attract them. On the one hand, the image of 'the religious' embodies a promise for 'wholeness' — security in one's full, ideologically consistent Jewish lifestyle. On the other hand, religiousness is seen as endangering one's personal liberty, threatening to become intrusive and coercive. Traditionists appear to solve this 'potential' dilemma in a rather decisive manner in the practical level: As agreed by the vast majority of my interviewees, in-spite of the 'spiritual' attraction of the religious identity, it represents an impractical and unrealistic lifestyle — at least not in a modern world. Orthodoxy is thus harshly judged as reclusive and extreme, and as introducing too many unnecessary and impractical restrictions on the individual's freedom. Hence, the final verdict is that a religious way of life, although valued, is simply impossible. Moreover, many of my respondents believe that modern Jewish orthodoxy has come to embody some restrictions and dictations which are not only irrelevant for the conduct of an authentic Jewish lifestyle, but also biasing and distorting the true meaning of Judaism. Roni's formulation was rather blunt in this regard:

> I believe everyone has his/her perversions. Last week I saw an ultra-orthodox Hassid in the shopping mall, and thought to myself: this twisted mutation of Judaism, are they the true successors of Judah Maccabee, Bar-Kokva and Moses? This is an absurd and ridicules claim. I have no doubt that me and my family are much closer, in many parameters, to the original Jews or to our fathers' tradition than those people who imitate a seventeenth century Polish-Galician lifestyle. I don't think they are the real Jews, but I do think that they are more adherent to halacha in its original form, because religion, in essence, is a conservative thing.

Against this image, the traditionist choice is reinforced as the 'normal', correct choice of a practical yet authentic strong Jewish identity. This identity, my respondent stressed, is both and at the same time just as 'Jewishly good' as the one enjoyed by orthodox Jews and preferable over secular detachment from Jewish content and meaning.

This last point — the image of secularism as being devoid of Jewish meaning — is probably the most salient of traditionists' criticism of Jewish-Israeli seculars. This dominant identity group emerges as a model of too severe a detachment from Jewish tradition and the authenticity associated with it. Traditionists, in other words, view secular Israeli-Jews as individuals who, in the name of the pursuit of personal liberty have lost their ties to their (collective) Jewish identity, on its customs, values, history, and future. As such, seculars are viewed as 'empty', lacking any true meaning to their life. Many of my respondents evoked this image of the secular as the ultimate expression of personal liberty — both positively (i.e. as embodying one's ability to pursue one's ambitions with no restrictions) and negatively (as this freedom can easily deteriorate into uninhibited hedonism).

This is the context in which the identification between Judaism or a Jewish way of life and ethics and morality reemerges as a central component of traditionalists' attitudes toward secular Israeli Jews. As aforementioned, my respondents tended to identify secularism with 'emptiness' and absence of values and meaning — which are a sure path to loosing one's moral humanism. The absence of belief in God (which is the ultimate mark of secularism in the eyes of many traditionists) is understood by traditionists whom I interviewed as signaling egoism and unbridled hedonism. 'The secular' was described by some as concerned only with him/herself at the expense of others and at the expense of national as well as universal values and principles.

One symbolic arena in which traditionists' identity in-relation to the two dominant poles finds expression is the issue of wearing (or neglecting to wear) the traditional Jewish headgear for men, the *kippa* (or 'yarmulke'). In the Jewish Israeli context, the *kippa* has come to symbolize the division mark between religious and secular in a rather straight forward way: the religious wear it, the secular do not. The attitude of traditionists to the *kippa* is hence of immense significance in manifesting their position outside of this dichotomy. And it appears to capture the complex attitude of traditionists to the whole world of religion. As my respondents clarified, from the traditionist point of view, the wearing of a *kippa* is a symbolic act signaling the division between the world of holiness and religion, and the world of the secular and mundane *in one's own personal life* (and not a public symbol of one's identification with either opposite pole). In donning the *kippa* the traditionist identifies himself as one who has entered, temporarily, the arena of religion, of the holy. Removal of the *kippa* signals his return to the everyday, where holiness is absent. By wearing the *kippa* and removing it (or not wearing it) the traditionist signals — to himself, rather than to the public — the boundaries of the holy and the different set of rules demanded of him. This symbolic meaning of the *kippa* constitutes a central component in the tendency of traditionists to compartmentalize the Jewish religion, to limit its sanctity and to draw the distinction between holy and profane. This symbolism is reinforced in the context of Israeli society where the wearing of a *kippa* denotes membership in the community of the religious. In this context, not wearing a *kippa* is of great significance for the traditionist because it distinguishes him from the religious. Amongst my respondents there was general agreement that one who always wears a *kippa* and does not maintain a religious life is a charlatan.

6. CONCLUSION

Multiculturalism necessitates, by its very nature (to adopt a somewhat essentialist tongue) — the opening up of public discourse beyond dominant polar opposites. Although helpful as an analytic tool, such dichotomous, binary constructs often distort our nuanced, complex view of the ways in which groups and individuals instill their life with meaning. Mary Douglas' warning seems to capture this sense in full: 'Binary distinctions are an analytic procedure, but their usefulness does not guarantee that existence divides like that. We should look with suspicion on anyone who declared that there are two kinds of people, or two kinds of reality, or process.'[46]

A sensitive, multicultural standpoint, one that is attentive to the varying ways in which individuals and groups strive for recognition[47] thus has to transcend such binary constructs. It has to recognize not only those who find it more meaningful to self-identify somewhere along the continuums suggested by those binary oppositions, but also those who transcend such dichotomous views of reality, and form their meaning-systems outside of a such dominant polar-opposites.

This paper dealt with but one example of such a binary, dichotomous identity construct — albeit an overtly dominant one — the distinction suggested by the 'modernization and secularization' narrative between the modern-secular and the traditional (or, rather, tradition*alizing*)-religious. This distinction, I have argued here, not only distorts our view of sociocultural reality, but also functions politically to silence a large group of Israeli-Jews who simply do not find themselves represented anywhere on the secular-religious dichotomy.

Contrary to the expectations encouraged by the use of the secularization versus traditionalization paradigm, traditionists are far from disappearing from the arena of Jewish identity in Israel. Both the academic and popular discourses have failed to provide traditionists and traditionism with the attention they deserve. On the contrary, when discussed, traditionism is often dismissed as an unmethodical, selfish preference of comfortableness over ideological substance and consistency. Against this background, as I have tried to show here, a multiculturalist perspective would highlight, to give but one, major example, the modern character of traditionist identity. This modern quality, I suggested here, is evident in the social fact of choice: traditionism and traditionist identity are far from being obvious. They are constantly criticized by both (dominate) polar opposites and cast as illegitimate mixture of two conflicting worldviews. The traditionist individual, lacking substantial public expression and support of her/his identity, finds her/himself in a constant minority status (even though people who self-identify as traditionists outnumber those who self identify as 'religious'), as constant cross pressures to 'solve' and 'dissolve' the un-normality of her/his identity are applied throughout the Israeli sociocultural field. Yet s/he chooses to identify as traditionist and conduct a traditionist lifestyle.

In this context, traditionist choice — which is an active and constant one — seems to be more viable than the one that characterizes the dominant polar opposites. In other words, I would contend that a comparison of the choice of traditionism with that of secularism on the one hand and tradition*alism* on the other demonstrates the greater complexity of the first. Traditionist identity is based on a choice that is of greater significance than the alternative choices because in most cases the secular and the religious Jew never really have the identity options of the traditionist. In many respects the traditio*nalist* and the secularist identities, to the extent that they are matters of choice and not simply givens from the home and the cultural environment, are formed as mirror images of their polar opposites.

It seems that the dominant alternatives from which most of those born into orthodox and secularist homes can choose is to either remain as they are or totally transform their identities — adopting the opposite pole's meaning-structure. As my interviewees stressed, such 'converts' tend to become extreme in their new identities. Traditionist identity, on the other hand, is always of a mixed, hesitant, tempered nature. It must always, so it seems, justify itself and, as I have noted, is often accompanied by feelings of guilt. The possibility of alternate choices is always present because the options are always present and fairly easy (socio-culturally speaking) to adopt.

In conclusion, a multicultural perspective would benefit from a post-secular stance, in which the dichotomous discourse of secularization versus traditionalization is no longer dominant. Such a perspective allows for a more nuanced and sensitive approach to the fundamental issues with which Israeli multiculturalism has to grapple, involving the complex relationships between modernity, religion, ethnicity, nationalism and collective identities. The relationship between national symbols, ceremonies and values and the system of Jewish-religious values, beliefs and ceremonies troubled the Zionist enterprise from its very outset, underwent many changes and has been the topic of research for quite some time now.[48] But the secularization versus traditionalization discourse renders traditionism and traditionists into something of an anomaly; something requiring a solution rather than an identity expression which sheds light on new ways to view Israeli society. In the context of a Jewish national state, the traditionist option may yet reveal itself as a solution to the continuing tension inherent in the Jewish national enterprise — the tension between a universal and a particularistic identity, between a state which is 'democratic' and one which is 'Jewish.'

NOTES

1 Shlomit Levy, Hanna Levinsohn, and Elihu Katz, *Beliefs, Observances, and Social Interaction Among Israeli Jews* (Jerusalem: Louis Guttman Israel Institute of Applied Social Research, 1993); Shlomit Levy, Hanna Levinsohn, and Elihu Katz, *Jewish Israelis: A Portrait* (Jerusalem: Avi Chai and the Israel Democracy Institute, 2002).

2 The Hebrew term, *masorti*, which can be also translated as 'traditional', was probably first coined during the 1950's by Israeli sociologists who focused on the fact that most traditionists immigrated to Israel from 'pre-modern', mostly Muslim, countries.

3   For example: Edward Shils, "Tradition and Liberty: Antinomy and Interdependence," *Ethics* 68, no. 3 (April 1958): 153–165; Jurgen Habermas, "Struggles for Recognition in the Democratic Constitutional State," in *Multiculturalism: Examining the Politics of Recognition*, ed. Amy Gutmann (Princeton, NJ: Princeton University Press, 1994), pp. 107–148.

4   Shils, "Tradition and Liberty"; See also: Struan Jacobs, "Edward Shils' Theory of Tradition," *Philosophy of the Social Sciences* 37, no. 2 (2007): 139–162.

5   Hans-Georg Gadamer, *Truth and Method*, 2nd ed. (New York: Crossroad, 1989), pp. 282–283; Alasdair MacIntyre, *After Virtue: A Study in Moral Theory, Second Edition*, 2nd ed. (University of Notre Dame Press, 1984), ch. 15; Charles Taylor, "The Politics of Recognition," in *Multiculturalism: Examining the Politics of Recognition*, ed. Amy Gutmann (Princeton, NJ: Princeton University Press, 1994), pp. 25–74; see also: Avi Sagi, *The Jewish-Israeli Voyage: Culture and Identity* (Jerusalem: Shalom Hartman Institute, 2006), pp. 87–122.

6   Confusingly, William Graham, following Joseph Levenson, uses the term "traditionalism" to denote a similar non-orthodox stance toward tradition. (I, too, have done so in several previous publications). I hope that my neologism solves this terminological confusion. See: William A. Graham, "Traditionalism in Islam: An Essay in Interpretation," *Journal of Interdisciplinary History* 23, no. 3 (Winter 1993): 495–522; Joseph Richmond Levenson, *Confucian China and Its Modern Fate* (Berkeley: University of California Press, 1958).

7   Mizrahi (pl. Mizrahim; an alternative term to 'Sephardic') Israeli Jews are those who originate, or whose parents originate from predominantly Muslim countries. 50% of all Mizrahim self-identify as traditionalist, whereas only 19% of Ashkenazim (Israeli Jews who originate, or whose parents originate, from Christian countries) so self-identify. Mizrahim constitute more than three quarters of those identifying as traditionalist.

8   Mordechai Bar-Lev and Peri Kedem, "Ethnicity and Religiosity of Students: Does College Education necessarily Cause the Abandoning of Religious Tradition?," *Megamot* 28, no. 2–3 (1984): 265–279; Harvey Goldberg, "A Tradition of Invention: Family and Educational Institutions among Contemporary Traditionalizing Jews," *Conservative Judaism* 47, no. 2 (1995): 69–84; Harvey Goldberg, "Religious Responses among North African Jews in the Nineteenth and Twentieth Centuries," in *The Uses of Tradition: Jewish Continuity in the Modern Era*, ed. Jack Wertheimer (New York: Jewish Theological Seminary with Harvard University Press, 1993), pp. 119–144; Harvey Goldberg, "Religious Responses to Modernity among the Jews of Jerba and of Tripoli: A Comparative Study," *The Journal of Mediterranean Studies* 4: 278–299; *Jews of the Middle East: Anthropological Perspectives on Past and Present*, ed. Shlomo Deshen and Moshe Shokeid (Tel-Aviv: Schocken, 1984); M. Shokeid, "The Religiosity of Middle Eastern Jews," ed. Shlomo Deshen, Charles S. Liebman, and Moshe Shokeid, *Israeli Judaism, Studies of Israeli Society* 7 (1995): 213–237; Shlomo Deshen, "The religiosity of the Mizrahim: Public, Rabbis, and Belief," *Alpayim* 9 (1994): 44–58.

9   Yaacov Yadgar, "Gender, Religion, and Feminism: The Case of Jewish Israeli Traditionalists," *Journal for the Scientific Study of Religion* 45, no. 3 (2006): 353–370; Yaacov Yadgar and Charles Liebman, "Beyond the Religious-Secular Dichotomy:

Masortim in Israel," in *Religion or Ethnicity? Jewish Identities in Evolution*, ed. Zvi Gitelman (New Brunswick, N.J: Rutgers University Press, 2009), pp. 337–366.

[10] For Example: Janet Jakobsen and Ann Pellegrini, "Times Like This," in *Secularisms* (Durham: Duke University Press, 2008), pp. 1–35; William H. Swatos and Kevin J. Christiano, "Secularization Theory: The Course of a Concept," *Sociology of Religion* 60, no. 3 (Autumn 1999): 209–228; Talal Asad, *Formations of the Secular: Christianity, Islam, Modernity, Cultural memory in the present* (Stanford, Calif: Stanford University Press, 2003); Talal Asad, "Religion, Nation-State and Secularism," in *Nation and Religion: Perspectives of Europe and Asia*, ed. Peter van der Veer and Hartmut Lehman (Princeton, NJ: Princeton University Press, 1999), pp. 178–196.

[11] See also: *Secularism and Its Critics*, ed. Rajeev Bhargava (Oxford University Press, 2005); P. L. Berger, "Secularism in Retreat," *The National Interest* 46 (1996): 3–12; David Martin, *On Secularization: Towards a Revised General Theory* (Aldershot, England: Ashgate, 2005); Rodney Stark, "Secularization, R.I.P.," *Sociology of Religion* 60, no. 3 (Autumn 1999): 249–273.

[12] William J. Keenan, "Post-Secular Sociology: Effusions of Religion in Late Modern Settings," *European Journal of Social Theory* 5, no. 2 (2002): 280.

[13] Yadgar, "Gender, Religion, and Feminism: The Case of Jewish Israeli Traditionalists"; Yaacov Yadgar, *Israeli Traditionists: Modernity without Secularization*, Israeli Judaism (Jerusalem: Hartman Institute/Bar-Ilan University, Faculty of Law/Keter).

[14] José Casanova, *Public Religions in the Modern World* (Chicago: University of Chicago Press, 1994).

[15] Charles Taylor, *A Secular Age* (Cambridge, Mass: Belknap Press of Harvard University Press, 2007); M. Lilla, *The Stillborn God: Religion, Politics, and the Modern West* (New York: Alfred A. Knopf, 2007).

[16] Asad, *Formations of the Secular*; Casanova, *Public Religions in the Modern World*; Ashis Nandy, "The Politics of Secularism and the Recovery of Religious Tolerance," in *Secularism and Its Critics*, ed. Rajeev Bhargava (Oxford: Oxford University Press, 1999), pp. 321–344; Jakobsen and Pellegrini, "Times Like This."

[17] Rodney Stark, "Secularization, R.I.P.," 1; See also: Rodeny Stark, "Atheism, faith, and the social scientific study of religion," *Journal of Contemporary Religion* 14, no. 1 (1999): 41–62; Rodney Stark and Roger Finke, *Acts of Faith: Explaining the Human Side of Religion* (University of CaliforniaPress, 2000).

[18] Danièle Hervieu-Léger, *Religion as a Chain of Memory* (New Brunswick, N.J: Rutgers University Press, 2000); Phillip E Hammond, *The Dynamics of Religious Organizations: The Extravasation of the Sacred and Other Essays* (Oxford: Oxford University Press, 2000); David Lyon, *Jesus in Disneyland: Religion in Postmodern Times* (Cambridge, UK: Polity Press in association with Blackwell Publishers, 2000); Keenan, "Post-Secular Sociology."

[19] Keenan, "Post-Secular Sociology."

[20] Lyon, *Jesus in Disneyland*.

[21] Zygmunt Bauman, *Liquid Modernity* (Cambridge, UK: Polity Press, 2000).

[22] William E. Connolly, *Why I Am Not a Secularist* (Minneapolis: University of Minnesota Press, 1999); Taylor, *A Secular Age*.

23   Taylor, *A Secular Age*, p. 431.

24   Connolly, *Why I Am Not a Secularist*.

25   Catherine M Bell, *Ritual Theory, Ritual Practice* (New York: Oxford University Press, 1992), p. 101; see also Jakobsen and Pellegrini, "Times Like This."

26   Casanova, *Public Religions in the Modern World*, p. 38.

27   Taylor, *A Secular Age*.

28   Bauman, *Liquid Modernity*.

29   Charles S. Liebman, *Aspects of the Religious Behavior of American Jews* (New York: Ktav Pub. House, 1974).

30   Yadgar and Liebman, "Beyond the Religious-Secular Dichotomy: Masortim in Israel"; see also H. Soloveitchik, "Rupture and Reconstruction: The Transformation of Contemporary Orthodoxy," *Tradition* 28, no. 4 (1994): 64–130.

31   See: Charles Taylor, "Interpretation and the Sciences of Man," in *Interpretive Social Science: A Second Look*, ed. Paul Rabinow and William M Sullivan (Berkeley: University of California Press, 1987), pp. 33–81; Hans-Georg Gadamer, *Truth and Method*, 2nd ed. (New York: Crossroad, 1989); Zygmunt Bauman, *Hermeneutics and Social Science: Approaches to Understanding* (London: Hutchinson, 1978).

32   See: Asher Cohen, *Israel and the Politics of Jewish Identity: The Secular-Religious Impasse* (Baltimore, Md: Johns Hopkins University Press, 2000); Charles Liebman, "Reconceptualizing the Culture Conflict among Israeli Jews," *Israel Studies* 2 (1997): 172–189; Charles S. Liebman, ed., *Religious and Secular: Conflict and Accommodation Between Jews in Israel* (Jerusalem: Keter Pub. House, 1990); Aviezer Ravitzky, *Religious and Secular Jews in Israel: A Kulturkampf?* (Jerusalem: Isreal Democracy Institute, 2000).

33   Taylor, *A Secular Age*, p. 431.

34   My discussion is based on 102 in-depth personal interviews conducted with Jewish Israeli men and women who self-identify as traditionists. The interviewees' ages range between 22 and 50. All of them have high school education, and about a third of them acquired college education. They live mostly in 'peripheral' towns and neighborhoods of the Tel-Aviv wider metropolitan area. All of them were born in Israel, and most of them (80%) — as is the case with Israeli traditionists in general — are of Mizrahi origin (that is they are descendents of Jewish immigrants from Muslim countries). The interviews were open-ended, and were conducted either personally by me or by one of three research assistants, usually at the interviewee's home. They revolved around issues that were deemed important by me as well as by the interviewees for understanding their identity as traditionists. The interviews were conducted in Hebrew, and translated into English by me, with the outmost attempt at preserving the relevant cultural nuances and contexts.

35   A comprehensive analysis of the issues raised here is to be published in Hebrew: Yaacov Yadgar, *Israeli Traditionists: Modernity without Secularization*, Israeli Judaism (Jerusalem: Hartman Institute/Bar-Ilan University, Faculty of Law/Keter).

36   Yaacov Yadgar and Charles Liebman, "Jewish Traditionalism and Popular Culture in Israel," *Iyunim Bitkumat Israel* 13 (2003): 163–180.

37 Shlomit Levy, Hanna Levinsohn and Elihu Katz, *Jewish Israelis: A Portrait* (Jerusalem: Avi Chai and the Israel Democracy Institute, 2002).

38 Rav Yosef Azran, a former Knesset representative from Shas (the bulk of Shas voters, I should mention, identify as Mizrahi traditionists) expressed this idea in a television panel discussing the findings of a major survey on the Jewish identity of Israelis. Azran reserved his criticism for the bulk of the traditionist, those who, in his opinion, were distancing themselves from the world of religion. (He excluded those who were originally secular and were now becoming more religious). In his words: "Why *masortim*? Because it was hard for the them to bear the yoke of religion, so they created an easy Judaism, whatever was easy for them. They keep cutting off more and more until all will be gone." Rav Yosef Azran in an interview with Aliza Lavi, in the program "Shavua Tov," Israeli TV Channel 1, May 4th, 2002.

39 Rivka Bar-Yoseph, "Desocialization and Resocialization: The Adjustment Process of Immigrants," in *Immigration, Ethnicity and Community*, ed. Ernest Krausz (New Brunswick, N.J: Transaction Books, 1980), pp. 19–27.

40 Some of the most brutal application of this formulation to the field of educational policy can be found in Reuven Feuerstein, *Children of the Melah: Cultural Underdevelopment Among Children of Morocco and Its Educational Implications* (Jerusalem: Szold Institute and the Department of Children's Immigration of the Jewish Agency, 1965).

41 Zygmunt Bauman, *Liquid Modernity* (Cambridge, UK: Polity Press, 2000).

42 It should be mentioned that the Conservative movement in Israel calls itself the "Masorti" movement. This often gives rise to a large measure of confusion. Conservatives themselves often address this confusion by identifying themselves as "Masorti with a capital M". This, by the way, is also a testimony to the ethnic (American-Ashkenazi) component in the movement's identity, which is, I believe, one of the major reasons for its failure to establish a close relationship with mizrahi-traditionalists in Israel.

43 Yaacov Yadgar, "Gender, Religion, and Feminism: The Case of Jewish Israeli Traditionalists," *Journal for the Scientific Study of Religion* 45, no. 3 (2006): 353–370.

44 See: Shlomo Deshen, "The religiosity of the Mizrahim: Public, Rabbis, and Belief," *Alpayim* 9 (1994): 44–58.

45 Charles Taylor, *A Secular Age* (Cambridge, Mass: Belknap Press of Harvard University Press, 2007), p. 431.

46 Mary Douglas, "Judgments on James Frazer," *Daedalus* (1978): 161; see also: José Casanova, *Public Religions in the Modern World* (Chicago: University of Chicago Press, 1994), pp. 40–74.

47 Charles Taylor, "The Politics of Recognition," in *Multiculturalism: Examining the Politics of Recognition*, ed. Amy Gutmann (Princeton, NJ: Princeton University Press, 1994), pp. 25–74.

48 Charles S. Liebman and Eliezer Don-Yehiya, *Civil Religion in Israel: Traditional Judaism and Political Culture in the Jewish State* (Berkeley: University of California Press, 1983).

SERVICE IN THE IDF
AND THE BOUNDARIES OF
ISRAEL'S JEWISH COLLECTIVE

ASHER COHEN and BERNARD SUSSER

The two subjects of this essay, military service and belonging to the Jewish ethnic/national collective, do not, ostensibly, have much in common with each other. The factors that set the boundaries for the collective, on the one hand, and the "symbolic rewards" that a society grants those who serve in its national army, on the other, do not appear to operate on the same intellectual/emotional plane. Gaining entry into the ethnic/national collective is not one of the "symbolic rewards" military service grants a soldier.

There is, of course, a voluminous literature describing the many elements that are involved in creating an ethnic/national collective. The list inevitably includes a common language and history, race, religion, culture, a geographic homeland, etc. Among these factors, an individual's service in the national army is rarely mentioned. Although military service is recognized as an important formative experience that strengthens one's identification with a specific nation-state, it is not normally considered a factor that bears on one's ethnic identity. Military service relates to one's formal duties as a citizen; it does not create a personal ethnic identity.[1]

In the United States, Canada, Australia, etc., where there is no distinction between citizenship and national belonging — as a matter of principle, the first entails the second — military service has no relevance in determining identity. In Israel, by contrast, ethnic belonging to the Jewish collective is sharply distinguished from citizenship. Some 20% of Arab and Druze Israeli citizens are not Jews and have no desire to be Jews. Virtually every ideological point of view in Israeli public discourse grants importance — even if for some it is not exclusive — to the Jewish identity of an individual's parents in determining Jewish ethnic belonging. Furthermore, virtually all agree that entering the Jewish collective requires some visible and dramatic actions that grant access to what tends to be a closed communal circle.

It goes without saying that there are millions of Jews world-wide who are recognized as such without having Israeli citizenship — indeed, even if they oppose the existence of the Jewish State. Jewishness may have a critical religious component but beyond this religious component it is also an ethnic identity that, in many cases, exists on its own. It is the sense of ethnic communalism which Jewish Israelis share, more than the Jewish religion *per se*, that lies at the foundation of the Jewish character of Israel. (This statement, however, requires reservations and modifications that would take us far from our subject.)

Israel certainly does have multi-cultural elements but at base it is an ethnic state.[2] As such, joining the ethnic collective is not a formal or technical matter as pledging allegiance or signing citizenship papers are.[3] It requires, as we put it, "visible and dramatic actions." Consider, for example, risking one's life in military service to defend the Jewish State.

This essay focuses on the unique Israeli case in which military service has become a significant and contentious element in the public discourse on the boundaries of the Israeli-Jewish national collective. We will argue that in those cases where the disjunction between national belonging and service in the Israel Defense Forces (IDF) is clear and impermeable, the boundaries of the national/ethnic collective are not affected by army duty. By contrast, in those cases where Jewish ethnic identity is in dispute — a phenomenon that has greatly intensified since the mass immigration from the Commonwealth of Independent States (CIS) — military service has become a charged issue. It has added yet another dimension to what is already a complex and thorny controversy about the boundaries of national identity. Military service is looked upon by a substantial number of Israelis as a rite of passage, an alternate, non-traditional route through which one acquires access into the Jewish-Israeli collective. In a word, our subject is the highly significant 'symbolic reward' granted to those whose very military service is thought to transform them into members of the national collective.

We are not analyzing a demographically marginal phenomenon affecting only a few individuals. As a consequence of the mass immigration from the CIS, roughly 310,000 immigrants who are not halachically Jewish and are not registered as Jews by the Israeli authorities are currently resident in Israel.[4]

They do not constitute a monolithic group but rather divide into a number of different sociological categories: At the 'Jewish' extreme of the continuum, there is the small minority of about 15,000 immigrants who have either undergone religious conversion or who are now in the process of undergoing one. At the opposite end, there are between 50,000 and 80,000 who are defined as ethnic Russians including about 30,000 who officially identify themselves and are registered as Christians. The largest group, in the center of the continuum, comprises between 200,000 and 250,000 immigrants who are in the process of being culturally 'assimilated'[5] into the Jewish/Israeli collective.

Among those in this large assimilating group, Jewish self-identification and practice spans a wide spectrum. There are those who adopt unmistakably traditional behavior that can often exceed the Israeli/Jewish norm. At the other end, there are many whose assimilation process is considerably more reserved and unenthusiastic. Our essay deals with those in this large intermediate group whose Jewishness is the subject of public debate — a debate exacerbated by their serving in the Jewish State's army. (It is important to note that at any given time between 5,000 and 6,500 'non-Jewish' soldiers are serving in the IDF.[6]) Do the hardships and dangers of their military service affect their being perceived and defined as belonging to the Jewish/Israeli collective?

(A very telling, not to say ironic, 'multi-culturalist' episode was reported in 2002 by the army's Chief Rabbi. In that year, the army rabbinate distributed 1000 copies of the New Testament that were requested by non-Jewish immigrants for the 'swearing in' ceremony conducted after the completion of basic training. This number represents 15% of all the 'non-Jewish' soldiers in regular military service which roughly accords with the Christian part of the Russian Ethnic component among the immigrants.)

1. ETHNO-NATIONAL BELONGING AND MILITARY SERVICE: A GENERAL AND TERMINOLOGICAL INTRODUCTION

The 'Who is a Jew?' question is, of course, among the most persistent and hotly debated issues in Israeli public life. It pits the Orthodox (and many 'traditional' Jews) against those who tend to more secular beliefs and practices. The Orthodox accept only the halachic standards for Jewishness — either a Jewish mother or conversion — while the secular would broaden and loosen these requirement dramatically. They insist that other, more 'modern,' criteria should be considered, such as: self-identification, the sense of belonging, Jewish genealogy even if it is on the father's side, behavior patterns, and so on. Military service, although not usually included in this list, is gradually becoming a lightening rod that presents the 'Who is a Jew' question in a novel and very pointed way.

The disjunction between ethnic belonging and military sacrifice is also present in the literature on the 'symbolic rewards' that military service grants a soldier. States and societies regularly grant compensations of various kinds to those who fulfill their military duties because of all the inconvenience and danger involved. It is clear as well, that the greater the threat to the populace of the country, the greater the 'symbolic rewards' are likely to be. 'Convertibility,' as it is called, means the ability to translate the resources accumulated in one context to assets that serve the individual in another. It is regularly claimed that the potentially 'convertible' symbolic resources for military service are related above all to social prestige, economic benefits or to enhance civil rights.[7] It must, however, be emphasized here as well that granting social prestige and privileges do not include the very weighty contention that military service can be "converted" into ethno-national identity.

It is worth noting that the IDF created a program of religious conversion for 'non-Jewish' soldiers. This program is considered 'friendly' and quick by comparison with the much stricter programs offered by the Israeli rabbinate for 'non-Jewish' civilians.[8] The 'compensation' given to the 'non-Jewish' immigrants serving in the army is, therefore, the ability to undergo a relatively uncomplicated religious conversion. This makes it all the more clear that to become part of the Jewish collective, religious conversion is a necessity. Military service by itself is insufficient — at least in formal terms — to establish membership in the national collective.

Moreover, it needs to be emphasized that the ethos of a people's army serving as a melting pot for Israeli Jewishness has weakened substantially in recent years. Even if there is controversy as to the scope and depth of the problem, there is little doubt that the process is well underway.[9] *Prime facie,* this would seem to bolster the argument that military service has no link to ethno-national identity.[10]

In the early decades of its existence, the Israel Defense Forces (IDF) was regularly described as a powerful consolidating force that helped unify the hundreds of thousands Jews who had come to Israel from dozens of countries and cultures. Military service created not only an effective fighting unit out of a motley group of conscripts; it was also an experience that converted far-flung immigrants into a single Jewish cultural unit. The very term '*gibush*' or 'consolidation' was a regular part of the vocabulary of military service and one of its prime objectives. If there was a melting pot in which Jewish Israeliness was forged, it was often identified with service in the IDF.

In those early years, the identity between consolidating a fighting army and socializing immigrants as Jewish Israelis could easily be taken for granted because virtually all the new immigrants were Jews. To be sure, there were non-Jewish soldiers in the new IDF. Druze and Bedouin units, for example, fought alongside the Jewish forces right from the start. In their case, however, there was no question of them becoming part of the new Jewish Israeli identity. There were also the Jews who did not serve in the IDF. The Haredi community rejected conscription. Nonetheless, there were none who would deny their Jewishness.

Our discussion begins with a short account of the early period in which there was no ostensible connection between military service and ethnic identity. Thereafter, we will present the historical debate regarding the 'Who is a Jew' issue as it was argued in the context of military service. We follow with an analysis of the singular phenomenon of immigrants from the former Soviet Union who although halachically non-Jewish, undergo intense processes of assimilation into Jewish Israeli society — perhaps most salient of which is service in the IDF. In this context, we explore the illuminating public debate regarding the status of these soldier-immigrants and their relationship to the Jewish Israeli collective.

2. Ethnic Belonging and Service in the Israeli Army: The Druze and Bedouin, and the Haredim

Although military service (or non-service) plays an important role in the public perception of the Druze, Bedouin, and Haredim, these perceptions do not relate to their position in the Jewish-Israeli collective. The service granted by the non-Jewish minorities to the State is presented as a model of loyalty but not even the most radical Israeli patriot among the Druze would claim that it makes them part of the Jewish Israeli collective. They would bridle at the very suggestion. By contrast, although Haredi non-service in the army is the object of rancorous public criticism no one would deny their ethnic Jewishness.

The only attempt in recent years to connect ethnic belonging to military service was made by Yosef (Tommy) Lapid of the Shinui Party in a raucous speech delivered to the Knesset in 2001:

> Mr. Chairman, I ask myself can it be, is it possible that Jews, Jews in the Jewish State, on days when Jews are being killed, on days when old people are being drafted into the reserves in order to protect Jews, on days when we are told that there is no money for soldiers who have completed their army service because the money is needed for the defense of the Jewish homeland — can it be that on such a day that Jews in the Knesset of the Jewish State propose a law to excuse

Jews from military service for a year or two? The only reasonable, logical answer to my question is that they are not Jews. (...) They are something like the Sabbateans, the Karaites, the Samaritans. The Haredim, a very strange sect that has survived in this land, does not identify with Judaism, with the Jewish State. They only pay attention to what the Jews do in order to extort, to injure, to take, to profit, but not, forbid it, to contribute anything to the state of the Jewish people. (...) When you understand that the Haredim do not belong to Judaism, then you understand their conduct. Because if they were Jews, what they do and what they inflict upon this state is absurd, inconceivable... " (Divrei Haknesset, 2001/3/6; 7/3/2001).

Clearly, Lapid's speech is more a reflection of his brash and belligerent style than an attempt to present a serious argument. It expresses anger that is broadly felt in Israeli society — even though the vast majority of Israelis would recoil from his hateful invective — but it has no bearing on the universal perception of Haredim as an integral part of the Jewish people.

3. A Jewish Father and a Jewish Motherland: The Case of Chanan Frank (1970)

German Rozhkov, a deputy company commander, who was killed in a battle with terrorists in 2002 — a story to which we will presently return — was not yet born when Chanan Frank, who suffered from 100% army disability, directed a number of trenchant questions to the then Prime Minister, Golda Meir in 1970. These questions cut to the heart of the complex roots of Jewish identity in Israel and expose the tortured boundary lines of the Israeli Jewish collective.

Chanan Frank wrote his letter to Golda Meir in early 1970 against the background of public debates regarding the alteration of the terms of the Law of Return. These debates began in the wake of the Supreme Court's decision to register the children of Major Benyamin Shalit as Jews despite the fact that their mother was not Jewish.

Until that year, the Law of Return declared that "all Jews are entitled to 'make aliyah' to Israel"[11] and automatically became citizens of Israel but it did not specify 'Who is a Jew?' and what the boundaries of the Jewish collective are. Israel conducts a population registry that records each individual's nationality[12] and religion and, until 2002, these identities appeared in every citizen's identity card as well.

Major Benyamin Shalit was married to a non-Jewish woman and, in halachic terms, his children were not Jewish. Shalit appealed to the Supreme Court against the Minister of the Interior demanding that his children be registered as Jews under the category of 'nationality' and 'no religion' in the category of religious belonging. In a five to four split decision, the court ruled to accept Shalit's appeal and directed the Minister of Interior to register his children as Jewish.

The National Religious Party (NRP) immediately declared that in dissociating Jewish identity from halacha, the court's decision had violated their most cardinal religious and national beliefs.[13] Given the centrality of the NRP to Israeli political coalition building, intense discussions were held with the purpose of changing the terms of the Law of Return to make it acceptable to the central political forces of the country.

The change that was proposed and finally accepted in the Knesset included two crucially important elements. The first was the clear definition of the term 'Jew' in religious halachic terms: "One who was born to a Jewish mother or who has undergone conversion and who was not a member of another religion." The second was the introduction of a *'family'* provision, which declared that the right to 'return' to Israel would apply not only to halachic Jews but also to their spouses, their children and spouses, and to their grandchildren and their spouses. [14] In effect, the law narrowed the definition of 'Jew' to its halachic boundaries but simultaneously broadened the Right of Return to include their non-Jewish family members. The new law awakened intense debate in the media and the case of Chanan Frank was perhaps its most charged instance.

Chanan Frank began his letter to Prime Minister Golda Meir recounting the story of his *aliya* to Israel, his joining the founding core (*gar'in*) of Kibbutz Revadim, his being the son of a Jewish father and a non-Jewish mother (hence not defined as a Jew according to the new version of the Law of Return) and the loss of both of his legs in a military action. He asks:

> Do you think I was right in coming to Israel? As one who is a non-Jew by law, is my place here? Do you think I did the right thing when I was drafted, like every Jewish citizen who must do military service in the IDF? ... Did I lose both my legs for the homeland or am I mistaken and this is not my homeland at all? Because I thought of myself as a Jew, I made 'aliya' to Israel and was drafted into the army but it seems that all this is not sufficient. What must I do to be a Jew?[15]

Chanan Frank's case was paradigmatic: he identified intensely as a Jew, his life had been lived in Jewish surroundings, his father was Jewish, he was a founder of a Kibbutz and, most dramatically, he paid a tragic price for his perception of himself as a Jew.

The letter was read at a demonstration against the Law of Return that took place opposite the Knesset in February 1970. When Frank's question "What must I do to be a Jew?" was read, a young religious man grabbed the microphone and shouted: "Convert!" Here then were the two positions expressed in their simplest and most dramatic form. Being a Jew in Frank's mind implied the throwing of one's lot in with the Jewish people. For the young religious man however, Jewishness was defined either by birth or by conversion.

A large front-page photo in one of the newspapers showed Chanan Frank sitting in a wheel chair. The text alongside the photo contained a scathing critique of the new Law of Return. It mentioned his being 100% disabled because of his military service and in a large headline added: "100% Jew." The intention of the headline was clear: the service in the army, especially when it involved such a heavy personal price, is a crucial factor in determining whether one is to be considered a Jew or not.

Referring to the Frank case, the religious scientist-philosopher Yeshayahu Leibowitz noted: "If a non-Jewish volunteer fights heroically, he should receive a medal of honor and, if he is disabled, a pension... But his volunteering and heroism do not make him into a Jew: *Waffenbruderschaft* (brothers in arms) is not the same thing as *Bruderschaft* (being brothers)." Leibowitz's position argues for the exclusivity of the religious position in determining membership in the Jewish collective. It makes a sharp distinction between Jewish belonging and the more general belonging to the collective of Israeli citizens. In the terms we used earlier, Leibowitz distinguished acutely between civilian 'symbolic rewards' that are appropriate for a wounded soldier and ethno-national belonging that is not open to negotiation outside the domain of halacha.

To this the philosopher Shmuel Hugo Bergmann responded: "The non-Jewish volunteer becomes a 'brother' to me by his volunteering because he fought for the God of Israel even though he is an atheist. The Jewish people cannot rid themselves of such people simply with a medal of honor and a pension." [16]

The link between Israel military security and the 'Who is a Jew?' question arose very pointedly in arguments between the Supreme Court judges in the Major Binyamin Shalit case. Justice Zvi Berenzon presented what appeared to him the absurdity of the halachic point of view that rests exclusively on birth and is entirely severed from the real world of national life:

> According to this teaching, the chief terrorist from East Jerusalem, born to a Jewish woman … who dedicated himself to kill, ravage and destroy the State of Israel, would be considered an ally and son of the Jewish nation while the son and daughter of a Jewish major who fights the wars of Israel would be lacking in Jewish nationality. The soul shudders to think that such a reality could prevail in the State of Israel.[17]

The judge was referring to an important Fatah activist of those days, Kamal Nimri, who was the son of a Jewish mother and a Palestinian father and who was involved in detonating a refrigerator stuffed with explosives in Jerusalem's Mahane Yehuda market. In objective halachic categories, Kamal Nimri, the terrorist, is a Jew. In subjective terms, i.e., those related to his self-perception and to his actions, his having a Jewish mother seems entirely risible. In Justice Berenzon's view, even those who comply with all the objective halachic standards but who act in an anti-Jewish fashion cannot be considered part of the national collective.

Justice Zilberg, loyal to halachic standards, responded to the paradox in a very different way:

> The son of the Jewish mother, a member of the terrorist Fatah, is a Jewish scoundrel, a wicked evildoer. Many like him are found in Jewish New Left circles. The petitioner's [Major Shalit's] children are, by distinction, nice but ill-fated. Because of the stubborn opposition of their parents to the (Jewish) religion, they have not been entitled to receive the entrance ticket to the Jewish nation.[18]

The Supreme Court's Chief Justice, Shimon Agranat, joined this debate in a way that expressed more hesitation than Justices Berenzon and Zilberg. On the one hand, he declared that:

> the present generation possesses an equality of rights with those of the past and, therefore, is not required to accept 'as a totality' the commandments of the latter since the present has its own dynamic and the current generation is free to act in accordance with its own views and in consideration of new necessities that have arisen.[19]

In the terms we have been using, Agranat understands Jewish identity as a 'construction', a developing perception influenced by historical processes and current assessments taking place among Jews who comprehend their Jewish identity in ways that are not necessarily bound only by halacha. Nevertheless, in that very same decision,[20] Agranat declares, "every deviation from the framework of halachic definition … is liable to scatter deep ideological divisiveness between the (Jewish) people in Israel and the Jews in the Diaspora or to cause widespread confusion among the latter." Agranat's formulation reiterates the obligation to the religious norm although it is not an obligation to halacha itself but rather to the desire to preserve Jewish unity between those who are committed to halacha and those who are not.

This was neither the first nor the last time that the fraught argument regarding the elements comprising Jewish identity and the boundaries of belonging to the Jewish nation arose in full force. At one end, as we have noted, there are those who insisted on the exclusiveness and permanence of halachic requirements: birth to a Jewish mother or conversion. At the other, there are those who define Jewishness in terms of self-identification, values and way of life rather than exclusively halachic considerations. What is crucial for our purposes is that for this latter view, military service and the self-sacrifice it entails, is one of the constitutive elements in the determination of one's Jewish Israeli identity.

Nonetheless, the Chanan Frank case reflects a far more intensely personal issue than the substantial demographic problems that have arisen with the mass immigration of ex-Soviet citizens in more recent years. In the Israeli society of 1970, it was rare for the phenomenon of a person's Jewishness to spark controversy. We may confidently estimate that within Israeli society at that time there were no more than a few hundred Israeli residents with questionable Jewishness — those who fell into categories like that of Shalit and Chanan Frank. Since the mass Soviet immigration, the unique problems of a few individuals have transformed into a wide-scale national challenge that relates to tens of thousands young people, officially considered 'non-Jews' who are either currently serving in the IDF or slated to serve in the coming years.

4. THE GERMAN ROZHKOV CASE (2002)

Lieutenant German Rozhkov, deputy commander of a company in the Nahal Brigade, an infantry combat unit, the only son to his non-Jewish mother Ludmilla, was killed in a battle with terrorists in the Upper Galilee in 2002. In the period before his death, he formulated, together with a friend, a letter to Prime Minister Ariel Sharon. The letter raised charged questions that although reminiscent of Chanan Frank's questions thirty-two years earlier, presented issues that were arguably even more complex. "Do I have to be killed," Rozhkov asked, "in order for my mother not to be deported from Israel, for her to get Israeli citizenship?"

As opposed to Chanan Frank, German Rozhkov did not appeal on behalf of himself and did not object to his own definition as a non-Jew. He was already born into the official reality of the Law of Return as revised in 1970. Rozhkov came to Israel with the full knowledge that the Law of Return did not define him as a Jew (whatever his self-perceptions might have been) although it permitted him to exercise his right of return and become an Israeli citizen because his father was Jewish. What he was requesting were 'rights' for his mother who did not fall into any of the Law of Return's categories.

The differences between the cases of Rozhkov and Frank are apparent. Frank explicitly demanded recognition as a Jew as is clear from his letter to Prime Minister Golda Meir. Moreover, Frank as well as the Shalit children represented rare instances in Israeli society rather than partaking in a large-scale social phenomena. Rozhkov, by contrast, demanded only basic residence and, at most, citizenship rights for his mother. In practice however, the Rozhkov case cannot be seen as a private matter. Whatever his own sense of personal identity might have been, German Rozhkov became a symbolic representative of a broad social and national issue that affected hundreds of thousands of immigrants who were in a similar halachic position as his own. Consequently, and as we shall see in the examples provided below, Rozhkov's case was immediately transformed into a lightening rod in the controversy over the boundaries of the Jewish collective. Its importance went far beyond narrow residence and citizenship issues and touched upon the core character of the Jewish/Israeli national collective.

The crisis related to German Rozhkov and his mother reflects one of the more trying cases that arose in the wake of the mass immigration from the ex-Soviet Union. Under the provisions of the Law of Return, many Jews came to Israel together with family members of the first order who were not themselves entitled to Israeli citizenship under the stipulations of the law. They were classified as 'temporary residents,' a status that needed to be periodically renewed.

The details of the complex case of German Rozhkov are as follows. He was the son of a Jewish father and a non-Jewish mother who had divorced before immigrating to Israel. On the strength of his being the son of a Jewish father, he was entitled to 'return' and receive Israeli citizenship. His mother fell into a different category entirely. The provisions of the Law of Return weren't applicable to her because the divorce deprived her of any Jewish family link — neither that of her ex-husband nor that of her non halachically Jewish son. She arrived in Israel as a 'temporary resident', a status she needed to apply for afresh every few months. This is to say that her status in Israel was uncertain and tentative. Again, a painful paradox arose, which formed the background for German Rozhkov's chilling letter to Prime Minister Sharon and explains what transpired afterwards.

In brief, the son (German Rozhkov) was entitled to citizenship because of the Law of Return's *family* provision. His mother, by contrast, had no determinate status at all. Hence German Rozhkov (and many others like him) struggled to obtain 'permanent resident' status for their parents. This was Ludmilla Rozhkov's unenviable position.

Rozhkov's macabre question — "Do I need to be killed in order to resolve my mother's status as a resident of Israel?" — turned out, tragically, to be more than rhetorical, and received an 'affirmative' answer. A day after his death, Ministry of Interior officials arrived with the desired 'stamp' for Ludmilla Rozhkov's passport. The press carried a photo with truly surrealistic qualities: A government official is stamping her documents with a 'permanent resident' permit on the hood of the taxi that had come to take her to identify her son's body. The media described Rozhkov as someone who fought on two fronts simultaneously: a military front in which he fought as an officer and a civilian front where he fought to assure his mother's right to stay in Israel.[21]

Maya Kaganskaya, an author and journalist in the Russian language, analyzing the complex reciprocal relations between civil rights, official administrative registration, national belonging and religious halacha wrote the following which clearly goes far beyond the technicalities of residence and citizenship:

> The bleeding State of Israel must come to peace with the new historical reality of the Jewish people in its historical homeland. This new reality makes it imperative to assert that a Jew in Israel is not only the one who has Jewish blood flowing in his veins. A Jew is also the one who is prepared to spill his blood for his people and his homeland ... A woman like this must be judged by one and only halacha: the halacha of the spilt blood of her son that seeped into the land.[22]

Ironically, Kaganaskya cites a halachic term familiar in the rabbinical discussion of 'military sacrifice' in making her appeal for German Rozhkov's Jewishness: "The Halacha of Spilt Blood."

The Minister of Interior, Eli Yishai from the ultra-Orthodox Sephardic party Shas declared:

This is a hard thing. We must help them. Without connection to the present case, there are thousands of people who would want to serve here in a foreign legion in order to live in Israel. The State of Israel must decide whether it wants to bring here thousands of foreign workers who will be drafted into the army.[23]

Bambi Sheleg, a religious Zionist publicist and editor of the Magazine *Eretz Acheret* did not hesitate to attack the religious establishment directly.

The story of German Rozhkov is a heart-rending example of the intolerable gap between the self-perception of Rozhkov and of the ex-Soviet community, who saw him as fully Jewish, and his status in the eyes of halachic authorities of this generation... Is there not in his action... an unqualified commitment, the affirmation of a covenant of fate and purpose with the Jewish people of this generation? Has the time not come for one of the rabbis who consider themselves as Zionists to say something courageous on this issue? If they say nothing, if they keep their silence at this time—if they continue to publicly shame the best of our sons—Jews will seek welfare and deliverance from other sources.[24]

Sheleg's argument is interesting for another important reason as well. She is arguing from within the context of the religious-Zionist movement for which military service is a national religious commandment (*mitzvah*) deriving from their credo that the State of Israel is permeated with deep religious significance. Military service is often spoken of as a sacred calling. (Not surprisingly, there are today disproportionate numbers of religious Zionist who choose to serve in 'active combat units.') It is not difficult to understand the quandary that must arise in the minds of these religious soldiers who serve alongside 'non-Jewish' Israeli citizens, soldiers who often fully identity themselves as Jews. They share the same mess and tents, fight as small units each protecting the other, and risk their lives as a team for the same goal.

One obvious question that needs to be addressed is this: to what extent is the 'intermediate' group of some 200,000–250,000 sociologically assimilating immigrants really interested in entering the Jewish/Israeli national mainstream? Are they perhaps concerned with Israeli citizenship and little else? Do they want to be recognized as a distinct group that has Israeli citizenship — 'non-Arab Israelis' — i.e., citizens who are broadly Israeli but without a distinct Jewish identity?

The results of research in this area are not conclusive. Different future scenarios — often contradictory — are presented without confidence as to which of them is most likely. For example, Baruch Kimmerling discusses three possible futures: first, assimilation into Jewish/Israeli society especially by the middle class younger generations with a concomitant decline in Russian uniqueness. Second, the preservation of Russian cultural distinctiveness as well as belonging to Jewish/Israeli society — much as has happened to other groups of immigrants over the years. Finally, an isolation and the sharpening of their Russian character while rejecting their Israeliness and their Jewishness.[25]

Commenting on the future of non-halachically Jewish *olim*, Lissak and Leshem, despite uncertainties, express a distinctly 'negative' (from the point of view of assimilation) perspective.

> We do not have data at this stage that can indicate in a meaningful way about the cultural identity of this Israeli group. Still, it may be assumed that behavior patterns that emphasize loyalty to their culture of origin and rejection of the absorbing culture will be relatively frequent among this population.[26]

Among the more traditional and religious sectors of Israeli society, the dominant perspective is that the Russian immigrants are becoming a part of Israeli society — a positive phenomenon they applaud. Israeliness provides a conveniently blurred identity that serves to occlude the far more thorny issue of Jewishness. For this large group of traditional and religious Jews (including much of the country's political leadership) there can be no entry into the Jewish collective apart from conversion — whatever the sociological and personal experiences, including military service, the *olim* may undergo.

A second approach, also with many adherents, depicts Israel as a multicultural society, even a multi-national society whose character as a Jewish State is gradually fading in importance. For example, Yifat Weiss, claims that the Law of Return, with its broad conception of 'returnees', has made Israel into a multi-ethnic state. "It is difficult," she writes, "to accept the view that in the global multi-cultural reality a few hundred thousand ethnic Russians, who immigrated and continue to immigrate to Israel, will assimilate into Israeli society." [27] Mark Kopovtzky notes: "It is possible to predict with a certain degree of security, that if the current tendencies among the *olim* continues… in ten or twenty years, another rather large ethnic minority will be created — with all the problems appertaining thereunto." He believes that the non-Jewish cohort is "liable to become a rather isolated ethnic minority with, possibly, a Christian orientation."[28]

There are however, other views and research as well that point in different directions. The work of Majid El-Haj and Elazar Leshem indicates that among the non-Jewish immigrants and their spouses there is a substantial group that perceives itself as Jewish in identity and belonging. 89% among the halachic Jews who were questioned reported that they feel Jewish either to "a great degree or a very great degree." Among those who are not halachically Jewish or who are married to non-Jews 57% declared themselves to feel Jewish to a great or very great degree.[29]

The charged nature of military service and the sacrifices it entails is visible in yet another highly sensitive arena. Conflicts have erupted from time to time regarding the burial of soldiers who were not halachically Jewish. Halachically, only Jews may be buried in a Jewish cemetery. The most famous of these cases, which sparked national controversy, took place in the summer of 1993. The soldier Lev Pesachov was killed in a battle in Lebanon and the media reported that he was buried in a fringe area of the military cemetery because he was not halachically recognized as a Jew. The revelation caused a storm of protest that persisted over the course of a number of days. After strident debate, Pesachov's body was exhumed and reburied in a regular (Jewish) army plot. What is remarkable about this case is the position of some rabbis who made it clear that no halachic problem exists: one may bury a soldier who has died in battle in a regular army grave.[30] To be sure, this does not signify a halachic pronouncement that one who falls in battle is transformed into a Jew. In this regard, Pesachov's case is indeed different. Nevertheless, the very willingness to advocate a halachic rule that opposes the conventional approach, reveals that even the religious community sees military service as a an important component in the debate on Jewishness.

On the human scale of values upon which individual contributions to societies, states, homelands, communities and nations are measured, Chanan Frank, Lev Pesachov and German Rozhkov not only fully fulfilled their duties, they paid the heaviest of personal prices. Frank's, Pesachov's and Rozhkov's deeds are appreciated beyond the normal admiration expressed for others who pay a high personal price in serving their country. The 'symbolic reward' that many are willing to bestow upon them is entrance into the Jewish Israeli collective.

5. SOCIOLOGICAL CONVERSION

One of the basic traits of Jewish Israeli society is its development and self-definition in the course of persistent military conflict — conflict usually seen in life and death terms. Hence, the IDF's dominance in the formation of Israeli culture is difficult to overstate. Patterns of military leadership, interpersonal relationships, modes of thought, and social norms have all been attributed to the centrality of the IDF experience in Israeli life.[31] Military service as well as the civilian experience of military and terrorist hostility has a deep formative and acculturating effect on the Israeli public mind. Nili Elias notes that among the ex-Soviet *olim*, the 'Al-Aksa' Intifada that broke out in September 2000 brought them closer to becoming 'Israeli.' According to most *olim*, the mass terrorist attacks made the new immigrants and the veteran Israelis "brothers in blood," belonging to the same communal family.[32]

Chanan Frank and German Rozhkov, the one with his severe wound and the other with his death in battle, underwent a form of 'sociological conversion' — tragic, focused and quick. It is not necessary however, to be wounded or killed in battle to become part of the sociological conversion phenomenon. To be sure, extreme cases such as those of Frank and Rozhkov raise the issue of Jewish/Israeli identity to its most incisive form, thrust it into the public's consciousness and make it a heated subject of media discourse. Nonetheless, the issue is far broader than military service *per se*; it has become another arena in which the 'Who is a Jew' controversy is debated.

In this debate, military service is a symbolic act with strong subjective connotations. Although by halachic standards, a particular soldier may not be Jewish, his/her own experience of IDF service together with the broad social perception that defending the Jewish State gives one some kind of Jewish standing is becoming commonplace in Israeli society. The day-to-day lives of those who are not halachically Jews are, in practice, full of personal, experiential feelings of Jewishness. The accumulation of these subjective sensibilities gives rise to a gradual and consistent process of sociological conversion.

6. Summary and Conclusions

Our discussion has shown that in cases where a soldier's Jewishness or non-Jewishness is clear, military service has no bearing on his identity. This general assertion is true so long as those in question are Druze, Bedouin, Christians or Haredim. The issue arises among the large number of halachically non-Jews who came to Israel from the CIS and who lead Israeli and to one degree or another Jewish lives, serve the country militarily, often at great personal risk.

It is important to note that even before the issue of military service further fanned the flames of dissension, their status as Jews was already controversial. In cases where they identify themselves as Jews and Israeli patriots, speak Hebrew, study in the Jewish/Israeli school system, where they live lives that can often be more traditionally Jewish than their halachic but secular Jewish neighbor next-door — it is difficult, even for some religious Zionists, to feel entirely comfortable with the very limiting categories provided by halacha. To say nothing of secular-liberal Israeli Jews. When these Israeli/Jewish signs of belonging are compounded by military service, when 'non-Jewish Jews' endanger their lives in the IDF alongside and without any distinction from their Jewish comrades — the 'Who is a Jew?' question becomes unavoidable.

Alexander Jacobson and Amnon Rubinstein relate to the claims for halachic exclusivity in determining Jewishness and to the necessity for conversion in cases where one's mother is not Jewish in the following way:

> These olim receive Israeli citizenship and, for the most part, integrate successfully into the Hebrew-speaking Jewish Israeli society. Although they are not registered as Jews, they comprise an inextricable part of this society ... The claim that Orthodox halacha and its interpreters are those who determine the boundaries of the Jewish national collective in Israel is today a claim that is cut off from the social reality of Israel.[33]

One safe, if unfortunate, assumption is that the security threats confronting Israel will not abate in the foreseeable future. Whether they are long range threats from Iran (physically and temporally) or short-range threats from Hamas-controlled Gaza or Syria, the IDF's role will remain paramount in Israeli society. With military operations a near certainty, the likelihood of growing 'symbolic rewards' for military service is substantial. 'Sociological conversion' gives every sign of becoming a growing phenomenon. The opportunities for 'non-Jewish Jews' gaining informal access to the Jewish collective by non-halachic means would appear to grow apace. The threat to the 'Who is a Jew?' *modus vivendi*, appears to become more intense as time passes. Although it abets the controversy, military service in itself, does not create it. Nevertheless, it presents the dilemma in a compelling and singularly stark fashion.

NOTES

1   In a broad theoretical survey of the literature, Tor Kaspa, Pereg and Mikulincer present a wide variety of components thought to be significant in determining identity and belonging to a national collectivity, with special attention to Jewish identity. They include all the familiar items mentioned above. Notably they do not mention military service despite the fact that Israel's army is regularly described as a "people's army" that is under the constant existential threat of attack. See, Michal Tur-Kaspa Shimoni, Dana Pereg and Mario Mikulincer, "Psychological Aspects of Identity Formation and Their Implications for Understanding the Concept of Jewish Identity: A Review of the Scientific Literature," *Research and Position Papers of the Rappaport Center*, no. 6, Ramat Gan, Bar Ilan University, 2004, pp. 38–71. (Hebrew)

2   On the disjunction between national belonging and citizenship in Israel's character as an ethnic democracy see, Sammy Smoocha, "An Ethnic Democracy: Israel as a Prototype," in Ruth Gavison and Daphna Hacker (eds.), *The Jewish-Arab Divide in Israel: A Reader* (Jerusalem: The Israel Democracy Institute), pp. 153–200. (Hebrew)

3   See, Eliezer Don Yehiya and Bernard Susser, "Nation-States in the West: Israel as a 'Deviant Case'" *Democratic Culture*, I (Spring 1999): 9–22. (Hebrew)

4   This data is correct for the spring/summer of 2007 according to Israel's Central Bureau of Statistics. The number includes not only those who themselves immigrated to Israel from the CIS but also their children born in Israel.

5   For further elaboration on this subject see: Asher Cohen, *Non Jewish Jews in Israel* (Keter Publishing House and the Hartman Institute, 2006).

6   According to the estimate of Yagil Levy, in *From 'People's Army' to Army of the Peripheries* (Jerusalem: Carmel Press, 2007), there were 5,000 'non-Jewish' soldiers serving in the IDF in 2005. The army's Chief Rabbi in an interview conducted in his office 30/12/2003 estimated the number at 6,500. See also Zvi Aloosh and Amir Rappaport's "6,500 Immigrant Soldiers in Regular Army Duty: Non-Jews," *Yediot Achronot* 13/3/2002, p. 20.

7   Yagil Levy, *From 'People's Army' to the Army of the Peripheries* (Jerusalem: Carmel Press, 2007), pp. 26–31; Yagil Levy "Militarizing Inequality: A Conceptual Framework," *Theory of Society*, 27 (6): 837–904.

8   Yagil Levy, *From 'People's Army' to Army of the Peripheries, op. cit.* p. 84; Edna Lomski-Feder and Eyal Ben-Ari, "From a 'People in Uniform' to 'Different Uniforms for the People': Professionalism, Diversity and the Israel Defense Forces," in M. Al-Haj and Uri Ben Ari (eds.), *In the Name of Security — The Sociology of Peace and War in Israel in Changing Times* (Haifa University Press, 2003), pp. 225–285. (Hebrew)

9   Stuart Cohen and Ilan Suliman, "IDF: From a People's Army to a Professional Army," *Ma'arachot* 341 (May 1995): 2–17; Stuart Cohen, "The IDF and Israeli Society: Towards the Diminution of the Army's Functions," in Moshe Lissak and Baruch Knei-Paz (eds.), *Israel Confronting the Twenty-First Century: Society, Politics and Culture* (Jerusalem: Magnes, 1996), pp. 215–232.

10   Some claim that in the face of the sociological diversity of its soldiers, multi-cultu-
      ralism has become one of the IDF's agendas. Edna Lomski-Feder and Eyal Ben-Ari,
      "From 'A People in Uniform to a 'Different Uniforms For the People': Professio-
      nalism, Diversity and the Israel Defense Forces," in M. Al-Haj and Uri Ben Ari (eds.),
      In the Name of Security — The Sociology of Peace and War in Israel in Changing Times
      (Haifa University Press, 2003), pp. 255–285 (Hebrew); Yagil Levy, *From 'People's
      Army' to Army of the Peripheries* (Jerusalem: Carmel Press 2007), pp. 209–211.

11   *The Law of Return*, 1950, *Sefer Ha'chukim*, 51, p. 159.

12   *The Law of Population Registry*, 1965, *Sefer Ha'chukim*, 466, p. 270.

13   It should be recalled that in the wake of a similar incident in 1958, the National
      Religious Party left the coalition in a storm of protest. See, Eliezer Don Yehiye,
      "Religion, Identity, Nationality and Politics: The 'Who is a Jew?' Crisis — 1958" in
      Mordechai Bar-On and Zvi Zameret (eds.), *Two Sides of the Bridge* (Jerusalem: Yad
      Ben Zvi, 2002), pp. 88–143.

14   *The Law of Return*, 1950, *Sefer Ha'chukim*, 586, p. 34.

15   Yonah Hadari, *Messiah Riding on a Tank* (Machon Hartman, the Tzivion Center — Bar
      Ilan University, the United Kibbutz Press, 2002), p. 170.

16   This incident and its broader context are described in Yonah Hadari, *Messiah Riding
      on a Tank*, pp. 170–172.

17   Pnina Lahav, "Personal Identity and Collective Identity: Modernity and Jewishness
      in the Shalit Case," in Menachem Mautner, Avi Sagi and Ronen Shamir (eds.), *Multi-
      Culturalism in a Democratic and Jewish State* (Tel Aviv: Ramot, Tel Aviv University,
      1998), p. 419.

18   Ibid.

19   Ibid., pp. 420–421.

20   An analysis of the judicial debate in the Shalit case in general and of Justice Agra-
      nat's position in particular is described and cited at length in: Pnina Lahav, op. cit.,
      pp. 439–409.

21   Avi Ashkenazi, "On the Way to Identity Her Son's Body She Became a Permanent
      Resident," *Maariv*, 14/3/2002, pp. 14–15.

22   Maya Kaganskaya "The Halacha of Spilt Blood," *Maariv*, 14/3/2002, pp. 12–13;
      Channel 2 News, 13/3/2002.

23   Glickman, Eytan, and Palter, Nurit, "The Good Sons to the Army, the Bad Parents
      to the State," *Yediot Achronot*, 24 Hours Supplement, 14/3/2002, pp. 2–3.

24   Bambi Sheleg, "Our People is Your People, Our God is Your God," *Maariv* (Maariv
      Today), p. 7.

25   Baruch Kimmerling, *Immigrants, Settlers and Natives* (Tel Aviv: Am Oved, 2004),
      pp. 430–431. (Hebrew)

26   Elazar Leshem and Moshe Lissak, "The Social and Cultural Consolidation of the
      Russian Jewish Community in Israel," in Moshe Lissak and Elazar Leshem (eds.),

From Russia to Israel: Identity and, Culture in Transition (Tel Aviv: Odem, 2001), p. 67. (Hebrew)

27   Yifat Weiss, "The Golem and its Creator or How the Law of Return Transformed Israel into a Multi-Ethnic State," *Theory and Criticism*, 19 (2001): 65. (Hebrew)

28   Marc Kopovtzky' "'Will they Both Walk Together?': The Post Soviet Jews and the Israeli Society," *Ex-Soviet Jews in Transition* 20–21 (2002): 61–64.

29   Majid Al-Haj and Elazar Leshem, *Immigrants from the Former Soviet Union in Israel: Ten Years Later* (University of Haifa Press, 2000), p. 59.

30   Yehuda Shaviv, "Beloved in Life — and in Their Death?," *Tchumin*, 14 (1994): 319–330. (Hebrew)

31   See Majid El-Haj and Uri Ben Eliezer (eds.), *In the Name of Security* (Haifa: University of Haifa Press and Pardess, 2003).

32   Nili Elias', *From the CIS to Israel and Germany: The Role of the Public Media in the Process of the Cultural and National Absorption of Immigrants* (Doctoral Dissertation, Tel Aviv University, 2003), p. 170.

33   Alexander Jacobson and Amnon Rubinstein, *Israel and the Family of Nations* (Jerusalem and Tel Aviv: Schocken, 2003), pp. 160 and 351–352. For elaboration of the non-halachic approaches that present 'secular' alternatives to joining the Jewish collective see, Asher Cohen, "Non-Jewish Jews: Non-halachic Approaches to the Question of Joining the Jewish Collective," in Stuart Cohen and Bernard Susser (eds.) *Ambivalent Jew: Charles Liebman in Memoriam* (New York: Jewish Theological Seminary Press, 2007), pp. 157–172.

IDEAS VS. REALITY:
MULTICULTURALISM
AND RELIGIOUS-ZIONISM

DOV SCHWARTZ

Religious-Zionism is a movement that has comprised different streams at different times. The movement, however, created a rather rigid frame in terms of consciousness and theology, which united the vast majority of its supporters until the end of the 1970s. This uniting frame includes several elements:

(1) An aim: Religious-Zionism set an external and general aim — establishing a state ruled by Halakhah — and an internal and personal aim — creating a new religious type with a complex consciousness. This type is involved in the modern world and genuinely strives to integrate, but also operates in a world of redemption.

(2) An ideological foundation: Religious-Zionism explicitly endorses several ideological conceptions, such as the ascription of religious value to Zionism and to the State of Israel, the redemption of the world through the redemption of the Jewish people, and a religious interpretation of history.

(3) Ideological intuitions: Religious-Zionism endorses several metaphysical outlooks such as the unity of the people of Israel (implying a hidden link between all Jews that is also extolled as a moral value); a divine presence in the world and in history, and a perception of Jewish secularism as a transient phenomenon.[1]

(4) Esotericism: Since history does not reflect the messianic interpretation of religious-Zionism, an esoteric approach emerges claiming that reality is driven by hidden Divine Providence. This is a crucial characteristic for the purpose of the current analysis, as noted below.

Given this defined consciousness, religious-Zionism could be expected to find the accommodation of multiculturalism a troubling notion. Multiculturalism assumes that even antithetical approaches deserve respect and legitimacy.[2] The religious-Zionist interpretation of history as a redemptive process, the deep belief in the movement's religious values, and the world view underlying religious-Zionist theology, all work against the idea of granting legitimation and respect to opposing views. For religious-Zionism, twentieth-century events are stages in the process of Israel's redemption. Every one of these events (the Balfour Declaration, the Holocaust, the establishment of the State of Israel, and so forth) brings the people of Israel closer to the messianic era. This interpretation presented the secularization of the Zionist movement in particular, and of most of the Jewish people in general, as temporary and transient. Secularization for religious-Zionism does not follow from an authentic recognition of modernity and it is implications for religion, but is perceived instead as a husk that covers the religious core. In the course of time, as redemption progresses, secularists will admit their mistake. The perception of secularization as temporary precludes any genuine recognition of other cultural groups' right to autonomy.

This article will present the following claim:

(1) Religious-Zionism is a movement founded on interpretation. Its reactions to historical decisions and events are deeply entrenched in the hermeneutical skills that the movement has managed to develop. This skill enabled an inversion of the process, and allowed its members to build a consciousness opposed to real facts. The reality is that Zionism is a secular movement, and the State of Israel is a liberal and democratic entity and, as such, far from being a state of Halakhah. Religious-Zionism, however, interpreted the national renaissance as the implementation of a divine plan and its aim as the completion of redemption. This interpretation precludes genuine integration in a multicultural environment.

(2) The idea of multiculturalism is currently being implemented, to some extent, in religious-Zionist society. Contrary to the expectations founded on the structure of religious-Zionism, reality can ultimately be said to have defeated consciousness. This statement relates to processes that have affected religious-Zionism in the last twenty years concerned with openness to, and experience in, areas that had previously seen as taboo (the media, the arts, the acknowledgement of democratic norms, and so forth). The processes reflect a reaction of "negotiation" to the secular world and the acceptance of some of its values. In a sense, religious-Zionism no longer ignores the stable, undeniable existence of a world outside religion, and ascribes value to its views. The processes recently affecting religious-Zionism compel a rethinking of its integration in a multicultural world.

(3) The following situation has therefore unfolded: in the first eight decades of its activity, interpretation outdid intransigent reality. In the last two decades, however, reality has begun to override interpretation.

The meaning of this argument, then, is that a trend of integration in a multicultural society has become discernible in religious-Zionism only in recent years. The details of this argument are clarified below, including an analysis of the linkage between religious-Zionism and multiculturalism.

1. PAST

The significant fact concerning the relationship between religious-Zionism and multiculturalism is that religious-Zionist consciousness is paternalistic, and thus unable to tolerate other cultural groups as independent. Given its pretension to provide a close and fully-fledged interpretation of Jewish history and of current Jewish existence, religious-Zionism maps and locates non-religious groups within this explanation. No cultural phenomenon relating to the Jewish people remains outside the all-inclusive interpretation suggested by religious-Zionism theology. Even what appears as "secular" or "multicultural" is part of the homogeneous explanation of religious-Zionism. Below is an outline of various stages in the development of the movement's patronizing attitude.

Esoteric Interpretation

The founder of the Mizrahi, Yitzhak Yaakov Reines, paved the way for the paternalistic approach toward Zionism.[3] In the wake of this approach, religious-Zionism developed an interpretation of modernity in general and of the Zionist renewal in particular that fits these basic assumptions.[4] The secularized Zionist idea, in this view, is not autonomous in the following senses:

(1) A religious core. The true meaning of the Zionist idea is religious. In a manifesto he published at the time of the Mizrahi's founding (1902), Zeev Jawitz explicitly stated the motivation for establishing the movement: "Because in the countries of our exile the soul of the nation, which is our holy Torah, can no longer prevail in its full power, nor can its commandments, which alone are the whole of spiritual life, be preserved in their purity."[5] He used the image of husk and core to illustrate the Mizrahi's mission. The secularization of Zionism and its various manifestations is the husk. But "in truth, all these things brought from the outside have no

relationship or genuine connection to the true essence of Zionism."[6] The perception of secularization as the husk of the "pure" religious core will also shape religious-Zionist consciousness in the future.

(2) *Religious source and religious continuity.* The Zionist idea does not appear *ex nihilo*, nor is it a rebellion against the past. Zionism is a continuation of the attachment to Eretz Israel, which Jewish religion had fostered over the centuries. Take, for instance, the following declaration of Judah Leib Maimon, a Mizrahi leader: "This is indeed obvious, and seemingly self-evident: Zionism is the offspring of religion. Were it not for religious Judaism, which tied the Hebrew nation to its historical land through historical threads, laws, and practices, such as 'memorials to the destruction of the Temple,' prayers and ritual songs, halakhot and aggadot — Zionism would have never come about."[7]

(3) *The idea of redemption.* Zionism is not only a continuation of the past but an expression of future religious faith. Over centuries, Jewish religion diligently endeavored to describe future redemption, and Zionism is the realization of these hopes. One instance is the formulation of Shmuel Hayyim Landau (Shahal), one of the leading figures in Ha-Po'el Ha-Mizrahi:

> Some have questioned the essence of Zionism. Yet, if we enter the depths of this issue and consider the very core of the idea, we will find it is a continuation of the Jewish messianic idea. The content of the messianic idea is also the content of Zionism. The content is — faith in the national redemption, in the idea that the Jewish people will return to their land and have an independent government.[8]

Religious-Zionism created a distinction between reality and the interpretation contradicting it. Historically, Zionism emerged as a movement of rebellion, not of continuity. The rebellion was not within but against the religious context: Zionist ideology related to religion as a symbolic source, and emptied it of its actual contents.[9] From the perspective of Zionist ideology, religious practice is merely an expression of exilic passivity. Religious-Zionism, however, interpreted reality antithetically: the true aim of the Zionist rebellion is a return to religious life. At its initial stage, religious-Zionism claimed that what really bothers secular Zionists is that the Torah in exile is incomplete, and only the wholeness of the Torah will satisfy them.

The religious-Zionist interpretation of the Zionist idea, as expressed by such leaders as Reines, Jawitz, and Maimon, gained deep theological support from an important thinker, R. Abraham Yitzhak Hacohen Kook. Although R. Kook never joined the movement officially, he provided a theological underpinning and a rabbinic cover. He developed a comprehensive interpretation of the Zionist endeavor through his impressions of the Second Aliyah pioneers. In his view, religious-Zionist youngsters seek no less than the return of prophecy. According to the Maimonidean principle, prophecy cannot be realized under persecution, so they chose freedom by rejecting what Judaism sanctifies. Their aspiration, however, is pure.[10] R. Kook's interpretation of these youngsters' ethos developed into an all-encompassing exegesis of the Zionist endeavor as a whole: the national awakening is a planned divine move. The heavenly response to Jewish redemption is paralleled by the response of the Jewish people. Even individuals who are distinctively secular inwardly wish to implement the divine plan.

Pronouncements by leading figures of early Zionism were also given a religious-Zionist interpretation at this time that presented, as it were, the inner core of the movement — religious renewal and the hastening of redemption. Theodor Herzl's speeches and his biography (from assimilation to nationalism) were favored objects of such interpretations, as fitting the religious-Zionist ideal. This was the starting point for the perception of Zionism as a movement of return to Judaism. The consciousness that developed through the hermeneutics of religious-Zionism was one of obliviousness to the concrete meaning of historical reality. Secular Zionism developed a similarly symmetrical consciousness: many of its leaders viewed religion as a transient phenomenon, holding that religious individuals would ultimately acknowledge modern national reality. Over time, however, many secular Zionists abandoned this interpretation, whereas the hermeneutical consciousness of religious-Zionism persists until this day and draws on the movement's conservative religious views.

The clash between interpretation and reality reached a pinnacle of intensity at the time of Israel's creation. Several leaders and ideologues of religious-Zionism led by Maimon and Shlomo Zalman Shraga'i, a key figure in Ha-Po'el Ha-Mizrahi, sought to implement the envisioned Sanhedrin.[11] The role of this judicial institution is to apply Jewish law (Halakhah) in all realms of life (civil and criminal law). Establishing a Sanhedrin as the supreme judicial institution is an essential step in the creation of a state of Halakhah. The idea received no support among the movement's leaders, who considered it unfeasible. This failure, however, had no effect on the religious-Zionist interpretation stating that the process of national awakening would ultimately lead to the creation of a state of Halakhah and to the Sanhedrin's renewal. The interpretation of the Zionist idea in the religious-Zionist camp reached absurd extremes. Many claimed that, after the establishment of the state and following the strategic balance reached after the wars, secular Zionism had concluded its role and had therefore left the stage. Henceforth, the only worthy ideology was religious-Zionism.

Religious-Zionist paternalism prevented a genuine dialogue with other cultural groups. The esoteric interpretation of the Zionist endeavor developed by the movement enabled the paternalistic approach to survive together with involvement in the modern world. The esoteric view had endowed secular Zionism with absolute meaning, as an element in the movement's comprehensive theology. The result was cultural dissonance between religious-Zionism on the one hand, and the cultural context of its action (and the Zionist movement above all), on the other. Whereas its cultural surroundings have largely abandoned metaphysical universal views upholding absolute truth and a shared ideal, religious-Zionism has persisted in clinging to a comprehensive interpretation of the one truth. "If we do not accept that Judaism has a 'truth,' that we as Jews accept this 'truth' because we believe that it is the one and only 'truth' that makes life and suffering worthy — does the fact that we were born Jews, that this land was once the land of our ancestors, that Hebrew was once our language, compel us to be Jews?!" This was the response of Shraga'i to Aaron Megged in the "Who is a Jew?" controversy.[12] The factors that had led to multiculturalism failed to influence the prodigious self-conviction of religious-Zionists. Members of the movement continued to develop a split consciousness: at the concrete level, they generally behave tolerantly and respectfully toward other cultural groups; internally, however, they support absolute principles that cannot tolerate alternatives.

The esoteric interpretation of religious-Zionism can probably be explained most fully by relying on psychoanalytic theory as a tool of cultural studies.[13] In this context, the underlying motivations of religious-Zionist philosophy and activity operate at three levels:[14]

(1) At the overt level, religious-Zionism affirms the concrete "normal" activity of social and political life.

(2) At the subconscious level, it views "normal" events as the realization of the naturalistic messianic vision in the Maimonidean version — political independence for the Jewish people and universal recognition of the wisdom and progress ideal. Religious-Zionism explains present events as a preparation for the establishment of a state of Halakhah or for turning the State of Israel into a state of Halakhah.

(3) At the unconscious level, it expects the realization of apocalyptic messianism, in the course of which God will be revealed in miracles and wonders and will bring about full redemption and the "new

world," entirely detached from the current world order. This apocalyptic level has been preserved in several isolated mentions in religious-Zionist writings, in a kind of parallel to Freudian slips.[15] Religious-Zionism holds that the second level is the corridor to a dream world of eternal life.

Religious-Zionists and their explanations of events are thus composed of depth layers, which daily activity covers up. Although the daily routine of religious-Zionists conveys an accommodation with secularization, the subconscious layer, for instance, views this routine as a realization of the first stages of natural redemption.[16] The gradual realization of the Zionist process created the basis for the national independence of the Jewish people from the outset, and the broad support of the world for this process is evidence of progress and enlightenment, all signs of universal messianism.

The layer that parallels the unconscious, implying the expectation of an apocalyptic messianic aim leading to a new world that is all good and from which evil has forever been eradicated, is complex and puzzling. The sexual contexts of Freudian theory do not provide a satisfactory explanation here, and Jungian theory provides a suitable alternative. The aspects of Jungian theory relevant to our discussion will be presented first, while analyzing their messianic implications. As we know, Jung viewed the unconscious as a rich structure of cultural symbols and contents ("archetypes"), while rejecting Freud's perception of it as solely a cluster of negative sexual drives. In this view, then, understanding the unconscious demands recourse to religious, mythical, and folkloric traditions that influence behavior. One component of the unconscious is the integration of entirely different natures, such as the divine and the human in the figure of Jesus.[17] What, then, are the messianic implications of the theory of archetypes?

Jung emphasized the eschatological aspect of the integration of natures in Jesus' Second Coming that, as noted, is a distinctive expression of the unconscious since it is accompanied by mythical descriptions.[18] Jung included eschatological motifs in the archetype of the "son of God." Formulating an ideal statement, he claimed that the desire of the unconscious to be exposed and revealed as integrated with the rest of the "self" is evident in Jewish messianic sources.[19] Apocalyptic motifs about the end of days also play a part in the contents of the unconscious, and Jung often discusses the role of the demonic Antichrist that will use these contents to struggle against Jesus in the future.[20] He also included extensive magical and mythical traditions among the contents of the unconscious.[21] Terrifying messianic struggles and the transformation of nature in the present and the future join together as elements of a distinctive archetype.

Jewish sources fostered an apocalyptic messianic tradition in midrashim of redemption and in systematic treatises such as Sa'adia Gaon's *The Book of Beliefs and Opinions*.[22] For prolonged eras, the apocalyptic version of messianism dominated Jewish creativity. One of the more crucial cultural characteristics of Jewish messianism, then, is the transformation of the real world, evil and turbid, into a redeemed, illusionary world; of the sinful earthly creature into the redeemed future type, lacking any evil disposition. Jung claimed that the unconscious is shaped according to its specific cultural habitat, although cultural uniqueness does not thwart the transpersonal nature of the unconscious, that is, the existence of archetypes common to all human beings. Messianic transformation is thus an important element in the understanding of the repressed drives at work in the Jewish world, and total apocalyptic messianism may be seen as an archetype of Jewish culture. Prosaic "normal" activity to establish a national home was accompanied, as noted, by repression mechanisms that operated in religious-Zionism to hide the expectations of apocalyptic messianism's immediate realization and of a new, dreamlike world. The contents of the unconscious, however, are constantly present below the surface, and at times erupt in the context of unique, heroic or tragic, events. The attitude of religious-Zionism to events such as the Holocaust on the one hand, or the Six-Day War on the other, sometimes shows traces of the unconscious apocalyptic element.

A certain downplaying ("repression") of blatant apocalyptic expressions in religious-Zionist thought was particularly evident at the time the State of Israel was established. By contrast, at the time the Mizrahi was founded as a faction within the World Zionist Organization (1902), when realization had not seemed so imminent, messianic expressions were more obvious and transparent. Nahum Grinhaus, a Hibbat Zion supporter and a leading personality at the time, wrote explicitly on this question:

> We will seek to prove that the land of our fathers is precious and beloved to us by placing workers atop the Judean mountains to build up the land through the sweat of their brow. Every single one will do his best to support our brethren as best he can by seeking to settle them and turn the desert into paradise. Our Lord will then pleasantly remember to favor us with hope and faith, and our merit and the merit of the Holy Land will stand us in good stead, because the Holy One, blessed be He, will show us miracles and wonders beyond nature.[23]

The context shows that this view rests on an apologetic element, which holds that Zionism does not replace divine redemption with planned human redemption but makes the latter an introduction to the former. Responding to the claims of non-Zionist Orthodoxy, religious-Zionists stated they were not seeking to blur the miracle element.[24] Grinhaus clearly points to the apocalyptic motivation underlying the Zionist process, to be realized in its wake. This sense of ultimate redemption is also found in the writings of Pinhas Rosowsky, who explicitly identified the nineteenth century with "the end of days."[25]

This attitude, as noted, had already been formulated at the dawn of the Mizrahi. Although Reines explained at length that the renewed creation of heaven and earth in days to come were to be understood allegorically, he too awaited an absolute eternal redemption whose fullness would entirely dismiss the past.[26] Jawitz wrote *Toledot Israel*, a broad historiography with recurrent allusions to exile and redemption that ends with a description of "messianic pangs."[27] R. Kook and Jacob Harlap also wove a magnificent messianic web, with the apocalyptic end playing an unequivocal and important role.[28] Both awaited a new, perfect world, where human creatures would live forever with a new body and a new mind. "Death is a flaw of creation, and the mission of the people of Israel is to eliminate it, it is an insult to our people, 'and the insult of His people shall He take away from off all the earth: for the Lord has spoken it' [Isaiah 25:8]."[29] Furthermore: "And not only that, but all the changes life has shown since Creation — all were a preparation for the vast change that will take place at the end of days."[30] R. Kook clarified that the echoes of the apocalyptic end resonate already in the present:

> And the light of the spiritual revival is progressively revealed, and the light of the powerful messianic revival flourishes, arriving to cleanse the iniquity of the flesh, the pollution of the snake and the root of all sin, bringing joy to the world and filling it with love and gaiety by removing the sadness of the flesh that is part of the natural sinfulness blocking the spirit of purity... The revival adds wisdom to the knowledge of eternity, to the knowledge of the stronghold of spiritual life, to the knowledge that death is deceit, removing all vain fear and all misleading sadness and [marking] the beginning of the resurrection of the dead era shining in its full strength.[31]
>
> I see the light of Elijah's life rising, his power gradually unfolding before God, the holy in nature breaking through its barriers, itself moving to unite with the holy beyond rugged nature, with the holy battling nature... Elijah comes to herald peace, and a living current of nature erupts in the nation's inner soul, and draws closer to the holy.[32]

This approach, which sees the incipient signs of an apocalyptic future realized in natural reality, demands "the union of miracle and nature," in

R. Kook's terms. In his wake, Harlap adopted Nahmanides' approach, which claims that natural reality is itself merely a composite of hidden miracles. Nature is a husk hiding a wondrous foundation:

> It is part of the order of the world that all spiritual wonders (peli'ot) will assume a natural garb, hence the mystery of nature's development at the end of days. These matters, which had appeared only as wonders beyond nature, are revealed in the natural world and become natural matters. Ignorant creatures relate only to their natural dimension, disregarding their miraculous aspect. But whoever has reason and knowledge of this matter will understand that, the more nature develops, the greater the true and sublime value of the wonders beyond the ways of nature. They know that nature too acquires power to develop only through the divine emanation, and becomes a garb for sublime wonders.[33]

R. Kook and Harlap, then, expanded the realm of miracle to include nature as well, characterizing redemption as a gradual process of transition from a miracle that is now hidden to one revealed in the future. R. Kook and Harlap disagreed on whether natural or apocalyptic redemption is higher, but neither doubted that at the final stages of redemption there would be another world, without suffering and death, guided by a miraculous order.[34] Their disciples then added details on the order and stages of redemption.[35]

Religious-Zionist thinkers preserved the messianic apocalyptic layer in their discourse as attested, for instance, by the long discussion of Ben Zion Meir Hai Uzziel, who emphasized apocalyptic characteristics such as eliminating aggression in animals.[36] For Uzziel, fundamental messianic belief requires "an expectation of redemption through miracle and wonder."[37] Uzziel's recognition of the State of Israel as the "beginning of redemption" evident in his writings, never thwarted or dimmed the expectation of redemption's last, apocalyptic stage. Hayyim David Halevy, who was Uzziel's secretary and eventually became the Chief Rabbi of Tel Aviv, unequivocally stated: "This is what He ruled in his wisdom, may He be blessed, that two stages will be reserved for future redemption — the first in the natural way, accompanied by suffering and hatred of the Jewish people, and the second miraculous and with great compassion."[38] Uzziel and Halevi thereby convey the world view of many religious-Zionist thinkers, who prayed and entreated: "Hear O Israel, Moses will rise and bring the dead of the desert to the Land of Israel... may God allow us to see this in our times in the State of Israel."[39]

Many religious-Zionist thinkers were wary of discussing these apocalyptic elements extensively and transparently. They did insist, however, on preserving elements of the miraculous dimension and preventing its assimilation and disappearance, as it were, given the naturalistic realization of redemption in the present generation. Some could not restrain these impulses, and persisted on seing natural events as apocalyptic messianic revelations. "I am sure," wrote Meir Bar-Ilan, a long-standing Mizrahi leader, "that if our forefathers and ancestors were to rise from their graves, they would see today the realization of Ezekiel's vision, the entire prophetic mission."[40] Yehudah Amital, the head of the Har-Eziyon yeshiva, asserted that belief in the realization of terrifying messianic events in the natural world must be a feature of the "*ben Torah*," that is, of the yeshiva world intellectual elite.[41] The realization of the messianic era here and now, then, is a recurring motif at the core of religious-Zionist action as well as of its world view.[42] Even a group such as the Religious Kibbutz Movement, many of whose leaders currently express reservations about a consistent messianic interpretation, upheld a perception of the state as "the beginning of redemption" and strove for the halakhic and conceptual changes required by this view.[43] Religious-Zionism was convinced that realizing the ideal it had developed would bring redemption to the entire world, and that cosmic and universal redemption depended upon it.[44] A distinction between its various streams is thus a function of the level of activism as opposed to the level of repression.

The messianic motif was indeed significantly enhanced following the Six-Day War. The messianic moment, however, had also erupted at other stations of religious-Zionist history. Among the many reactions of rabbis and thinkers to the *hallukkah* controversy (1937), for instance, some were no less intense than those expressed after 1967. Traces of the messianic element are also evident in the Mizrahi's strong opposition to the Zionist Organization's acceptance of the White Paper that split off Transjordan from the British Mandate (1922), and certainly in its closeness to the political right wing in Israel many years later. The strenuous political course of religious-Zionism did go through several eruptions and suppressions. Abstract and theological religious-Zionist thought, however, never agreed to a gradual realization of the messianic idea. It sought to realize all its aspects and dimensions, all now. The apocalyptic dimension, then, becomes a kind of messianic archetype in the deep consciousness of the religious-Zionist thinker.

An analysis of the structure of religious-Zionist consciousness and its modes of interpretation present the action of its members as resulting from complex hermeneutical layers. This analysis does not allow us to explain religious-Zionist activity as reflecting a compartmentalization, that is, a separation of realms.[45] Religious-Zionists indeed engage in "normal" activity, but the messianic interpretation of "normal" events still prevails and continues to seep in. In this perspective, paternalism clearly emerges as anchored in the structure of religious-Zionist consciousness, making integration in a multicultural world a hopeless endeavor.

2. PRESENT

In the last two decades, religious-Zionism has undergone several crises and processes that eroded the unity of consciousness and theology presented in the previous section. Some of the movement's current directions do enable recognition and toleration of other cultural contexts. Other directions, however, have become further entrenched within the borders of religious-Zionist consciousness as it developed from the outset. The following outline presents the new and renewing trends in religious-Zionism in the present.

Over the last twenty years, religious-Zionism has come to include several trends that differ in their character and their manifestations. Each of these trends points to horizons previously marginal or unknown. Although the trends differ from one another in the extent of their influence and the level of support for them, together they present a multifaceted mosaic eroding the image of unity that had typified religious-Zionism:[46]

(1) *Religious-Zionist feminism.* The awakening of women calling for a reconsideration of the status of women and for a re-examination of Orthodoxy's borders in this regard is not as yet an inclusive organization. It has, however, emerged from several directions and is coalescing into a movement. This awakening has directly influenced rabbinic and judicial echelons, and its central expressions are the following:

(a) Torah study. Establishing a system of *midrashot* for women parallel in character to the institution of the yeshiva for men.[47]

(b) Women's *miniyanim* (prayer quorums). In more extreme cases, the *miniyanim* are egalitarian and, with certain constraints, allow women to participate in leading the synagogue and the prayers.

(c) Institutionalization. The establishment of "*Kolech*" ["Your Voice"] and the efforts of "*Emunah*," the women's movement, to promote ideological progress among Orthodox women, have made the feminist trend a substantive element of religious-Zionism.[48]

(2) Centers of study and research. A series of previously marginal institutions involved in academic pursuits have become central and are formulating a new agenda. The Yaakov Herzog Center for Jewish Studies
founded by the Religious Kibbutz Movement and, in Jerusalem, the Shalom
Hartman Institute and Beith Morashah, are examples of institutions seeking
to focus attention on the adaptation of Halakhah to modern reality, and
are in many ways adjacent to the rabbinic yeshiva world. These institutions
are centers for the study of Judaism, and their teachers and scholars are
rabbis and academics with a modern Orthodox world view. The closeness
of some of these institutions to the *"Ne'emanei Torah va-Avodah"* movement,
aiming to promote pluralistic values in a national religious context, is not
a mere coincidence. Ideologically, they seek to create a pluralistic discourse
concerning existential problems. They publish extensively and have
developed a network of classes and lectures intended for the community,
extending the circles targeted by the religious-Zionist public. They have
also legitimized the academic connection; their members have university
degrees or are professional academics, and many of their students attend
Israeli universities. In public life, they are seen as supporting an intellectual
and moderate religious-Zionist line.

(3) The mamlakhti ideology. Until the mid–1980s, the national perception
of religious-Zionism had hallowed the State of Israel as "the beginning of
redemption." This perception is also a direct result of the "unity of Israel"
metaphysics of religious-Zionism. But after Zvi Israel Tau and his disciples
broke away from the Merkaz Ha-Rav yeshiva and created Har Ha-Mor, the
mamlakhti principle assumed renewed intensity. The distancing of religious-
Zionism from the national consensus and its association with defined
political movements (Ha-Ihud Ha-Leumi) was particularly troublesome to
supporters of the *mamlakhti* ideology. Some of them expressed their concern
in this regard by supporting Shas rather than the National Religious
Party-Ichud Leumi. The line endorsed by the Har Ha-Mor yeshiva is also
supported, even if partially, by yeshivot such as the one at Mitspeh Ramon.
Another development worth noting is that the pre-army preparatory courses
(*mekhinot kedam-tsva'iot*) began to flourish from the end of the 1980s. These
courses, which prepare youths for full army service, focus on issues of faith,
identity, and personality development. Some of the leading figures in these
pre-army courses support the *mamlakhti* approach noted above.

(4) The hilltop youth. Distinctive groups composed of young people
who grew up in the settlements, immigrants from North America, newly
observant elements, and others. To some extent, they have retreated from
the religious-Zionist ideal of openness and involvement and have called

for a return to the sources and to nature. They meticulously observe certain commandments, and their spiritual sources are also inspired by Hasidism. These youths have established outposts and settlements detached from cultural centers and from the spiritual leadership of religious-Zionism,[49] and have sought institutional and rabbinic sanction from the yeshiva at Yizhar and from rabbis associated with it, such as David Dudkewitz. They are also influenced by figures such as Yitzhak Ginzburg (see below).

(5) Movements in the political right. A series of radical right-wing movements, which despise the relatively flexible political orientation of the official religious-Zionist establishment, offer alternative options for spiritual and political identities. The right wing no longer coalesces into a monolithic movement such as Gush Emunim but spreads over a series of ideologies and world views. Two entirely different expressions of this new kind of right-wing religious-Zionism are:

(a) Yitzhak Ginzburg, who established groups of disciples drawing inspiration from Hasidic sources, and particularly Habad, as well as from several grandiose political and theocratic approaches. His outlook supports a radical activist messianism.[50] Among his disciples are also some who define themselves as religious-Zionists.

(b) The *"Zu Artsenu"* [This is Our Land] movement, which developed into the *"Manhigut Yehudit"* [Jewish Leadership] movement. This movement called its supporters to join the Likud party, and eventually submit a religious candidate as prime minister. Its ideologues, such as Hillel Weiss, Moshe Feiglin, and Motti Karpel, call for the creation of a "faith consciousness," meaning a return to the "authentic" religious messianic interpretation of Zionism.[51]

These trends reflect organizational attempts at various levels, attesting to diversity within religious-Zionism. Even if some of them are marginal, the arrival of the Internet about a decade ago makes the marginal and the anti-establishment conscious and influential.[52] The Internet makes once distant authorities close and accessible. Internet responsa are today one of the most influential factors in the lives of religious youths. Contrary to the responsa's original character, which had focused mostly on halakhic issues, Internet responsa address issues of leadership, ideology, and theology. Rabbis such as Shlomo Aviner, Shmuel Eliyahu, Eliyakim Levanon, and Yuval Sherlo are available and online to answer questions of religious-Zionist youths. The official rabbinic establishment has recently expressed opposition to this phenomenon, claiming it leads to superficiality and even to contempt of responsa.

These organizational attempts point only to general directions. Undercurrents continue to be at play in the religious-Zionist public, exposing the changes that have affected it in the last two decades. Several facts and processes reflecting social changes in the religious-Zionist public are presented below:

(1) *The "new wave."* Openness to cultural fashions is reflected in the promotion of a view that advocates incorporating Hasidism into the ideology and the day-to-day life of religious-Zionism on the one hand, and incorporating mysticism and new age trends in general into its values on the other.[53]

(2) *Expansion.* The penetration of religious-Zionism into realms that had previously been blocked. These realms had been seen as dominated by left-wing elements or groups identified with the government (media, senior army appointments, and so forth).

(3) *Education.* The number of national yeshivot is currently six times greater than their number twenty years ago.[54] The Amit network, for instance, which offers a moderate alternative to the educational model of yeshiva high-schools, has gained considerable strength.

(4) *Traditional religiosity.* Observance had been an unequivocal aim of religious-Zionism from the outset. Although levels of observance had been a matter of discussion and of daily ethos, the very definition had never been questioned. Recently, a phenomenon of "light" religiosity has become widespread, involving declared norms of non-strictness in the observance of halakhic and semi-halakhic obligations.[55] This religiosity is becoming an ideology.

(5) *Experiential religiosity.* The prayer ritual is a central element in religious life, which is conducted in a conservative framework and in set patterns (a cantor facing the community, a rabbi preaching, and so forth). One expression of the search for a fresh experience is the growth of prayer *miniyanim* in the "Carlebach" style. The prayer is accompanied by singing and dancing, collapsing the rigorous frontal framework.

(6) *Leisure patterns.* Religious-Zionist youngsters no longer recoil from recreation options such as pubs, and some have indeed opened up specifically for this public. Religious "rock stars" have begun composing alternative religious music (Aharon Raza'el, Sinai Thor, Shivi Keller, Uri Davidi, Gabriel Hason, Adi Ran, the groups *"Rev'a le-Shev'a," "Ha-Madregot,"* and others), which has spread to the center of religious-Zionist consciousness. Reports of religious-Zionist youngsters experimenting with (apparently soft) drugs have also surfaced in recent years.[56]

These developments place religious-Zionism at a new crossroads. Peter Berger noted that one of religion's reactions to modernity is negotiation, that is, religion renounces certain demands in order to accommodate the modern world.[57] Religious-Zionism had never been as involved in negotiation as in the period that began in the late 1980s. We could try evaluating to what extent the postmodernist climate has been a decisive influence on religious-Zionism. The behavior of many religious-Zionist youths can be explained according to their opposition to a specific ideology.[58] The hilltop youth, for instance, does not search for an ideology but intuitively sees the natural surroundings of Judea and Samaria as its home. And in the style of Shimon Gershon Rosenberg (Shagar): "The 'hesdernik' is no longer the good boy he had once been."[59] On the one hand, different ideologies have increasingly become part of the religious-Zionist world, and on the other, the postmodernist situation is also leaving a mark on the religious-Zionist retreating from the rigid ideology of the past. The diversification of religious-Zionism can also be ascribed to several crisis-like events, such as the uncovering of the Jewish underground, the Oslo accords, the murder of Prime Minister Yitzhak Rabin, and the evacuation of the settlements in Gaza and Amona. The diversification, however, is not exhausted by crises and must be viewed against the background of involvement in a postmodern and multicultural world.

From the 1980s, as noted, religious-Zionism has been at a crossroads. Since this is a theological movement, it relied not only on ideological pronouncements but on a theological foundation. Until the late 1980s, the theological backbone of religious-Zionist thought had been R. Kook's writings (at least in the 1960s and 1970s). Recently, however, we have witnessed a trend to promote the teachings of R. Joseph B. Soloveitchik, a leading Torah scholar and the honorary president of the Mizrahi in the United States, whose work displays features of individualism and subjectivity.[60] A stream of books comprising R. Soloveitchik's writings has been published over the last few years, and popular literature on his work has also begun to flourish.[61] This endeavor is promoted not only by the Har-Etziyon yeshiva, who counts among its leaders Aaron Lichtenstein, R. Soloveitchik's son-in-law, but also by Torah institutions, universities, and various study centers.

The foundations of R. Soloveitchik's thought are entirely different from R. Kook's outlook, as well as that of his disciples and their disciples. Whereas these approaches offer comprehensive and cosmic explanations of existence, explaining political and current situations in their light, R. Soloveitchik's teachings deal with the phenomenology of the religious experience and with the individual's existential and intimate situations. R. Soloveitchik's outlook focuses on the dialectical poles between which religious consciousness and actual existence fluctuate, marginalizing the resolution between them. The very focus on the dialectic as an independent value presents, to some extent, an attempt to contend with a postmodern world.[62] R. Soloveitchik's teachings fit some of the recent organizational developments in religious-Zionism presented above.

Furthermore: until about a decade ago, the canon of R. Kook's writings had included only philosophical works. These works created a conceptual, metaphysical, and messianic atmosphere that has been extensively discussed. The writings lacked any personal, autobiographical, or emotional tone. The book *Hadarav*,[63] published in 1998, includes personal passages exposing an emotional and individualistic facet of R. Kook whose son, Zvi Yehudah Kook, had struggled not to publish. This publication is part of a trend that has increasingly intensified in recent years, seeking to publish R. Kook's writings without any editing. The first harbinger of this trend was the publication of eight compilations, from which Ha-Rav Ha-Nazir (David Cohen) had edited *Orot Ha-Koddesh*. Contrary to the defined directions in which Zvi Yehudah Kook and Ha-Nazir had taken R. Kook's writings through their editing,[64] the prominent trend in recent years has been to return to the pluralistic and multifaceted source. Eight of these compilations were published in 1999, the thirteenth was published from the manuscript version by Ben-Zion Shapira, and further ones appeared in 2006 through Boaz Ofen (*Kevatsim Mi-yad Kodsho*). The "competition" for the publication of R. Kook's manuscripts covers up various tensions bubbling under the surface, but the result is the same: R. Kook emerges as an individualistic and experiential thinker, beside the national religious doctrine he had preached. These trends are also part of the expanding horizons and the collapse of long-standing solid frameworks.

The deeper expression of changes in the religious-Zionist camp in the last twenty years is the problem of identity. From its inception, the parameters of religious-Zionism remained quite homogeneous, notwithstanding its involvement in momentous historical events throughout various periods. The ideological and theological grounds that the movement had relied upon colored many of its years of activity with a hue of unity. In recent years, however, the solid structure has been threatening to crack. In this section, we present the areas of change in religious-Zionism, considering first the issue of identity, and then the factors jeopardizing its continuity.

Any definition of identity in a movement such as religious-Zionism will invariably be simplistic and involve generalizations. But from 1902, the year of the Mizrahi's foundations, two elements have been part of religious-Zionist identity:

(1) A messianic interpretation of current events, that is, a perception of the national awakening as a stage in the redemption process.

(2) Institutionalized cooperation with transgressors, that is, with a secular organization (the World Zionist Organization).

These characteristics conveyed the united theological layer of religious-Zionism, whose principles we presented above. The theological basis enabled the monolithical image of religious-Zionism, despite the various currents coexisting within it. This basis has also been at the foundation of religious-Zionism's widespread support for Gush Emunim and its enlistment behind it.[65]

From the 1980s onward, however, religious-Zionism has changed and has become far more diversified. Currents and undercurrents previously latent have surfaced, new trends have emerged, and horizons have expanded, all striving for a renewed and more minimalist model of religious-Zionist identity. From that period onward, some religious-Zionists have argued that the characteristics of religious-Zionist identity are the following:

(1) An adherence to Orthodoxy that recurrently examines its borders.

(2) Granting some religious value to the State of Israel.

The first supporters of changing the identity characteristics were a group of people at the religious-Zionist "center," assisted by prodigious resources and media talents. The motivation for changing these characteristics was, above all, dissatisfaction with the messianic feature accompanying the religious-Zionist narrative, and particularly with its strengthening since the beginning of the settlement endeavor.[66]

The facts supporting changes in the characteristics of identity are that the ranks of religious-Zionism have diversified throughout the spectrum of the social and political map and not only at its center. A parallel phenomenon is the electoral decline of the religious-Zionist party. Diversification, then, led to non-sectarian political identification. Social and ideological openness have influenced the political identity.

3. FUTURE

The preceding discussion analyzed the clash between two trends in religious-Zionism today. In many regards, the confrontation is between the past and the present. On the one hand is the religious-Zionist consciousness that crystallized in the past, which included defined identity characteristics and supported an approach of absolute truth in its interpretation of history and of the Zionist idea. On the other are the alternative trends that have developed in the present, meaning in the last two decades, supporting the realization of identity and the toleration of other cultural groups. The present trends reflect a climate of curiosity about the outside, an attempt to conduct a dialogue with others at various levels, and a rejection of hermeneutical paternalism toward the surrounding cultural groups.

Will religious-Zionism indeed change in the future? Can we point to a clear shift from a "one truth" perception and an (esoteric) absolute interpretation to integration into the multicultural situation? An evaluation of the integration possibilities of religious-Zionism in a multicultural society shows it depends on at least two factors:

(1) A quantitative factor. The weight of the new trends vis-à-vis the conservative trends within religious-Zionism is yet to be decided. It is not yet clear whether the "silent" religious-Zionist camp is gradually attaining liberation from the deep hermeneutical dimensions of consciousness, as described above, or whether the breakthrough is only taking place at the margins. It is not yet clear whether, in Chomsky's terms, the "surface structure" of today's religious-Zionism reflects its "depth structure."

(2) A qualitative factor. The question of whether religious-Zionism, with its solid theological foundation, could be truly integrated in a pluralistic culture is vital. Moreover, we have no guarantee that the conscious past, including its hermeneutical assumptions, will not reawaken. The paternalistic approach and its interpretive derivatives are alive and prospering in many national yeshivot.

Ignoring the cultural and interpretive trends of religious-Zionism could lead to a superficial view, which confines itself to the actual integration of the movement's members in modern life. The involvement of religious-Zionists in the economy, the media, the army, and other areas of Israeli life does not compel the erasure of the traditional paternalistic interpretation. Religious-Zionism is a movement with currents and undercurrents operating openly and covertly. The fascinating question is whether the new trends within religious-Zionism point to a new future of true integration in a multicultural society, or whether the conservative-interpretive consciousness that has been dominant for so many decades will also be uppermost in the future.

NOTES

This article was translated by Batya Stein.

[1]   Dov Schwartz, *Faith at the Crossroads: A Theological Profile of Religious-Zionism*, trans. Batya Stein (Leiden: E. J. Brill, 2002). See also idem, *The Land of Israel in Religious Zionist Thought* [Hebrew] (Tel Aviv: Am Oved, 1997); idem, *Religious Zionism Between Logic and Messianism* [Hebrew] (Tel Aviv: Am Oved, 1999), Part 1; idem, *Challenge and Crisis in Rabbi Kook's Circle* [Hebrew] (Tel Aviv: Am Oved, 2001).

[2]   See Charles Taylor, *The Ethics of Authenticity* (Cambridge, MA: Harvard University Press, 1992); Will Kymlicka, *Multicultural Citizenship: A Liberal Theory of Minority Rights* (Oxford: Clarendon Press, 1995). For Jewish and Israeli implications, see Menachem Mautner, Avi Sagi and Ronen Shamir, eds., *Multiculturalism in a Democratic and Jewish State* [Hebrew] (Tel Aviv: Ramot, 1998).

[3]   See Dov Schwartz, "From Early Onset to Realization: The History of the Religious-Zionist Movement and its Ideas" [Hebrew], in *Religious-Zionism — The Era of Change: Studies in Memory of Zvulun Hammer*, ed. Asher Cohen and Israel Harel (Jerusalem: Bialik Institute, 2004), pp. 30–31.

[4]   See Schwartz, *Faith at the Crossroads*, ch. 5; Avi Sagi, *A Challenge: Returning to Tradition* [Hebrew] (Tel Aviv: Hakibbutz Hameuhad, 2003), ch. 7.

[5]   Judah Leib Maimon (Fishman), "The History of the Mizrahi and its Development" [Hebrew] in *Sefer Hamizrahi* (Jerusalem: Mossad Ha-Rav Kook, 1946), p. 99. See also Ehud Luz, *Parallels Meet: Religion and Nationalism in the Early Zionist Movement*, trans. Len J. Schramm (Philadelphia: Jewish Publication Society, 1988), pp. 232–233.

[6]   Maimon, "The History of the Mizrahi," p. 100.

[7]   Ibid., 8.

[8]   Shmuel Hayyim Landau, *Writings* [Hebrew] (Warsaw, 1935), p. 66.

[9]   Peter Berger defines this type of reaction as "reductionist. " See Schwartz, *Religious Zionism Between Logic and Messianism*, pp. 110–111.

[10]   Zvi Yaron, *The Philosophy of Rabbi Kook*, trans. Avner Tomaschoff (Jerusalem: WZO, 1991), ch. 10; Schwartz, "From Early Onset to Realization," p. 48.

[11]   Asher Cohen, *The Prayer Shawl and the Flag* [Hebrew] (Jerusalem: Ben Zvi Institute, 1998), ch. 3.

[12]   Shlomo Zalman Shraga'i, *Immediacy and Eternity: Expositions on Religion, Zionism, and the State of Israel* [Hebrew] (Jerusalem: Mossad Ha-Rav Kook, 1960), p. 85. Aaron Megged's answer was that "a national experience is not to be identified with any particular world view, religious or other, or in other words, with a 'truth' that is exclusive to a people" (ibid., p. 87).

[13]   Shoshana Felman, ed., *Literature and Psychoanalysis: The Question of Reading, Otherwise* (Baltimore: Johns Hopkins University Press, 1982).

[14]   See Schwartz, *The Land of Israel in Religious Zionist Thought*, ch. 11. On the use of Freudian theory to explain the crisis of traditional society at the time of the Zionist movement's expansion, see Shlomo Aaronson, "Bialik and Ben-Gurion:

Between Words and Politics" [Hebrew], in *Hebrew Literature and the Labor Movement*, ed. Pinhas Ginossar (Beer Sheva: Ben Gurion University 1989), p. 28. Finally, on psychoanalysis as a social model, see Peter L. Berger, "Towards a Social Understanding of Psychoanalysis," in *Facing up to Modernity: Excursions in Society, Politics, and Religion* (Harmondsworth: Penguin, 1977).

[15] Schwartz, *The Land of Israel in Religious Zionist Thought*, pp. 216–217.

[16] See also Yosef Salmon, *Religion and Zionism: First Encounters* (Jerusalem: Magnes Press, 2002), pp. xix–xxiii.

[17] See C. G. Jung, *Psychology and Religion: West and East* (Princeton, NJ: Princeton University Press, 1969), pp. 406–409.

[18] Ibid., 440. Compare Paul Bishop, *The Dionysian Self: C. G. Jung's Reception of Friedrich Nietzsche* (Berlin: W. de Gruyter, 1995), pp. 229–230.

[19] C. G. Jung, *Mysterium Coniunctionis: An Inquiry into the Separation and Synthesis of Psychic Opposites in Alchemy* (Princeton, NJ: Princeton University Press, 1970), p. 414. Jung related to the rabbinic saying "the son of David shall not come until all the souls that were in the body have fully gone out" (TB Yevamoth 62a; and see Genesis Rabbah 24).

[20] Jung, *Psychology and Religion*, pp. 432–435. On apocalyptic messianism, see Malcolm Bull, *Apocalypse Theory and the Ends of the World* (Oxford: Blackwell, 1995).

[21] The hermetic tradition, founded on magical and alchemic conceptions, plays a central role in Jung's theory of archetypes. See, for instance, C. G. Jung, *Psychology and Alchemy* (Princeton, NJ: Princeton University Press, 1980), pp. 131–137.

[22] My book *Messianism in Medieval Jewish Thought* [Hebrew], second expanded edition (Ramat-Gan: Bar-Ilan University Press, 2006) is devoted to systematic expressions of apocalyptic messianism.

[23] Maimon, "The History of the Mizrahi," p. 57.

[24] This approach was presented by Yeshayahu Avi'ad (Wolfsberg) as follows: "Jews had always feared this sharp turning, because of the suffering and the hard trials preceding redemption. The natural source, the natural light of restoration and redemption, which were not invented by Hibbat Zion and Zionism and had already been considered by rabbis and eminent *rishonim*, were not to the liking of those who had distanced themselves too far from the 'natural' ways of life. Not only did they rely on miracles but they also founded redemption on miracles and wonders that would release them from the pangs of change and from the sufferings of the past." *Studies in Judaism* [Hebrew] (Jerusalem: Mossad Ha-Rav Kook, 1955), p. 152. Avi'ad, a leader of the Mizrahi in Germany, preferred to focus on the natural dimensions of messianism in his writings.

[25] Maimon, "The History of the Mizrahi," p. 80.

[26] "Hence, when the prophet promised in God's name that the future redemption would be complete, without any remembrance of the past, he said, I create new heavens and a new earth [Isaiah 65:17]... For the joy will be perfect, and eternal, and no more exile and enslavement will follow after it." Yitzhak Yaakov Reines,

A New Light on Zion [Hebrew] (New York: Posy Shoulson, 1946). The sense that the current redemption is eternal accompanied Isaac Nissenbaum's thought as well. See Abraham Rubinstein, "Messianic Portents and Messianic Pangs in R. Isaac Nissenbaum's Teachings" [Hebrew], in *Sefer Shraga'i*, ed. Mordechai Eli'av and Yitzhak Raphael (Jerusalem: Mossad Ha-Rav Kook, 1982), p. 121.

27   See Reuven Michael, *Jewish Historiography from the Renaissance to Modern Times* [Hebrew] (Jerusalem: Bialik Institute, 1993), p. 462.

28   On R. Kook's approach, see Aviezer Ravitzky, *Messianism, Zionism, and Jewish Religious Radicalism*, trans. Michael Swirsky and Jonathan Chipman (Chicago: University of Chicago Press, 1996), pp. 108–109; Schwartz, *The Land of Israel in Religious Zionist Thought*, pp. 80–81. On Harlap's view, see Schwartz, *Faith at the Crossroads*, pp. 163–165.

29   Abraham Yitzhak Kook, *Orot ha-Koddesh*, ed. David Cohen (Jerusalem: Mossad Ha-Rav Kook, 1963), p. 386. R. Kook intended eternal life at the material level, as evident from his previous remarks in this passage, where he specifically speaks of the soul at the center of an actual concrete body: "Why should the soul not unite with the dead body to resurrect it forever?" (Ibid., p. 385).

30   Jacob Harlap, *Mei Merom: Mi-Ma'ynei ha-Yeshu'ah* [Hebrew] (Jerusalem: Bet Zevul, 1977), p. 35.

31   Abraham Yitzhak Kook, *Orot* (Jerusalem: Mossad Ha-Rav Kook, 1963), pp. 27–28.

32   Ibid., p. 78. In these passages, R. Kook again presents the "true" inner content of the nation. In his view, at the advanced stages of redemption, it will be revealed that "all that has illuminated and all that will illuminate everything that lives and will live within it [the nation], all is the eternal divine light of the God of Israel" (ibid., p. 79). On Elijah's messianic associations see, for instance, Hayyim Milikovsky, "Elijah and the Messiah" [Hebrew], *Jerusalem Studies on Jewish Thought* 2 (1983): 491–496.

33   Harlap, *Mei Merom: Mi-Ma'ynei ha-Yeshu'ah*, p. 83. See David Berger, "Miracles and Natural Order in Nahmanides," in *Rabbi Moses Nahmanides (Ramban): Explorations in his Religious and Literary Virtuosity*, ed. Isadore Twersky (Cambridge, MA: Harvard University Press, 1983), pp. 107–128. On the influence of Harlap's approach, see, for instance, Eliezer Waldman, *Or Israel*, ed. Yishai Aviezer (Hevron: Keren Hagii, 1985), pp. 632–633.

34   Abraham Yitzhak Kook, *Epistles* [Hebrew] (Jerusalem: Mosad Ha-Rav Kook, 1962–1965), pp. 19–22. See also Uriel Barak, *Rabbi Yaakov Moshe Harlap: The Development of his Theory of Redemption* [Hebrew] (M.A. Thesis: Touro College, 1997).

35   See, for instance, Zvi Israel Tau, *Faith in our Times: An Outline for the Understanding of the Era* [Hebrew], ed. Mordechai Hass, Yair Diamant and Zeev Neumann, vol. 1 (Jerusalem: Hossen Yeshu'ot, 1994), pp. 58–69.

36   "And when the world is repaired at the time of the Messiah, everything will return to the way it was at the time of Creation, and even the beasts will go back to proper ways." Ben Zion Meir Hai Uzziel, *Hegiyonei Uzziel*, vol. 1 (Jerusalem, 1993), p. 186. Uzziel was aware of the disputes over the allegorical interpretation concerning the

change in the nature of animals, but decided: "and I have already cited R. Saadia Gaon, who concurs with Nahmanides, and I agree with them." Uzziel, then, favored the view assuming an actual change in the nature of animals, and he added: "The realization of this view [in the messianic era], when even animals will return to their original nature, will certainly come after man attains perfection through knowledge of the true God" (ibid., p. 188). His agreement with Sa'adia Gaon and Nahmanides is also evident in the dispute on the resurrection of the dead, a stage involving many miraculous motifs in apocalyptic literature (ibid., pp. 188–189). Compare Schwartz, *Messianism in Medieval Jewish Thought*, p. 104.

[37]   Uzziel, *Hegiyonei Uzziel*, vol. 1, p. 305.

[38]   Hayyim David Halevi, *Aseh Lekha Rav* (Tel Aviv, 1981), p. 101.

[39]   Zeev Gold, *Nivei Zahav* (Jerusalem, 1949), p. 543. These dramatic remarks end Gold's homiletic work.

[40]   Meir Bar-Ilan, *The Writings of R. Meir Bar-Ilan* [Hebrew], vol. 1 (Jerusalem: Mossad Ha-Rav Kook, 1950), p. 264. Assumptions about the presence of miracles in natural activities are particularly evident concerning Israel's wars. See, for instance: "Even the heroes and the soldiers who were at the forefront and led the battle admitted that they could not find a natural explanation for the defeat of Israel's enemies and for Israel's victories except for the "secret weapon" [*neshek sodi*], whose acronym is *nes* [miracle]." Shlomo Zalman Shraga'i, *Processes of Change and Redemption: Problems of the Emerging State* [Hebrew] (Jerusalem: Mossad Ha-Rav Kook, 1959), p. 380. Compare Schwartz, *Faith at the Crossroads*, pp. 215–216. Against this approach is a reductionist view, which established victory solely on strategic considerations. Moshe Dayan, who was then Minister of Defense, analyzed the Israeli victory in the Six-Day War in distinctively reductionist terms. Controversy still rages around Uri Milstein's provocative views.

[41]   "We must endorse this belief [in the struggles between the Messiah son of Joseph and the Messiah son of David]. And anyone who comes into contact with a *ben-Torah* must be inspired to faith from such an encounter." Yehudah Amital, *Ha-Ma'a lot Mi-Ma'amakim* (Jerusalem: Alon Shevut, 1974), p. 32. The background of this statement was the trauma of the Yom Kippur War. Amital further claimed that action in a redemptive period requires a different ethos. "And however hidden it might be that we are living in a redemptive stage, this is still the compelling belief. Our expectations and our speech must accordingly be different" (ibid., p. 75).

[42]   In this context, note that Arieh Leib Gelman attacked Ben-Gurion for his topical interpretation of messianic prophecies. In his view, it is impossible to draw out current human and cultural elements from the messianic idea and ignore its unique and specific dimension. See Aryeh Leib Gelman, *Netsah Ha-Umah* (Jerusalem: Mossad Ha-Rav Kook, 1958), pp. 144–145. Gelman concludes, as usual, by disparaging Ben-Gurion and stating that Spinoza is no less than "Ben-Gurion's teacher and mentor in the doctrine of Zionism" (ibid., p. 146). Gelman was one of the very few who negated Spinoza's outlook altogether, although his arguments did not rest on a deep study of it but rather on his stormy and controversial style. See Schwartz, *Faith at the Crossroads*, p. 92.

43 One example are the prayers instituted for Independence Day and Jerusalem Day.

44 "The messianic goal is a universal one. The Messiah ushers in universal justice and world peace. But the universal expectation is inseparable from Israel's home-coming." Eliezer Berkovits, *Faith after the Holocaust* (New York: Ktav, 1973), p. 146. See also Schwartz, *Faith at the Crossroads*, pp. 160–168.

45 On this position, see Yedidia Z. Stern, *Law, Halakhah and Pluralism: Living with Normative Duality* [Hebrew] (Ramat-Gan: Avichai Foundation, 2000), p. 6.

46 Some of these developments are reviewed in Yair Sheleg, *The New Religious Jews: Recent Developments among Observant Jews in Israel* [Hebrew] (Jerusalem: Keter, 2000), Part 1.

47 See Tamar El'or, *Next Passover: Women and Literacy in Religious-Zionism* [Hebrew] (Tel Aviv: Am Oved, 1998); Tamar Ross, *Expanding the Palace of Torah: Orthodoxy and Feminism* (Hanover, MA: Brandeis University Press, 2004).

48 See, for instance, various articles in the proceedings of the yearly conferences of "Kolech: Religious Women's Forum" ed. Margalit Shiloh, *To Be a Jewish Woman — Proceedings of the First International Conference: Woman and her Judaism* (Jerusalem: Urim, 2001) and *To Be a Jewish Woman — Proceedings of the Second International Conference: Woman and her Judaism* (Jerusalem: Urim, 2003) ; Lilakh Rosenberg-Friedman, ed., *From Faith to Action: On the Seventieth Anniversary of the Emunah Movement* [Hebrew] (Jerusalem: Emunah, 2006). See also Yoram Kirsch, "The Status of Women in Religious-Zionist Society: Struggles and Attainments" [Hebrew], in *Religious-Zionism — The Era of Change: Studies in Memory of Zvulun Hammer*, ed. Asher Cohen and Israel Harel (Jerusalem: Bialik Institute, 2004), pp. 386–421. See also Dov Schwartz and Judith Tydor Baumel, "Reflections on the Study of Women Status and Identity in the Religious Zionist Movement," *The Review of Rabbinic Judaism* 8 (2005): 189–209. An entire issue of *Democratic Culture* [Hebrew] 10 (2006) was devoted to gender and society in Israel. Particularly relevant in this context are Zehavit Gross, "The Mute Feminist Psychological Template of Girl Graduates of Religious-Zionist High Schools in Israel" [Hebrew]: 97–133, and Tovah Cohen, "Jewish Women's Leadership: Israeli Modern Orthodoxy as a Test Case" [Hebrew]: 251–296.

49 See Shlomo Kaniel, "The Hilltop Youth — Biblical Sabras? An Exploratory Study of the Residents on the Hills of Judea and Samaria" [Hebrew], in *Religious-Zionism — The Era of Change: Studies in Memory of Zvulun Hammer*, ed. Asher Cohen and Israel Harel (Jerusalem: Bialik Institute, 2004), pp. 533–558.

50 See Yehiel Harari, *Mysticism as a Messianic Rhetoric in the Works of R. Yitzhak Ginsburg* [Hebrew] (Ph.D. dissertation: Tel Aviv University, 2005).

51 On these movements see Motti Inbari, *King, Sanhedrin, and Temple* [Hebrew] (Ph.D. dissertation: Hebrew University of Jerusalem, 2006).

52 Harari, *Mysticism as a Messianic Rhetoric*, pp. 225–226.

53 See, for instance, Nahum Langental and Nissim Amon, *When Moses Met Buddha* [Hebrew] (Tel Aviv: Maskel, 2005); Odeya Tzurieli, ed., *Prophesy, O Son of Man: On*

the Possibility of Prophecy [Hebrew] (Jerusalem: Reuven Mass, 2007), Introduction. See also Jonathan Garb, *"The Chosen Will Become Herds": Studies in Twentieth Century Kabbalah* [Hebrew] (Jerusalem: Shalom Hartman Institute and Carmel, 2005).

54   See, for instance, Eliezer Don-Yehiya, "Religious Fundamentalism and Political Radicalism: The National Yeshivot in Israel" [Hebrew], in *Independence — The First Fifty Years: Collected Essays*, ed. Anita Shapira (Jerusalem: The Zalman Shazar Center for Jewish History, 1998), pp. 431–470. Note that, two decades ago, all soldiers doing their military service in *hesder* yeshivot served in the same divisions and the same units. Entire cohorts enlisted one time in the armored corps and another in the Giv'ati brigade. Today, youths from *hesder* yeshivot have many options of military service. The multiplicity of options has contributed to attitudes such as that of General Elazar Stern, head of the Army's Human Resources Division, who is striving to break up the homogeneous units and scatter the soldiers serving under this arrangement in various units. On the eve of the 2007 Shavu'ot holiday, Stern sent a personal letter to all the *hesder* soldiers asking to dismiss the rumors that he was seeking to undermine the entire arrangement of the *yeshivot hesder* with the army. At the time of writing this paper, a dialogue is ongoing between the representatives of the *yeshivot hesder* and Stern, with obvious displays of mutual suspicion. The yeshivot leaders, even those who endorse Stern's position, are opposed to a forced implementation of his recommendations. This event is a further expression of the opening up of the ranks and the expanded horizons of the religious-Zionist public in recent years.

55   This pattern conforms to the patterns of religious practice common among broad segments of the Mizrahi (Middle-Eastern and North-African) public. Contrary to the traditionalism typical of these communities, however, in this case we are dealing with an ideology involving the selective choice of specific norms and the rejection of others. Note also that some of the changes in the norms of halakhic behavior are ascribed to the student body at Bar-Ilan University and include, for instance, symbolic head covering for married women. See Dov Schwartz, "Bar-Ilan, the Idea of the University, and Religious-Zionism" [Hebrew], in *Bar-Ilan University: From Concept to Enterprise*, vol. 1 (Ramat-Gan: Bar-Ilan University, 2006), p. 79.

56   See, for instance, Shaul Schif, *Be-Sod Siach*, Ha-Tsofeh, 15/06/2007.

57   Peter L. Berger, *A Far Glory: The Quest for Faith in an Age of Credulity* (New York: Free Press, 1992).

58   On the youths' connection to secularization processes, see Shraga Fischerman, *The "Formerly Religious"* [Hebrew] (Elkana: Orot Israel, 1998).

59   Shimon Gershon Rosenberg, *Broken Vessels: Torah and Religious-Zionism in a Post-modernist Environment* [Hebrew] (Efrat: Yeshivat Siah Yitzhak, 2004), p. 113. Students at *hesder* yeshivot are perceived in this context as the elite of the religious-Zionist camp.

60   See Dov Schwartz, "'*Kol Dodi Dofek*': A Religious-Zionist Alternative," *Tradition* 39, 3 (2006): 59–72.

61   R. Soloveitchik's books are published in Hebrew by Toras HoRav Foundation, in a series known as "Me-Otsar Ha-Rav." The popular literature includes the book by Yuval Sherlo, *From Dialectics to Harmony in the Teachings of R. Joseph Dov Halevi*

Soloveitchik [Hebrew] (Alon Shevut: Tevunot, 2000), and the book by Hayyim Navon, *Caught in the Thicket: On the Thought of Rav Soloveitchik* [Hebrew] (Ma'aleh Adumim: Ma'aliot, 2006). Aaron Lichtenstein wrote in his introduction to the latter book that it serves as an introduction "to the novice, who has had no experience reading the philosophical works of the Rav, and is not familiar with the man and his thought" (ibid., p. 11). A radical popularization of his teachings is thus intended. The editors of "Me-Otsar Ha-Rav" have indeed invested significant effort in attempts to introduce the unspecified term "the Rav" in reference to R. Soloveitchik (as he is known in the United States), whereas this term is today reserved in Israel for R. Kook. Until now, R. Soloveitchik's family had opposed the intensive publication of his writings, but this has no longer been the case in recent years.

62   See, for instance, Sagi, *A Challenge: Returning to Tradition*; Gili Ziwan, *Religion without Illusion: An Inquiry into the Thought of Soloveitchik, Leibowitz, Goldman, and Hartman* [Hebrew] (Jerusalem: Shalom Hartman Institute, 2005).

63   Abraham Yitzhak Kook, *Hadarav: Personal Chapters Gleaned from his Writings* [Hebrew], ed. Ran Sharir, second enlarged edition (Ramat-Gan: Re'ut, 2002). On the controversy evoked by this treatise see Jonathan Meir, "Lights and Vessels: A New Inquiry into the 'Circle' of Rav Kook and the Editors of his Works" [Hebrew], *Kabbalah: Journal for the Study of Jewish Mystical Texts* 13 (2005): 245.

64   Schwartz, *Religious Zionism Between Logic and Messianism*, pp. 198–233; Udi Abramowitz, *The Ideology of Rabbi Zvi Yehudah Ha-Cohen Kook in Editing the Writings of Rabbi Abraham Isaac Kook* (M.A. thesis: Bar-Ilan University, 2007).

65   The literature on Gush Emunim is extensive, ranging from Zvi Ra'anan, *Gush Emunim* [Hebrew] (Tel Aviv: Sifriat Ha-Poalim, 1980) up to Michael Feige, *One Space, Two Places: Gush Emunim, Peace Now, and the Construction of Israeli Space* [Hebrew] (Jerusalem: Magnes Press, 2003).

66   In line with this trend, those identifying with the religious-Zionist political center have also tried to change the perception of the past arguing that, in its early days, religious-Zionism had also included a non-messianic stream, meaning one describing current events as resulting from Divine Providence but not as part of a messianic process.

THE SUFFERING OF THE OTHER: TEACHING THE HOLOCAUST TO ARABS AND JEWS

AVIHU RONEN

1. The Politics of Recognizing the Suffering of the Other

Recognizing the suffering of the other is a difficult and complicated issue. It is difficult not only for two nations fighting each other, but also for people who believe in democratic values like tolerance and human rights.

It seems that many democratic societies internalized the idea that ethnic or religious minorities deserve several rights usually concerning culture, language and education. At the same time the minority is called upon to respect the authenticity of the majority and its right to realize its beliefs and values according to its own cultural norms. Mutual respect and bilateral recognition of different groups have become necessary conditions for the constitution of a multi-cultural society.[1]

However, these presumptions of a multi-cultural society become problematic when the issue is the suffering of the other, especially if the groups involved have bitter collective memories of each other. It sometimes happens that recognition comes too late, when the problem of co-existence becomes irrelevant, as in the case of post-war Germany. The Germans recognized the Jewish suffering only when German Jewry was all but eliminated. Sometimes, there is no recognition in spite of the extended time that has elapsed. The refusal of the Turks to admit the mass murder of the Armenians during the First World War is a sad example of this.

In other cases, one group is ready to recognize the suffering of the other only if it is not considered responsible for it, as in the belated recognition of the Jewish massacre by their Polish neighbors in Jedwabne during Word War Two.[2] In some societies recognition of the other's suffering may involve a long process. A case in point is American society's acknowledgement of the suffering inflicted by white Americans on other groups, mainly Native-Americans and Afro-Americans. But again, such recognition usually takes place only when fear of each other no longer exists.

Two main barriers stand in the way of recognizing the suffering of the other: a practical one and a psychological-moral one. The first is the unwillingness of one side to be the subject of compensation or reparation claims of the other side. The second is the psychological difficulty of one side to admit his moral responsibility for the suffering of the other, giving up by this the uniqueness of his own suffering. No one wants to be conceived as the aggressor but rather as the injured party.

These barriers are crucial within the context of Arab — Jewish relationships in Israeli society. Both groups, Arabs and Jews, are heavily burdened by historical memories of suffering and being victims. These two memories are anchored in two different narratives which are asymmetrical and incomparable: the Jewish narrative of the Holocaust and the Palestinian narrative of being deprived of their homeland (*El Nakba*). It seems to both groups that recognizing the other narrative means giving up the authenticity of their own narrative. As Dan Bar-On and Saliba Sarsar commented in their article "The Holocaust and El Nakba":

> There is an underlying fear that the acknowledgement of the tragedy of the "other" will justify their moral superiority and imply acceptance of their collective rationale.[3]

Illan Gur Ze'ev and Illan Pape', see the situation as a battle between two rival collective memories:

> The destruction of the collective memory of the Other, through the construction of one's own, is a central element in the formation of national identities. ... In the case of Palestine/Israel, control of the collective memory is part of the internal and external violence each of the rival collectives applies to secure its reconstruction. ... Within this dialectic, each side sees itself as a sole victim while totally negating the victimization of the Other.[4]

Though Gur Ze'ev and Pappe's argument is a radical one, their conclusions are quite similar to those of Bar-On and Sarsar: Both Jews and Arabs are afraid to be deprived of their own existential cause as victims by admitting the other's narrative.

2. AVOIDING A FRIGHTENING SUBJECT

For many years the subject of the Holocaust was not part of Jewish-Arab discourse. The memory of the Holocaust was a "Taboo" issue in Jewish-Arab relationships in Israel. The feeling of both groups was that it is better to avoid this frightening issue than to openly discuss it. The Holocaust was conceived as a mere Jewish affair which was best not discussed with the Arabs. "Don't Touch My Holocaust" was the ironical title of a 1994 Israeli movie.[5] Indeed the Israeli Arabs didn't touch it: the Holocaust as a subject matter was only rarely studied in Arab schools and until the early nineties Arab intellectuals only seldom dealt with it. As Gur Ze'ev and Pappe' pointed out: "We hardly find any systematic study on the subject during the 1970s and 1980s in the central Palestinian academic stages".[6] The same was true about Jewish intellectuals and politicians who did not wish to discuss the subject openly with Arab colleagues.

On the other hand, there was much discussion about the *Mufti* of Jerusalem, Hajj Amin el Husayni, who supported the Nazis during the Second World War. Jewish historians studied the Mufti as an enemy[7], Arab intellectuals dealt with his pro-Nazism in an apologetic manner.[8] These studies were typical to the atmosphere of avoiding the crucial questions: it was not the Holocaust which was discussed, but rather its frightening shadow.

Azmi Bishara was the first to explain the problem from the Arabic point of view. In his 1995 paper he pointed out that "The Arabs and the Holocaust" is a "subject which is not only mysterious but provocative and suspicious as well."[9] According to Bishara, Arab restraint of dealing with the Holocaust was the result of several reasons:

a. The Holocaust as a European event was irrelevant to the Arabs and did not raise any essential problem for them.

b. The Palestinians were the indirect victims of the Holocaust, because "their homeland was taken away by the direct victims of the Holocaust."

c. The emphasis placed on Jewish suffering might diminish the Palestinian suffering.

d. The memory of the Holocaust is instrumentally used to legitimize the State of Israel.[10]

Although Bishara has moved in the last years to a much more radical position, emphasizing the Zionist manipulation of the Holocaust memory,[11] his main argument still seems a clear presentation of the Israeli Arab attitudes towards the Holocaust. These attitudes are located on a spectrum ranging from absolute avoidance (the Holocaust is irrelevant) to suspicion (the Holocaust is used for political reasons). One can add to it another attitude (though Bishara didn't mention it in 1995) — denial. According to a new poll made by Prof. Sami Smoocha of Haifa University 28% of Israel's Arab citizens believe the Holocaust never happened.[12]

The Jewish attitudes towards the issue of "Arabs and the Holocaust" seem to be as follows:

a. Exposing the Holocaust as something that happened to the Jews might raise "dangerous" ideas among Arabs. Rehavaam Zeevi clearly exposed this fear when Yassar Arafat wished to visit the Holocaust Museum during the late nineties:

> What is this murderer looking for at the Holocaust Museum? ...Does he want to study Adolph Hitler's exploits so he can learn from him?[13]

b. There were several Arab leaders, like the Mufti in Palestine and Rashid Ali al-Kaylani in Iraq who supported the Nazis, and thus the Arabs seem to stand on the side of the perpetrators. For years the Mufti photo was shown in the "collaborators" exhibitions in Yad Vashem museum, and as is mentioned above several books concerning his activities have been published in Israel.

c. Arab leaders who wish to destroy Israel are following Hitler and the Nazis who tried to annihilate the Jews. As Moshe Zuckermann pointed out, the comparison between Hitler and arch-enemies of Israel like Saddam Hussein was most popular during the Gulf War.[14]

d. Discussing the Holocaust with Arabs could lead to a comparison between Jewish suffering and Palestinian suffering, and thus diminish the uniqueness of the Holocaust. On the same occasion of Arafat's plea to visit the Holocaust Museum, MK Shmuel Halpert of United Torah Judaism called the idea:

> A defamation of the memory of those who were killed in the Holocaust; a trampling of Jewish dignity and a terrible insult to the last remaining survivors.[15]

The range of Jewish attitudes towards the issue are located on the spectrum between avoidance (don't give the Arabs the chance of comparison), implicit blame (some of the Arabs supported Nazism) and explicit blame (Arab leaders are followers of Hitler).

Although there is no symmetry between the two kinds of fears, one can find a single clear element that associates the two: this is the element of the "victim." It seems that both groups are afraid to loose the monopoly of being the victim. The lack of open Jewish — Arabic discourse about the Holocaust is due to this motive. Both Arabs and Jews want to be recognized as the sole and the absolute victim. Not sometime victim, sometime perpetrator, or sometime bystander but as a victim only. The Holocaust survivor, from the point of view of many Jews, is the ultimate and the absolute victim. The Palestinian refugee is the only victim in the framework of the Palestinian collective memory. He is again the ultimate and absolute victim.

This idea was clearly expressed by the Arab intellectual, Hazem Saghieh in his 1997 article published in *Dar El-Hayat*: "Once The Devil was an Angel":

> Becoming victims not only prevents the solution of the Palestinian problem, it again emphasizes it endlessly. The victims spare no sympathy to the other, because, according to their argument "we" are "all" the victims.[16]

Saghieh's argument exposes the problem of recognizing the suffering of the other: a pre-condition for such recognition is the giving up of the feeling of being the absolute victim. One has to recognize that although he has been or, he is a victim, there are other victims as well. Moreover: the refusal to recognize the other as a victim impedes the solution to one's own problem as a victim. Hazem Saghieh's argument is applicable to Palestinians and Jews as well.

3. Changing Attitudes

The suspicious atmosphere concerning the issue still exists, as can be inferred from the Teheran conference of Holocaust "revisionists" held in December 2006 under the auspices of Iranian President Mahmoud Ahmedinejad.[17] On the other hand, the same Ahmedinejad is conceived by many Israelis as the new "Hitler".

Nevertheless, following the experiences of the first Intifada (1989) and the beginning of the peace process with the Palestinians (1993), a shift was noted in Israeli attitudes towards the Holocaust as part of the Jewish — Arab discourse. Several Israeli intellectuals produced works trying to understand the links between Holocaust memories and the suffering of the Palestinians. Moshe Zuckermann, in his book, *Shoa in the Sealed Room*[18] exposed the existential fears of Israelis associating the Arabs with Holocaust images during the Gulf War. Duddi Mayyan produced *Arbeit Macht Frei*, a total-theatre play concerning the impact of the Holocaust upon Arab-Jewish relationships in Israel.[19] Illan Gur Ze'ev published several works concerning the Other's Genocide.[20] Idith Zertal, in her book *Death and the Nation*, analyzed the impact of the Holocaust upon Israeli policies in the occupied areas.[21] The suffering of the Palestinians as standing for itself was also studied thoroughly during these years by Benny Morris in *The Birth of the Palestinian Refugee Problem, 1947–1949.*[22]

These works can be viewed as first steps towards giving up the self-image of the "absolute victim" and recognizing the "other" as a victim. According to Moshe Zuckermann, the real lesson of the Holocaust is that the victims' successor should not victimize others:

> The Zionist collective in Israel cannot escape of facing the horrifying truth that … every act of brutal oppression directly or indirectly drawn from the Israeli occupation disconnects the Zionist collective from its ethical-humanistic identity, received as a binding inheritance from the Holocaust victims, and connects itself more and more to the mentality incorporated in the perpetrators' identity.[23]

A similar trend was noted among some Arab intellectuals. Several Arab leading intellectuals started relating to the Holocaust in the late eighties and the early nineties: the late Feisal Husseini, a leading Palestinian figure paid a visit to the Ghetto Fighters' Museum. The philosopher (later Knesset Member) Azmi Bishara, the journalist Hazem Saghieh and the poet Salem Jubran published papers dealing with the Holocaust. Salem Jubran, in his paper, "The Arabs and the Holocaust — Historical and Actual Perspectives" wrote:

> The Arabs should study the issue of the Holocaust, as part of the universal human commitment to act against racism and extreme nationalism, and as an integral part of Arab—Jewish appeasement and establishment of co-existence and good neighborliness.[24]

Azmi Bishara, although being critical about the instrumental use of the Holocaust memory in Jewish — Israeli society wrote:

> 1) Every possible compromise with the State of Israel necessitates consideration of two collective memories, that one of them includes the Holocaust … 2) The History of the Holocaust and its lessons are not a "capital" of the State of Israel, but of all humanity. Arab intellectuals who sought democracy and social and national justice have to

represent a clear position concerning racism and Anti-Semitism issues, likewise other minorities' issues. 3) The cooperation of the national Palestinian movement with Nazism [during WW II] was a serious mistake and should be criticized.[25]

Father Emil Shufani expressed similar ideas during the second Intifada (2000). Shufani, who conducted meetings of Arab students from Nazareth and Jewish students of the Hebrew University in Jerusalem, noted the following at one of the meetings:

> I realized that there is no chance for true dialogue and reconciliation unless we have in-depth understanding of this matter of the Holocaust; unless we touch the suffering, the memory, the terminology. It may be not sufficient to get us out of the mud we're stuck in, but it's definitely necessary."[26]

In spite of the differences between the humanistic approach of Jubran, the critical approach of Bishara and the emotional approach of Shufani, they all agreed about the necessity of studying the Holocaust. It is the recognition of the suffering of the other that can constitute a real dialogue.

4. COURSES FOR ARAB TEACHERS STUDYING THE HOLOCAUST

The first course for Arab teachers dealing with the Holocaust was held in 1993 at Givat Haviva,[27] in the framework of teachers on a sabbatical program. The idea to arrange such a course was a consequence of the previous year's experience in which five Arab teachers participated in a course entitled "Jewish Leadership during the Holocaust." Actually, the 1992 course was intended to be mainly for Jewish teachers, and the five had enlisted in the course quite incidentally, looking for new courses to fill up their sabbatical program. However, during the studies the five Arab Teachers became most involved and active in studying the Holocaust. Three of the Arab teachers also joined their Jewish colleagues on the trip to Poland to visit the death camps, and came back moved and stimulated.[28]

Following the positive conclusions of this primary experience, a special course intended for Arab teachers was programmed at Givat Haviva. The course, entitled "Racism and the Holocaust" was guided by three lecturers: Salem Jubran, Olek Netzer, and myself. The course's topics included historical and psychological perspectives of racism and historical and sociological perspectives of the Holocaust. The program ran for several years with an annual average of 20 participants.

In 1995, "The Center for Humanistic Education" was established as a department at The Ghetto Fighters' House (GFH) in the Galilee.[29] The Center is headed by Mrs. Raya Kalisman, and aimed for Arabs, Druze and Jewish teachers and students. The center proclaims:

> Our fundamental outlook is that dealing with the subject of the Holocaust leads to an understanding of the importance of humanistic and democratic values, and instills tools for moral judgment and civic responsibility ... We believe that dealing with the subject of the Holocaust raises fundamental questions of the existence of the human race and human nature; it can bring about empathy, bridge between individuals of differing backgrounds and cultures, and clarify what they have in common.[30]

From its very beginning, some of the main programs of the Center have been courses concerning the Holocaust for Arab teachers. There are also courses concerning Humanism and Racism for Arab and Jewish teachers. Most of the teachers are from Northern Israel: Christian Arabs, Moslem Arabs, and Druze — from the area of the Galilee, the Carmel, and Haifa, and Jews — from Akko, Nahariya, Haifa, Hatzor Haglilit and Kibbutzim in western Galilee. The lecturers were Salem Jubran, David Netzer, and myself. Since 1996, about 500 Arab teachers have participated in the first program and about 600 Arab and Jewish teachers have participated in the second.

A project for Arab teachers also began at Yad Vashem in 1995 and was entitled "Teaching the Holocaust to Israeli Arabs." According to Irit Abramski the starting point was fostered by the climate of the post-Oslo accords when "the atmosphere of mutual dialogue encouraged Arab educators and intellectuals to openly express curiosity about the Jewish tragedy." During the second Intifada (2000), many of the participants left the project, but as Abramski points out "Nevertheless, Yad Vashem instructors and guides continue to present this topic in front of Arab students and teachers in various Israeli colleges throughout Israel."[31]

Since 2003, another project of Arabs studying the Holocaust has been under way in Nazareth headed by father Emil Shufani. The project has held seminars for Arab and Jewish intellectuals, educators and political activists and organized visits to the death camps in Poland.[32] However, the discussion below will mainly concentrate on the GFH and Givat Ha-viva activities.

The Students

The motivations of Arab teachers to attend the Holocaust courses can be seen as mixed: instrumental and intellectual. As an instrumental motive, one can note the Arab teachers' drive for advancement in the Israeli educational system. This advancement is achieved by participation in training courses and accumulating more credits in available courses held near their neighborhood: both Givat Haviva and the Ghetto Fighters Museum are located in areas densely populated by Arabs. The willingness of Jewish institutes to open their gates to Arab teachers and to initiate special programs for them is an important factor in attracting Arab teachers to the courses dealing with the Holocaust.[33] For some of the Arab teachers it has been the first opportunity to study or to be trained in a Jewish educational institute. As a matter of fact, most of them have been graduates of Arab Teachers' Seminars and have never had a chance to attend a higher educational center with Jewish lecturers and students. Thus, the instrumental factor has some extra educational value of its own: through the Holocaust studies, the Arab teachers have become much more involved in the Israeli educational system. Certainly, the situation is different with the Father Shufani's project which was initiated by Arab intellectuals, and holds no instrumental motive at all.

Nevertheless, during the study sessions at GFH and Givat Haviva, the intellectual factor became the crucial one. Actually, most of the Arab teachers who chose to study the Holocaust had little previous knowledge of it. The more the studying process progressed, the more their intellectual curiosity was aroused, and they became more and more interested in the subject. This process was corroborated by the findings of an attitudes research carried out by Neomi Shiloah, Edna Shoham, Raya Kalisman. Shiloah et al. studied the attitudes of 35 Arab teachers who participated in the GFH courses during 1998–1999. According to this research the main motivation in studying the Holocaust was the Arab teachers' interest in the subject and their curiosity about it.[34]

The courses became a tour of discovery for the Arab teachers. Their first and most important finding was that the Holocaust really happened. This lesson was not obvious at all: before these courses the Arab teachers rarely heard anything about the Holocaust, and they considered it either as propaganda or as an exaggeration. Attending lectures, reading documents, listening to oral testimonies, watching documentary movies, the Arab teachers found the reliability and the truth of this story.[35]

The second insight was that of the historical Jewish suffering and the heavy impact of the memory of the Holocaust upon so many Jews in Israel. It contradicted the traditional Israeli-Arab's image of the strong, tough and dominant Israeli-Jew. The Arab teachers learned to know that the Jews were once weak, helpless and oppressed. In short, the "Jew" is like them — sometimes strong, sometimes weak — but always a mere human being. Shiloah et al. quote several sayings of the course's graduates:

> "Whoever takes the course will feel the terrible suffering undergone by the Jews and will forgive them ... In the past I almost hated Jews, but now much less so;" and "It helped me understand the Jews better ... I think that I felt very close to the feeling of a Jew who suffered. It enabled me to better understand the meaning of the word 'Holocaust.'"[36]

The third insight was the universal aspect of human suffering. As Zigmunt Baumann and Primo Levi put it, nothing like the Holocaust could teach us so much about human nature, about the suffering that one human being can cause another, and the human ways of facing it.[37] Studying the Holocaust, the Arab teachers faced the entire human suffering, as one of the teachers commented:

> To see people being deceived, separating mothers and fathers (selection), putting them into gas chambers, and loading them onto carts, causes you to shudder. It has made me be more human, I will relate to people with more respect. When I can help — I will.[38]

Last but not least, the Arab teachers revealed that they can openly speak about their own suffering. The discussion about Jewish suffering opened the door for discussing Arab and Palestinian suffering. Usually, their comments were not comparative. Admitting the uniqueness of the Holocaust, and the pointlessness of comparing wounds they used to ask: how could people of a nation which suffered so much inflict so much suffering on other nation?[39] Referring to their interviews with the Arab teachers Shiloah et al. note that:

> half of the interviewees contended that the Holocaust and the Palestinian 'Nakba' cannot be compared, because in the Holocaust there was the systematic and planned murder of the Jewish people, whereas in the 'Nakba' the Palestinians suffered because they were evicted, but they were not annihilated as a people.

Other teachers made connections between their personal-family suffering and that of the Jews:

> "I also underwent a 'holocaust' in 1948; my parents' home was destroyed, two of my brothers died of hunger, I felt that feeling, therefore ... I always compare the two ... " and "The Jews should also know what happened in 1948. It hurts me that my land was confiscated."[40]

Nevertheless, the comparative attitude was not the dominant one during the courses. It was rather the drive to study this unique story which has so many human implications. Sometimes, documentary movies had to be stopped midway. With tears in their eyes, the Arab teachers said — "it is too much, we can't stand it." Yet they came back and kept studying, and the following year they returned for more advanced courses. Some joined the trips to Poland, others began to note the Holocaust commemoration day in their Arab high schools. Many of them still keep in contact with the lecturers or with the Humanistic Centers in the Ghetto Fighters' House and Givat Haviva.

Teaching Methods

The concepts and educational methods that were developed in these programs are supposed to deal with the special problems of the Arab teacher facing the Holocaust. The first principle underlying these methods is that teaching be done by both Arab and Jewish instructors. In order to eliminate prior suspicions of ideological manipulations, propaganda or paternal authority of solely Jewish lecturer, this method seems a necessary condition for the studies' effectiveness. By means of Arab-Jewish teaching these prior suspicions were overcome. Note also that some of the lectures were presented in Hebrew and other in Arabic. The poet Salem Jubran who was a leading lecturer in these courses noted:

> As a person, as a humanist, as a leftist, I cannot be indifferent to an ideology of extermination. In my seminars, at first the people do not let go of their national affinities, but after two or three sessions, it becomes harder to think in terms of being only Jews or only Arabs. We are human beings first of all ... Learning about the suffering of the Jews doesn't take anything away from our national identity ... If I say that you are a true victim, does that have to mean that I am not a true victim?[41]

Similar methods were applied with Arab high school students, following the experience of Raya Kalisman in The Holocaust Memorial Museum in Washington. The Arab and Druze high school students who participated in long-term workshops (12 weekly sessions) were trained as guides in the Museum. The highlight of the workshop is a meeting of the workshop graduates with their own families and friends, in which the workshop seniors guide the others in the museum. The idea is the same as the Arab-Jewish co-teaching: the Arab students of the Holocaust studies are the best educational agents for their own society.

The Humanistic Center program emphasizes the study of the Holocaust and humanistic education as an ongoing process. It aims not only at expanding the knowledge of the student, but also at training him as an educator for others:

> Training is given only to those who study the subject in depth, who then go on to teach what they have learned to their communities.[42]

Consequently many of the final papers, which were submitted by the students at the end of the teachers' courses, dealt with educational issues of teaching the Holocaust, humanism and anti-racism in the Arab sector.

The teaching methods also aimed to expose the emotional level of the students at first, moving gradually into rational discussions, and achieving conceptualization only at the last stage of the study process. This method proved to be very effective with Jewish students whose own personal feelings were taken as the starting point of the learning process. Emotional release was effective with Arab teachers who exposed their own biased feelings towards the Holocaust at the beginning of the course. Following the sessions with survivors, the movies and the discussions they experienced a transformational process in their perception of the Holocaust. Nevertheless, this method has its shortcomings especially when establishing the truth about the Holocaust. Therefore, the students attend lectures of historians, read historical documents and study archival materials.

Finally, the teaching is open to discussion of every relevant and/or controversial question. During the courses, discussion in many sessions has related to current events and contemporary political culture in Israel. One of the most dramatic discussions was held in the Humanistic Center at the start of the second Intifada (2000), following events which frightened Jews and Arabs as well. Students and teachers were skeptical at that time about the future of the Humanistic Center. But due to the open talk, it ended successfully: the activity at the center has not ceased for a single day.

The programs

The programs of the courses have been shaped according to various concepts that are inter-dependent but focus on different aspects of the subject:

1. "The Holocaust and its significance." A basic course intended for Arab teachers. The main subject of the course is the Holocaust as an historical event, and its implications on humanism and anti-racism.[43]

2. "Teaching the Holocaust in Arabic-speaking High Schools." A course focuses on didactic and educational methods of teaching the Holocaust in Arab and Druze high-schools.[44]

3. "Racism." (in Givat Haviva only.) A course for Arab and Jewish teachers. Study of the universal problems concerning human nature: racism, stereotypes, xenophobia, chauvinism, and genocide. The Holocaust is studied as the central case study of the above, but other modern phenomena of racism, chauvinism etc. are discussed.[45]

4. "Humanism versus Racism." An advanced course for Arab and Jewish teachers, mainly graduates of the basic courses. Studying the Holocaust and its impact on modern society as the background, emphasize is placed on contemporary issues such as humanism in post-war society, religious tolerance, humanism and racism in Israeli society.[46]

5. "The Humanistic Challenge for Jews and Arabs in the Israeli Society." A new advanced course for Arab and Jewish teachers, dealing directly with Arab Jewish relationships in Israel, taking for granted the lessons of the Holocaust.

In the above programs it is sought to maintain a balance between studying the uniqueness of the Holocaust as an historical event and studying its universal significance. This changing balance reflects the dialectics of the two aspects of the Holocaust within an educational context.

Was the Holocaust a unique or universal event? The philosophical and historical discussion of this question is far beyond the scope of this paper. However, according to the experience of teaching the Holocaust in the Arab sector, it seems that the answer is more practical than theoretical. On one hand it is impossible to teach this historical chapter without referring to its particular features and its unique aspect: the systematic mass annihilation of the Jews by the Nazis. The Arab students will be able to recognize the Jewish suffering only by studying the Holocaust as a unique and particular story. On the other hand, studying the universal aspects of the Holocaust, for example the crisis of modern civilization, modern racism, stereotypes etc. enables the Arab students to face contemporary issues including their own national suffering. It also enables a much more open discussion with their Jewish colleagues.

How much do these programs deal with the Arab or the Palestinian suffering? While being conducted within historical institutes for Holocaust studies, the courses cannot extend their subject matter too deeply into Arab-Jewish history. However, most of the programs include chapters concerning Arab suffering (*El Nakba*) and Arab humanism. Some of the lectures do deal with issues of racism, tolerance and human rights in the Israeli society in respect to the Arab minority. Other chapters emphasize mutual calls for humanism, for example Martin Buber as a Jewish voice, and Nagib Mahfuz as an Arabic voice.[47] Other chapters concern inconvenient issues: Fascist and racist movements in the Jewish sector and the Arab sector during the 1940's.

Several events were held concerning the destructions of Arab villages in the Galilee. For example, in 2003, The Center held a reunion dedicated to the evacuated Arab village of Ikrit. About 50 Arab and Jewish students attended the gathering where they listened to testimony concerning the evacuation of the village in 1948. One of the Jewish students asked the witness:

> "Are you embittered, is this why you brought up the issue?" He answered: "I brought up this story because it is very important to me. But I am not embittered, especially on this afternoon, after you have all come to this meeting, listened carefully to my story, [and] expressed your empathy."[48]

5. CONCLUSION

Recognizing the suffering of the other is still a difficult task. When it recently became known that the Education Ministry has approved school text referring to "1948" as "El Nakba," the media was inundated with angry responses.[49] As mentioned above, in 2007, still 28% percent of the Israeli Arabs don't believe that the Holocaust really happened. It seems that the efforts of the Moreshet in Givat Haviva, the Humanistic Centre in the Ghetto Fighters House and the Shufani's project are only the first attempts towards a more comprehensive program of recognizing the suffering of the other.

However, the experience obtained in these programs can lead to some preliminary conclusions:

a. Studying the suffering of the other within the Jewish-Arab framework is possible only by relinquishing the feeling of being the "absolute victim."

b. The attitude towards the subject matter (Holocaust and/or El-Nakba) has not to be comparative one, but rather one of sharing and empathizing with different narratives.

c. The teaching methods must depend heavily on mutuality, namely, co-teaching (by Arab and Jewish instructors), syllabi including subjects and authors relevant to both Arabs and Jews, and readiness to discuss any controversial subject.

d. The study is an ongoing process. The aim is not only to increase the student's knowledge, but also to train him as an educator for others.

e. Studying the suffering of the other can lead to a better understanding of the other, and it is most effective in establishing a real dialogue between two nations in a multicultural society.

The linkage between these conclusions and the peace process is quite clear, but only the future will reveal whether peace can foster more understanding between Arabs and Jews, or whether education for such understanding and empathy can bring about peace.

NOTES

1   Charles Taylor, *Multiculturalism and the politics of recognition* (Princeton, N.J.: Princeton University Press, 1994).

2   See: Jan T. Gross, *Neighbors: The Destruction of the Jewish Community in Jedwabne, Poland* (Princeton, NJ: Princeton University Press, 2001).

3   Dan Bar-On and Saliba Sarsar,"Bridging the Unbridgeable: The Holocaust and Al-Nakba," *Palestine — Israel Journal of Politics, Economics and Culture* vol. 11 (No. 1) (2004).

4   I. Gur-Ze'ev & I. Pappé. "Beyond the Destruction of the Other's Collective Memory: Blueprints for a Palestinian-Israeli Dialogue," *Theory, Culture & Society* 20, 1 (February 2003): 93. Note: the paper was published at the same year when the Hebrew version of this paper was published.

5   *Don't touch my Holocaust*, a documentary film, directed by Asher Tlalim, Israel 1994.

6   Gur-Ze'ev and Pappé, ibid., p. 96.

7   See: Moshe Pearlman, *Mufti of Jerusalem: The Story of Haj Amin el Husseini* (London: V. Gollancz, 1947). Eliyhau Eilat, *Hajj Muhamed Amin el-Husayni, the ex-Mufti of Jerusalem* (Tel Aviv: Reshafim, 1968); Karmon Yigal, *The Mufti of Jerusalem, Hajj Muhamed Amin el-Husayni and Nazist Germany during the Forties,* dissertation (Jerusalem: The Hebrew University, 1987).

8   Gur-Ze'ev and Pappé, ibid., p. 95.

9   Azmi Biahara, "The Arabs and the Holocaust, Analysis of a Problematic Connective" (Hebrew), *Zemanim*, Vol. 53 (1995): 54.

10   Bishara, ibid.

11   Azmi Biahara, "Lessons from the Holocaust: Ways of Denial," *CounterPunch,* December 23–24, 2006.

12   Fadi Eyadat, "Poll: Over 25% of Israeli Arabs say Holocaust never Happened," *Haaretz,* 18/3/2007.

13   Aviv Lavie, "Arabs Study the Holocaust," *CounterPunch,* February 12, 2003 (published first in *Haaretz* 7/2/2003).

14   Moshe Zuckermann, *Shoa in the Sealed Room* (Tel Aviv, 1994), pp. 77–83.

15   Aviv Lavie, ibid.

16   Hazem Saghieh, "Once The Devil was an Angel," *Haaretz,* 21/3/1997, translated from *Dar El-Hayat.*

17   See the revisionist site: http://www.adelaideinstitute.org.

18   Moshe Zuckermann, ibid.

19   *Arbeit macht Frei fun Toitland Europa,* Akko Theatre, 1991–1992.

20   See: Ilan Gur-Ze'ev, "The Morality of Acknowledging/Not-acknowledging the Other's Holocaust/Genocide," *Journal of Moral Education* 27(2) (1998): 161–177.

21   Idit Zertal, *Death and the Nation* (Jerusalem: Dvir 2002), pp. 223–284.

22   Benny Morris in *The Birth of the Palestinian Refugee Problem, 1947–1949* (Tel Aviv: Am Oved, 1991).

23   Zuckermann, ibid., p. 30. See also: Avihu Ronen, "The Courage to be Alone," *Haaretz,* 30/1/1989.

24   Salem Gubran, "The Arabs and the Holocaust — Historical and Actual Perspectives," *Shvilei Hzikaron,* Yad Vashem, vol. 17 (November 1996): 15.

25   Bishara (1995), p. 69. In his 2006 paper Bishara became much more critical about the monopoly of the Holocaust memory claimed by Zionist movement calling it "another face of denial". Still he argues that "Holocaust denial does not undermine the moral justifications for the existence of the state of Israel, as some imagine. What it does do, however, is hand the European right and Israel a convenient enemy upon which to unload their problems." Bishara 2006, ibid.

26   Aviv Lavie, ibid.

27   Givat Haviva was founded in 1949 as the national education center of the Kibbutz Artzi Movement, a federation of 83 Kibbutzim throughout Israel. Givat Haviva conducts seminars and offers formal and informal educational programs for teachers and children — including Jewish-Arab relationship, socialist thought and the Holocaust heritage. http://www.givathaviva.org.il.

28   Rona Raanan Shafrir, "An Arab in Auschwitz," *Hadashot,* 29/1/1993.

29   The Ghetto Fighters' House — Itzhak Katzenelson Holocaust and Jewish Resistance Heritage Museum was founded in 1949 by a community of Holocaust survivors, members of the Jewish underground in the ghettos of Poland, and veterans of partisan units. The museum operates an educational center for Holocaust and Jewish resistance studies. http://www.gfh.org.il.

30 Ghetto Fighters' House/ Humanistic Education/ Our fundamental outlook, http:// www.gfh.org.il.

31 Irit Abramski, "Overcoming the Prejudice — Teaching the Holocaust to Israeli Arabs," http://www1.yadvashem.org/education.

32 Aviv Lavie, ibid.

33 Rona Shafrir, ibid.

34 Neomi Shiloah, Edna Shoham, Raya Kalisman, "Arab teachers and Holocaust education: Arab teachers study Holocaust education in Israel," *Teaching and Teacher Education* 19(6) (2003): 609–625.

35 Shiloah et al., table 1.

36 Shiloah et al., ibid.

37 Zygmunt Baumann, *Holocaust and Modernity* (Cambridge, Mass., 1981); Primo Levi, *The drowned and the Saved* (London, 1988).

38 Shiloah et al., ibid.

39 Rona Shafrir-Raann, ibid.

40 Shiloah et al., ibid.

41 Aviv Lavie, ibid.

42 Ghetto Fighters' House/ Humanistic Education/ Educational Principles and Working Methods, http://gfh.org.il.

43 The educational department, Moreshet.

44 The Center for Humanistic Education's Archive, see also Shiloah et al.

45 The educational department, Moreshet.

46 The Center for Humanistic Education's Archive.

47 A most important contribution to this subject is the new book by Robert Staloff who studied Arab righteous among nations during the Holocaust. See: Robert Staloff, *Among the Righteous: Lost stories from the Holocaust's long reach into Arab lands* (New York: Public Affairs, 2006).

48 The Center for Humanistic Education's Archive.

49 *Haaretz,* 22/07/2007.

THE JEWISH HOLIDAYS AS A PLATFORM FOR A MULTICULTURAL DISCOURSE OF IDENTITY

RINA HEVLIN

1. GENERAL INTRODUCTION

The culturally pluralistic character of Israeli society has given rise to two opposite approaches. There are those who deplore it, viewing it as a divisive and alienating factor, and an obstacle to the formation of an overarching "Israeliness." Others welcome it, recognizing its intrinsic worth as a manifestation of cultural authenticity and an instrument of self-identity.

The present article proposes that a dialogic encounter between members of different cultural groups has great potential for self-growth without blurring the distinctive cultural differences between them. This point is demonstrated by a series of dialogic meetings between Jewish and Arab students in Ohalo Teachers College in Katzerin, the Golan Heights, Israel. The meetings were conducted in the course of a seminar in Jewish Studies I coordinated, and this article, which presents and analyzes them, has been written from the standpoint of a researcher whose field of study coincides with her academic teaching of Jewish tradition. Thus, while the given encounters are subject to analysis and interpretations, the point of departure for their theoretical consideration is personal experience, my own as well as that of the team and the students working with us.

The research herein presented applies some insights gained by my previous theoretical studies.[1]

2. PROJECT DESCRIPTION

The Structure, Objectives and Components of the Course

The arena for the encounters presented in this article was a seminar entitled "The Holidays in Jewish Tradition in Sound and Movement," which was designed for all students training as teachers of physical education and fulfilled the requirement for Jewish studies, as determined by the Ministry of Education. (This has since been changed to require the study of a cultural heritage, in order to allow each student to study his or her own tradition.)

The curriculum was designed as a two-year program that combines academic studies with workshops in two-hour sessions once a week. The contents of the seminar were carefully selected to make the course suitable for the target audience, its purpose, and the time limits.

The content of the course was organized around the Hebrew Calendar. Why was this particular subject chosen? For the college, this was a matter of professional necessity. Teachers of physical education are sometimes required to relate to the Jewish holidays and to coordinate holiday events and ceremonies at their schools. I, as the head of the Jewish Studies Department, had additional objectives in mind. I wanted to choose a subject that would provide the students with the tools to understand the multiplicity and the complexity of the socio-cultural realities in Israel. In Israel, the Jewish holidays serve as milestones introduced by the Jewish time dimension to guide Israeli society.[2] They are a marked presence in our lives, and an academic consideration of their meaning offers the learners the opportunity to discuss the nature of Jewish tradition and relate it to their lives as individuals and as part of the Jewish collective, and by doing so to explore questions of society, culture, and identity. The Jewish holidays convey the narrative that society tells about itself and its past and transmits to its children down the ages. They are one of the central and efficient channels of values and perceptions of reality.[3] Furthermore, the discourse of the generations on how to shape the holidays is actually *a discourse about the collective "I."* The holidays reflect the collective identity of society[4] and construct the identity of its members. Thus, the holidays are not only expressions of culture, but also the channels through which the Jewish identity is bequeathed and inherited. They embody the strong relationship between culture, tradition, and identity in the Jewish world.

The discussion in the course focuses on demonstrating the nature of the holidays as situations that establish identity. The course participants — teachers and students alike — are engaged in an identity discourse, in the process of which they open up to each other and reshape their identities.

Three important choices made this course multicultural: First, the content of Jewish and national holidays as manifestations of culture and tradition and their significance to the participant's sense of identity; second, the teaching methods, which involved the participants with a complex dialogue with each other and in relation to their heritages; third, the open and creative spirit of the teaching staff, which engaged the participants in productive interaction.

The Participants in the Project: Composition and Attitudes

The Team

The teaching staff consisted of a music teacher and a teacher of movement — both of whom had only a rudimentary knowledge of the Jewish holidays but were extremely open and ready to learn — and me, a lecturer in Judaism, and the course coordinator.

The three of us were anxious to work together. We were all willing to deal with areas of knowledge with which we were unfamiliar. Our working assumption was that within the framework of this multidisciplinary program, movement and music should be treated as languages in their own right, with concepts and skills that should be taught for the purpose of self expression. Joined together they necessarily become an even more powerful tool for conveying messages.

Significantly, these are the very languages that the students will be teaching in their future professional work.

The Students: Variation and Complexity

Each year, 80 students of different cultures and religions take part in the program. In 2002, half of the students in the program were Jewish. The others were mostly Arabs — Christians, Muslims, and Druze — with a small number of immigrants from the Russian Federation, who were officially registered as Christians by the state authorities but viewed themselves as part of the Jewish people. The Jewish students came mostly from traditional or religious homes, with some of them having attended religious elementary or high schools, and only a minority of them was estranged from tradition. The Arab students all described themselves as not religious, but (with the exception of one student) expressed respect for tradition and religion. The immigrants from the former Soviet Union, Christians and Jews alike, attached great importance to the knowledge of Jewish heritage as a vital element in their integration into Jewish-Israeli society. They sometimes even expressed their desire to be integrated into the Jewish people as a whole, as opposed to being part of Israeli society alone.

The quantitative weight of Arab students participating in the program was from the beginning a determining factor which influenced program planning and was viewed as a limitation. However, at the planning stage, we did not correctly appreciate the complexity of the situation. The team was forced to decide whether to exempt the Arab students from the course or face the difficulties head on.

From a Course in Jewish Studies to a Multi-Cultural Project

Theories of tolerance, pluralism, and multiculturalism[5] contributed directly to one of the important goals of the program: dealing with pluralism and multiculturalism as attitudes. Thus, in working with different cultural groups we made no attempt whatsoever to narrow the gap between groups at the legal, social or cultural levels, or insofar as the group interests, rights or obligations were concerned. Rather, we strove to affect their personal attitudes towards one another. We felt that in-depth work of developing tolerance toward others could not be achieved through attending theoretical lectures or poring over scholarly texts. The transition had to be constructed gradually, as the participants experienced situations that enabled them to interact with the other as a person with a full inner world.

Whenever expressions of disrespect for the world of the other came up during the course, the team refrained from uttering rebuke or criticism, preferring to deal with them in a matter-of-fact way or sometimes simply to ignore them. The team felt that a restrained response to these expressions would promote openness to the other as an attitude. Judging by the students' own testimony during the summary lesson and in personal discussions, this approach indeed proved to be effective.

During the first stage of the biennial course, our main tool in encouraging openness to the other was to expose the participants to the multiplicity of Jewish traditions, their nuances, and their development. The pertinent texts were presented with factual explanations and with emphasis on the similarities and differences between the various traditions, and a deliberate effort was made to accord respect and legitimacy to the many expressions of tradition originating in different places and at different times.

The move from culture to multiculturalism was unplanned. It occurred as a natural result of the process and the accompanying reflection on it. This enabled us to progress in new and rewarding directions.

3. The Nature of the Current Research

The Choice of Paradigm and the Type of Research

The dominant paradigm in this research, as in my two previous studies,[6] is hermeneutic. Hermeneutical research[7] combines a description of events, a theoretical-conceptual analysis and critical reflection, moving smoothly from one to another with almost no demarcation of boundaries between them. Accordingly, the present research is presented from the standpoint of the team who developed and implemented the program, and especially from my standpoint as a researcher. By acting both as a team member and a researcher of the same project, I played the role of an observer-participant, thus breaking the accepted dichotomy between the researcher and the object of her research.

Although this research investigates events, it would not be correct to define it as classic field research since it is primarily based on team reflection, especially mine. However, it combines features of two types of field research, both connected to the researcher's analytic self-report: action research and self-case report. Action research investigates the effects of intervention and usually includes a first-person account of the research by the individual who has initiated the action and has been involved in it.[8] As such, this is one of the axes around which the present article revolves. Thus, the research discussed here is presented as a self-case report and as a first-hand explanation. It gives an account of my experiences, my actions, and my personal interpretations, whereby I, the writer, take the role of the main actor in the narrative.[9] As is usual in action research and in self-case report, I simultaneously serve as the research tool and as the researcher.[10] Those engaged in qualitative research view this combination as the only tool flexible enough to integrate the complexity, sensitivity, and constant change that characterize human experience.[11]

The Research Data Base

The data base for the research was not constructed systematically. In addition to the questionnaires filled out by the students at the beginning and the end of the academic year, I had at my disposal material that had aided me in my daily activity: a number of participant observations written immediately after the occurrence of the events in which I took part, reports of team meetings, written reflections composed by the team members, field reports written during my discussions with students and with my team partners as well as during the participant observations, and a diary in which I wrote comments and reminders to myself for planning team meetings.

The analysis of the data and the research material is based on a self-reflective analysis I wrote for myself over the regular course of work. This led my two co-workers and myself to insights and to changes as the work proceeded, as is customary in the classic spiral of action research.[12] Indeed, in this case, as stated, I was both the researcher and simultaneously, the object of the research. Moreover, I was in a position to influence the reality being researched and sometimes even to create it.

Qualitative research accompanied the formulation of the curriculum[13] and the application of its two central in-depth topics: (1) A discussion of the multiplicity inherent in Jewish culture and of the gap between this multiple reality and the uniform image people have of it; (2) The participants' dialogue with the texts and the contents of tradition, and the dialogue with their classmates on the issues brought up in the texts. Due to lack of space, this article makes scant references to the encounter of the Jewish students with the gap between tradition and their image of tradition, although this constituted one of the foci of the course and the research. Indeed, this actually became the foundation for what follows.

The research process continued for a few years, proceeding through a continuing dialogue between conceptual thought and the research findings. The research is based on the documentation that accompanied the implementation of the program. However, its documentary character is limited, among other reasons, because the description of the implementation of the program applies to two or even three years and covers groups that worked simultaneously side by side.

Research Questions

The central question in planning and teaching the course was how can the meanings that Jews over generations accorded their holidays be expressed in an academic situation whose participants come from different cultures and religions? From this question derived other, secondary questions, such as, what do the participants experience in such a situation? How do they react? What insights do they take with them? How can we shape the program so as to encourage an open learning situation that invites a dialogue?

All of these questions came up in situations where an identity discourse took place.

4. THE INTER-JEWISH DIALOGUE: THE FIRST STAGE IN OPENING UP TO THE OTHER

In planning the course, emphasis was placed on gradually exposing the students to a variety of traditions. This was meant to construct the concept of tradition through a continuous process, whereby the common notion of tradition as one single and stable enduring truth would be rectified without threatening students' loyalty to their own heritage.

Exposing the multiplicity of traditions and their dynamic and dialogic elements was one of the learning objectives for each of the holidays, and at least one section of each topic was devoted to this study. One method I used for this purpose was to introduce traditional interpretations that reflected diverse and even contradictory perceptions concerning various matters. The students were surprised. As far as religious matters were concerned, they were used to a dichotomous understanding: "traditional" versus "un-traditional," but not to a dichotomy within tradition itself.

Little by little, the students learned to listen to the different voices of Jewish tradition and to take part in a dialogue with them. The music and movement lessons enriched the listening and the empathetic skills of the students, as well, and provided them with the courage to express their inner truths to others.

In retrospect, I can say that opening up to the varieties in Jewish studies, and the ability to carry on an inter-Jewish dialogue provided a foundation for integrating the Arabs into the program. It paved the way for discussion among people of different cultures on subjects concerned with their collective identity.

5. FROM CULTURE TO MULTICULTURALISM

Integrating the Arab Students into the Program

One of the first difficulties of the Arab students, which became apparent at the very first meeting, was the language problem. By this I mean vocabulary and communication skills as well as language in the wider sense of the word, language as an expression of culture and of a multi-layered multi-generational heritage. In addition to their problems in using modern Hebrew, they faced difficulties in dealing with the vocabulary and syntax of the Hebrew sources. These were shared by the Jewish students as well, though not to the same extent. One example of this occurred at the beginning of the first year of the program. During the study of the Sabbath, we read the biblical commandment regarding the Sabbath day in the book of Exodus and its parallel in the book of Deuteronomy. We explained words, ideas, and even basic terms, such as the Ten Commandments. Towards the end of the lesson, which seemed particularly prolonged for students who had studied in the Israeli school system, it seemed that everything was clear. And then, someone asked a question which indicated the depth of the problem: "I understood everything you explained. The only thing

I didn't understand was this: what are Exodus and Deuteronomy?" This made me aware of two additional difficulties for the Arab students: The first was they had no knowledge of either the basic units of the Bible or its different literary genres, such as prophecy, law, the biblical story, poetry, and the literature of wisdom. The second difficulty was that they were not familiar at all with the biblical stories, including the Sinaitic Revelation and its foundational status in Jewish tradition.

After this and other such instances, it seemed that if we were to suit the pace of the academic lessons to the students with limited knowledge of Hebrew, most of the Jewish students would lose interest. This problem was compounded with the arrival of new immigrants, whose limited Hebrew made it difficult for them to follow the lessons, not to speak of their content, which was largely foreign to them. After a month, I wrote a note to myself in my diary: "I fear that the great heterogeneity of the class will not let us progress at a reasonable pace. How can we deal with that? Bring it up for discussion with the team." As the students were, in any case, studying in two groups due to their large numbers, we decided to solve the problem by breaking up the groups and re-dividing them, but were unsure of what criteria to use in forming the subgroups — language level or culture of origin — and what impact this sub-grouping would have on the students.

And so we chose not to change the make-up of the groups. However, we decided to check the study program for the next holiday — texts, concepts, and ideas — and to form different groupings of students for a specific lesson, for a defined purpose and/or for a specific objective. During the summary team meeting at course midterm, we recommended that, even if this year we had decided not to re-divide the groups, the following year, students would be divided into groups using one of the methods mentioned above. The fact that, at the end of the year, we chose not to do so, identifying the benefits of a mixed group in contrast to a relatively homogeneous group, bears witness to the transformation[14] which all of the participants, including the team, had experienced during the year.

In the music workshops, another problem became evident. When the subject matter of the lessons were the *piyyutim* (Jewish religious hymns), or more modern Hebrew songs, both inalienable assets of Israeli-Jewish culture, the Arab students and the new immigrants felt alienated by these expressions of a culture not their own. But when they were asked to use musical instruments which included the darbuka drum, everyone was carried away with enthusiasm, especially the Arab students. Playing the darbuka drums linked them to the lesson and removed their sense of alienation. Therefore, a decision was made to use these instruments as much as possible.

Movement was the area with which everyone felt most comfortable. Through it the participants felt connected and free to express themselves in their preferred language, with no words and content to separate them from others.

The Requirement for Jewish Studies

Difficulties of another type were posed by the complex demographic characteristics[15] of the course participants. As stated, almost half of the students during the first year of the program were Arabs. But some of the Arabs were Christian, others were Muslim and some were Druze. The requirement of learning Jewish studies created many difficulties for them. The first difficulty was the requirement itself, to study a religion or culture that was different from their own. This difficulty was intensified by two unconnected factors. On the one hand, the conflict between Israel and its Arab neighbors. On the other, the deep inner connection between religion and nationality in Jewish tradition.

The decision of the Ministry of Education to compel all students in teachers' training colleges to participate in courses on Jewish Studies was met with discontent by the Arab students and they asked to be released from these courses (as stated above, this decision has been cancelled). In the past, a practical solution had been found. Non-Jewish students were excused from participation in Jewish Studies courses on their second year in college and were required to hand in a short written paper relating to their own cultures. This solution was accepted by the students. The requirement for *all* students to participate in these lessons for two years was a change in the status quo and was viewed as a threat to previous achievements.

It would have been easy to decide to excuse Arab students from the lessons, and to give them an alternative requirement. This solution would have left the team with the Jewish students, who themselves were very heterogeneous in their levels of previous knowledge and in their attitudes to the subject matter. However, our perception of the program as a part of the students' professional training tipped the scales, and so the requirement to participate in "The Holidays in Jewish Tradition, in Sound and Movement" was applied to all students. In doing so, we were guided by two reasons, both basically utilitarian. First of all, during their studies, all students do student training in the Israeli general educational system, and they are often assigned to teach there after graduation. As these schools teach the holidays, it is important to prepare all physical education teachers to deal with the subject. Second, and perhaps more important, the course is constructed primarily to provide tools, skills, and principles for dealing with the holidays and the ceremonies in the educational system. Although the subject of the course is the Jewish holidays, the basic assumption was that these tools and skills could be applied to holidays in every religion or culture. Moreover, the instructions for the final project recommended that Arab students deal with their own holidays in accord with the examples that had been developed in the course.

The initial indecisions, the final decision and the considerations leading to it served as a point of departure for the team. Indeed, the students discovered very quickly that the team was attentive to them and respected their wishes, requests, and arguments. However, tolerance, trust, and mutual respect among the individuals did not solve the difficulties stemming from the very complexity of the participants' demographics.

The Complexity of the Demographic Features of Course Participants

To a great extent, I owe my insights into this complexity to Walzer's book *On Toleration*.[16] The book, which focuses on the cultural or religious differences between two groups in one society, and distinguishes between different types of group differences, provided my co-workers and myself with a broad conceptual framework for dealing with the difficulties arising from the complex demographic characteristics of the course participants. In addition, the conceptual tools we derived from this essay helped us distinguish between various types of difficulties and analyze them. The insights we gained and the conceptual tools we acquired largely shaped how we coped with the problems that came up in the course. Due to its significance and influence, I have chosen to bring the conceptual discussion on the complexity of the demographic characteristics as a background for discussing the milestones rather than as a summary.

In his discussion of tolerance, Walzer explains that the state of Israel is deeply divided on three issues, as follows:[17]

(1) The state of Israel is a *national state* established by a classic national movement of the 19th century. It has organized its public life in a way which reflects the history of the Jewish people, its religion and culture, by using language, the state educational system, and the Hebrew calendar, along with its holidays, symbols, and rituals. Among the Israeli citizens there is a rather large minority of Arabs, whose history and culture find no expression in the public life of the state. Moreover, the long-term conflicts between the State of Israel and its Arab neighbors, including the Palestinian Authority, have nourished resentment in the Jewish public to the Israeli Arabs' national

attachment and sense of belonging to the Arab nation and, as a result, have led to intolerance toward the Arab Israeli citizens themselves.

(2) The Jewish society in the State of Israel is an *immigrant society* whose population came to Israel from all over the world. Although the members of this society claim to have a common past — the cultural link which led them to settle down in Israel — this common past goes far back to ancient times, while the marked differences in their historical and cultural background remain intact. The numerous ethnic communities in Israel have different customs and traditions which find their expressions especially in ritual celebrating life cycles and family events and in rituals associated with the Jewish holidays. These ethnic and communal differences sometimes serve as a divisive factor in Israeli society despite the overall Jewish cultural orientation that is common to all of the Jewish communities in Israel. Another divisive factor is the existence of different Jewish spiritual currents and movements, including the secular stream, as well as different levels of obligation towards the Halakhic traditions (Jewish religious law).

(3). The existence of different religious groups is not unique to the State of Israel. Walzer attributes the autonomy granted to the various religious groups, as far as family law and school programs are concerned, to the persistence of the Ottoman millet system, which was the abiding law in Palestine until the Ottoman rule was replaced by the British Mandate at the end of World War I.

The Arab educational system exercises partial autonomy and is one of several educational systems in Israel. A simple questionnaire which was filled out by the participants in our program elicited that they had come from a wide range of school systems, each having its own curriculum: the state-sponsored general and religious system, and the sectorial Druze, Muslim, and Christian educational systems. In addition to this variety, there were students who immigrated to Israel after they had completed their primary or secondary education elsewhere.

The heterogeneous learning group as a whole formed a kind of microcosm of Israeli society. Dealing with the holidays within such a framework both revealed and emphasized the cultural, religious, and national differences between the participants. The joint effort of the group as a whole, the constructive interaction between its multicultural members, were made possible by the participants' openness to the "others" and acceptance of their differences, by their determination to know the culture and world of the "other" without blurring their own uniqueness, and by giving expression to the things that they all had in common. Exposing the difficulties and the disputes between the groups served as an important stage in dealing with them once the lesson was transformed into a dialogic situation. This marked the beginning of the identity discourse between the members of the various cultural groups.

Milestones in the Development of Identity Discourse

If, at the beginning of the program, the problem of language was prominent, the study unit about Chanukah revealed tensions of a different kind. These were intensified by the atmosphere in Israel in 2002, the first year of the program. At that time the Second Intifada (Palestinian uprising) broke out, resulting in severe terror attacks in Israel and increased activity of the Israeli army in the occupied territories. The sense of security among Israeli citizens was deeply harmed. Tensions rose, and along with them, the level of suspicion and negative feelings of the groups towards each other. This had a significant effect on how we planned and dealt with some of the course topics, and on our planning for the following year (the second year of the course).

Chanukah — First Attempt at Teaching in a Pressure Cooker

The study of the ancient sources dealing with Chanukah went more or less smoothly. God who saves his nation in the "*Al ha-Nissim*" (For the Miracles) prayer, the miracle of the flask of oil, and even the ethos of Hanna and her seven sons, who lost their lives as martyrs — all of these matters were understood and accepted by the course participants, most of whom had been brought up in traditional societies.

Clarifying the words to Chanukah songs, which were known to the Jewish participants from childhood, created confusion among most of the students, Jews and Arabs alike. For the Jewish students, the common holiday songs[18] express the Zionist shift in the content of Chanukah from a holiday that commemorates the miracle of God saving His people to a holiday commemorating the bravery of the Maccabees, the national heroes fighting against a foreign conqueror and martyring themselves for the freedom of their nation. A first look at the words of Zionist Chanukah songs suggested the absence of God. Placing them alongside the text of the prayers and the blessing over the Chanukah candles illuminated the intertextual dialogue between them and hinted at the interpretive possibility that not only was God absent from the story of the events; His traditionally acknowledged role in explaining and shaping reality was entirely denied. By replacing God as the heroic figure of the festival with a human hero, the story establishes Chanukah as a national holiday.

The Jewish students were completely unaware of the deep chasm separating the religious perception that had led to the "*Al ha-Nissim*" prayer, the blessing over the candles, and the religious hymns (*piyyutim*) such as *Maoz Tzur* (Rock of Ages), and the national-secular perception expressed and reflected in the classic Israeli songs. The secular interpretation of Chanukah revealed to the Arab students that the Zionist-secular public accepted Chanukah as a national Jewish-Israeli holiday celebrating the nation's freedom fighters and the unity of the people in its struggle for freedom in every generation.

Amidst the Israeli realities of the beginning of the new millennium, faced with a study group polarized along social, cultural, national, and religious lines, the team felt a certain discomfort with some of the aspects of the Zionist ethos of Chanukah.[19] This applied to the ethos of the Jewish revolt against the Hellenists, beginning with the actions of Matityahu the Hashmonai, who refused to obey the conqueror's command and killed a Jewish collaborator. And the same held true of the Zionist ethos of Judah Maccabee and his guerilla fighters, who defeated the cumbersome army of the oppressive Greek conquerors. We asked ourselves some difficult questions: What was going through the heads of the Arab students while listening to these stories? Were there some who would see a similarity between the Greek conquest and the Israeli occupation of the territories conquered in 1967, or a similarity between the characters of Matityahu ha-Hashmonai, Judah Maccabee and his guerillas and the terrorist leaders of the Palestinian armed struggle against Israel? Were they adopting the Zionist approach, which embraced the ancient freedom fighters as its heroes, and applying it uncritically to those Palestinians who are engaged in hostility acts against Israelis? Will any of them raise these issues and speak of them in class? And how will the others react?

The atmosphere in the lesson was good, but we, the team members, were tense. The potential for conflict over one of the divides in Israeli society was there. Thus, our sensitivities to the verbal and non-verbal reactions of the participants were understandable. We achieved both an immediate and a long-term success.

In the immediate sense, the lesson did not turn into a wrestling arena, and I wonder whether this was because the participants did not see any similarities between the Zionist ethos and the national-Palestinian ethos. Alternatively, they may have been careful to avoid anything that would involve problems for them and would interfere with their integration in a Jewish college. We cannot answer that question with certainty. In retrospect, I assume that at such an early stage of the program (the beginning of the year), the participants were not ready to conduct an open and productive discussion of the given issues without turning them into a bone of contention that would force each group to withdraw into its own position.

In the long term, the study of Chanukah provided the team with a point of departure from which to clarify the complex nature of the program we had undertaken: Encouraging discourse about culture and identity among multicultural groups in Israel, where cultural diversity often has a divisive effect.

It should be emphasized that the description of learning about Chanukah reflects the indecision of the team, their fears, their doubts, and their feelings about what took place rather than reflecting the actual events themselves. It testifies to a process of development by awareness and insight, because the Jewish holidays embody general structures of meaning, which reflect, among other things, the "collective self" and even construct it.[20] The learning process clarified to the two teachers of music and movement the extent to which the holidays actually express socio-cultural contents and themes and serve to clarify the "collective self." In order for the team to create situations in which the differences and contrasts between different groups could be safely expressed, it was necessary not only to develop a high level of sensitivity but also to gain an insight into the nature of the holiday as a cultural institution.

Constructing such a situation became possible during the study of the fifteenth of Shevat (*Tu bi-Shevat*), the "New Year of the Trees."

Seder Tu Bi'shvat — The First Attempt at Multi-Cultural Activity

The Tu bi-Shevat *Haggadah* (the text of the ceremony) served as the focus of our studies about this festival. This presented us with two salient problems: (1) Language difficulties in terms of vocabulary and cultural references. The *Haggadah* version we used contains a selection of excerpts from rabbinic literature, from the *piyyutim* (religious hymns), and from recent Hebrew literature. Written mostly in multi-layered literary Hebrew, these texts relate to each other through the use of biblical and rabbinical allusions that form an interesting intertextual dialogue. They are not easy to understand for native Hebrew speakers who are inexperienced in reading this type of text, let alone for those who are not fluent in Hebrew. (2) The content. One of the important aspects of the *Tu bi-Shevat Haggadah* is love of the land of Israel,[21] its nature and landscape, along with an emphasis on the *mitzvah* (religious commandment) to settle the land. Love for the Land of Israel is a seemingly neutral subject. But in order for it to remain neutral, it had to be neutralized from contemporary political connotations concerning the ownership of the land. For the Land of Israel, or to be more specific, the sovereignty over parts of its territories and the settlement in them is an issue charged with tension. It is disputed internally and also lies at the heart of an international conflict, a conflict between two nations, each claiming ownership of the same territory and struggling over its land, not the least by settling it.

The perception of the potential for tension when studying the *Haggadah* constituted the first stage of organizing the studies. The three teachers were aware of the need to stress the commandment to settle the land as a value in itself and not as a contemporary political expression of one position or another. This was made completely clear from the beginning, and set the tone for the study of the *Haggadah*.

Among the topics appearing in the *Haggadah*, we chose to work with the Arabs on the olive tree. The olive tree is a multi-layered and multi-generational symbol in the Mediterranean cultures in general, and not specifically in Jewish culture. Thus, it enables people of different cultures and different eras, from ancient times up to the present, to identify with it. Israeli artists of the first decades of the 20th century, such as Nahum Guttman, Reuven Rubin, Anna Ticho and others, viewed the olive tree as symbolizing the Land of Israel, its landscapes, and its settlement. Its appearance in their art expressed the yearning to strike roots in the land. For Arabs, however, the olive tree represents not only roots and the connection to the land. It constitutes a stage in the agricultural-economic progress and it is important in their cultural/familial traditions and in their way of life. The Arabs spoke of the olive tree with deep feeling and expressed their warm connection in writing about it. They happily agreed to bring a variety of olive products to the *Seder*, and on the day of the *Seder* they proudly displayed the products of their own family industry. In this respect, the decision to divide the participants working on the Haggadah into socio-cultural groups (Jews and Arabs) was successful. This division enabled each of the groups to focus on its own culture. Re-uniting the groups for celebrating the occasion together created a multi-cultural whole. The choice of the olive theme was suited to the Arab group and enabled its members to express their unique cultural attachment to the tree. Along with their happiness and pride, there was an undertone of pain. One of the Arab students wrote of a painful childhood experience associated with the olive. He wrote how olive trees near his village were uprooted by Israel Defense Force soldiers. He described his feelings as a child, seeing his father's helplessness in face of the soldiers who were demolishing the trees; and how helpless he felt as a child, witnessing the death of the innocent (i.e., the olive trees). In his writing, a cry of pain could be heard, the cry of a child for what was being done to him, to his family and to the trees, which were considered part of his family.

We were glad that we had created a learning situation that enabled the students to express their cultural uniqueness through empathetic joy and pride, along with some sorrow, and perhaps even protest, from the point of view of a child who had experienced what seemed to him lack of sensitivity and non-acceptance of the other. This marked the beginning of a multicultural attitude to the program: the recognition of the principle of cultural difference and the obligation it entails to grant legitimacy and respect to the culture of the other; creating the possibility to learn about this culture; and finally, creating a situation that invites a meeting between cultures in which both sides get to know each other.

Entering the Lion's Den

In studying the festival of Purim, we focused on the Book of Esther which tells of the events which provide the basis for celebrating Purim and describes its heroes. The discussion of the conflict between two main characters, Mordecai, the respected Jew, and Haman, the head of the Persian King's ministers, who plotted to destroy the Jewish people and, in the end, was destroyed himself, focused on the *relations* between the Jewish nation and "Haman"/"Amalek" — the ultimate enemy. It investigated the attitude of the Jewish people to the figure of Haman and the nature of the struggle between them, a struggle for the very survival of the Jewish people. We discussed the demonic enemy of the Jewish people, the "absolute other," without mentioning the term itself.

The term "absolute other" conveys *an attitude towards the other as such*, an attitude that excludes any possibility of dialogical relations. In the case of the Book of Esther, the conflict is between two nations whose existence is mutually exclusive. This absolute nature of the conflict makes it different from any other struggle, however stubborn or cruel, over specific resources: territory, water, possessions, and so forth. These are all perceived as struggles in pursuit of specific interests, which can be met through viable solutions, which do not involve the complete destruction of the enemy. In contrast, the objective of a struggle with a *demonic enemy* is to wipe it out.

It was a risky business to present our course participants with a struggle between nations. Here was a group of students with mixed, politically hostile nationalities, and a hint of tension was already palpable in the classroom. During the lesson, the students identified Adolf Hitler as "Haman" and the other enemies of Israel as historical enemies against whom the struggle is temporary and specific — even though the pain is prolonged and is accompanied by great bloodshed. With hesitation, which derived from sensitivity to the demographic characteristics of the group, the question was raised as to which pattern of the two could describe the struggle between the Israeli-Jews and the Palestinians. Some students presented a reasoned proposal for seeing Yasser Arafat and the Palestinians as "Haman." Most of the students did not adopt this position, and they, too, substantiated their position. At the end of the academic part of the lesson, the story of the Book of Esther was divided into sections, and the material was given to groups (which were balanced in gender and in religion-culture) to be turned into a play.

The kernel of the story, the plot to destroy the Jews and the way in which the opposite occurred, that is, the Jews were saved and their enemies were killed, was constructed with the dominant motif of "the opposite happened." Thus, Purim is often presented through a reversal of roles. As expected, our attempts to turn the story into a play were characterized by role reversal. Queen Esther was played by a young man and some of the male roles were played by women. In one group, an Arab student was chosen to be Mordecai the Jew and a Jewish student played Haman. This group received the section of the story that expresses the conflict between Mordecai and Haman: Mordecai refuses in principle to bow down to Haman and does not surrender. Haman reacts with hatred for the entire Jewish people and issues a decree to have them killed. The group wrote a text for W., the Arab student, which had him saying proudly while surrounded by the people bowing to Haman: "We, the Jewish people, do not bow to anyone. I will not bow to you, Haman."

Rehearsals began, and then an excited student, G., came up to me. She was a pleasant girl, intelligent and dominant in her group. "I can't go on with the play." "What happened?" I asked her to explain. In the end she agreed to answer: "I am an extremist in my political opinions. And I am not ashamed of it. During the lesson, I said that the Arabs and the Palestinians are "Haman." And now I can't look into W's eyes as he plays a Jew. And I have heard that he is an extremist in his nationalist opinions." (Later I found out that W. was moderate in his political opinions, and was not at all an extremist.) I calmed G. down and suggested that she change the text in coming rehearsals from "We, the Jewish people…" to "The Jewish people…" and that is what she did. No one in the group knew of the girl's strong feelings and no one was conscious of the minor change in text. The student was persuaded, returned to her group, and nothing remained of her flurry of emotions.

The following week, the performance took place. There was no visible trace of G.'s strong emotions. The others had not been aware of what had occurred nor did they share her feelings. W. played "Mordecai, the Jew" proudly — his body language was even clearer than the words he spoke. And the Jewish student was a great Haman. The forty students cheered this version of the Book of Esther, and especially the reversal of roles.

At this point, I would like to analyze the events. The story of the conflict between Haman and Mordecai moves the Jewish reader into the past, to the world of the King of Persia, to Haman and to Mordecai. But the contemporary reader is required to move between the past and the present. This is how a holiday works: it creates a strong connection between the events of the present and the past, and leads the reader to identify with the position of the attacked that have been saved. Reference to a holiday as a symbolic form, which embodies a pattern of meaning, sharpens not only the sense of identification with the eternal victim of attack but also creates an initial identification with the present conflict between Palestinians and Jews as a concrete expression of this form. The discussion which distinguished between Haman and other enemies provided the group of mixed nationalities and cultures with effective thought patterns and a natural but controlled situation in which the present conflict between two nations was discussed from another perspective. Most of the students accepted the characterization of this dispute as a difficult historical conflict between two peoples over a number of issues. There was almost complete agreement that the existence of one people does not exclude the existence of the other.

What is reflected in the choice of the Arab student as Mordecai the Jew? What is reflected in his acceptance of this role? What led G., who had expressed a minority opinion during the lesson, to become so emotional during the dramatization of the Book of Esther about the reversal of roles? Was her perception of the Palestinian as "Haman" connected to her stereotyping him as a nationalist extremist?

Perhaps the transition from the theoretical discussion to the interpersonal meeting on this issue enabled G. to move from an intensification of the conflict to a stage of cooperation with the other, who had stopped being the "absolute other." Some of the participants had gone through this stage during the theoretical discussion, while others had seen this, from the beginning, as a historical dispute, difficult but solvable.

It would seem that none of these questions can be answered, but it is highly important to raise them, and in so doing to create a dialogical situation wherein the participants discuss their "collective I" and its existential difficulties.

From the perspective of a weekly workshop and dialogue on the Jewish holidays over a span of a year or two, we can identify the development of a complex discourse on several levels. One level is inner-cultural. This involves discourse among young people about their heritage using canonic texts and their interpretation, and a dialogue with classmates who have different perceptions about the same heritage. Another level is the discourse between cultures and nations through which the participants develop openness towards their peers and achieve inner growth.

Preparing the Project: A Turning Point

Each academic year ended with a final project consisting of individual academic study of a holiday, coupled with the construction of a movement activity for schoolchildren and its demonstration to the student group. In the first year of the program, while the Jewish students were busy with their projects, their Arab counterparts — Christian, Muslim and Druze alike — were bickering about the project in obvious discontent.

In light of the positive relations with these students, and as the project was supposed to apply what was learned to their own holidays, the team did not understand their opposition. In brief conversations with the students, they raised a few arguments: "We have very few holidays"; "We don't know anything about the content of the holidays because we are not religious"; "We don't do anything special on our holidays except for festive meals and family visits"; "We don't have holiday songs as the Jews do"; "We don't do anything special in our educational system regarding our holidays the way you Jews do." The teachers reacted to these statements with respect and attention to each student and to each request. We answered every argument. It seemed that the disquiet had passed. But we were wrong.

In the end, the teachers called the Arab students together for a discussion. We opened the discussion by insisting that the tools, the approaches, and the skills which were learned during the year were significant in the program no less than the content of the holidays. The students respectfully made every effort to explain what we had never understood — namely, that instead of actually listening to them, we had been busy answering their arguments.

This was an exceptional lesson. But this time, we were the ones who had benefited from it. By listening to our students we learned an important lesson from them, a lesson in listening, in "multicultural rules," and in relating to the "other." We also learned something about the place of the holidays in Arab cultures. At the end of the meeting we understood that we had drawn conclusions about Arab culture from the Jewish culture which we knew, and we had not been aware of this. Jewish culture is based on an internal connection between religion and nationality; the Hebrew calendar, along with its holidays, symbols, and ceremonies, reflects the collective memory of the Jewish people, the contents and themes that have been transmitted down the ages. The general Israeli educational system recognizes the importance of instilling the socio-cultural values of the Jewish people and therefore places great emphasis on incorporating the holidays into the curriculum. As stated at the beginning of this article, the program was planned with this educational need in mind. We did not realize that this was not the case in the Arab sector.

In my usage in this context, "Arab" refers to Muslim and Christian Arabs alike, as well as to the Druze, and this generalization characterizes all those who fall under this category as a national group. But as far as this group is concerned, there in no correlation between nationality and religion. The holidays observed by Arab Israelis are religious holidays, celebrated separately by the different religions, and they have no national features. In addition, in the conservative Arab society the role of the family in transmitting tradition is more significant than in the predominantly secular Jewish society, and the educational system does not deal intensively — if at all — with holidays. Thus, giving the Arab students the option to deal with one of their own holidays did not solve their problem. One of our basic assumptions in constructing the course was that the essential difference between their holidays and ours was in content and practices, but now this assumption proved to be utterly wrong. Having this insight, we reduced our demands from the Arab students to writing a paper on one of their holidays and presenting it to the group. The students were relieved and were willing to do what we requested. The crisis had ended.

At this point, there was a dramatic change of direction.

During the presentation of the projects, in a bustling atmosphere of activity, one of the Arab students asked if she could teach the students the *debka*, despite the fact that she had not included this in her paper. She had come up with the idea while watching the previous presentation of an activity. "The debka is *the* dance we do on holidays and happy occasions," she explained. In seconds, the darbuka drums were taken out of the cupboard and all of the Arab students cooperated in teaching the dance and playing the darbukas. Without speaking, they took over the lesson and all of the students were enthusiastically swept away. Everyone in the room was left panting and excited, and there was a sense that the ice had been broken, that we were witnessing a breakthrough. At that moment, it was not clear what the effect of breaking the ice would be, and whether there would be a continuation. In the weeks that followed, the change of atmosphere did continue. One after another, the Arab students created activities which carried the other students away in the excitement of their holidays. Distributing sweets, an important custom in Arab culture, accompanying holiday celebrations in all of the religions, contributed another dimension to the lessons, as did the multicultural experience of togetherness. In this cooperative spirit, it was only natural that the students would express their desire to learn about the other cultures and to get to know them. This affected all of us.

At the end of the second year of studies, participants were again given a final project. This time, there were no refusals.

During the third year of the program three Arab students presented the month of Ramadan. They explained the content of the holiday and its customs. Their activity involved the other students in a demonstration of the calls of the early risers to have breakfast before the sun came up, of the meal itself and the different types of dishes eaten, the calls of the muezzin at the end of a given day of fasting, and finally, the stages of serving the meal that ends the fast. Their project highlighted values and notions reminiscent of Yom Kippur, the Day of Atonement. The end of the presentation was met with loud applause by the other students. During the feedback which was given after every presentation, the group expressed special thanks to the three Arab students for the opportunity they had provided to become acquainted with the ideas and contents of the holiday through the combined effect of music, movement, and the sense of taste. The lesson was over before we had managed to fully clarify the ideas, values, and customs associated with Ramadan, especially with Id al-Fiter, its peak day — which are reminiscent of those of the Jewish Yom Kippur. However, the students remembered this activity and when, later in the year, we studied the Jewish Yom Kippur, we discussed similar elements that are found in the Muslim holiday.

The immediate conclusion of the team after the successful presentation of the three students was that we should consider having the non-Jewish students present their holidays in a broader framework than usual, and to see this as a preferable alternative to inviting guest lecturers. This idea was reinforced when we saw the affection and the appreciation for the three students in the halls of the college and their own feelings of pride.

6. SUMMARY AND REFLECTIONS

The final meeting of the first year of the program was creative and productive, involving all of the participants in an exciting experience of dealing with cultural, religious, and national multiplicity in the group.

This experience was reflected mainly by the atmosphere in the class during activities: in what was said, in the enthusiasm and gaiety with which the students expressed themselves, in the cooperation among them, and in their body language. On the other hand, the words that they chose to add to their creative written projects mainly reflected their attitudes toward the integrative character of the course, the combination of movement, music, and Jewish Studies and its contribution to their training as teachers, and how each of the course elements had contributed to their own knowledge. Indeed, both the multidisciplinary nature of the program and its framework, which enabled a discussion between different groups in Israeli society, gave the program its uniqueness and were placed at its center.

A different balance between these issues was reflected in an activity that took place a few months later, at the beginning of the second academic year. The students were asked to refer to two subjects: closing and opening. Thirteen of the 61 statements referred to the issue of integrating Arabs and Jews, with a focus on attitudes towards the other. This was the subject which received greater reaction than any other single subject. The variety of statements clarified the lesson as a multicultural situation, that is, as a situation in which *dialogical relations* exist among the various cultures, which recognize their differences and respect one another.

The "relations" we have tried to develop between the different groups provide a salient concept for understanding the meanings involved in the approach to an individual and a society whose identity is established multiculturally.[22] By this I do not mean a negative or paternalistic attitude, but rather an attitude that recognizes the difference of the other and respects those who are different. Furthermore, *multiculturalism is characterized by dialogical relations with the other*, that is, by a significant dialogue between those who are different in culture. This dialogue takes place with the willingness of the participants "to risk dismantling the identity which they know for a new identity, with the knowledge that if they continue to maintain their old identity, they will have to do so with consideration for the other."[23] We tried to create this kind of dialogue in a slow and prolonged process.

The students' evaluative statements revealed the process they had experienced and importance they attached to it. Jews and Arabs alike referred to the way Arabs were integrated into the course, although the percentage of Arabs who brought up this point was higher than that of the Jewish students. Why so? It seems to me that those who belong to the cultural minority in Israel, those who are labeled by the majority as the "other" and are generally treated with apathy, rejection or contempt, were more sensitive to the instances of dialogical relations, which the course provided. The following are a few of the comments written by the students: "Closing the problems and relating to the important thing, that we learn all of the lessons together, Jews and Arabs and we become friends. Because in the final analysis, we are all human beings who have the same pleasant days and the same sad days"; "Ending everything that relates to racism in the class because, in my opinion, it doesn't matter what religion we adhere to. In the end, there is only one God who cares for us all. So there is no significance to these things"; "Ending hypocrisy and discrimination, hatred and unsportsman-like rivalry"; "Closing the gate of hatred and discrimination"; "Closing the gate of war" ; "Closing arguments and unfounded hatred"; "To divide the groups so that there are mixed groups of Arabs and Jews, so that Arabs know about the holidays and customs of the Jews and the Jews know the same about the Arabs"; "To lead to open relations among students, regard-less of race, gender or religion"; "To open the gate of peace, love, tolerance, and the understanding of the other"; "More comradeship and affection"; "To know better those who learn together with me."

These statements reveal a desire to develop different social relations from what is usual for most of the respondents. Indeed, the Physical Education Department is open to all, with no consideration of differences of religion, culture and ethnicity, with possibilities for working together for sports achievements on a personal level and on a college level. However, the point of departure for these activities is what *is common among the participants as individuals*. Their wish to attain sports achievements is dependent on cooperation, and in this area they are used to it. The program we have been discussing is different in principle. The cultural group is not the framework within which the sportspeople are participating in order to achieve. The group — its culture, its identity and what distinguishes it from other groups — is the focus. The program does not focus on what is common, and overcoming the differences between groups, but *exposes these differences and enables an identity discourse*.

To summarize — In a lengthy and complicated process combining study, discussion and seminar in three areas of knowledge, *the learning groups dealt with the dissentious foundations of multiplicity, narrowed them down and strengthened the factors inspiring creativity*. The participants varied in their awareness of the process they had experienced during their studies. Nevertheless, an outside observer could identify a change in the tone of voice, and even a greater number of explicitly positive expressions, while addressing others. It was important to the participants to insist on the value of understanding the culture of the other. Such statements increased precisely when there were disagreements that were connected to the given differences. For example, during a lecture about Christmas given by a high-ranking personality in the Department of Religions, the Office of Christian Communities, a sharp verbal dispute broke out in one of the groups. During the argument, all of those involved emphasized that they were criticizing certain parts of the lecture and the course, but not the actual exposure to the holidays of other religions. They expressed unreserved support for getting to know the holidays of the religions of other course participants and even spoke warmly of the learning situation which the course provided.

At the end of the first year of studies, one of the team members wrote the following summary for the college newspaper: "Now, at the end of the school year, after having observed the students' lessons, we can summarize by saying that all of us (both the students and the team) have certainly come a long way, but there is still much work ahead of us."[24] From my personal viewpoint, as a person dealing with the theoretical level of culture, multiculturalism and Jewish culture, and as a person who experienced this process as one of its leaders, it had clearly been a process of change.

Notes

1   See Hevlin Rina, *Jewish-Israeli Time — The Jewish Holidays as a Key to Identity Discourse* (Tel-Aviv: Hakkibutz Hameuchad, 2009), Chapters 1, 2, 3 (Hebrew) and note 6 (infra).

2   See A. Harel-Fish, *The Zionism of Zion* (Tel Aviv, 1982), pp. 11–17 (Hebrew).

3   Arieh Ben Gurion states: "A holiday cannot be bequeathed. The verb form does not work in Hebrew. Holidays are inherited. When you experience the holiday [...] in any case, it is gradually absorbed, acquired, accumulates memories, and afterwards, it is put into practice, as a continuation of the sequence." Aharon, Yogev, Chefetz, *An Excuse for Arieh, King of Holidays* (Beit-Hashitta, 1996), p. 10 (Hebrew).

4   The existence in Jewish-Israeli society of a wide range of subgroups, which emphasize different elements in their Jewish identities, is mirrored in the celebration of the holidays. Exposing this multiplicity, while granting legitimacy and respect to the other, was one of the objectives of the course.

5   Especially noteworthy are two very different theories. The first, formulated by Avi Sagi, differentiates three types of relations between social and cultural groups: tolerance, pluralism, and multiculturalism. The second is formulated by Michel Walzer and in spite of its limitations is important for our analysis. (See also Nissim Calderon, "Israeli Hunger for Abstract Thought," *Haaretz- Literature and Authors Supplement* 31/12/99). Walzer's principal importance is in its approach to historical situations and to well-known political realities using concepts of relationships among different groups. Perhaps its most important contribution toward analyzing the process of constructing and implementing a course program lies in clarifying how to view given situations as concrete expressions of tolerance, pluralism, and multiculturalism.

6   These studies provide a detailed discussion of the concepts of hermeneutic theories dealing with culture, tradition, and identity; and a discussion of the developments

in the celebration of the Jewish festivals due to the changes in the Jewish tradition throughout the generations, and especially upon the renewal of Jewish settlement in Israel. See Hevlin (supra, note 1), Chapters 1, 2, 3 (Hebrew).

7   For the characteristics of hermeneutic research see Dargish Ruth and Tzabar Ben-Yehoshua Na'ama, "Hermeneutics and Hermeneutic Research," in *Traditions and Streams in Qualitative Research*, ed. Tzabar Ben-Yehoshua Na'ama (Tel-Aviv: Dvir, 1992), pp. 77–100 (Hebrew).

8   Louis Cohen, Lawrence Manion and Keith Morrison, *Research Methods in Education*, 3rd ed. (London: Routledge & Kegan Paul, 1989).

9   J. H. Shulman, "Toward a Pedagogy of Cases," J. H. Shulman (ed.), *Case Methods in Teachers Education* (New York: Teachers College Press, 1992), p. 19.

10   Lincoln & Guba, *Naturalistic Inquiry* (Thousand Oaks, CA: Sage, 1985).

11   Shkedi Asher, *Words of Meaning, Quality research-theory and practice* (Tel-Aviv: Ramot, 2003).

12   Tzabar Ben-Yehoshua Na'ama (ed.), *Genres and Tradition in Qualitative Research* (Tel-Aviv: Dvir, 2001) (Hebrew).

13   On this characteristic of qualitative research see Hazan Haim, "A Different Voice: On the Qualitative Sound," *Traditions and Streams in Qualitative Research*, ed. Dargish Ruth and Tzabar Ben-Yehoshua Na'ama (Tel-Aviv: Dvir, 1992), pp. 9–12 (Hebrew).

14   This process, its stages and its difficulties are described later in the paper.

15   The use of the term "demographic characteristics" refers only to features of religion, society, culture, and nationality, and not to other features such as age, and gender.

16   Michael Walzer, *On Toleration* (New Haven: Yale University, 1997). Walzer points to many possible expressions of tolerance that can be discussed, but they are beyond the scope of this paper.

17   Ibid., pp. 40–43. The concept of tolerance and the difficulty with using it in Walzer's descriptions will be discussed further on in the paper.

18   Songs like "*Mi Yimalel*" (Who Can Retell), *Yemei Ha-Ḥanukkah* (The Days of Chanukah) and "*Banu Hoshekh Legaresh*" (We Have Come to Chase Away the Darkness) among others.

19   My field notes while building the curriculum for the Chanukah holiday and my lesson summaries reflect our indecision and discomfort.

20   For a more detailed view of this, see Hevlin Rina, *Jewish-Israeli Time — The Jewish Holidays as a Key to Identity Discourse* (Tel-Aviv: Hakkibutz Hameuchad, 2009), Chapter 3.

21   There are several versions of the *Tu Bi-Shvat Haggadah*, with different content emphases.

22   See: Menachem Mautner, Avi Sagi and Ronen Shamir (eds.), *Multiculturalism in a Democratic and Jewish State* (Tel-Aviv: Ramot, 1998), p. 7.

23   Ibid.

24   Gayger Ora, "Judaism, Sound, and Movement: Connected in an Interdisciplinary Experiential Course for Physical Education Students," summary for 2002, *Ohalo Journal* (June 2002).

THE MULTIPLE-ETHNIC SYNAGOGUE IN ISRAEL

NISSIM LEON

1. INTRODUCTION

The multicultural trend in research and politics is a response to the effects of the melting-pot policy that prevailed for many years in Western nation-states that attracted immigrants or included prominent ethnic and religious minorities. This trend encourages emphasis of an ethnic, religious, or local "micro-identity" in various social domains — politics, culture, education, and so on. In these domains, cultivation of the micro-identity and recognition of it as a legitimate focal point for a sense of belonging is felt to be an important component of the reformulation of collective identities.[1] The assumption is that "identity" is not something predetermined but something political; i.e., it is subject to constant social and cultural formulation that emphasizes a fundamental element of a person — the desire to belong and recognition of this belonging as legitimate.[2] But the content of this belonging is frequently subject to political bargaining. Therefore democratic societies should protect micro-identities from the integrative tendencies of a national macro-identity that pressure them from above, from the direction of the nation-state.[3]

Despite the attempt to view "identity" as an inherently elusive and variable concept, with respect to encouragement of the multicultural trend it seems that micro-identity, which is perceived as being threatened by attempts at integration from above, is described as something stable that does not change with the vicissitudes of time. And if it does change, this is due to the nation-state's overall idea of order. It seems, then, that the attempt by supporters of multiculturalism to cultivate micro-identities and recognize them as an integral part of an overall, dynamic collective identity rests, somewhat paradoxically, on the assumption of non-variability over time of micro-identity — that of immigrants, of religious people, of members of minority groups, of those whose identity is regarded as different, disturbing, and posing an inherent challenge to the national order. In the case of the multicultural reaction, the attempt to fashion an agenda around the cultivation of micro-identities and in the name of recognition of these identities seems to ignore de facto changes in daily life that have moved the micro-identities toward integration and turned some of them into new integrative focal points for a sense of belonging, located between the old micro-identity and the national macro-identity.

As an example of this assertion, we present the case of multiculturalism and the Mizrahim in Israeli society. *Mizrahim* is another name for Jews from Islamic countries. The prevailing view seems to be that the integrationist efforts of the dominant culture in the Zionist enterprise sought to erase the ethnic identities of the Mizrahim.[4] But the very use of the term *Mizrahim* implies a change in the ethnic identity of Jews from Islamic countries in Israel — a change located between the processes of ethnic integration among Jews from Islamic countries and the salient ways in which they differ from Jews from eastern and central Europe (the Ashkenazim). What is important for our purposes is that this change does not necessarily occur solely in response to demands from above[5], i.e., from the nation-state or the dominant Ashkenazic culture; it also occurs in response to the integrative ethnic dynamics from below. After all, although the melting-pot policy was already a failure in the mid–1950s when it was exerted top-down, daily religious, political, and socioeconomic encounters between ethnic groups developed into a broader ethnic milieu that was catalogued by sociologists under the term *Mizrahim*. In practice, the contexts of these encounters reflect day-to-day coping with a multicultural situation that gets its life from below and produces new identities. One context in which this process is reflected is the conversion of the Israeli ethnic synagogue from a mono-ethnic to a multi-ethnic institution. At first glance one might think that the synagogue is a place that preserves the ethnic and religious micro-identities that make up the group known to Israeli sociologists as Mizrahim. This is where ties to the ethnic micro-identity are ostensibly maintained; this is the place that guards against integration from above and even prevents the formation of a multicultural milieu. But as I shall show in this paper, it is in the ethnic synagogue that the ethnic identity of Mizrahi Jews was reshaped as a multiple identity that develops in keeping with integrative social processes associated with daily religious and socioeconomic life under local conditions.

An ethnic synagogue is a place of worship organized around the preservation of its founders' cultures of origin. In scholarship on Israeli society, the term "ethnic synagogue" refers to a house of worship for Jews from Islamic countries (Mizrahim).[6] Whereas Israeli synagogues established by European Jews (Ashkenazim) are perceived as being organized on the basis of ideology and social support systems, synagogues of Jews from Islamic countries are described as striving mainly to perpetuate the heritage and culture of the community of origin. Although one can disagree with this assertion on the grounds that religious Zionist and haredi synagogues are also ethnic synagogues, I believe that the assertion is true. Nevertheless, it is not part of the discussion in this paper. The discussion here focuses mainly on changes in the sociology of Mizrahi ethnic synagogues.[7]

In the following pages I discuss two salient trends in congregational sociology in the "generation of the State," i.e., the second and third generations following the mass immigration from Islamic countries. The first trend is the heterogenization of congregations. It stems from geographical moves, secularization, and the evolution of a Mizrahi discourse that reflects the common sociocultural experience of many Jews from Islamic countries in the environments in which they grew up. Heterogenization has led to a more complex model of an ethnic synagogue, changing it from a place that expresses the culture and heritage of a single ethnic group into a multi-ethnic place. The second trend is the religious homogenization of the Mizrahi ethnic synagogue in the generation of the State. This trend originates in haredization and Orthodox socialization processes among some of the Jews from Islamic countries, as well as local responses to these processes. This trend has resulted in four types of ethnic synagogues, distinguished not by place of origin but by religious character: synagogues based on traditionalist Jews, spiritual centers of the teshuva movement, *batei midrash* (prayer and study centers) of Sephardic *bnei Torah* (haredi yeshiva graduates), and Sephardic synagogues in religious Zionist communities.

This paper is based on a large number of observations that I conducted in recent years in approximately 34 ethnic synagogues and on changes in the liturgy of Mizrahi synagogues in Israel. From an inductive standpoint, the findings are limited to (1) synagogues that follow the "Sephardic and *edot ha-mizrah*" rite; (2) urban synagogues; (3) ethnic synagogues founded by Jews who arrived in Israel during the mass immigration of the 1950s and still rely on a fairly active population. In other words, the paper does not tell us anything about ethnic synagogues of Jews from Yemen and Aden; nor does it tell us about ethnic synagogues in the rural periphery or synagogues that are merely historical monuments whose unique character is being preserved in part by outsiders for tourism purposes or other reasons.

The paper consists of two parts. In the first part I discuss the major trends in ethnic synagogues in the generation of the State — the change from mono-ethnic to multi-ethnic synagogues and from synagogues based on ethnicity to synagogues based in part on religious divisions. In the second part I show how the liturgy, as seen in prayer books, reflects these processes.

2. The Sociology of Mizrahi Ethnic Synagogues in the Generation of the State

Mizrahi[8] Ethnic Synagogues in Israel

Israeli society is a society of immigrants, and Mizrahi ethnic synagogues reflect this trait. The stories I have heard about the founding of ethnic synagogues attest to a commitment to the repertoire of traditions and customs of the ethnic group to which the founders — immigrants in the past or present — belonged. For instance, the founders of the Kol Yehuda synagogue in Tel Aviv — Jews from the city of Salonika — describe its establishment as follows:[9]

> When we founded our synagogue [Kol Yehuda] and added the words "in memory of the Salonika community" to its name, we undertook to maintain the customs, prayers, and melodies of our ancestors from Spain as manifested over the generations in the great city of Salonika.

After the mass immigration to Israel, the ethnic synagogue served as a strategic device for preserving cultural identity. It was a place of stability amidst the cultural, social, and political changes experienced by the immigrants from the East. The synagogue was not just a place to pray. It was a place through which one could semi-independently regulate the cultural crisis that had resulted from the move to Israel and from internal and external pressure to assimilate.[10]

In terms of the sociology of the collective memory, the ethnic synagogue served as a "memorial district," i.e., a space where the biography and traditional knowledge of the community of worshippers is reconstructed in view of the distance in time and space from the country of origin and its culture, and in view of the desire to establish a source of group cohesion on an ethnic basis. Through the synagogue, the immigrants stopped being people tested by the culture to which they had immigrated and become people who create a local culture by constructing a continuous identity.[11]

This is manifested in the fact that in addition to new synagogues built in local architectural styles, some founders of ethnic synagogues reconstructed precisely the original structure of the synagogue in their place of origin. For instance, the synagogue of the Jews of Djerba in the Yad Eliezer neighborhood of South Tel Aviv was reconstructed as it was on the island of Djerba from which the founders came.

Scholarship on ethnic synagogues in Israel reveals two salient patterns associated with the religiosity of the Mizrahim. One pattern is that of the family synagogue. For the most part, such synagogues originated in an initiative by one or more families to create a place for public prayer based on those families' culture of origin and unique customs. This pattern, scholars argue, also had a political side to it in view of the desire of extended or dominant families to create their own boundaries and resources in order to establish their power in their new environment.[12] The pattern also reflected the local balance of power between family-based factions and served as a source for demarcating borders between them and other family-based factions.

The second salient pattern is that of the ethnic synagogue. These synagogues were based mostly on the logic and initiative of ethnic activists who wanted to preserve the unique culture of their ethnic group. These were a variety of individuals or a few families that shared a desire to pray and practice their religion as they had done in their country of origin.[13] If the ethnic family synagogue was based mainly on a small, local ethnic tradition familiar to Jews from a relatively small region, the purview of the ethnic synagogue was broader.

If we return to the case of the Kol Yehuda synagogue of Jews from Salonika, we find that its worshippers do their best to preserve their unique style of prayer by meticulously following certain rules. In other synagogues, too, the founding generation made sure to incorporate in the services melodies and songs used in the country of origin. Evidence of this can be found in old editions of prayer books for the afternoon and evening services that are still on the shelves of Israeli ethnic synagogues. If we extricate them for a moment from the heaps of dust that have piled on top of them, we can see how the editors maintained a connection with the culture of the community of origin. For instance, from time to time they remind worshippers of a particular practice in the old country. Some of the prayer books contain instructions written in Judeo-Arabic or Ladino. In later, more Israeli editions, prepared with the generation of the State in mind, these references are few and far between and may not even exist. Notes in Ladino and Judeo-Arabic are part of a vanished past. But the geographical dispersion of families, the diminution of the devout commitment to religious and ethnic traditions, cultural assimilation, and economic change have all contributed to the erosion of the ethnic and family synagogue configuration and the appearance of a new pattern — the multi-ethnic synagogue.

From Mono-Ethnic to Multi-Ethnic Synagogues

Mizrahi ethnic congregations in the generation of the State have undergone processes of ethnic and religious change that have eroded their ability to maintain the mono-ethnic tradition of the founders. This erosion is pointed out in the early ethnographic studies of Moshe Shokeid and Susan Sered, carried out in the early 1980s. Shokeid, for example, draws our attention to the difficulty faced by *gabbaim* in ethnic synagogues in getting a quorum of worshippers (*minyan*) for daily services.[14] They would recruit members of other ethnic groups, thereby stabilizing the minyan but undermining the mono-ethnic tradition. In a footnote in her doctoral dissertation, Susan Sered notes[15]:

> Ethnic synagogues in Israeli society are currently in a state of change. While a synagogue may be affiliated with one ethnic group, people from other ethnic groups might conceivably also attend. In the neighborhood where the club is located, there are many synagogues that represent a large number of ethnic groups. Nevertheless, there is a certain degree of mixing.

The continuity of ethnic synagogues in the generation of the State has suffered from a combination of two social trends. One is a natural dwindling of the number of worshippers from the founding generation, those who had direct knowledge of the tradition and its emphases. The second is a deepening of secularization and an erosion of religious observance among Mizrahim in the generation of the State — but not necessarily abandonment of the commitment to the religious and ethnic tradition.

The founders of the synagogue, i.e., the first-generation immigrants, try to preserve the unique identity of the synagogue as much as possible in terms of the ethnic and family tradition. This is manifested in the recruitment of worshippers and in vibrant ethnic activity based on the ethnic group's liturgy. Cantors are hired who are familiar with the specific liturgy of the country of origin, and the synagogue serves as a place where the symbols and portrait of the religious tradition come to life in a meaningful way. But in the generation of the State (the second and third generations in Israel) things change. The "pure" ethnic patterns are gradually lost. This process is manifested in its dialectic form in the Sisyphean attempts of the second generation of the State to reconstruct the "pure" pattern, although in fact it was often fluid under the influence of the move to Israel.

In the old country, the next generation would normally take the place of the previous generation in synagogue life, but in Israel things became more complex. First of all, the ethnic synagogue lacks the social backing of an established community that is vital to its continuity. A look at Ashkenazic synagogues such as shtiebels and haredi *batei midrash* or at religious Zionist synagogues shows that the ethnic rites in these places are backed by a religious educational system. The Mizrahi Jews did not have such a system, and insofar as they did, it mostly existed within the local synagogue, a wholly voluntary place that lacked any enforcement ability amidst modernization and secularization processes. Second, we have to take into account the impact of secularization. Even in some of the countries of origin, secularization had begun under the influence of colonial modernization. But the synagogue was still a place organized around a fairly solid community of worshippers and believers whose lives were pretty consistent. Moreover, it was a place around which "Jewish" symbols often developed; i.e., it was a place of Jewish identity.[16] In Israel and other countries where Jews moved en masse from Islamic countries, secularization picked up speed and the synagogue was perceived as a place of sweet nostalgia and nothing more. But among Mizrahim a pattern of "soft secularization" became common. It was certainly more comfortable than the rigid, confrontational secularization that characterized Ashkenazi communities.[17] But still it should be kept in mind that it meant greater distance from consistent religious observance, and this has had a direct impact on the day-to-day survival of a Jewish institution that depends on the participation of at least ten men aged 13 and above to meet the halakhic requirement of public prayer. In addition, the synagogue was no longer needed to express one's Jewish identity. The State of Israel was itself an important, significant expression of Jewish identity. Moreover, due to direct exposure to Zionist modernization, the ethnic synagogue came to be seen as a reflection of a past that was over and done with, a place without a future, with no organizing outlook on life. Third, some people would say that geographical mobility was a factor, whether as an integral part of processes of economic constraints or due to a desire for class mobility; but while this mobility led to the decline of existing ethnic synagogues, it also caused new ones to open.

As anthroplogists show, in the late 1970s and early 1980s the ethnic synagogue underwent a transformation. At its center was the ethnic heterogenization of congregations, whether due to the recruitment of new worshippers to keep the synagogue going or due to the desire of worshippers who had moved to a different area to pray in a synagogue that was similar — and I stress the word "similar" — to that in their culture of origin. The result was the evolution of what can be termed "multi-ethnic" synagogues. These synagogues combine ethnic traditions, liturgies and piyyutim that cross boundaries within the world of Mizrahi Judaism.[18] But within this context, dominant liturgical rites are constructed. My observations show that what makes a particular ethnic rite dominant in the diversifying ethnic synagogue is not the number of worshippers from that ethnic group but the ability to support this rite with appropriate texts and the hiring of rabbis and cantors who are familiar with the culture of origin. Also worth taking into account is the ability of the synagogue to create a synthesis of cross-ethnic sounds and customs relevant to the various aspects of the congregants' lives. The construction of an ethnic and class culture that distinguishes Mizrahi Jewish groups in Israel from Ashkenazim is another salient factor in the maintenance of multi-ethnic synagogues. These synagogues have melodies, customs, and petitional prayers (*bakkashot*) associated with the ethnic, class, and political environment in which Mizrahi Jews in the generation of the State live their lives. There are two main ethnic styles of prayer: the Jerusalem-Sephardic style and the Moroccan-Andalusian style. These reflect the spread of two dominant cantorial styles, which are often expressed at the expense of other ethnic heritages. The Moroccan-Andalusian style is powerful due to the large number of worshippers that use it, since the Moroccan community is the largest and most prominent group of Jews from Islamic countries; the Jerusalem-Sephardic style derives its power from its synthetic ability to adopt tunes from local Israeli daily life and come up with "Mizrahi" arrangements of them.[19]

From a Comfortable Religiosity to a Tense Religiosity in the New Ethnic Synagogue

Ethnic diversification is not the only change that Mizrahi ethnic synagogues have undergone. The religious character of these synagogues has changed as well. Here we touch on one of the important insights of scholarship regarding Mizrahi Jews. According to Shlomo Deshen,[20] Zvi Zohar,[21] Moshe Shokeid,[22] and other scholars, one of the traits that distinguish Mizrahi religiosity from Ashkenazic religiosity concerns religious character. The religiosity of the Mizrahim is described by the scholars as "comfortable." This comfort, they maintain, contrasts sharply with the devout, confrontational religious character that they see as typifying the religiosity of Ashkenazim.

They see the comfort, the religious moderation, manifested in the ethnic synagogues of the segment of the population referred to in Israeli sociology as "traditionalist." These Jews are prominent in ethnic synagogues.

Mizrahi traditionalists perceive the ethnic synagogue as a focal point for religious life, a place where the ethnic and religious tradition is maintained by those loyal to the ethnic or family heritage.[23] This attitude leads some of them to view themselves as members of the congregation, not necessarily because they participate regularly and directly in the rites, but because they participate in synagogue maintenance. The result is often extremely ornate synagogues that are obviously well maintained but have few worshippers. *Gabbaim*, even in congregations of newly haredi Jews, told me how traditionalist Jews who do not attend services regularly are of great economic significance in maintaining the ethnic synagogue. Although they may not take part much in synagogue practices, their estrangement from synagogue life, combined with their attachment to the religious tradition, leads them to help with the physical and financial maintenance of the ethnic synagogue, either on a regular basis or when called upon.

Nevertheless, the ethnic changes in ethnic synagogues and their conversion into multi-ethnic synagogues are also involved in a complex way in the spread of Orthodoxy and haredism in the ethnic synagogue and in an intrinsic conflict with traditionalist segments of the population. Thus, the comfortable religiosity turns into a tense religiosity. The change in the religious character of ethnic synagogues is driven by the religious renewal movements active among Mizrahi Jews. One prominent movement that has had a major impact on ethnic synagogues is the haredi teshuva movement. Less well known is the religious Zionist movement, although it has been increasingly significant in recent years in the life of ethnic synagogues. Both of these movements are based on a historical trend of growing involvement by haredi society and the religious Zionist community in the traditional education of Mizrahi Jews. The result is two conflicting trends in the ethnic synagogue: an insular one and an expansionist one.

Adoption of a haredi or religious Zionist way of life has led to the founding of ethnic synagogues within these societies. Synagogues of Sephardic *bnei Torah* can be found in many haredi neighborhoods. There are also ethnic synagogues comprising alumni of religious Zionist socialization and acculturation tracks. Mizrahi synagogues in which alumni of Orthodox institutions are involved are religiously homogeneous; their congregants are mainly yeshiva graduates and their families. This affects the religious character of the synagogue, the place occupied by religious discourse in synagogue life, and of course the development of a religious outlook to be passed on to future generations. The attitude of Mizrahi haredim toward ethnic synagogues differs from that of Mizrahi religious Zionists. The attitude of the former is underscored by the inferior place of Mizrahim in haredi society. Mizrahi religious Zionists, in contrast, are somewhat ambivalent on the subject due to the community's perception of them as not entirely accepting the ideology that sanctifies ethnic integration as part of a new Zionist reality in Israel (even though, paradoxically, the Ashkenazic prayer tradition is followed in that supposedly integrated space).

In addition to the trend of consolidating the new enclaves, organizations, activities, and initiatives are being established in an effort to change the religious lives of Mizrahim outside the haredi or religious Zionist enclaves. These activities are known as the "teshuva movement.[24] In the past three decades, the most prominent teshuva movement has been the haredi one. It has been a leading, substantial force in shaping the individual and collective religious agenda of many Mizrahim in the 1980s, the 1990s, and the present decade. At times the local agenda of teshuva movement activists and subsequently groups of newly religious Jews has involved the local ethnic synagogue. The re-establishment or revitalization of ethnic congregations was perceived as an integral part of "restoring the crown to its former glory," to use a phrase favored by the ethnic haredi party Shas, which promotes this as part of its agenda. People from the teshuva movement have been significant in reviving the hard core of the ethnic synagogue minyan outside haredi enclaves. A few have even served as *gabbaim* or held other religious leadership positions in the synagogue. Now, for instance, the *gabbai* no longer has to gather a minyan on weekdays as in the case presented by Moshe Shokeid in his famous paper about change in urban ethnic synagogues in the late 1970s. He can rely on the devoutness of the newly religious to ensure the stability of the minyan.

But despite the attempt to depict the day-to-day state of affairs encountered by the people in the teshuva movement as a desert and a place of spiritual desolation, reality shows otherwise. Rabbis, teshuva movement activists, and newly religious Jews have become immersed in the crisis of the ethnic synagogue that I described above. But we must keep in mind that it is not as if there was no one around before. In fact, the continuity of the ethnic synagogue depended both on the recruitment of new worshippers and on the comfortable atmosphere the synagogue offered traditionalist Jews who attended. Ethnic synagogues were known for being places where traditionalists and observant Jews could have a shared religious and community life. But this sort of comfortable situation found itself facing an inherent challenge due to the impact of the teshuva movements, especially the haredi ones.

The culture of religious stringency and the culture of selective religiosity found that they could coexist under one roof. The pious people from the teshuva movement who want the synagogue to follow what they consider the "correct" religious practices, in accordance with their commitment to a particular agenda and way of life that are not always compatible with the comfortable religious character of the traditionalist Jews in the ethnic synagogue, have caused this institution to become plagued by internal tension that affects its conduct and its survival. This does not mean that the dividing lines are sharp. Sometimes there are complex relationships, as I will discuss in connection with the religious liturgy; but sometimes the disagreements lead to crises and the breakup of minyanim. On the one hand, minyanim are formed that are dominated by people from the teshuva movement and its culture; on the other hand, synagogues are formed in which traditionalists and their patterns of comfortable religiosity play a significant role.

In recent years there has been another source of tension in ethnic synagogues outside the haredi and religious Zionist enclaves. The tension originates in the competition between the haredi teshuva movement and the religious Zionist renewal movement, which has been trying to gain a foothold in Mizrahi congregations, especially those with traditionalist worshippers.[25] The tension is manifested in clashes over ideological and nationalistic issues and over the fact that many of the local young activists in the religious Zionist teshuva movement have an advanced halakhic and talmudic education, in contrast to the lesser religious education of the activists in the haredi teshuva movement and the Jews who became religious through that movement. This quickly leads to a clash between these two trends. But the religious Zionist teshuva movement is relatively young and it is not yet clear how significant a role it will be able to play in ethnic synagogues.

As a result, alongside the division of ethnic synagogues by ethnic group, in the past three decades four religious patterns of Mizrahi synagogues have emerged. These can be distinguished by their religious character and the religiosity of the population groups that make up their hard core. The first pattern is that of the "traditionalist ethnic synagogue," where most of the worshippers are traditionalist Jews. This type of synagogue is characterized by a comfortable, moderate religious atmosphere and a more moderate reaction to the increasing devoutness promoted by the haredi teshuva movement. The second pattern is that of synagogues of the haredi teshuva movement. These are often former local ethnic synagogues that have been converted into centers for Torah study or spiritual centers rather than simply synagogues. In addition to these two patterns, which can be found outside the Orthodox religious enclaves, there are two other prominent patterns. The first is the synagogue of Sephardic *bnei Torah*, i.e., Mizrahi yeshiva graduates who, after getting married, establish synagogues separate from the traditionalists, whom they do not consider religious. This type of synagogue is common in haredi cities and neighborhoods. The second is the ethnic synagogue in a religious Zionist community. In these synagogues most of the worshippers are Sephardic alumni of religious Zionist educational institutions. They can be found in religious Zionist rural and community settlements and in urban neighborhoods.

3. CULTURAL CHANGES IN ETHNIC SYNAGOGUES AS SEEN IN THE LITURGY

Changes in Prayer Books

The Orthodox homogenization trend in ethnic synagogues can be seen in the prayer books. The old ethnic prayer books published by Bakkal, Mansour, and Livorno have been replaced by new prayer books. The change is associated with the rising status of the newly haredi rabbis — those who received their yeshiva education in the haredi society of scholars. Most of the prayer books published since the mid–1980s and used in Mizrahi synagogues are connected to some rabbinical halakhic project. Those arranged according to the rite followed by Rabbi Ovadia Yossef, one of the leading figures in the Mizrahi haredi world and the spiritual leader of Shas, are obvious. But one can also find prayer books from the Kisse Rahamim yeshiva and the *beit midrash* of Rabbi Mordechai Eliyahu, as well as other, less well-known rabbis. Every prayer book of this sort reflects a halakhic or ethnic project associated with the rabbi who endorsed the book.

One characteristic of the new prayer books is their attempt to promote a change from an oral tradition to a written tradition. Virtually all of them reflect a switch, noted by the publishers, from the oral tradition of the founding generation to a written tradition essential to population groups that are not so knowledgeable about the details of the service. As we know, a prayer book is really a guide to the prayer service. Its purpose is to lead worshippers safely through the service. The editors of new prayer books used in ethnic synagogues in recent years are aware of the religious and ethnic identities that come together in this space. For example, in the revised edition of the *Or Yesharim* prayer book, published in the late 1970s, the editors state[26]:

> Unfortunately, the young generation tend not to be experts in praying orally and do not know the order of prayers, because each ethnic group prays with additions passed down over the years from father to son.

Or Yesharim and the newer prayer books, including *Yehaveh Da'at*, *Kol Eliyahu*, and *Or Ha-Hayyim*, are user-friendly. They have been a big help to worshippers who are not sufficiently familiar with the service. Unlike old prayer books, such as the Livorno, Bakkal, and Mansour editions, the new ones stress the flow of the service without skipping around. As a quick glance will show, the old prayer books assumed that readers understood the rules of prayer and knew their way around the service. Therefore they often told worshippers to skip from one service to another, or from one page to another. The new prayer books do not do this; instead, they follow the sequence of the prayers. Thus, even someone who is not sufficiently familiar with the service can keep up without much effort. The following are two salient examples, one taken from the Rosh Hodesh service, and the other from the "dialogue" between the cantor and the congregation in the reader's repetition of the Shemoneh Esreh.

The Rosh Hodesh service includes Hallel and a few changes in the standard daily prayers. Those who are unfamiliar with these changes may quickly find themselves confused and depending mainly on the religious literacy of those who are more knowledgeable than they. The old prayer books, despite instructions in the text telling worshippers to skip to specific places, hampered the continuity of the service. This was remedied in the new prayer books such as *Or Ha-Hayyim*, published by the Or Ha-Hayyim yeshiva for the newly religious in Jerusalem. The only skipping it requires is to Hallel, which is the main axis of the Rosh Hodesh morning service. After Hallel, the book continues with the service to the end, i.e., until the Aleinu prayer.

The second example concerns the way the relatively new prayer book *Ve-Zarah Shemesh*, for the Moroccan community, treats the traditional "dialogue" that accompanies the Shemoneh Esreh prayer. This prayer — the main element in the morning, afternoon, and evening services — has two parts. The first part is said silently, each person to himself. The second part is the repetition of the prayer by the cantor out loud. In this part, known as the "reader's repetition," a dialogue takes place in many ethnic synagogues between the congregation and the cantor. In addition to responding "Blessed is He and blessed is His name" in the middle of each blessing and "Amen" after the blessing, some people add other responses that are not found in most prayer books. For instance, when the cantor says "You bring down the dew" or "You make the wind blow and the rain fall," the congregation responds, "For a blessing!" When the cantor says, "And all the living shall acknowledge You," the congregation responds, "Blessed is the Life of the Universe." This dialogue is not in the prayer books; it is part of the oral tradition practiced in Israeli Mizrahi synagogues. *Ve-Zarah Shemesh* is one of the few prayer books that has added this dialogue to the text in recent years; the additions are in insets in bold type. This is an interesting approach, since the responses are basically a custom with no halakhic significance. Their purpose is to involve the congregation in the service. Perhaps this ease of use is why *Ve-Zarah Shemesh* has become prevalent even in many synagogues that do not follow the Moroccan rite.

Changes in the Melodies of the Prayers

The ethnic heterogenization in synagogues is evident in changes in the tunes used in the service. On more than one occasion I was told that the cantors whom worshippers consider the best are the ones who treat their congregations to new melodies that reflect the cultural and religious world of the people around them — not only their religious world but also the everyday sounds and songs that they hear on a daily basis. These may be tunes associated with popular Mizrahi singers or "songs of Eretz Israel." "Enough of the unfamiliar tunes," is the cry from the public. "We have to be more modern, to create up-to-date things." "Forget about the old-fashioned tunes," the congregation tells the cantor. "Bring us something more modern."

Anyone who pays attention to the melodies in modern-day Mizrahi ethnic synagogues, especially on Shabbat, will find that whether the synagogue is Moroccan, Tunisian, or Iraqi, the prayer "El Adon" will be sung to the tune of "Ze Ha-Zeman Lisloah" by the Mizrahi singer Yoav Yitzhak. And "She-Lo Nevosh Ve-Lo Nikalem" will be sung to the tune of the Mediterranean song "She-Lo Te'atsvi Od." The popular sounds of Mediterranean music, familiar from weddings, the cassette tape market, and places of entertainment, have linked the ethnic synagogue with the ethnic-class state of affairs that I discussed above. These melodies are so much a part of the service that young worshippers — especially those who are becoming more religious — sometimes think the opposite is the case:

that the singers are using sacred melodies for their songs. They often regard this as one more sign that the Redemption is imminent.

All these factors serve as a foundation for the erosion of the nuances of micro-ethnicity, i.e., ethnicity based on a city, area, or country of origin. The micro-ethnic rites and melodies are replaced by ones that seem to the worshippers to be more relevant to a multi-ethnic synagogue, more up-to-date given their environment (which they describe as "modern" and "Israeli"), and better able to involve the different groups of worshippers in the congregation. The congregation demands and the cantor supplies. Thus there is an interesting dialogue between the congregation and the cantor. The cantor uses familiar melodies and the worshippers find themselves not only participating but also complimenting the cantor for being up-to-date. This situation is expressed in a reflective statement by the veteran cantor and *paytan* Ezra Barnea, who writes in an article: "Non-Jewish tunes have always influenced synagogue music, but in our generation these influences have multiplied and become more diverse. They include Israeli songs, and recently Greek- and Turkish-style melodies as well."[27] Similarly, Essika Marks describes how in the old Sephardic Abouhav synagogue in Safed the cantors incorporate Ashkenazic tunes in the prayers, perhaps to make people from Ashkenazic congregations part of the local community life.

A study by the historian Simcha Goldin on Ashkenazic synagogues in the Middle Ages shows how making the worshippers active participants in the service was one of the strategies used by rabbis and community leaders in central Europe to counter the pressures and temptations of their Christian surroundings.[28] Amidst the challenges of modernization, this same strategy became a means of preserving congregations in danger of dissolution, whether due to secularization or due to demographic trends. Ethnic synagogues in Israel started out with limited participation by congregants in leading the prayers. But we find increased participation by the congregation in the singing, based on a constant dialogue between the congregation and the cantor. Therefore, the cantor is often responsible not only for the quality of the service but also for the very existence of a minyan. I have heard several *gabbaim* say that a good cantor — a "modern" one, as they put it — can attract many worshippers to the synagogue. By "modern," they mean one who is in touch with the melodies of the congregation and their world. From the cantor's perspective, he is thereby fulfilling not only his mission as a prayer leader but a religious mission as well — since by means of his pleasant voice and, more importantly, his ability to get the worshippers to participate in the experience of prayer, he does his job of making the congregation meritorious.

This insight is significant with respect to the fact that many haredi kollel students and *bnei Torah* have taken positions in recent years as cantors in ethnic synagogues. The development of multi-ethnic Mizrahi synagogues stresses growing dependence on the experts in the tradition, who are hard to find among the vanishing older generation and must be sought in the world of the Mizrahi haredi yeshivas. The economic crisis in the society of scholars, combined with the crisis of the ethnic synagogues, has impelled yeshiva students to turn their mastery of the tradition and Jewish law into a religious profession that can add to their earnings or even give them an income equivalent to a kollel stipend. Although the original motivation may be primarily functional and financial, the status of the cantor and the complex interaction between him and the congregation can put the cantor in a position to go beyond his liturgical function and engage in "rabbinical" leadership of the local community. Involving the worshippers in the service and giving them guidance and direction are part of what the teshuva movement calls *zikkuy ha-rabbim* (literally, "making the people meritorious"). This is a highly meaningful practice with the charisma of religious activity and influence, and the cantors/kollel students learn about it in their society of scholars from the activist myths of hasidism and the Mussar movement.[29]

4. CONCLUSION

The religious renewal of the ethnic synagogue has not led to the establishment of "pure" ethnic congregations. Ethnic heterogenization and religious homogenization of congregations have together had a major impact on the erosion of the mono-ethnic pattern, which has been replaced by the pattern of the multi-ethnic synagogue. The advantage of the multi-ethnic pattern was its heterogeneity — not its ability to find ethnic similarities among participants in synagogue life but the capacity to create these similarities to a large extent and call them "ethnic." These similarities were taken from the mundane daily lives of the worshippers in the ethnic synagogue — not necessarily from their religious repertoire but from their weekday activities. Thus we saw melodies from the country of origin being replaced by local Israeli tunes; we saw the "ethnic heritage" being replaced by "ethnic halakhah" in form of new prayer books and updated, accessible halakhic literature. This does not mean that all participants in an ethnic synagogue have become halakhists. But it has given them the ability to stabilize the boundaries of the place.

The ethnic heterogenization and religious homogenization trends in the ethnic synagogue are thus shaping this institution in a new fashion. It is hard to say what the future holds. Research on ethnic synagogues should address the enigma of continuity in the traditional ethnic synagogue. After all, synagogues shaped by the teshuva movement and by alumni of haredi yeshivas have what traditional ethnic synagogues lack: a congregation of observant Jews who attend services regularly, and especially backing from socialization institutions. Here we have a paradox that is worth some attention from scholars of Israeli ethnic synagogues. The ability of traditional ethnic synagogues to survive as halakhic synagogues depends to a large extent on the incorporation of trends of greater Orthodoxy. The route to symbiosis deserves a separate study. Also worth a separate study are ethnic synagogues in religious Zionist communities. This is a complex issue since such synagogues are frequently faced with the integrationist ideological challenge of religious Zionism and are not always rooted in ethnic socialization efforts that could give them some continuity. In this respect, too, they find themselves in a paradox in view of their dependence on ethnic or multi-ethnic identity efforts originating in Mizrahi haredism.

NOTES

1   Craig Calhoun, *Social Theory and The Politics of identity* (New-York: Wiley Blackwell, 1994).

2   Charles Taylor, *Sources of the Self* (Cambridge: Mass, 1989); Joseph Raz, *Ethics in the Public Domain: Essays in the Morality of Law and Politics* (Oxford: Oxford University Press, 1996); Amy Gutmann, "The Challenge of Multiculturalism in Political Studies," *Philosophy and Public Affairs* 22 (3) (1993): 171–206; Avi Sagi, "Identity and Commitment in Multicultural World," *Democratic Culture* 3 (2000): 167–186.

3   Mautner Menachem, Avi Sagi & Ronen Shamir, "Reflections on Multiculturalism and Ethnicity in the Israeli Society," in *Multiculturalism at a Democratic and a Jewish State*, ed. Mautner Menachem, Avi Sagi and Ronen Shamir (Tel-Aviv: Tel-Aviv University, 1996), pp. 67–76 [Hebrew].

4   Yossi Yona & Yehouda Shenav, *What is Multiculticuluralism? The Politics of Difference in Israel* (Tel-Aviv: Babel, 2005) [Hebrew].

5   Eliezer Ben-Rafael, *The Emergence of Ethhnicity: Cultural Groups and Social Conflict in Israel* (London: Greenwood Press, 1982).

6   Shlomo Deshen, "The Ethnic synagogue Patterns of Religious Change in Israel" in *The Integration of Immigrants from Different Countries of Origin in Israel*, ed. Shmuel Noha Eisenstadt (Jerusalem: Magness Press, 1969), pp. 66–73; Moshe Shokeid,"The

Religiosity of Middle Eastern Jews," in *Israeli Judaism,* ed. Shlomo Deshen, Cahrles Liebman, Moshe Shokeid (London: Transaction Publishers, 1995).

7   Ephraim Tabory, "Religion and Ethnicity among Jews," *Journal of Jewish Communal Service* 69(2/3) (1993): 39–49; Ephraim Tabory, "Americans in the Israeli Reform and Conservative Denominations: Religiosity under an Ethnic Shield?" *Review of Religious Research* 24 (3) (1983): 177–187.

8   Mizraci Jews: Jews whose families came from North Africa and western Asia have been referred to by different terms, *Sephardim, edot ha-mizrah, Mizrahim,* and *Arab Jews.* Each term expresses a scholarly attitude, which takes into consideration the history and sociology of these Jews and their encounter with Israeli society. For convenience I use *Mizrahim, Mizrahi Jews,* and *Jews from Islamic lands.* Clearly, these terms are biased. Many so-called Mizrahi Jews prefer to use other terms, such as *Sephardim, edot ha-mizrah,* or specific mention of the region or country of origin. Nevertheless, as analytical categories, the terms *Mizrahim* and *Mizrahi Jews* are widely used to simplify the discussion of issues pertaining to these Jews. For a recent discussion on approaches to referring to the *Mizrahim,* see: Sammy Smooha, "Mizrahim in Israel: A Critical Observation into Israel's Enthnicity," *Iyunim Bitkunat Israel* 13 (2003): 397–412 [Hebrew]; Yehouda Shenhav, *The Arab Jews: A Postcolonial Reading of Nationalism, Religion and Ethnicity* (Stanford: Stanford University Press, 2006).

9   *Mahzor Saloniki,* Tel-Aviv, 1962/63, preface.

10 It should be noted that synagogues organized around the worshippers' culture of origin are not unique to the Israeli case. Throughout the generations we find ethnic synagogues organized on the basis of migration, whether voluntary or forced, determining the history of Judaism. This pattern is familiar from the time of the Second Temple, as well as from Mediterranean Jewish society in the Middle Ages. Ethnic synagogues were also established after forced migrations such as the expulsion of the Jews of Spain and after voluntary migrations of Jews from central and eastern Europe in the nineteenth and twentieth centuries.

11 Moshe Shokeid, *The Dual Heritage: Immigrants from the Atlas Mountains in an Israeli Village* (Manchester: Manchester University Press, 1971).

12 Moshe Shokeid & Shlomo Deshen, *The Generation of Transition: Continuity and Change among North African Immigrants in Israel* (Jerusalem: Yad Izhak Ben-Zvi, 1999), pp. 141–153.

13 Shlomo Deshen, "The Ethnic synagogue Patterns of Religious Change in Israel" in ibid.

14 Moshe Shokeid, "The Religiosity of Middle Eastern Jews," in ibid.

15 Susan Sered, *Religion among Eeatern Jewish Women,* Ph.D. Dissertation (Jerusalem: Hebrew University of Jerusalem, 1986) [Hebrew], p. 223.

16 Harvey Goldberg, "Religious Responses among North African Jews in the Nineteenth and Tewntieth Centuries" in *The Uses of Tradition — Jewish Continuity in The Modern Era,* ed. Jack Wertheimer (Cambridge: Harvard University Press, 1992), pp. 119–145; see also Zvi Zohar, *The Luminous Face of the East: Studies in the Legal and Religious Thought of Sepharadic Rabbis of the Middle East* (Tel-Aviv: Hakkibutz Hameuchad, 2001) [Hebrew].

17   Shlomo Deshen, "The Religion of the Mizrachim: People, Rabbis and Faith," *Allpayim* 9 (2000): 44–58.

18   Sociologists have shown that the boundaries of this heterogenization are limited by the boundaries of the major ethnic division between Ashkenazim and Mizrahim, between Jews from eastern and central Europe and Jews from Islamic countries. See: Eliezer Ben-Rafael & Steven Sharot, *Ethnicity Religion and Class in Israeli Society* (Cambridge: Cambridge University Press, 1991).

19   Ezra Barnea, "Music and Liturgy in the Sepharadic Synagogue," *Duchan* 16 (2006): pp. 180–194 [Hebrew]; Essika Marks, "The Liturgy in the Habuav Sepharadic Synagogue," *Duchan* 16 (2006): 255–266 [Hebrew].

20   Shlomo Deshen, "The Religion of the Mizrachim: People, Rabbis and Faith," ibid.

21   Zvi Zohar, ibid.

22   Moshe Shokeid, "The Religiosity of Middle Eastern Jews," ibid.

23   Yaakov Yadgar & Charles Liebman, "Beyond Religious-Secular Dichotomy: Traditional Judaism in Israel," in *Israel and Modernity*, ed. Uri Cohen, Eliezer Ben-Rafael, Avi Bareli, Ephraim Ya'ar (Beer-Sheva and Tel-Aviv, 2006), pp. 337–366 [Hebrew]; Yaakov Yadgar and Charles Liebman, "Jewish Traditionalism and Popular Culture in Israel," *Iyunim Bitkumat Israel* 13 (2003): 163–180 [Hebrew].

24   Kimmy Caplan, "Israeli Haredi Society and the Repentance (Hazarah Biteshuvah) Phenomenon," *Jewish Studies Quarterly* 8 (4) (2001): 369–398.

25   The obvious reasons for this are ideological and political — ideological in the sense that there is a desire to exert a cultural and religious influence on population groups that are outside the spectrum of religious Zionist life, and political in that, as in the case of Shas, ties with these population groups can yield a decent electoral return in the future that would strengthen religious Zionist groups outside their enclaves in urban neighborhoods and religious settlements. The less obvious reasons include the generational maturation of young religious Zionists from Mizrahi ethnic groups who want an influence on the places where their extended families live, and ideological soul-searching regarding the argument that religious Zionism has based its educational and ideological efforts primarily on a commitment to the settlement movement, while neglecting urban neighborhoods, development towns, and rural settlements.

26   *Syddur Or Yesharim*, 1977/78, introduction.

27   Ezra Barnea,"Music and Song in the Sephardic Synagogue," ibid, p. 194.

28   Simcha Goldin, *Uniquencess and Togetherness: The Enigma of the Survival of the Jews in the Middle Ages* (Tel-Aviv: Tel-Aviv University, 1997) [Hebrew].

29   Nissim Leon, "Benefitting the Public: The Wider Influence of R. Ovadia Yoseph's Halakhic Project," *Studies in Contemporary Jewry* 22 (2008): 150–168.

"WE PAY OUR TAXES AND SERVE IN THE ARMY": ETHNOGRAPHY AND THE CHALLENGE OF MULTICULTURALISM

MEIRAV AHARON

1. INTRODUCTION

In the last decade of the twentieth century, theories developed concerning the flourishing of cultural enterprises, and treating them as demands for the recognition of cultural difference.[1] Multicultural citizenship seemed to be a way to define and understand how people settle their identity, both as citizens and as ethnic subjects, identities that often "run up against one another."[2] Hence, Kymlicka's notion of multicultural citizenship appeared to be a promising tool for analyzing one of the cultural enterprises of the second generation of immigrants to Israel from North Africa — the Israel Andalusian Orchestra.

However, every attempt to fit the field research on which this paper was based into the language of multicultural citizenship raised more questions than answers. It became clear that multiculturalism has to be viewed as a constructed category, rather than a natural phenomenon, raising questions of how people use it, what contribution it makes to different social groups and under what conditions. Thus, a research project that began as an exploration of multicultural citizenship turned into ethnography of the politics of classification.

Early in my research it became clear that "multiculturalism" was not only the language of researchers. The subjects of this research, the founders of the Israel Andalusian Orchestra, were familiar with it and with its implications. The way they interpreted the experience of the first generation of immigrants led them to reject the use of it. They refused to adopt difference, the central component of the multiculturalist way of thinking, demanding instead recognition as an integral part of Israeli society, not merely by right of their ethnic identity. They rejected uniqueness as the basis of their claim, on the grounds that "nowadays everybody is unique," to use the words of one of them. Furthermore, establishing the orchestra was not an effort to revive a culture, but rather one more case of invasion of tradition.[3] From this perspective, multiculturalism can be explored as one strategy among others that people use to gain recognition. Indeed, as far as these founders were concerned, it is not even a very successful one. They were knowingly constructing a culture by asking themselves how a tradition that their immigrant parents brought with them could be accepted as high culture by mainstream Israeli society.

In the course of establishing the orchestra, a number of methods of presentation were examined. The method which the founders chose, what they called "the right model," was to perform Andalusian music within the outward forms of a western classical orchestra, that is to say in formal suits and bow ties, with a preponderance of string instruments, under a conductor, with a printed program, and with a Friends of the Orchestra association, all of which were absent from the source. They saw this as a new way to make use of their inherited culture to become a modern national enterprise.

It was this understanding that brought the research back to its starting point for review, this time investigating not only citizenship as it was experienced by the second generation of North African Jews, but the theories of multiculturalism as well. A study of the relationship between the state and the Andalusian Orchestra involves a close look at a struggle for classification that identifies the institutions that operate in the field. The question of what multiculturalism is (both as an idea and as a set of institutionalized practices) in the eyes of the second generation of Jewish immigrants from North Africa to Israel, brings multiculturalism into question as an empirical reality that has to be understood in the wider context of economy and politics.

Several steps are required to create new research tools as Vertovec[4] urges us to do in his important introduction to the special issue of Ethnic and Racial Studies.

The first step is to distinguish between the language of the field and the language about the field. In the course of writing field diaries it became clear that multiculturalism is emic, the language of the field. Comaroff and Comaroff (ibid.) suggest that the concept of "polyculturalism" provides a more useful tool for analyzing social variety than the term "multiculturalism". The concept of polyculturalism includes both multiplicity and the politicization of the relations that arise from that multiplicity.

The second step is to analyze a cultural phenomenon at the meeting point of the structures and the agents — that is, between state institutions and its subjects[5]; in this case, not so much the orchestra and the state themselves as the relationship between them. The state is both the source of funding and the source of social recognition and legitimization[6], and hence it is not a matter of the ethnography of the state or of a particular cultural enterprise, but of the meeting point of the two. It is here that bureaucracy, nationalism, law and liberalism come into the picture, together with social aspirations.

The third step, emphasizing analysis within the wider social context, is to ask what multiculturalism means to groups of minorities whose rights are recognized but who experience poverty under a neo-liberal policy.[7] The social climate during the period of this research was formed by years of economic depression and the second *intifada* (Palestinian revolt). The Jewish public discourse in Israel during that time was dominated by nationalism, on the one hand, and neo-liberalism (the ruling policy in the field of economy, under the Minister of Finance, Benjamin Nethanyahu), on the other. The budget for cultural enterprises was cut progressively from $95 million in 2003 to $56.4 million in 2004. In the second year of the research, the players of the orchestra were not paid for seven months. Thus, even ten years after it was founded, the orchestra was still struggling for its existence and for official recognition.

The Subjects: Between the promise of belonging and social marginality

> *"Minority individuals suspended in limbo between the promise of full integration and the fear of continued exclusion"*
>
> Geoff Dench.[8]

The current section discusses a second generation of immigrants into the modern nation state, Israel, whose national and religious identity enables them to take part in state and society, but whose social marginality is nevertheless preserved by strong social forces.

It is impossible to understand the story of the Andalusian Orchestra without taking into account the suppression of local cultures that non-European immigrants brought with them to Israel in the 1950s and early 1960s. To a great extent, the orchestra was a response to this cultural and social fracture, when they were lumped together under the term "Mizrahim" [a term denoting immigrants from Islamic countries].[9] "Country of origin" became a useful category for sociologists in describing the ladder of class in Israel, with European and North America Jews at its head, followed by the Jews from Asia, then Jews from Africa, Palestinian citizens of Israel and, at the bottom, Palestinians living in the West Bank and Gaza Strip.[10]

Cultural suppression was made possible by the total dominance that the established forms of culture held over art and culture,[11] including the field of music.[12] The culture of the Mizrahim, insofar as it enjoyed the status of culture at all, was not granted the resources that would enable it to flourish or maintain any quality. From this perspective, culture can be seen as a political mechanism for excluding minority groups. Cultural oppression constructs social marginality and is reinforced by it.

The history of Moroccan Jewish music in Israel typifies the extent of this deliberate cultural destruction and what arose from the dramatic circumstances of this great wave of immigration.[13] This suppression of "alien cultures" led to the near-extinction of the customs of Moroccan Jewry in Israel. Many of the musicians and singers of sacred music became a part of the proletariat of the predominantly secular Zionist revolution, with the result that many of them were forced to abandon their music just to earn a living. In such circumstances there was no chance of forming musical ensembles and playing professionally. In addition to this process, the leaders of the musical scene were split up, in the name of settling peripheral areas of the country, putting the older generation of musicians into an impossible situation. Dr Eilam-Amzalig, musicologist and first conductor of the orchestra, stated:

> The human element of Andalusian music was very low, both culturally and musically. This is easy to show: they were limited to playing at parties and celebrations. They were capable of banging on an oudh or a violin, but the musical continuity, the musical knowledge and culture were lost to them. Look at the players who are used to playing loudly: the nobility of the instruments has got lost over the years of playing at Bar Mitzvahs, weddings and parties. What you have to do there is to play over everything else, over the eating and the noise of the crowd.

Nonetheless, there were still some among them who were recognized over the years as special phenomena, due to their expertise in classical Arabic and Hebrew and the esoterics of music. However, any chance of bringing up a second generation without a conservatory, without music groups for young people and without documented music was doomed to failure. Even the few who continued with this musical activity treated their work as if they belonged to a closed guild and took on no pupils.

The Israel Andalusian Orchestra was founded by Dr Yehiel Lasri and Motti Malka in two stages in Ashdod, a pre-planned immigrant city. In 1988, together with Sammi Almagrabi, Eli Ben Hammo and Aryeh Azulai, they established the Center for Sacred Songs and Poetry, which became, and remains to this day, a training school for singers of sacred songs and musicians who play the traditional instruments. In 1994, there was a division, and the orchestra was put on a new footing. It was established as a classical orchestra, with a preponderance of string instruments absent from the original format. There were forty-five instrumentalists, consisting of two groups. The first was called, in local usage, 'the authentics', and all the rest "the orchestra." Most of the "authentic ensemble" were, and still are, immigrants from North Africa and Israelis of Mizrahi origin. The First Violin, however, was a Palestinian, an Israeli citizen from Majd el Krum in Western Galilee, and most of the "orchestra" consists, to this day, of immigrants from countries of the former Soviet Union or native-born Israelis.

How could the second generation found an orchestra under conditions of cultural oppression? How could they dream about a classical orchestra, with its preponderance of string instruments, when very few of their people knew how to play the violin? During the early nineties, there was a huge wave of immigration to Israel from the countries of the former Soviet Union. Among them were many musicians who, under the state policy of dispersing the population, were settled in Ashdod. These new immigrants provided the founders of the orchestra with cheap, professional western musicians. The second generation of immigrants from North Africa were able to empower their 'burden' and present it as 'culture', in order to gain social status, only thanks to these immigrants from the CIS.

By 2006, the orchestra had 4,000 subscribers. Most of these were first or second generation Moroccan Jews. Most of the musicians played from notes, on classical instruments, such as the violin, viola, cello and double bass, but next to these was an ensemble of traditional Andalusian musicians who played the oudh, mandolin, guitar, camandja, darbuka and tahr drums. Integral to Andalusian music is the accompanying vocal. For hundreds of years, both Muslims and Jews wrote lyrics to the music, in Arabic and Hebrew, and over the years these lyrics became the main part of a tradition of worship among Moroccan Jewry. Texts in Moroccan Arabic were interwoven into the Hebrew, so that the content would be understandable. This genre was known as "*al-matroz*" (the weave). In the program that were distributed at concerts, the words appear in Arabic, but written in Hebrew letters, since most of the audience can not read Moroccan Arabic — though perhaps half can speak it.

Even ten years after the orchestra was established, its founders were busy morning to night in defining their vision and their form. The raison d'être of the orchestra was an ongoing process of constructing a cultural identity. It became apparent early on that there was no common knowledge available: there was no common understanding of 'This is how we usually do things'. In one conversation Malka spoke about his meeting with Dr. Buzaglo, a philosopher and the son of one of the important musicians of North African Jewry, Rabbi David Buzaglo. "You have to help me to create a language," Malka told him, "I need more words and arguments, we have to write a new dictionary." This developmental flux facilitated our investigation into the politics of classification.

2. Methodology

The present paper is based on four years of ethnographic study in the city of Ashdod, Israel.[14] After a year of preliminary exploration, the study concentrated on the Andalusian Orchestra, over a period close to three subscription seasons (2002–5). This involved attendance at many concerts, sitting side by side with the subscribers, recording backstage events, talking to the musicians in their dressing rooms and traveling with them. Interviews were held with dominant figures in the municipality. The research even involved attendance at synagogues at four o'clock of a winter's morning. It also involved inquiries concerning the history and music of North African Jewry.

In a first telephone conversation with Malka, the managing director of the orchestra, I asked his permission to visit the orchestra. His answer was surprising: "I've been waiting years for this telephone call." It was an answer that opened the door to a deep and frank dialogue. Malka and Lasri, the founders of the orchestra, came to Israel from Morocco as toddlers. Both of them are religious, charismatic and able in the fields of politics and power. They were very welcoming, viewing the fact that a researcher saw fit to devote the topic of a doctorate to the orchestra provided them with authoritative proof of its importance. As a result, the research on the orchestra itself became an important part of their quest for recognition. For example, when Malka was told that the work had been presented at the AAA conference in Washington D.C, he requested the Abstract in order to put it on the Orchestra's web site, "You see," he smiled, "It's not every day that people talk about the orchestra in Washington."

In the majority of ethnographic studies there is a distance between the researcher and the reality under study, but in this case the distance was minimal. The discourse concerning multiculturalism represents a meeting of an enlightened subject and political academia. Major Israeli academics have been requested by state authorities to write papers on the topic of policy regarding culture; others led the establishment of social organizations that became dominant in the demand for multiculturalism. Malka, Dr. Lasri, Dr. Avi Ilam Amzalig (first conductor) and Asher Canfo (chairman of the orchestra) took part in the intellectual discourse concerning multiculturalism. They attended discussions and conferences, and published essays and papers in a variety of publications. Thus, my position as the one who wrote about them became yet another voice in a field in which the writers and the subjects of research constantly changed places.

The condition of second-generation immigrants at the time provided a unique methodological moment which gave observers, including social scientists, a standpoint from which to analyze culture both within and beyond the borders of culture, thereby helping them to explore the construction of major social categories such as ethnicity and citizenship.

Theory: Between "ideals," "empirical reality," and "concepts"

It was Walter Benjamin who proposed the use of the meeting point between the "ideals," "empirical reality" and "concepts' as a research tool:[15]

State and statements (ideals)

[Citizenship]

People and concepts   Empirical reality

This triangular model will be followed to analyze the citizenship undertaken by this second generation of immigrants who were looking for both social recognition and making a living. At the point of the triangle is the utopian ideal of modern nationalism, which promises a national culture that embraces everyone. On one side of the base is the empirical reality, which is how the ideal actually works out on the ground (where it will be shown how state actions often contradicted formal state pronouncements), and at the third point we find the people themselves, that second generation whose very existence embodies multiple identities. It is in the space between these points that different categories of citizenship are negotiated and can be classified.

Hence, the model can help us to explore the experience of citizenship in a new light. It turns attention from constituent elements as entities in themselves to the relationship between them, reminding us that social categories, promises and power struggles play out at their meeting point.

The triangle reflects tension between its point and its base, between the "'big time,"[16] the national time of promises, declarations and ceremonies and the "small time" of the daily round.

> The state and society meet at the point where citizenship is found, that is to say at the point where rights, duties and institutions overlap... citizenship is located at the medial point between state and society, exercising the normative control of the relations between the state and the individuals that constitute society [17]

3. FINDINGS

Part 1: Statements and state: enlightened nationalism and the politic of exclusion.

Culture, like every social phenomenon, is always stratified. Just as no social movement has succeeded in deleting social stratification, so too no social-cultural movement has succeeded in deleting cultural stratification. Hence, the principal of equality of value may be a heartfelt catchword, but it is never brought to reality in any cultural system.[18]

In more recent years, the official pronouncements of the state, which also form a part of the public discourse, aim to present enlightened nationalism by shuttling between the demand for homogeneity and tolerance toward groups of minorities. In this case, multiculturalism came to be a discourse of mere politically correctness. State officials adopted multiculturalism under an interpretation that preserved the core (Western) culture, while yet making some room for other cultures. At the same time, the state practiced a bureaucracy of exclusion by adopting so-called objective criteria, based on official reports and carried into practice by budgetary policy. The orchestra, as a result of its refusal to accept the label "ethnic," became a serious problem, because it blurred the establishment strategy to budget the orchestra, not under the category of "classical orchestra" but as a "special-native-case."

Two reports on culture were written at the beginning of the present century by major academics in Israel, at the request of the government, called the Bracha Report[19] and "Vision for 2000."[20] Another document was the budgetary policy, which became known as 'the criteria'. It is in those parts of the documents, in the small print which the reader tends to pass over, that the fate of whole groups was decided. Why did the government ask for reports on culture? Firstly, to neutralize the power of politicians to interfere with the budget for cultural matters, secondly it was a result of examining the tension between preserving the old institutions and encouraging new enterprises, and thirdly out of a desire to strengthen the connection between the national budget and national objectives, especially social unity.

By presenting a policy of enlightened nationalism, the reports try to tread a path between the desire to preserve the ethos of one national culture by protecting the budget for so-called "national institutions" (i.e., the national theater, Habima, and the national orchestra, the Philharmonic) while at the same time showing "tolerance" by promoting what were seen as "other" cultures. They rejected the main and basic demand of the Andalusian Orchestra to be considered as a classical orchestra, as we can see in the following quotation:

> In 1998, some 40% of the Jewish population attended the cinema, a museum, a popular music show or an evening of light entertainment at least once. Twenty-five percent went to a concert of classical music, 13% to a dance performance, 5% to the opera and 5% to a concert of the Israel Andalusian Orchestra.[21]

The Andalusian Orchestra is in a separate category that the report refuses to consider as classical music. In rejecting this demand, its writers repeated their position that the orchestra belongs in the "ethnic" category. At the same time, the orchestra went through a process of delegitimization, under the label "ethnic symbolism," which placed the Mizrahi identity into the category of an invented one, and its leaders into representatives without a public. "The claim of Mizrahis who demand equality is more statistical (50% of the population) and sociological (identity) than substantial" (ibid.). In "Vision for 2000", too, Mizrahi identity is negated as an artificial construct. The writers of the report continue to look for a mono-ethnic national identity.[22] The orchestra was stigmatized as threatening to split Israeli society.

An attempt to understand the overall picture arising from the many details reveals a bureaucracy of exclusion. The policy known as "the criteria" involves supposedly objective support by the state of its national culture. The main parameters for awarding budgets are (a) assessment of quality, which the Cultural Administration mostly divides into "pass; or fail;" (b) seniority, on the basis that the old should not have to give way to the new. For example, a cultural enterprise can gain the support of the state only after showing two years of activity. The latter criterion of course closes the door to groups who need support from their outset.

The research revealed a formal machinery of ranking that lets the Authority maintain and protect what it calls national projects. This system gives the Philharmonic Orchestra the advantage of being "national," while the official policy of multiculturalism provides a lower ranking factor, called "special," that enables the Authority to give relatively tiny grants to groups on the fringes of the hegemonic society.

Part II: people and concept

Next, we come to the subjects, the people concerned, who play a major role in defining the situation. The director of the orchestra, Malka, was busy from morning to evening with questions of self-definition and strategic location; not as a therapeutic exercise, but to win recognition and financial support. For example, when asked whether he considered their music as "world music," he answered:

> As far as I am concerned, our music is world music, in the sense that all the music in the world comes into that category. If mine is world music and his is classical music, then mine is not world music at all. And if his is Western classical music, then mine is Mizrahi classical music. When I define my music, I don't use the notion of world music.

In other words, ethnic identity has nothing to do with the culture of a particular group, nor indeed with the country of origin of that group. The need to maneuver in a wide range of discourses involved the heads of the orchestra and its players — Moroccans and Russians alike — in questions of ethnic identity, specifically as it concerns movement from the margins toward the center of society.

This is a different definition of ethnic identity: the attempt to "get in," to be "correct," to win a budget, to gain recognition. Such an identity — in this case, Mizrahi identity — does not arise from the question of origin, but from the desire to move from the social periphery to the central, established positions.

The "Vision for 2000" Report brings into discussion the need to preserve the national core culture. Groups that do not belong to Western culture were promised funds in return for their recognition of the centrality of Western culture.

This was Malka's reply:

> Someone wanted western, Ashkenazi [i.e., European] culture to be THE Israeli culture. In my opinion, they failed. The facts speak for themselves. There is a struggle going on, both concealed and open, about what Israeli culture is to be. My contribution is to say: let every

cultural sector come out in all its glory, in full force, in its fullest expression, with its strength and its people, and from the junction of them all we will get one good central power. In one of my articles, I asked, what is culture for your understanding? Mozart? Rachel the Poetess? What about David Avidan and Hanoch Levin? [This refers to three Israeli writers who could be considered to typify the established culture.] That's the heart of the matter!

Tell me — don't hold back. I say that the core will come from both this one and that one. David Avidan — I've nothing against him, but his poetry does nothing for me. The poetry of Rabbi David Buzaglo is what does it for me — it's canonical. They say that the core is Ashkenazi stroke western culture, and on the fringes let the Beduin, the Druze, the Maimuna [a Mizrahi festival] come out with their mats and dances and we'll take a look and say Oi, oi, oi, natives [Malka used the English word] and so on. Oi, oi, oi, I'm not having that!

Malka went on more quietly:

The problem is one of resources. If all that culture were carried on with private money, if they were to bring a hundred million dollars, they could do what they like. But the moment that it's a question of public money of all the shareholders, both mine and theirs, in my opinion it should be divided out in a way that all the shareholders can enjoy the dividends. That's not what happens.

In saying this, Malka expressed the central standpoint of the orchestra, that it is central to Israeli society and the Israeli culture. They did not seek to select or point to differences, and thereby adopt the category of ethnicity. In their understanding, the dangers of the ethnic label lay behind all talk of differences. Hence, the orchestra refused both the bait and the stigma of "difference." Malka saw clearly that every controversy on the topic of culture came down to a controversy on resources. The experience of the previous generation taught him that any expression of willingness to accept the ethnic label would forever leave them on the periphery of society.

As a case study, let me go into details concerning a meeting between the heads of the orchestra and the Culture Administration. This meeting took place in the summer of 2003, and encapsulates the politics of classification. The context of the meeting explores a new facet of analysis: the summer of 2003 was the summer of the second *intifada* (Palestinian revolt), a time of terror, fighting and deep economic recession. It was at a time when the orchestra had not been able to pay the wages of its musicians for seven months. Malka opened the meeting by saying:

It was important to us, as heads of the orchestra, not to come to the meeting as members of a needy minority. What we wanted was to be a proper part of Israeli society. After all, we pay our taxes, we do our army service.

In other words, their request for a budget was not based on difference, but on their desire for legitimacy and equal partnership. As they saw it, emphasizing the difference might bring advantages in the short term, but it would harm them in the long term.

Where multiculturalism is concerned, it's a matter of the "special" factor. We objected to that. We don't want to be labeled as natives, with an agreement for the 6% allocated to special cases, which ended up at 4%. That was supposed to be divided up between all non-Western classical orchestras, and in the end, they added baroque groups and groups that play period instruments as well. It's nothing but fraud.

From a legal point of view, the special factor simply doesn't work. Besides, I don't want to be treated like one of the natives. How much are you giving to multiculturalism?

Dr. Lasri added:

It bothers you that we compare the Andalusian Orchestra with the Philharmonic.

The head of the Cultural Administration answered: "The nation isn't divided into Andalusian and Philharmonic. We've only just paid for an east-west concert. There is only one national orchestra, and that's that. Don't try to compete with it."

An argument about the status of the Philharmonic as the national orchestra developed. "Where is that written?" asked Malka. "I'll take it on myself to clarify that point. It has to be documented somewhere," answered the vice-chair. She was forgetting that the unwritten agreements are the strongest ones.

Malka asked her to say in her own voice that the orchestra is Mizrahi Classical Orchestra. She refused. "You don't understand what classical means," she answered, and Malka responded: "Classical means anything that is excellent, in the sense of that particular taste. Those mistaken assumptions are embedded into the Establishment, and there's no way that it won't influence your decisions if you won't define us as classical."

That made her angry. She banged on the table: "It's ethnic. It belongs to a particular group. It's just fashionable at the moment."

Malka got angry too and banged on the table. "That's just labeling. It's not labeling on one condition, though: if I'm ethnic, then Beethoven is ethnic too."

This made everyone laugh in amazement.

The meeting was closed on the understanding that the head of the council, who had been trying to calm the sides down throughout the meeting, would examine the possibility of adding to the budget under the heading of "needy cultural institutions."

What comes out of this discussion is that, contrary to formal pronouncements by the state on "culture for all," the moment that some cultural enterprise tries to get support in the name of national unity, the state protects the hegemonic groups, and affixes the label "ethnic" on to even the second generation of immigrants, and then grants them their lesser budgets accordingly. Malka's question, "How much are you giving to multiculturalism?" puts the actual use of the term into a ridiculous light. Contrary to multicultural expectations, Malka refused to talk in terms of different cultures. He was perfectly well aware that if he accepted that term, he would be put right back into the ethnic niche, a "native," as he put it.

Why did the officials repeatedly demand that the heads of the orchestra define their music as ethnic or east-west music? According to Regev,[23] this classification is a continuation of the "melting pot" ideology: "Its creators serve the national idea and in fact make a form of music that is subordinated to the concept of building an Israeli identity." This contention gains reinforcement when comparison between the Philharmonic and the Andalusian Orchestras is treated as the ultimate threat. The officials of the Authority demanded again and again that the orchestra should not compare itself to the Philharmonic, that the latter was something special, and when they were pressed made it clear that they considered this to be a basic understanding that required no documentation. Shenhav and Yonah[24] explain this phenomenon: The dominant culture in Israel was envisaged and engineered from the beginning as an ethno-national Zionist one, and not as a people's culture. The established élite and the state institutions conferred on its creators such kite-marks as "national poet," "national theater," "national museum," "national library" or "national literature."

However, in view of the policy of criteria, a whitewash of the cultural and social priorities was revealed, in that the committee was forced to invent a special status for the Philharmonic Orchestra in order to preserve the level of its budget. The chairperson of the criteria committee declared to the people of the Andalusian Orchestra, "We made our judgment without any preconceived ideas, don't be suspicious." Lasri and Malka tried to tear off the disguise of objectivity, asking "Who are the judges? Who are these people who sit on the committee?" and the chairperson turned the whole question on its head by declaring, "It's you, by claiming to represent women, Mizrahis, Arabs to the committee, who have introduced a subjective and alien element into the system." For a moment, the heads of the orchestra were tempted to make their demands on the grounds of being a "special case," but Malka recognized that this strategy would be a failure, because "everyone's special now." He went back to the main track, declaring that they were the equals of the big orchestras and should receive their budget accordingly.

Part III: empirical reality

It is not enough to record and analyze "front of the stage" interactions: they are only one side of the picture, and not the most important one. Behind the scene, in the places that concrete decisions are taken, another kind of policy is shaped. There are key people in the bureaucracy whose position enables them to deal with the reality of a polycultural society. They are not people who are out to change the world, but aim to keep things quiet by means of mechanisms that bypass bureaucracy and by using personal connections.

When a number of key persons work that way over a period of time, a new Establishment statement is created, one that often flies in the face of the formal pronouncements, but never publicly opposes them. The case of the criteria committee shows how opening side-doors to granting a budget gave birth to major social categories, which in turn gave rise to shadow policies that encouraged the politics of identities and, at the same time, to formal pronouncements on the importance of "social glue." For instance, if you came from the CIS and wanted to set up an Israeli theater, you could get a budget from the Ministry of Absorption, as a Russian. A Druze who wanted to set up an Israeli dance group, had to declare himself a member of a minority, and get his budget from the Council for Minority Culture.

In other words, these key people did not announce a new agenda. They adopted the existing one, and were able to recite the chain of events that brought it into being. However, they were aware of exceptions, inherent mishaps that, according to them, were neither deliberate nor the result of error. In point of fact, by their long drawn-out handling of such exceptions, they created a new agenda for the bodies dealing with recognition and connections, where cases fell into bureaucratic and organizational gaps. This activity gave rise to a new reality, as the reports on culture themselves reveal.

For example, according to Katz and Sela,[25] in order to obtain financial support from the Ministry of Culture, it was necessary to prove continuous existence for at least two years — and even that was conditional on the Ministry receiving a higher budget, since it would not be at the expense of any existing body. In that case, how is it possible to become a supported body? How is it possible to "get in" in the first place? How can one support oneself for those two years? One answer given by the report (ibid., p. 48) is that one can first obtain a modicum of support as a special project, and become a regular, fully supported institution at the end of the period. Another solution is to gain support under a different fiscal heading, for instance as a religious body, or as an organization of new immigrants (as the Gesher Theater did), and thereby gain support from another government ministry. In other words, to become a candidate for support, the body or institution concerned is forced to go through the very politics of identities that it opposes.

Hence, the identity of cultural enterprises in Israel has been defined by slipping them through the cracks in the bureaucratic obstacles, cracks that enabled new immigrants from the CIS to obtain support for the Gesher Theater, or a grant being given to a sale of Judaica, justified by calling it artwork. When the Culture Administration rejected a request for support of "neighborhood art," new resources were found to set up councils for neighborhood culture. The result has been that bureaucrats have created routes that bypass the criteria — by right of the politics of difference — and have thereby won peace and quiet.

As a result, the first request of the orchestra to be treated as an equal among orchestras failed, on the grounds that, according to those who made the decisions, it did not meet the criterion of quality. The Ministry would only grant it the status and budget of an "ethnic project."

4. Conclusions

> "Ethnic minorities are first and foremost the product of enclosure from outside, and only secondly, if at all, the outcome of self-enclosure."[26]

This research began as an Israeli case of multicultural citizenship and ended up as ethnography of the politics of classification. It explored the experience of citizenship as a struggle for existence and recognition, where the process of classifications became the turning point to win legitimacy and budget. The founders of the Andalusian Orchestra rejected the option of winning their claim as "natives." By rejecting this, they rejected any claim on behalf of difference, a category that, in their understanding would preserve their social marginality. Consequently, multicultural citizenship failed to define citizenship as it is experienced by second generation North Africa Jews in Israel.

Multiculturalism should have come under the academic microscope as an empirical reality, as one of many strategies that people use to present and advance their case. Instead, it became a theory, a tool for analyzing social reality in polycultural societies. Under the influence and authority of American academic discourse, this way of thinking became widespread in Israel too.

The following questions arise on public and academic floors: "Does multiculturalism threaten the very existence of the modern nation state?" and "Is multiculturalism the last chance of the state to deal with its internal variety in a moral way?" Questions like these are essential to committed academic discourse, that is, any scholarship that accepts the responsibility of being involved in society. The point is, though, that such questions do not contribute to research on the expanded variety of cultures in a society.

In our analysis of the policy of funding the arts in Israel, it is argued that by its public statements the state present enlightened nationalism, and yet at the same time the state practiced a bureaucracy of exclusion by adopting "objective criteria" for funding. The refusal of the heads of the orchestra to accept the label "ethnic" and their demand for equal treatment were seen as a threat to the status quo.

The narrative and actions of the orchestra make it clear that its leaders were full partners to the definition of the situation. Contrary to what intuition might suggest, they did not make their demands on the basis of the right to be different, or for their uniqueness, but fought for the right to be recognized as equals in Israeli culture. But the whole point is to be recognized as equal as who you are — Arab, Moroccan, Jew, or whatever. The sole contribution of the Culture Administration to multiculturalism was its proposal to grant the orchestra a budget as a special case. The orchestra recognized this as a trap that condemned it to the periphery, where it would have to share limited finances with dozens of other special cases. In rejecting the proposal, the heads of the orchestra rejected the concept of multiculturalism, which they saw as just one of the strategies of the hegemony to advance its own interests. It is worth noting that this standpoint in no way involves any rejection of the concepts of nation and state, in a country where nationalism has always been a major factor. Indeed, its spokesmen stressed its fulfillment of the duties to the state: "We pay our taxes and serve in the army," he said. They based their claims on excellence, but also on representing half of the Jewish population, a proposition that negated any assertion that the Mizrahi identity is "special." Their standpoint was that they were therefore entitled to centrality in society.

The concept of multiculturalism blossomed among radical intellectuals because it provided them with a new language for talking about democratic utopia and moral society, but it ignores the ideological power of these concepts and the fact that it is useless when it comes to explaining the activities of groups which reject talk about the right to difference, and want to play on center stage. Theoreticians of multiculturalism would no doubt claim that this was the policy of the liberal state, preserving the distinction between the center and the periphery, between the hegemonic culture and sub-cultures, whereas the heads of the orchestra treated multiculturalism as polycentric, as if aiming to multiply centers.

The motivation and driving force of the orchestra are expressions of human, political and cultural hunger for recognition and reward. In fact, it was not the aim of the heads of the orchestra to create a multi-centered society, or to redefine the relationship between the center and the periphery. The explosive nature of the dialogue between them and officials of the state was the outcome of the tension between a sense of being under threat and losing power, on the part of the agencies of the nation state, and the experience of its subjects that the nation state is a powerful and relevant player. Although transnational links were established by the orchestra with Jewish communities in Canada and Europe, these did not present any real alternative to links with the state

The dynamics behind the scenes presented above document and analyze how the shadow policy, created through complex organizational and personal processes, feeds the politics of identities, even while public declarations oppose such a thing. The result is that the imaginary community — and it makes no difference whether it retreated in the face of globalization, as Appadurai[27] says, or changed its appearance while hanging on to its power — paves the way to an imaginary community of differences.

NOTES

1   Will Kymlicka, *Multicultural Citizenship* (Oxford: Clarendon Press, 1995).

2   John Comaroff and Jean Comaroff. "Reflections on Liberalism, Polyculturalism, and ID-ology: Citizenship and Difference in South Africa," *Social Identities*, vol. 9, no. 3 (2003): 1–33.

3   Eric Hobsbawm and Terence Ranger, *The Invention of Tradition* (Cambridge University Press, 1992).

4   Steven Vertovec, "Introduction: New Directions in the Anthropology of Migration and Multiculturalism," *Ethnic and Racial studies* vol. 30 (2007): 961–978.

5   Ibid.

6   John Comaroff, "Reflections on the Colonial State, in South Africa and Elsewhere: Faction, Fragments, Facts and Fictions," *Social Identities* vol. 4, no. 3 (1998).

7   Nancy Postero Grey, *Now We Are Citizens* (Stanford University Press, 2007).

8   Zygmunt Bauman, *Community: Seeking Safety in an Insecure World* (Cambridge: Polity Press, 2001), p. 94.

9   Ella Shohat, "Sephardim in Israel: Zionism from the Point of View of its Jewish Victims," *Social Text*, no. 19–20 (1988): 1–35.

10 Moshe Semyonov and Noach Levin Epstein, *Hewers of Wood and Drawers of Water: Non-citizen Arabs in the Israeli Labor Market* (Cornell University: ILR Press, 1987).

11 Yehuda Shenhav and Yossi Yonah, *What is Multiculturalism? On the Paucity of the Narrative in Israel* (Tel Aviv: Bavel Publications, 2005).

12 Edwin Sarussi, "Change and Continuity in the Prayer Songs of Moroccan Jews," *Pa'amim* no. 19 (1984): 113–29. Galit Sa'ada-Ophir, "Between Israeli and Mizrahi Identities: Musical Hybrids from Ashdod," *Israeli Sociology*, vol. 3, no. 2 (2001): 253–76. Motti Regev, *Oudh and Guitar: the Musical Culture of Israeli Arabs* (Ra'anana: Center for the Study of Hebrew Society in Israel, 1993). Inbal Pearlson, *Great rejoicing tonight': Jewish-Arab music* (Tel Aviv: Resling Publications, 2006).

13 Edwin Sarussi, "Change and Continuity in the Prayer Songs of Moroccan Jews" *Pa'amim* no. 19 (1984): 113–29. Edwin Sarussi and Eric Carasanti, "Researching the Liturgical Music of Algeria," *Pa'amim* no. 91 (1991): 31–50. Gila Pelem, "Reflection of the East in Hebrew Songs," in Mordecai Ben-Or (ed.), *The Challenge of Sovereignty: Creation and Thought in the First Decade of the State* (Jerusalem: Ben Zvi Foundation Publications, 1999).

14 Meirav Aharon, "Planning and Living in the Modern National City: The Limits and Limitations of Israeli Citizenship," in 2000. PhD diss. (Tel Aviv University, Department of Anthropology and Sociology, 2005).

15 Stefan Moses, *Walter Benyamin and the Spirit of Modernism* (Tel Aviv: Resling Publications, 2003).

16 Zali Gurevitz, "The Double Site of Israel," in *Grasping Land*, Eyal Ben Ari and Yoram Bilu (eds.) (New York State University Press, 1997).

17   Gershon Shafir and Yoav Peled, *Being Israeli: The Dynamics of Multiple Citizenship* (Cambridge Middle East Studies, 2005), p. 26.

18   Zohar Shavit and others, *Culture Certificate, Vision 2000, Jerusalem* (Ministry of Science, Culture and Sport, 2000).

19   Elihu Katz and Hed Sela, *Bracha Report* (Jerusalem: Van Leer Institute, 1999).

20   Zohar Shavit and others. Op. cit.

21   Elihu Katz and Hed Sela. Op. cit.

22   Zohar Shavit and others. Op. cit.

23   Motti Regev, "From 'Camel, My Camel' to Tippex, Faces," *Teachers' Union Publications* vol. 5 (1998): 72.

24   Yehuda Shenhav and Yossi Yonah, *What is Multiculturalism? On the Paucity of the Narrative in Israel* (Tel Aviv: Bavel Publications, 2005) p. 301.

25   Elihu Katz and Hed Sela. Op. cit.

26   Zygmunt Bauman, *Community: Seeking Safety in an Insecure World* (Cambridge: Polity Press, 2001) p. 94.

27   Arjun Appadurai, "Disjuncture and Difference in the Global Cultural Economy," *Public Culture* 2(2) (1990): 1–24.

MULTICULTURALISM IN ISRAEL: A LINGUISTIC PERSPECTIVE

MICHAL TANNENBAUM

Multicultural and multilingual societies such as Israel offer great opportunities for in-depth sociolinguistic research, including studies focusing on language maintenance and language shift. This article describes Israel's linguistic reality, using as a conceptual framework Richard Ruiz's renowned analysis of language planning and its implications for multilingual societies.[1] It then offers an alternative perspective on language maintenance, pointing out its relevance for language policy-makers in general and in Israel in particular.

1. The Discourse of Language Maintenance

Language maintenance and language acquisition among members of ethnolinguistic minorities are widely researched subjects. Mastering the majority language is an integral part of the acculturation process, and various studies have pointed to the positive relationship between proficiency in the majority language shown by immigrants or members of indigenous minorities, and their economic, academic, professional, or personal well-being.[2]

Acquiring the new language, however, is only one side of the coin in the problem confronting members of minority groups. The other relates to the issue of language maintenance. In his influential article "Orientations in Language Planning," Ruiz points out the strengths and weaknesses of three different perspectives from which to approach multilingualism: "language-as-problem," "language-as-right," and "language-as-resource." Ruiz's model refers to issues of language policy and language planning, elucidating "different underlying beliefs about language that ground efforts to influence linguistic behavior through language policy making and subsequent implementation planning."[3] Studies focusing on various aspects of language maintenance have adopted perspectives from several other disciplines — sociology, psychology, education, economy, and law. Although Ruiz and his followers take other viewpoints as their starting point and focus on different problems, I adopted his model in this paper because most of the arguments that are raised in the discourse of language maintenance fit the conceptual framework Ruiz proposes, as the following section will show.

a. Language-as-right arguments

The language-as-right orientation draws on arguments from sociology and social psychology and emphasizes issues of group integrity, group membership, and collective identity. In this discourse, integrity refers to factors that contribute to group cohesiveness, and membership refers to factors that identify a person as belonging to a particular group. More often than not, linguistic characteristics serve as membership attributes in a group, and language plays a key role as a powerful uniting factor and a strong indication of group integrity.[4] Language maintenance is perceived as a natural right, hence purportedly to be encouraged.

Another group of arguments related to this orientation focuses on issues of cultural heritage, mainly with regard to indigenous groups.[5] The ecological approach, which often uses metaphors from biology and evolution, points out that thousands of languages are in danger of disappearing in the coming decades, together with the cultures associated with them. As phrased by Suzanne Romaine, "Because the preservation of a language in its fullest sense ultimately entails the maintenance of the group that speaks it, the arguments in favor of doing something to reverse language death are ultimately about preserving cultures and habitats."[6] These claims have led to programs aiming to promote language maintenance, saving indigenous languages from extinction.[7]

Language emerges in this orientation as a "God-given right," providing access to formal processes and affecting personal freedom and enjoyment. Ruiz claims that discrimination against individuals because of their use of a specific language constitutes a violation of their civil rights, liberty, and pursuit of happiness, and scholars have raised a series of arguments bearing on issues of linguistic rights. Will Kymlicka, for instance, defends the cultural and national rights of minorities, claiming that cultural membership provides people with a clear context of choice and a secure sense of identity and belongingness, which they call upon when confronting questions about personal values and perception. He argues that reliance on *individual* rights is often insufficient for ensuring language maintenance and, without an effective protective setting and a perception of linguistic rights as *collective* rights, languages could not survive.[8]

b. Language-as-problem arguments

Another significant set of arguments in the language maintenance discourse rests on economic models, focusing mainly on the majority and discussing these issues in cost-benefit terms. These arguments usually emphasize that, for society as a whole, investing in minority groups and in their heritage or indigenous languages is not economical.[9] Similar arguments often emerge with regard to minority groups, emphasizing the importance of fluency in the majority language to their members' future success.[10] These arguments, which tend to emphasize acquisition, result in policies opposing language maintenance, as if the two processes of acquisition and maintenance were necessarily mutually exclusive.[11]

Moreover, from a socio-political perspective, societies are usually reluctant to endorse ostensibly segregationist policies. Language maintenance could potentially result in quasi-ghetto lifestyles, dividing society rather than promoting assimilation and unity.[12] Attempts to counteract such trends led to the promotion of the melting pot ideologies that characterized most immigration countries at least until the 1980s, ideologies that do not allow for language maintenance or at least do not encourage it.[13] At present, less direct and perhaps more manipulative ways of achieving basically similar outcomes are pursued in many countries, in the form of language tests as a requirement of citizenship while ignoring other significant measures such as official status, length of residence, income level, educational background, and the like.[14] Furthermore, as Joshua Fishman notes, "even the much vaunted 'no language policy' of many democracies is, in reality, an anti-minority-languages policy, because it delegitimizes such languages by studiously ignoring them, and thereby, not allowing them to be placed on the agenda of supportable general values."[15]

c. Language-as-resource arguments

Three clusters of arguments can be placed under this rubric. The first takes economics as its starting point, emphasizing the benefits accruing to multilingual societies and leading, in turn, to programs that promote minority languages. The focus, however, tends to be on languages that the *majority* perceives as central to the economy in terms of trade (e.g., Chinese,

Japanese) or security (e.g., Arabic, Farsi, Urdu and the like).[16] Based on such arguments, minority languages are indeed perceived as a resource, though not exactly in the way meant by Ruiz, for whom this orientation is the best way of defending linguistic pluralism.[17]

Another "resource" perspective points to the advantages of bilingualism. Researchers almost unanimously agree that bilingualism is a positive phenomenon, including such benefits as improved school performance, creativity, cultural enrichment, meta-linguistic awareness, cognitive flexibility, and psychological resilience.[18] Minority languages may thus be viewed as a resource, since their maintenance may lead to additive bilingualism and all its rewards.

Last, and more strongly related to Ruiz's conceptual framework, this orientation is tied to arguments that truly promote minority — and especially endangered — languages, promoting maintenance programs conducive to dialogue between native speakers that would be unfeasible without them.[19]

All of these arguments, regardless of their orientation, have been and continue to be part of a heated controversy. As Cavallaro aptly notes, "minority groups must still rely on the majority group's sense of justice and morality to ensure the survival of their own languages."[20] In other words, Ruiz's paper describes majority orientations that, basically, tend to view minority languages as a problem. The majority may decide to grace minorities with options for maintaining their language, or even institute educational programs that promote language maintenance and diversity, and may also decide it will not.

Analyzing the situation of language planning and the stance towards language maintenance amongst minorities in the United States, Ricento states that "the history of languages in the U.S. is very much enmeshed with national development and especially with the construction of (a particular) American (national) identity."[21] He argues that, for a resource-oriented approach to gain any currency in the United States, hegemonic ideologies associated with the roles of non-English languages in national life would need to change, and alternative interpretations of American identity would need to be legitimized. American policy makers have consistently viewed language as the best medium for achieving national identity and unity. Claims demanding public space for non-English languages have been and continue to be viewed as threats to national unity. Within the liberal tradition of the nation-state, one can be a citizen of only one (American) nation (even though that "nation" is an imagined community).[22] Americanizers have viewed language as the essential instrument for accomplishing "thought sharing," ensuring (through English) a common understanding about American identity to be shared by immigrants and native-born, irrespective of their "ethnicity." A similar situation prevails in Australia, where multilingualism is not being actively or effectively promoted, and the first-language skills of non-English speakers in Australia are allowed to disappear with little thought to their maintenance.[23]

2. THE ISRAELI LANGUAGE CONTEXT

Israel's multicultural and multilingual setting is a fascinating locale for the exploration of language maintenance patterns and ideologies as a country with high rates of incoming immigration, absorbing Jews from all over the world. The largest group of immigrants is that of immigrants from the FSU (Former Soviet Union), which brought about one million immigrants to Israel during the 1990s.[24] Israel also includes a large Arab minority of close to twenty percent of the population, and small enclaves of ultra-Orthodox Jews who use Yiddish for daily communication.[25]

On the whole, the Israeli discourse on language policy is closely related to the revival of Hebrew as a spoken language as a key element of Zionist ideology. This discourse is essentially based on the idea that one language, namely Hebrew, is necessary for national unity, and multilingualism is therefore perceived as divisive.

During the long Jewish exile, Hebrew basically lost its function as a vernacular and was mainly reserved for literary-religious usage. In most Jewish communities around the world, Hebrew was the holy tongue, while the local language or one of the several so-called Judeo languages (based on a mélange of Hebrew and local languages) that developed in the Diaspora, served for day-to-day communication. Its revival within the Zionist context was accompanied by a strong effort, backed by a melting pot ideology, to force immigrants to abandon their many heritage languages and establish Hebrew as the main language of communication. Hebrew became the unifying factor in the evolving society, the symbol of the new Jewish identity, and melting pot policies were stringently implemented to make sure everyone spoke it. Hebrew is now an official language in Israel (alongside Arabic), and functions as a mother tongue or as a second language for most of the population.[26]

Together with these developments, the social atmosphere and the official stance have gradually changed in Israel. Signs of multiculturalism and pluralism have become increasingly evident in the last two decades, and melting pot policies are in decline. These changes reflect the effects of globalization, together with top-down trends urging multiculturalism and bottom-up pressure, mainly from the large immigration wave from the FSU.[27]

Despite these apparent similarities between Israel and other immigration countries, a comparison between Israel's circumstances and language policies and those endorsed in such countries as the United States or Australia reveals three main divergences, whose effect on the language maintenance discourse deserves special attention. The first relates to the existence of a large Arab minority that is excluded from the equation between Hebrew and Israeli identity. Israeli Arabs,[28] who are neither Jews nor immigrants, differ from immigrant groups in their position vis-à-vis the majority, and they often point to *exclusion* as an aspect defining them as a group.[29] These emotions may involve implications for language, with many Israeli Arabs viewing Arabic as a positive symbol and Hebrew as a more complex and conflictually loaded one. Identification with the Palestinian cause, which characterizes many members of this group, underscores that they are not immigrants, meaning they belong to the land in ways members of immigrant groups do not.[30]

The second divergence is that, for most immigrants to Israel, their first language (L1) does not usually serve as proxy for their ethnic identity. In most countries of immigration, the majority language (L2) usually functions as a neutral or instrumental aspect of the absorbing society, a vehicle associated with the immigrants' new (presumed) identity. In Israel, however, the language that immigrants are supposed to acquire and master is Hebrew, a pivotal symbol within Judaism and within Zionist ideology. The usual equations of L1=heritage and tradition, whereas L2=new/ neutral communication tool, do not apply in the Israeli context where, attached to the acquisition of L2 are ideological strings, usually bearing positive connotations for Jewish immigrant groups. Becoming part of the majority, then, is not driven merely by a motivation to assimilate, as is true for immigrant groups in general, but also by a desire to join a wider social context that carried symbolic significance even when these immigrants had been considered part of a minority in their countries of origin.

This brings us to the third divergence. Typically, immigrants leave a homeland where they are part of the majority in terms of ethnic, religion, and language background, and become a minority on their arrival to a new place, a situation that confronts them with new dilemmas related to their acculturation process and to ways of constructing their identity. Jewish immigrants, however, had also been (or had been considered by others) members of a minority in the countries they left, at least religiously. In some Diaspora communities, Jews may also feel that their communal survival is precarious, intensifying their self-awareness as members of a minority.

Although this feature does not predict the specific course of the acculturation process that Jewish immigrants will go through in Israel, it does suggest this process will be somewhat different from the one more typically followed by immigrants to many other immigration countries such as the United States, Australia, or Canada, to mention just a few. This feature leads at times to stronger feelings of resentment towards the "minority" tag, and at others to a more efficient merging of the two identities. Many are often surprised and even shocked to find themselves yet again part of a minority, when their expectation had been that, upon arriving in Israel, they would finally merge within their "natural" collective.[31] Failure to realize this expectation may affect their ways of structuring their affiliation with their countries and cultures of origin, and to the language associated with them.

In a recent study exploring the position of language in the value systems of different minority groups in Israel (Arabs, immigrants from the FSU, and immigrants from Ethiopia), language emerged as a central value for all the groups explored, but for very different reasons.[32] Among Arabs, Arabic emerged as significant for their group identity, strongly related to their national identity, and mainly offering a clearly different channel of communication and expression from hegemonic Hebrew, which they generally perceived as representing the majority, the oppressor, the colonizer, or the enemy.[33] This is consistent with the overall position of this minority group, which is to remain distinct from the Jewish majority. Even politically moderate Israeli Arabs often oppose the country's Jewish-Zionist character.[34] Since Hebrew is a primary element in the Zionist ethos, Israeli Arabs often express strong commitment to Arabic and opposition to Hebrew and to Hebrew-Arabic code-switching. To conclude from this that they reject Hebrew altogether, however, would be wrong. Indeed, the opposite is true: this is clearly a bilingual group, whose members use Hebrew in a variety of contexts and have borrowed many Hebrew words for use in Arabic discourse.[35]

Immigrants from the FSU relate to Russian in extremely positive terms, consider it beautiful and essential for them to retain contact with the treasures of their culture of origin, including literature and theater, and representing education, literacy, knowledge, and high status. Members of this community tend to view language as a means for reaching broader, perhaps more "cultured" realms. These indications are consistent with other features of this group documented in other studies, showing a tendency toward segregation and even elitism on various cultural issues.[36] By and large, this community seeks integration within Israeli society but from a position of strength, and their perception of language as a bridge to their culture of origin helps them to sustain this position vis-à-vis the Israeli majority. The presence of a relatively large percentage of non-Jews within this group has affected their acculturation processes and their attitudes towards Russian language and culture as well as towards Hebrew.[37]

Another group is that of relatively recent immigrants from Ethiopia and their descendants. Generally speaking, this group has experienced harsher acculturation problems than those of other immigrant groups due to several reasons, including the big gap between Israeli culture and their own, the fact that arrival in Israel was for many of them their first encounter with "white" people and white Jews, and a high percentage of illiteracy. Many suffered from prejudice due to their skin color, which singles them out as a separate group that in a sense can never become an integral part of the majority, and from formal and informal religious authorities in Israel that questioned their status as Jews because their practices differed from canonic patterns on several counts.[38] Language for this group represents mainly communication with family, enabling to promote key values of kinship ties, and especially the position of adults in the community. Their worries about language loss, their difficulties in communicating with the older generation, and the importance of intergenerational transmission are all related to the centrality of language as a means of preserving and supporting these values.

In sum, Israel's multilingual situation offers an interesting challenge for policy makers and educators. The interweaving of ideological positions and attitudes prevalent among members of different minority groups results in a broad spectrum of views regarding language policy and language planning, and enriches the current research on language maintenance.

3. LANGUAGE AS AN EMOTIONAL SYMBOL

The linguistic situation in Israel and in other immigration countries shows a persistent gap between declared policies and reality. This outcome might have been expected, given the widespread adoption of Ruiz's *language-as-problem* orientation, which has led to policies of melting pot, assimilation, and emphasis on the relationship between a new language and a new identity. The other two orientations, however, also appear to lead to similar results and, in a sense, act as two-edged swords. Specifically, the arguments of the *language-as-right* orientation, emphasizing the contribution of language maintenance to the sense of collective identity and cultural heritage, may actually lead to recommendations to abolish all programs that promote maintenance because of their divisive potential. Arguments supporting the *language-as-resource* orientation, and particularly those stressing the usefulness of minority languages for trade or security matters, often lead to foreign language programs that tend to address acquisition by non-speakers rather than maintenance. Teaching Arabic as a foreign language to Jewish students in Israeli high schools or to soldiers in the army, with military intelligence concerns foremost in mind, is just one example.

In this section, I would like to suggest another orientation from which to view minority languages and the significance of their maintenance — *language-as-a state of mind*. This orientation focuses on the well-being of individuals that, in turn, affects the majority, by contrast with orientations that start from the majority, with (or without) potential implications for individuals.

Language shift, as part of an immigration process or as a consequence of a strict assimilationist/melting pot approach is not a simple or technical act, nor does it reflect only the acquisition of a new language and the broadening of one's horizons. Language loss involves emotional, interactional, and psychological dimensions. Most studies exploring language maintenance and language shift focus on characteristics of the ethnolinguistic group, on the language *per se*, or on demographic variables associated with language maintenance, and rarely consider the emotional significance of this process. The few studies that do address language maintenance as associated with emotional aspects or internal representations of significant others describe mainly clinical case studies, psychological theories, or personal literary narratives. For instance, in Eva Hoffman's fascinating autobiography, *Lost in Translation*, she describes the helplessness that accompanied the acquisition of a new language as part of her immigration experience:

> But mostly, the problem is that the signifier has become severed from the signified. The words I learn now don't stand for things in the same unquestioned way they did in my native tongue...The worst losses come at night. As I lie down in a strange bed in a strange house...I wait for that spontaneous flow of inner language which used to be my night time talk with myself...nothing comes. Polish, in a short time, has atrophied...Its words don't apply to my new experiences; they're not coeval with any of the objects, or faces, or the very air I breathe in the daytime. In English, words have not penetrated to those layers of my

psyche from which a private conversation could proceed... Now this picture and word show is gone; the thread has been snapped. I have no interior language, and without it, interior images... those images through which we assimilate the external world, through which we take it in, love it, make it our own become blurred too...[39]

Leon and Rebecca Grinberg described the mother tongue as containing the experiences of infancy, including memories and feelings related to first object relations, and as one of the most traditional components of culture, highly resistant to change.[40] Julia Mirsky posited that losing the mother tongue in immigration is accompanied "by a deep sense of loss of self-identity and of internal objects."[41] J. Stern describes immigrants who felt they were betraying their mother tongue by shifting to a new language. Often, they were unable to describe their emotions and the world they had lost, feeling that the new language failed to apply to the old world.[42] Confronted with a new, unintelligible language, immigrants may feel excluded, as a child who does not understand the parents' secret language, a feeling likely to elicit alienation, anger, or frustration.[43] The dramatic implications entailed by language shift may even be inferred from the "mother tongue" concept found in many languages.

Studies exploring the main impact of immigration on family life indicate that certain aspects, such as identity conflicts, alienation, and inter-generational discord are uniquely magnified in the immigration process.[44] Children may also be faced with a conflict of loyalties, when their parents simultaneously expect them to acculturate and succeed while retaining their sense of tradition and family values.[45] Writers such as Philip Roth, Jumpa Lahiri, and others offer nuanced accounts of these conflicts. In shifting to a new language, the younger generation may often be cut off from its roots, possibly leading to estrangement between family members. Parents may feel unqualified to teach their children all the things parents usually teach, to transmit to them the cultural values and beliefs that the family and the group hold dear, and to support the development of a strong sense of self or culture in their children.[46]

In most studies that explored immigrant families where the parents' generation is the first to migrate and the children were either born in the new country or arrived at a young age, the parents' generation tends to have very positive attitudes towards their first language and wish to maintain it and transfer it to next generation(s). Children tend to associate the parents with their mother tongue, consciously or unconsciously grasping its personal importance. Parental acceptance, caring, and warmth may lead to similar emotions in the child, including acceptance of the parents' language, whereas parental rejection, hostility, or distance may lead the child to avoid or reject the parents, as well as their language. In other words, children who feel part of a cohesive, unified family system are more likely to internalize the values and behaviors of that system. Language will naturally be one aspect of this process and, consequently, children in such families have higher chances of maintaining their parents' language. By contrast, feeling more detached in the first place may lead a child to feel "freer" to go ahead and use the new language, with less motivation to maintain the old one. In turn, becoming competent in the new language may facilitate the child's sense of belongingness to the new group, which may be of particular importance for children without a cohesive family to provide comfort. Thus, close relations between family members may correlate with a tendency of family units to maintain their first language.[47]

Nevertheless, and this is where language planning and language policy come into play, language maintenance by children may also *contribute* to family closeness and to positive relationships between family members.[48] Viewing language as a state of mind means that language is perceived as closely associated with one's psyche, and thus with one's childhood as well as with personal past and memories. It also means perceiving language as tied to a collective identity and a collective ethos, as associated with personal processes of identity formation and personal development. It means viewing language as closely associated with psychological coping mechanisms and with social interactions. The ability to communicate in this language in intimate interactions, above all with one's children, will naturally lead to the promotion of language maintenance. If language maintenance in the second generation is accompanied by a positive message from the *majority* — by encouragement, by a range of options that may even include programs that promote it amongst members of the majority — then the odds of minority languages survival will increase dramatically, with positive effects for the personal and familial well-being of minority group members. As Daniel Nettle and Suzanne Romaine warn, however, "conferring status on the language of a group relatively lacking in power doesn't necessarily ensure the reproduction of a language unless other measures are in place to ensure intergenerational transmission at home [...] conferring power on the people would be much more likely to do the trick."[49] Family relations and psychological motives, then, should be viewed as meaningful variables in the language maintenance and language policy discourse, rather than as minor by-products of these processes.

4. CONCLUSIONS

An examination of current and past language policies in light of the above analysis in Israel and in other migration settings raises serious issues. When immigrants are banned from speaking their language or, in less extreme examples, are not encouraged to do so; when educational language policies focus on teaching immigrant children the new language but do not offer serious options for promoting their first languages; when children of the majority are either not exposed to minority languages or are encouraged to view them only from pragmatic perspectives; in sum, when this is the prevalent reality, these policies have severe effects on the relationship of minority members with the majority, but even more so, on their family relations and their personal well-being.

The current linguistic situation in Israel is now purportedly more pluralistic and multicultural. Compared with Zionism's early days, when immigrants were forbidden to speak their first languages in public domains and the motto was for all to speak Hebrew in order to become "new Jews," we are indeed in a different setting, which may feel less threatened. As Shmuel Yosef Agnon writes in *Only Yesterday* describing the 1920s:

> In those days, Jaffa was full of young fellows who had studied Talmud and had practiced exegesis, and when they gathered together, and their hearts would assail them, they would sweeten their sitting with Hasidic stories and Hasidic tunes or with homilies. The generation before them sang songs for Zion, for this generation those songs became trite, and when the yearning soul yearned it went back to seek what was lost. Anyone who could sing sang tunes he had brought with him from his hometown, and anyone who could tell tales sat and told tales [...] because of the desire to exalt the soul. Out of their affection for those things whose tang is mostly in Yiddish, they sometimes gave up Hebrew, on condition that the things were not said in public; in a small party of friends they weren't sticklers about their language.[50]

True, speakers of minority languages no longer need to hide. Declared educational language policy in Israel as reflected in the official documents of the Ministry of Education's Absorption Department calls for sensitivity and tolerance toward newcomers. And yet, policies still focus mainly on the significance of acquiring Hebrew and becoming acquainted with Jewish tradition,[51] with no serious attempt to consider the association between maintaining first languages and the well-being of their speakers.

As in other countries,[52] in Israel too, "schooling is still virtually synonymous with learning a second language."[53] Other languages (except for English), do not enjoy privileged status, and people whose dominant language is not Hebrew are in a sense expected to justify or explain how they can maintain "divided loyalties."

For large groups, such as immigrants from the FSU, this attitude has less dramatic (or traumatic) consequences since, due to their size, there are various extra-curricular options for promoting language and aspects associated with it (mainly Russian culture, but also study norms and specific areas of interest).[54] And still, top-down processes are different from bottom-up ones.

Abstention from addressing language maintenance issues within the educational system has more serious implications for immigrants of Ethiopian origin. Not only has this group confronted difficult experiences upon arriving in Israel, but it also copes with severe problems related to the younger generation in terms of school achievement, high rates of juvenile delinquency, high rates of school dropouts, high rates of adolescence suicide,[55] all closely related to feelings of alienation from the majority but also from their community, where the family is not perceived as a significant protector. Developing serious programs to promote minority languages, including Russian and Amharic in Israel, or other minority language in other countries of immigration, could make a positive contribution to family relations and to the personal well-being of group members.

This plan is also relevant to Israel's Arab minority. Studies have shown a gradual decline in the status of Arabic within the Arab minority in Israel, high rates of code switching, and a lower motivation to study literary Arabic in high schools.[56] Indeed, Arabic is in no danger in terms of its survival as a language in the world, but it is losing its status and position in the Israeli context within the Arab minority. Realizing the significance of language to the sense of self, language policy in Israel should also be sensitive toward Arabic. Hebrew is a compulsory subject from Grade Two until the end of high school within the Arab sector, and more than seventy percent of Arab students sit for their matriculation exams in Hebrew, with an average final score of about 80 for those who choose the highest, five-point level.[57] Their curriculum extends beyond linguistic skills and covers broad aspects of Hebrew and Jewish culture.[58] During their school years, Arab-Muslim pupils are more exposed to the Bible and the Mishnah than to the Qur'an; they learn more poems by Hebrew poets such as Bialik or Uri Zvi Grinberg than by contemporary Arab poets.[59] In light of the language planning and policy orientation developed in this article, the current approach may easily prove more harmful than beneficial to the aims considered desirable by Israel's educational system.

In sum, this article sought to emphasize the advantages of *additive* bilingualism, highlighting psychological, emotional, and familial angles that are often neglected. Just as acquiring the majority language does not entail abandoning one's heritage language,[60] neither does maintenance imply *not* acquiring the majority language.

Different studies have found support for practically all the arguments mentioned in this paper: some emphasize how language maintenance is important to preserve culture while others point that maintenance is harmful because it is potentially divisive; some claim that countries should demand language proficiency as a condition for citizenship while others stress that setting such conditions is injurious to human rights. My focus was on language maintenance within the context of Israel's multicultural and multilinguistic society, stressing the potentially dramatic implications of language shift primarily for the individual members of ethnolinguistic minorities and, in turn, for society as a whole.

In much of the research on language policy issues, language planning orientations, or educational programs, the main concern is the future of endangered languages, their chances of survival or revival, and the many complex factors involved in and affecting these processes. My main interest, however, is in the speakers, not in terms of their responsibility to future generations and to the world to maintain and transmit these languages, but in terms of their well-being in the course of their lifetime and in terms of the significance of language maintenance for themselves and for their children.

The unique characteristics of the multilingual Israeli context place a further responsibility on official institutions to promote issues of language maintenance. The unique features of the Jewish-Arab relationships, the distinctive features of Jewish and non-Jewish immigrants to Israel, the exceptional position of Hebrew in the history and present of Israeli culture and ethos — all these elements merge to create a multilingual and multicultural society that should embrace its diversities rather than erase them. Realizing the contribution of language maintenance to members of minority groups as well as to the majority, as emphasized in the new orientation suggested in this article, can genuinely enrich Israeli society.

NOTES

1   Richard Ruiz, "Orientations in Language Planning," *NABE (National Association for Bilingual Education) Journal* 8 (1984): 15–34.

2   See for example, Fred Genesee, Kathryn Lindholm-Leary, William Saunders and Donna Christian, "English Language Learners in U.S. Schools: An Overview of Research Findings," *Journal of Education for Students Placed at Risk* 10 (2005): 363–385; Anne-Marie Masgoret and Robert C. Gardner, "A Causal Model of Spanish Immigrant Adaptation in Canada," *Journal of Multilingual and Multicultural Development* 20 (1999): 216–236; Barry C. Chiswick, "Hebrew Language Usage: Determinants and Effects on Earnings among Immigrants in Israel," *Journal of Popular Economy* 11 (1998): 253–271; Enedina Garcia-Vázquez, Luis A. Vázquez, Isabel C. López, and Wendy Ward, "Language Proficiency and Academic Success: Relationships Between Proficiency in Two Languages and Achievement among Mexican American Students," *Bilingual Research Journal* 21 (1997): 334–347.

3   Solange G. Taylor, "Multilingual Societies and Planned Linguistic Change: New Language-in-Education Programs in Estonia and South Africa," *Comparative Education Review* 46 (2002): 315.

4   See for instance, Sarah Lawson and Itesh Sachdev, "Identity, Language Use and Attitudes: Some Sylheti-Bangladeshi Data From London, UK," *Journal of Language and Social Psychology* 23 (2004): 49–69; Jerzy J. Smolicz, "Minority Languages as Core Values of Ethnic Cultures: A Study of Maintenance and Erosion of Polish, Welsh, and Chinese Languages in Australia," in *Maintenance and Loss of Minority Languages*, ed. Willem Fase, Koen Jaspaert and Sjaak Kroon (Amsterdam: John Benjamins, 1992), pp. 277–305.

5   In the formulation of Joshua A. Fishman: "Quite clearly, language loss is often felt to involve profound changes in the continuity of preferred life styles and customary cultural acts." See *In Praise of the Beloved Language* (Berlin: Mouton de Gruyter, 1997), p. 27.

6   Suzanne Romaine, "The Impact of Language Policy on Endangered Languages," *International Journal on Multicultural Societies* 4 (2002): 22. See also Nancy H. Hornberger, "Language Policy, Language Education, Language Rights: Indigenous, Immigrant, and International Perspectives," *Language in Society* 27 (1998): 441.

7   As James Crawford notes, endangered species and endangered languages "fall victim to predators, changing environments, or more successful competitors," are encroached on by "modern cultures abetted by new technologies," and are threatened by the "destruction of lands and livelihoods; the spread of consumerism, individualism, and other Western values; pressures for assimilation into dominant cultures; and conscious policies of repression." James Crawford, "Endangered Native American Languages: What Is To Be Done and Why?," *Journal of Navajo Education* 11 (1994): 5. See also Nancy Hornberger, "Multilingual Language Policies and the Continua of Biliteracy: An Ecological Approach," *Language Policy* 1 (2002): 33: "Some languages, like some species and environments, may be endangered and the ecology movement is about not only studying and describing those potential losses, but also counteracting them." See also Joshua A. Fishman, *Can Threatened Languages be Saved?* (Clevedon, UK/Philadelphia: Multilingual Matters, 2001), ch. 19.

8   Will Kymlicka, *Multicultural Citizenship: A Liberal Theory of Minority Rights* (Oxford: Clarendon Press, 1995), pp. 51–52. See also Stephan May, "Language rights: Moving the Debate Forward," *Journal of Sociolinguistics* 9 (2005): 319–347; Ilan Saban and Muhammad Amara, "The Status of Arabic in Israel: Law, Reality, and Thoughts Regarding the Power of Law to Change Reality," *Israel Law Review* 36 (2004): 1–35; Ayelet Harel-Shalev, "The Status of Minority Languages in Deeply Divided Societies: Urdu in India and Arabic in Israel — a Comparative Perspective," *Israel Studies Forum* 21 (2006): 28–57.

9   Hornberger, "Language Policy, Language Education, Language Rights," pp. 441–446; John E. Petrovic, "The Conservative Restoration and Neoliberal Defenses of Bilingual Education," *Language Policy* 4 (2005): 395–416. See also several relevant examples in Fishman, *Can Threatened Languages be Saved?* focusing on economical aspects of maintenance concerning Irish (ch. 8), Catalan (ch. 11), and Australia's indigenous languages (ch. 17).

10 For a review see, for instance, Chiswick, "Hebrew Language Usage."

11 An interesting example in this context is that of post-apartheid South Africa. The new democratic regime has recognized the linguistic reality of multilingualism that had been ignored under apartheid. The new constitution contains a decree promoting the state's equal use of eleven official languages (nine indigenous languages plus the colonial languages Afrikaans and English). Romaine, "The Impact of Language Policy on Endangered Languages," pp. 13–14. Yet, many among those who are entitled to be educated in their indigenous languages would prefer to study English, and in English. Raj Mesthrie, "Language, Transformation and Development: A Sociolinguistic Appraisal of Post-Apartheid South African Language Policy and Practice," *Southern African Linguistics and Applied Language Studies* 24 (2006): 158; Theodorus du Plessis, personal communication, January, 2009. Mesthrie, however, warns against politicians who use the argument of the attraction of English to their own ends, that is, to promote Anglo-European-American values, norms and culture at the expense of indigenous languages and cultures, ignoring that people do indeed want English but *they want their language as well.* For further discussion on an intermediate position between overemphasis on English and overemphasis on multilingualism, see Stanley G. M. Ridge, "Language Planning in a Rapidly Changing Multilingual Society: The Case of English in South Africa," *Language Problems and Language Policy* 28 (2004): 199–215.

12 See for example Ceri Peach, "The Ghetto and the Ethnic Enclave," in *Migration and Immigrants: Between Policy and Reality*, ed. Jeroen Doomenik and Hans Knippenberg (Amsterdam: Het Spinhuis, 2003), pp. 99–122.

13 The "English only" movement is only one instance of such an ideology. See, for instance, James Crawford, *At War with Diversity* (Clevedon, UK: Multilingual Matters, 2000), p. 10: "In the American experience, English-only campaigns can be classed in two categories: as proxies for intergroup competition and as mechanisms of social control. Discrimination against minority language speakers can serve both as a means of privileging certain groups over others and as a tool for maintaining the hegemony of ruling elites." For a critical analysis of this phenomenon with regard to the notion of ethnolinguistic vitality, see Valerie Barker et al. "The

English-Only Movement: A Communication Analysis of Changing Perceptions of Language Vitality," *Journal of Communication* 51 (2001): 3–37. For various examples from Europe, Australia, and America, see Romaine, "The Impact of Language Policy on Endangered Languages," particularly the extreme example of a member of the Vlach minority in Greece, who was arrested after he distributed publications of the European Bureau for Lesser Used Languages mentioning the existence of the Aroumanian language and four other minority languages in Greece (9), and her reference to Turkey, which "still maintains that it has no minorities" (10).

14 For an extensive discussion, see Elana Shohamy, *Language Policy: Hidden Agendas and New Approaches* (London: Routledge, 2006), particularly chapters 2 and 3; Tim McNamara and Elana Shohamy, "Language Tests and Human Rights," *International Journal of Applied Linguistics* 18 (2008): 89–95. See also various links related to official government sites presenting details of tests, such as Latvia (http://www.alte.org/members/latvian/lltalc.php), Canada (http://www.cic.gc.ca/ english/citizenship/cit-test.asp#about), or Finland (http://www.oph.fi/english/ page.asp?path=447,574,51431), to mention but a few.

15 Fishman, *Can Threatened Languages be Saved?* p. 454.

16 Nevertheless, see Terrence G. Wiley, "The Foreign Language 'Crisis' in the United States: Are Heritage and Community Languages the Remedy?," *Critical Inquiry in Language Studies* 4 (2007): 179–205, who notes that this perception is extremely controversial since it classifies speakers of minority languages as "useful" and at the service of state agendas. See also Thomas Ricento, "Problems with the 'Language-As-Resource' Discourse in the Promotion of Heritage Languages in the U.S.A.," *Journal of Sociolinguistics* 9 (2005): 360–363; Petrovic, "The Conservative Restoration and Neoliberal Defenses of Bilingual Education," p. 405.

17 For a critical analysis of this orientation and further discussion of this point, see ibid.

18 See, for instance, Ellen Bialystok, "Cognitive Complexity and Attentional Control in the Bilingual Mind," *Child Development* 70 (1999): 636–644; Kenji Hakuta and Rafael M. Diaz, "The Relationship Between Degree Of Bilingualism and Cognitive Ability: A Critical Discussion and Some New Longitudinal Data," in *Children's Language*, vol. 5, ed. Keith E. Nelson (Hillsdale, NJ: Erlbaum, 1985), pp. 319–344; Renzo Titone, *On the Bilingual Person* (Ottawa: Canadian Society for Italian Studies, 1989), pp. 93–109.

19 See, for instance, Hornberger, "Language Policy, Language Education, Language Rights," who elaborates on the activities in a program designed to promote maintenance of ethnic languages in the Amazonian rainforest of Brazil: "One activity of the course … is the 'profesores índios' (e.g., indigenous teachers) authorship of teaching materials in the indigenous languages that reflect indigenous culture, history, and artistic expression; these materials serve as documentation of the professors' own learning while also serving as a teaching resource for their own classrooms" (p. 440).

20 Francesco Cavallaro, "Language Maintenance Revisited: An Australian Perspective," *Bilingual Research Journal* 29 (2005): 563.

21   Ricento, "Problems with the 'Language-As-Resource' Discourse," p. 349.

22   Ibid., p. 350. See also May, "Language Rights," particularly pp. 322–327.

23   Cavallaro, "Language Maintenance Revisited," p. 562; Romaine, "The Impact of Language Policy on Endangered Languages," p. 10.

24   Elazar Leshem, *Former Soviet Union Immigrants in Israel 1999–2003: Status Report* (Jerusalem: Joint Israel, 2003), p. 81.

25   Bernard Spolsky and Elana Shohamy, *The Languages of Israel: Policy, Ideology, and Practice* (Clevedon: Multilingual Matters, 1999), ch. 1.

26   Ibid., ch. 3.

27   See, for instance, Dan Caspi, Hanna Adoni, Akiba A. Cohen and Nelly Elias, "The Red, the White and the Blue," *The International Journal for Communication Studies* 64 (2002): 537–556; Tamar Horowitz, "The Integration of Immigrants from the Former Soviet Union," *Israel Affairs* 11 (2005): 117–136; Leshem, *Former Soviet Union Immigrants in Israel 1999–2003*, p. 81.

28   I am using here the term "Israeli Arabs" in this article, although many Arab citizens in Israel feel uncomfortable with this label and prefer alternative definitions, such as Palestinian citizens of Israel or simply Palestinians. These definitions, however, entail other shortcomings. For a broader discussion of this issue, see Dan Rabinowitz "Oriental Nostalgia: How the Palestinians Became 'Israel's Arabs'" (Hebrew), *Theory and Criticism: An Israeli Forum* 4 (1993): 141–152.

29   Many scholars stress the exclusion dimension with regard to the status of Arabs in Israel, addressing such issues as political power, land confiscation, discriminating laws, and identity issues. See for example, Samy Smooha, "Ethnic Democracy: Israel as an Archetype," *Israel Studies* 2 (1997): 199–200, 226–227; Dan Rabinowitz, "The Palestinian Citizens of Israel, the Concept of Trapped Minority and the Discourse of Transnationalism in Anthropology," *Ethnic and Racial Studies*, Vol. 24 (1) (2001): 64–85. See pp. 66–79; Ahmad H. Sa'di, "Catastrophe, Memory and Identity: Al-Nakbah as a Component of Palestinian Identity," *Israel Studies* 7 (2002): 181–185; Ahmad H. Sa'di, "Construction and Reconstruction of Racialised Boundaries: Discourse, Institutions and Methods," *Social Identities* 10 (2004): 144.

30   This issue has been extensively discussed in the literature. See, for instance, Salim Abu-Rabia, "Towards a Second-Language Model of Learning in Problematic Social Contexts: The Case of Arabs Learning Hebrew in Israel," *Race, Ethnicity and Education* 2 (1999): 109–125; Muhammad Amara and Izhak Schnell, "Identity Repertoires among Arabs in Israel," *Journal of Ethnic and Migration Studies* 30 (2003): 175–193; Dan Rabinowitz, "The Palestinian Citizens of Israel, the Concept of Trapped Minority and the Discourse of Transnationalism in Anthropology," pp. 64–85. See also the renowned book of David Grossman, *Sleeping on a Wire* (New York: Farrar, Strauss, and Giroux, 1993), which deals at length with identity issues unique to Israeli Arabs.

31   For an interesting analysis related to the unique Israeli discourse on immigration, *aliyah*, and return, see Edna Lomsky-Feder and Tamar Rapoport, "Homecoming, Immigration, and the National Ethos: Russian-Jewish Homecomers Reading Zionism," *Anthropological Quarterly* 74 (2000): 1–14.

32 See Michal Tannenbaum, "Language as a Core Value of Immigrant Groups in Israel: An Exploratory Study," *Journal of Ethnic and Migration Studies* (In press).

33 Jews in Israel often express similar negative attitudes towards Arabic. They view it as representing the "language of the enemy" and their motivation to study it is definitely lower than that of Israeli Arabs to study Hebrew. See, for instance, Michal Tannenbaum and Limor Tahar, "Willingness to Communicate in the Language of the Other: Jewish and Arab Students in Israel," *Learning and Instruction* 18 (2008): 288; Muhammad Amara and Abd el-Rahman Mar'i, *Language Education Policy: The Arab Minority in Israel* (Dordrecht: Kluwer Academic Publishers, 2002), pp. 7–9.
An interesting angle from which to consider these relationships is a new bill proposed in the Knesset's Education Committee requiring all Jewish students to take Arabic as a subject in their matriculation exams (http://www.nrg.co.il/online/1/ART1/527/947.html). A report on this proposal was also published in the newspaper's website. Very few of the talkbacks supported the suggestion, and most were negative, cynical, and downright hostile. Some examples:
— "Another suggestion: Compel them to pray in a mosque, and convert to Islam altogether!"
— "The only reason to learn Arabic: know thy enemy."

34 Sammy Smooha, "Minority Status in an Ethnic Democracy: The Status of the Arab Minority in Israel," *Ethnic and Racial Studies* 13 (1990), particularly pp. 395–400; Oren Yiftachel, "The Arab Minority in Israel and its Relations with the Jewish Majority: A Review Essay," *Studies in Comparative International Development* 27 (1992): 57–83.

35 Amara and Mar'i, *Language Education Policy: The Arab Minority in Israel*, pp. 46–58. See also Michal Tannenbaum and Limor Tahar, "Willingness to Communicate in the Language of the Other: Jewish and Arab Students in Israel," *Learning and Instruction* 18 (2008): 283–294, particularly pp. 289–292.

36 See for example, Majid Al-Haj, "Identity Patterns among Immigrants from the Former Soviet Union in Israel: Assimilation Versus Ethnic Formation," *International Migration* 40 (2002): 49–69; Horowitz, "The Integration of Immigrants from the Former Soviet Union," pp. 129–131.

37 Since 1989, more than a quarter were not registered in Israel as Jews on arrival. The proportion of non-Jews among the FSU immigrants has grown from 5% in 1990 to over 50% since 2000. See Al-Haj, "Identity Patterns Among Immigrants from the Former Soviet Union," p. 56; Yair Sheleg, *Not Halakhically Jewish: The Dilemma of Non-Jewish Immigrants in Israel* (Hebrew), Policy Paper No. 51 (Jerusalem: Israel Democracy Institute, 2004), pp. 10–12.

38 Uri Ben-Eliezer, "Becoming a Black Jew: Cultural Racism and Anti-Racism in Contemporary Israel," *Social Identities* 10 (2004): 245–266; Gadi Ben-Ezer, *Like a Light in The Urn: Immigrant Ethiopian Jews in Israel* (Hebrew) (Jerusalem: Rubin Mass, 1992), particularly pp. 138–159; Steven Kaplan, "Everyday Resistance and the Study of Ethiopian Jews" (Hebrew), *Theory and Criticism: An Israeli Forum* 10 (1997): 163–173; Meir Perez, "Chronicles of Linguistic Absorption of Ethiopian Immigrants" (Hebrew), *Hed Ha-Ulpan* 80 (2000): 12–20.

39 Eva Hoffman, *Lost in Translation: A Life in a New Language* (New York: E.P. Dutton, 1989), pp. 106–108.

40   Leon Grinberg and Rebecca Grinberg, *Psychoanalytic Perspectives of Migration and Exile* (New Haven and London: Yale University Press, 1989), p. 99.

41   Julia Mirsky, "Language in Migration: Separation-Individuation Conflicts in Relation to the Mother Tongue and the New Language," *Psychotherapy* 28 (1991): 620.

42   J. Stern, "Mother Tongue, Shift of Language and Psychotherapy," *Israel Journal of Psychiatry and Related Sciences* 23 (1986): 202.

43   Grinberg and Grinberg, *Psychoanalytic Perspectives of Migration and Exile*, p. 110.

44   George K. Hong and Marry Anna Domokos-Cheng Ham, "Impact of Immigration on The Family Life Cycle: Clinical Implications for Chinese Americans," *Journal of Family Psychotherapy* 3 (1992): 27–40; Michael Ritsner and Alexander Ponizovsky, "Psychological Distress Through Immigration: The Two-Phase Temporal Pattern?," *International Journal of Social Psychiatry* 45 (1999): 125–139.

45   Mali A. Mann, "Immigrant Parents and Their Emigrant Adolescents: The Tension of Inner and Outer Worlds," *The American Journal of Psychoanalysis* 64 (2004): 143–153; Dorit Roer-Strier, "Socializing Immigrant children: Home and School Coping with Cultural Differences," in *Language, Identity, and Immigration*, ed. Elite Olshtain and Gabriel Horenczyk (Jerusalem: Magnes Press, 2000), pp. 65–80.

46   Lesley Koplow and Eli Messinger, "Developmental Dilemmas of Young Children of Immigrant Parents," *Child and Adolescent Social Work* 7 (1990): 121–134; Lili Wong-Fillmore, "When Learning a Second Language Means Losing the First," *Early Childhood Research Quarterly* 6 (1991): 323–346.

47   See Michal Tannenbaum, "Viewing Family Relations through a Linguistic Lens; Symbolic Aspects of Language Maintenance in Immigrant Families," *Journal of Family Communication* 5 (2005): 229–252.

48   Relevant quotes from immigrants' memories emerge in several studies. For instance, see the statement of an Ethiopian immigrant in Israel: "If the teenagers of today will not insist on maintaining their parents' language, they will not be able to communicate with their parents and with other people in the community (…) there will be communication problems." Tannenbaum, "Language as a Core Value of Immigrant Groups in Israel." Another example is that of an Italian immigrant in Australia saying: "My parents spoke no English and spoke a southern Italian dialect. I learned this dialect very quickly from them and it had a great deal of meaning to me. It meant that I was like my parents and belonged to the group that they did." Jerzy J. Smolicz, Margaret J. Secombe, and Dorothy M. Hudson "Family Collectivism and Minority Languages as Core Values of Culture Among Ethnic Groups in Australia," *Journal of Multilingual and Multicultural Development* 22 (2001): 163.

49   Daniel Nettle and Suzanne Romaine, *Vanishing Voices: The Extinction of the World's Languages* (New York: Oxford University Press, 2000), pp. 39–40.

50   Shmuel Yosef Agnon, *Only Yesterday*, trans. Barbara Harshav (Princeton and Oxford: Princeton University Press, 2000), p. 83.

51   http://cms.education.gov.il/EducationCMS/Units/Olim/TahalichHaKlita/ThalichyKlita.htm.

52   See for example, Wiley, "The Foreign Language 'Crisis' in the United States"; Ricento, "Problems with the 'Language-As-Resource' Discourse."

53 Romaine, "The Impact of Language Policy on Endangered Languages," p. 13.

54 See for example, Caspi et al., "The Red, the White and the Blue"; Horowitz, "The Integration of Immigrants from the Former Soviet Union."

55 http://noar.education.gov.il/main/upload/.nituk/nituk15e.doc. See also the research report of Tamar Levin, Elana Shohamy, and Bernard Spolsky, *Academic Achievements of Immigrant Children in Israel* (Hebrew) (Jerusalem: Ministry of Education, Culture, and Sport, 2003); Leshem, *Former Soviet Union Immigrants in Israel*, pp. 82–83.

56 Amara and Mar'i, *Language Education Policy*, pp. 46–58.

57 *Background Document for Discussion: Arab Citizens of Israel Study Hebrew*. Submitted to the Knesset Education and Culture Committee, January 2002, p. 2.

58 http://www.biu.ac.il/HU/lprc/home/HEBTARA.htm.

59 http://www.tzafonet.org.il/kehil/tzafonet_arabic/estaba-2001/Takhal/ToknetH2006.doc. Nevertheless, although the Ministry of Education developed innovative programs for teaching Hebrew and Arabic in the Arab sector, these programs are not implemented and the more revolutionary changes do not seem to reach the textbooks. See Omer Barak, "Palestinian Literature Vanished on the Way to the Classroom," *Haaretz*, 23/05/2004.

60 On this question, see my comment above regarding the South African context.

ABSTRACTS

1. HANNA LERNER:
CONSTITUTIONAL INCREMENTALISM AND MATERIAL ENTRENCHMENT

The article focuses on the relationship between the controversy over the character of Israel as a "Jewish and democratic state" and the continuous abstention from drafting a formal constitution. It traces the constitutional debates during the first Knesset, showing how Israel's founding fathers preferred to adopt an incrementalist approach to constitution-making, deferring for the future controversial decisions on the state's ultimate values and shared norms. In light of the deep internal divisions between the religious and secular perspectives, they chose to transfer controversies over issues of Israel's identity from the constitutional sphere of entrenched law to the more flexible realm of political deliberation. This constitutional incrementalism, however, may unintentionally have led to the entrenchment of a material constitution lacking a formal mechanism of amendment. Indeed, more than six decades after independence, no consensus prevails in Israeli society over the appropriate relationship between religion and state. The rigidity of the existing informal arrangements in the religious sphere was reflected in the Knesset's recent attempt to draft a written constitution to the State of Israel.

2. MEITAL PINTO:
WHO IS AFRAID OF LANGUAGE RIGHTS IN ISRAEL?

The article argues that granting language rights to Israeli Arabs is wrongly perceived as a controversial political matter, from which Israeli courts should abstain. This perception rests on four distinctive dimensions of language rights viewed as threatening the Jewish-Zionist character of Israel, a fear the author describes as unjustified. The first is the positive dimension of language rights, requiring the state not only to grant Arabs the right to speak Arabic but also to actively support Arabic. The second dimension is their selective nature, requiring the state to privilege the Arab minority over other linguistic minorities in Israel, such as the Russian Jewish minority. The third is their public dimension, requiring that Arabic be visible in the Israeli linguistic landscape. The fourth dimension is their collective nature, which brings to mind other allegedly collective rights such as the right of return and the right of Israeli Arabs to self-determination. The fear of language rights is unjustified, however, since many other legally recognized rights that protect Israeli-Arab interests involve one of these dimensions. Only because language rights may simultaneously bear more than one dimension are they perceived as threatening. Yet, the difference between language rights and other well-acknowledged minority rights in Israel is a difference of degree and not of kind. Courts, therefore, should not leave language rights to the political system but address them as every other right.

3. TAMAR HOSTOVSKY BRANDES: THE VOICE OF THE PEOPLE: LANGUAGE AND STATE IN ISRAEL

The article examines the issue of language in Israel and challenges the traditional distinction between immigrants and national minorities in the context of Israel. It rejects the traditional justifications often brought for this distinction and argues that alternative justifications that were offered to justify this distinction in the case of Israel are equally problematic. It then examines, borrowing the concepts of self-determination and self-defense, an alternative justification, which is based not on the nature or characteristics of the members of each of the two groups but on the cultural nature of the state and the demands it presents to its members. The conditions for admission of Russian immigrants into Israeli society, it argues, contain an implied expectation that these immigrants abandon their culture and language of origin and identify with the Hebrew language and culture. This expectation, however, is not always realized, and, standing alone, is a poor basis for upholding the distinction between immigrants and national minorities and rejecting on a sweeping basis the possibility of recognizing the language rights of Russian-speaking immigrants in Israel.

4. MUHAMMAD AMARA: THE HAND-IN-HAND BILIINGUAL EDUCATION MODEL: VISION AND CHALLENGES

The Center for Jewish-Arab Education in Israel initiated a new model of bilingual education in the Israeli landscape. The new model is based on balanced bilingualism, using both Arabic and Hebrew equally as languages of instruction in three integrated schools of Jews and Arabs learning together. The main purpose of the new model is to offer dignity and equality to the two national groups. The basic idea behind the initiative is to create egalitarian bilingual educational environments. The paper deals with the following questions: What are the characteristics of the new model? What differentiates it from other bilingual models in Israel? To what extent do both groups, Arabs and Jews, remain loyal to their own linguistic heritage, and in what ways?

5. YEDIDIA Z. STERN:
CULTURAL AND NORMATIVE DUALITY
IN ISRAELI SOCIETY

The article argues that Jewish life in Israel is deeply affected by both Western-liberal civilization and Jewish-traditional civilization. The question of how to function in a reality of dual cultural commitments affects the cohesion of Israeli society and its ability to survive. Different Jewish communities endorse different strategies to cope with cultural duality: the religious choose compartmentalization (avoidance), the ultra-Orthodox, alienation (withdrawal), and the secularists, abdication (oblivion). All three strategies are equally ineffective, and none offers an inclusive model that integrates both cultures. This intercultural tension has led to increasing recourse to the law: state law vs. religious-halakhic law, when each group — secular and religious — seeks to validate its inner identity and end the cultural struggle through judicial decisions. The "lawlization" and "halakhization" of Israeli society allows each side to twist the arm of the cultural "other" while absolving itself of any responsibility for the aggressive and intolerant connotations of this act. This paper engages in a parallel analysis of the use of state and halakhic law in Israel, revealing that the two legal systems have contrary attitudes to values. Despite their opposite approaches, both adopt a clear rhetoric of judicial imperialism, both consider their theoretical and practical scope as all-inclusive, and both claim exclusivity in the regulation of reality. In order to stabilize Jewish society in Israel, however, both groups must now come to terms with Israel's cultural duality.

6. AVI SAGI:
SOCIETY AND LAW IN ISRAEL:
BETWEEN A RIGHTS DISCOURSE
AND AN IDENTITY DISCOURSE

Since its foundation, Israeli society has been engaged in an incisive discourse about fundamental issues regarding the relationship between its various groups, which this article examines in light of two key concepts: the discourse of rights and the discourse of identity. These two modes of discourse both reflect and shape different types of relationships between the parties engaged in the relationship.The central claim in this article is that Israeli society speaks mainly through a discourse of rights, as evinced by its frequent recourse to the legal system and to arguments emphasizing legal language, appealing to the Supreme Court on issues that could be resolved by dialogue and negotiations between the parties. The rights discourse allows Israeli society to evade central questions of Jewish identity, on which it is essentially divided.

7. YAACOV YADGAR:
TRANSCENDING THE "SECULARIZATION VS. TRADITIONALIZATION" DISCOURSE: JEWISH-ISRAELI TRADITIONISTS, THE POST-SECULAR, AND THE POSSIBILITIES OF MULTICULTURALISM

One of the major impediments to the maturation of a viable multiculturalism has been the predominance of binary, dichotomous distinctions, which divide the world into allegedly "coherent" and "systematic" constructs of polar opposites. As critics have pointed out, such polar opposites are artificial constructs whose merit is limited mostly to the social-scientific world, which is preoccupied with formulating universally applicable theories. Overcoming the predominance of such dichotomies as the guiding coordinates for interpreting the socio-cultural world entails obvious advantages for the development of a viable multicultural atmosphere. A more nuanced, tolerant approach that allows for the existence of complex, multilayered, and often self-contradictory constructs of identity is essential for multiculturalism to take hold. This paper discusses the predicament of maintaining an identity that does not fit into either pole of a predominant dichotomous distinction, together with the possibilities if offers for the (re)construction of a more tolerant, multicultural mindset. The dichotomy at hand is the one devised by the secularization and modernization thesis, and the alternative discussed in this article is what has come to be identified in Jewish-Israeli discourse as "traditionism" (*masortiyut*). The first part opens with a discussion of the socio-cultural phenomenon at hand and a brief account of how the secularization paradigm misrepresented and misinterpreted this phenomenon, considering the post-secular turn in the social sciences as a possible fruitful alternative to the secularization thesis. The second part of the paper offers an alternative interpretation of main components of the traditionist identity, including its potential for transcending the dichotomous worldview at hand.

8. ASHER COHEN and BERNARD SUSSER:
SERVICE IN THE IDF
AND THE BOUNDARIES
OF ISRAEL'S JEWISH COLLECTIVE

The question of defining the boundaries of the Jewish collective has been at the focus of debate ever since the appearance of significant social forces that questioned the authority and exclusive right of Halacha to determine these boundaries. The foundation of the State of Israel as the nation-state of the Jewish people significantly escalated the potential conflict over this matter. The State of Israel, as an expression of an unmistakably secular modern Jewish nationality, offered genuine alternatives to the exclusive authority of halachic tradition to determine the boundaries of the Jewish collective: life within the Jewish collective, which is a sovereign majority society, acquiring Hebrew language and culture, socialization processes within various frameworks, and Jewish self-awareness have all become potential options. In this context, service in the IDF is a decisive factor in determining the boundaries of the national collective. Endangering one's life and the willingness to engage in self-sacrifice are the highest price that can be demanded from individual members of the collective. The article examines several debated cases from the 1970s (the Shalit children and Chanan Frank) and from a more recent context (deputy company commander German Rozhkov), concluding with a review of religious conversion procedures in the IDF, which functions here as a social-national factor of primary importance despite the general tendency to professionalize it and relieve it of civilian roles that had been assigned to it in the past.

9. DOV SCHWARTZ:
IDEAS VS. REALITY: MULTICULTURALISM
AND RELIGIOUS-ZIONISM

Since the 1990s, the religious-Zionist movement in Israel has been undergoing a process that marks a collapse of its traditional borders,, a development that still awaits investigation. After presenting an account of the movement's development prior to these changes, the article exposes the new trends affecting its development, such as: the penetration of cultural strongholds that had been considered off-limits (media, television, cinema, and so forth); the emergence of the "hilltop youth," a group that represent a revolt against conventional frameworks; a breakdown of the traditional yeshiva structure (with a focus on new areas such as faith and Hasidism) and, consequently, a collapse of the Torah authority directly relying on the aura of "genius" or charisma (the Tsohar rabbis, and so forth). This paper argues that the breakdown of these frameworks indicates that the firm messianic interpretation of history has been shattered. Disappointment with this interpretation is reflected in a number of events: the Jewish underground; the murder of Prime Minister Rabin; the shift in the secular public's perception of religious Zionists as no longer an admirable vanguard but as a burden and a barrier to peace; the withdrawal from the territories, and the implementation of the disengagement plan.

These developments have led to the abandonment of the traditional structure (based on the Torah authority of the yeshiva heads, the political authority of the National Religious Party, and so forth). This breakdown of authority leads to individualism and cultural assimilation, with the concomitant acknowledgement of a variety of cultural options and the disappearance of the monolithic model of authority. And yet, the messianic interpretation is still alive below ground, fostered in yeshivot and in women's colleges and threatens to surface.

10. Avihu Ronen:
THE SUFFERING OF THE OTHER:
TEACHING THE HOLOCAUST
TO ARABS AND JEWS

This article analyzes the difficulties in recognizing the suffering of other groups in general, and the difficulties of such recognition among Jews and Arabs in particular. While the recognition of rights or ways of life is relatively simple, recognition of the other group's formative traumas may give rise to severe problems (as evident in the Turkish refusal to recognize the Armenian genocide). In the Israeli Palestinian case, these difficulties stem also from the fact that these traumas were formative of the other's group identity. As the Jewish Holocaust is constitutive of Jewish identity in Israel, so the events of 1948, called Nakba by the Palestinians, were constitutive of the Palestinian identity. The article presents the reasons for refusing to deal with the Holocaust among both Jews and Arabs, who feared that such common discussion would undermine the sense of absolute sacrifice. Recognition of the other's sufferings requires giving up the exclusiveness of suffering and martyrdom, accounting for the difficulty as well as the grounds for encouraging and building such mutual recognition. This is the background to a description of workshops and courses for acquainting Arab teachers with the Holocaust at the Givat Haviva Seminary and at Beit Lochamei Ha-Getaot.

11. Rina Hevlin:
THE JEWISH HOLIDAYS AS A PLATFORM FOR A MULTICULTURAL DISCOURSE OF IDENTITY

A description of two types of long-term multi-cultural encounters is enhanced by reflective discussion and accompanied by an interpretation of their meaning. The first type of encounter involved different Jewish cultural communities, and the second included Jewish and non-Jewish cultural groups. Despite the complexity of the second type, the author's experience with meetings between Jewish cultural groups is exposed as more problematic. These encounters require greater sensitivity and awareness from the participants toward the ongoing processes and their fragility. Encounters between different cultural communities — the variety of Jewish cultures, and the varied religiously based Arab cultures, Christian, Muslim and Druze — moved more effortlessly from a very tense atmosphere to greater openness.

12. Nissim Leon:
THE MULTIPLE-ETHNIC SYNAGOGUE IN ISRAEL

"Identity" tends to be viewed as an inherently elusive and variable concept. By contrast, micro-identity, which is perceived as threatened by attempts at integration from above, is described as a stable element unaffected by the vicissitudes of time. Change, if it does take place, is usually ascribed to the nation-state's overall idea of order. The attempt by supporters of multiculturalism to cultivate micro-identities and recognize them as an integral part of an overall, dynamic collective identity therefore appears to rest, somewhat paradoxically, on the assumption of non-variability of micro-identity over time — that of immigrants, of religious people, of members of minority groups, of those whose identity is regarded as different, disturbing, and posing an inherent challenge to the national order. The multicultural attempt to fashion an agenda around the cultivation of micro-identities and invoking their recognition seems to ignore de facto changes in daily life that have moved micro-identities toward integration and turned some of them into new integrative focal points for a sense of belonging, located between the old micro-identity and the national macro-identity. As an instance, this article presents the case of multiculturalism and Mizrahim in Israeli society. Although the melting pot policy was already a failure in the mid–1950s when exerted top-down, daily religious, political, and socio-economic encounters between ethnic groups developed into a broader ethnic milieu catalogued by sociologists under the category of *Mizrahim*. In practice, the contexts of these encounters reflect day-to-day coping with a multicultural situation drawing sustenance from below and producing new identities. One context in which this process is reflected is the conversion of the mono-ethnic synagogue in Israel into a multi-ethnic institution.

13. Meirav Aharon:
"WE PAY OUR TAXES AND SERVE IN THE ARMY": ETHNOGRAPHY AND THE CHALLENGE OF MULTICULTURALISM

The Israeli Andalusian Orchestra was established in 1994 by children of immigrant Jews from North Africa in the city of Ashdod. The paper explores the experience of citizenship as a struggle for existence and recognition, where the process of classification became the turning point in the struggle for legitimacy and state financial backing. It offers a way of understanding citizenship in a polycultural society by adopting Walter Benjamin's proposal to look for the meeting point between the "ideal," the "empirical reality," and the "concepts of the people." The founders of the Andalusian Orchestra rejected the option of defining themselves as an ethnic minority, thereby rejecting any claim on behalf of "difference," a category that, in their understanding, would preserve their social marginality rather than change it. Consequently, in this case, a politics of difference employed by the state failed to deliver a genuine feeling of citizenship.

14. Michal Tannenbaum:
MULTICULTURALISM IN ISRAEL: A LINGUISTIC PERSPECTIVE

Multicultural and multilingual societies such as Israel offer great opportunities for in-depth sociolinguistic research, and this article focuses on aspects of language maintenance and language shift. It describes Israel's linguistic reality, using as a conceptual framework Richard Ruiz's renowned analysis of language planning and its implications for multilingual societies in general and for Israel in particular. It then offers an additional perspective and develops the concept of *language as a state-of-mind*, which emphasizes the emotional and familial connotations of language maintenance and their meaning for language policies, with specific reference to Israel.

CONTRIBUTORS

AVI SAGI is Professor of Philosophy and the Director of the graduate program in Hermeneutics and Cultural Studies at Bar-Ilan University.

OHAD NACHTOMY is a Senior Lecturer in Philosophy at Bar-Ilan University.

HANNA LERNER is a Lecturer of Political Science at Tel-Aviv University.

TAMAR HOSTOVSKY BRANDES is J.S.D of Law from Columbia University.

MEITAL PINTO is a Post-Doc fellow at The Minerva Center for Human Rights, Faculty of Law, The Hebrew University.

MUHAMMAD AMARA is a Senior Lecturer of Linguistics at Beit Berl Academic College.

YEDIDIA Z. STERN is Professor of Law at Bar-Ilan University and co-editor of *Democratic Culture*.

ASHER COHEN is a Senior Lecturer of Political Studies at Bar-Ilan University.

BERNARD SUSSER is Professor of Political Studies at Bar-Ilan University.

DOV SHWARTZ is Professor of Jewish Philosophy at Bar-Ilan University.

AVIHU RONEN is a Senior Lecturer of History and Philosophy at Tel-Hai Academic College.

RINA HEVLIN is a Lecturer and Head of the Jewish Studies Department at Ohalo Academic College.

NISSIM LEON is an Instructor at the Department of Sociology and Anthropology at Bar-Ilan University.

YAACOV YADGAR is a Senior Lecturer at the Department of Political Studies, Bar-Ilan University.

MEIRAV AHARON is Adjunct Lecturer at the Department of Sociology and Anthropology at the Hebrew University of Jerusalem.

MICHAL TANNENBAUM is a Senior Lecturer at the Department of Education at Tel-Aviv University.

INDEX OF SUBJECTS

INDEX OF NAMES